C. S. LEWIS

PRE-EVANGELISM FOR A POST-CHRISTIAN WORLD

FOREWORD BY BRUCE LITTLE

WHY NARNIA MIGHT BE MORE REAL THAN WE THINK

BRIAN M. WILLIAMS

Brian M. Williams

C. S. LEWIS
PRE-EVANGELISM FOR A POST-CHRISTIAN WORLD
Why Narnia Might Be More Real Than We Think

Brian M. Williams

Christian Publishing House
Cambridge, Ohio

C. S. LEWIS PRE-EVANGELISM FOR A POST-CHRISTIAN WORLD

Copyright © 2021 Brian M. Williams

All rights reserved. Except for brief quotations in articles, other publications, book reviews, and blogs, no part of this book may be reproduced in any manner without prior written permission from the publishers. For information, write, support@christianpublishers.org

Unless otherwise stated, Scripture quotations are from English Standard Version (ESV) The Holy Bible, English Standard Version. ESV® Text Edition: 2016. Copyright © 2001 by Crossway Bibles, a publishing ministry of Good News Publishers.

C. S. LEWIS PRE-EVANGELISM FOR A POST-CHRISTIAN WORLD: Why Narnia Might Be More Real Than We Think by Brian M. Williams

ISBN-13: **978-1-949586-15-2**

ISBN-10: **1-949586-15-4**

Brian M. Williams

Table of Contents

FOREWORD 9

INTRODUCTION 12

CHAPTER 1 C. S. Lewis: The Man 15

CHAPTER 2 C. S. Lewis's Sacramental View of Reality 79

CHAPTER 3 C. S. Lewis's Romantic View of the Human Imagination 136

CHAPTER 4 C. S. Lewis's Use of Fiction as Pre-Evangelism: Exploring The Space Trilogy and The Chronicles of Narnia 190

CHAPTER 5 Towards a Lewisian Pre-Evangelistic Approach Today Through the Medium of Imaginative Fiction 268

INDEX 295

Book Dedication

For Dr. Bruce Little, who, far more than anyone else, taught me how to think, and whose mentorship, friendship, and example of a well-ordered life remain some of my most treasured blessings.

C. S. LEWIS PRE-EVANGELISM FOR A POST-CHRISTIAN WORLD

Book Endorsements

In my view, this is probably one of the best books on C.S. Lewis that has come into my hands. Not only does Brian Williams grasp Lewis, what is all the more impressive is that he begins to grasp Barfield.

No Inkling scholar can truly call themselves such without at least a passing understanding of how Barfield influenced his fellow Inklings. As Brian has shown by this lucid account, he does indeed fulfil this basic requirement and does so at the highest levels by courageously being able to discuss Barfield's ideas without the fear that previously pervaded the generations before him. In this, Brian demonstrates that he is a man for our times. Only by facing truth with fearlessness, will humanity find its way out of the current tribulation in which we find ourselves. — **OWEN A. BARFIELD**, Grandson & Trustee, Oxfordshire, England (www.owenbarfield.org)

In *C. S. Lewis: Pre-Evangelism for a Post-Christian World*, Williams introduces the reader to Lewis's imaginative fiction and philosophical works that combine to illustrate both the great professor's worldview and a model that can be used by Christians today to reach our culture. When so many are wondering how to share the Gospel with a world that is seemingly less receptive to its message, Williams puts forward a hopeful picture of how this can be done by looking to one of the greatest to ever do it. — **Zachary D. Schmoll**, Managing Editor, *An Unexpected Journal*

In this well-researched study of Lewis, the apologist-fiction writer, Williams demonstrates how Lewis's sacramental view of creation and romantic view of the imagination equipped him to smuggle a kind of pre-evangelistic Christian theology into his fiction that has the power to open the minds and hearts of modern and postmodern readers to the universal nature of goodness, truth, and beauty and to the fullness of God's presence in the world. It is well worth the read! — **LOUIS MARKOS**, Professor in English and Scholar in Residence, Houston Baptist University; author of *Restoring Beauty* and *On the Shoulders of Hobbits*

People know C. S. Lewis as a great writer of Christian fiction (the Narnia books, the Space Trilogy, '*Til We Have Faces*) and a great popular apologist. Not so well known is his role as a careful philosopher of reality and imagination. In *C. S. Lewis: Pre-Evangelism for a Post-Christian World*, Brian Williams explores the ways in which Lewis's fiction flows from his philosophy. That is, he explores the ways in which Lewis's views of reality and of the human imagination undergird a well-thought-out strategy for evangelism that can help us be effective in meeting the challenges of our own day. Not a mere rehashing of Lewis, this book offers insight that can help us follow in Lewis's footsteps. And that is a great gift indeed.

— **DONALD T. WILLIAMS**, Professor Emeritus at Toccoa Falls College; author of twelve books, including *Deeper Magic: The Theology Behind the Writings of C. S. Lewis*

Far more than just another introduction on the Oxford don, *C. S. Lewis: Pre-Evangelism for a Post-Christian World* explains why Lewis is an indispensable resource for a post-Christian culture. Boring deeply into Lewis's metaphysics, Brian Williams lifts up the key notion of desire. He rightly contends that by turning to the sacramentality of nature and the imaginative power of fiction, we can stir the "immortal longings" of our contemporaries as Lewis did his. — **HANS BOERSMA**, Saint Benedict Servants of Christ Professor in Ascetical Theology, Nashotah House Theological Seminary

This is a lively treatment of Lewis' vision of reality and of the human imagination. It is also bold - arguing that Lewis' implicit 'pre-evangelistic' strategy is worth reviving in the current cultural climate. A stimulating read. — **JEREMY BEGBIE**, Thomas A. Langford Distinguished Research Professor of Theology, Duke University

Dr. Brian Williams reminds us that the Platonic tradition is not one of many philosophical traditions throughout Western society. Rather, it is the central and perennial tradition of Western society. Christians such as Augustine, Aquinas, and the late C. S. Lewis each embraced philosophical realism as a means to ground their theology. Williams presents Lewis's view of reality and the role metaphysical realism has upon our views of both the imagination and pre-evangelism. Lewis's approach provides a robust alternative to both the secular understanding of philosophical naturalism and the prevalent embrace of Analytic philosophy by many Christians. This book offers a classical solution to our confused philosophical climate, while providing a method to evangelize our post-Christian world. — **WILLIAM C. ROACH**, President, *International Society of Christian Apologetics*

Brian Williams' *C. S. Lewis: Pre-Evangelism for a Post-Christian World: Why Narnia Might Be More Real than We Think* is a thoughtful and well-written exploration how Lewis employed fiction in the service of the Gospel. Williams begins by discussing Lewis's sacramental view of reality and then deftly moves to an exploration of Lewis' romantic view of the human imagination. He then examines these notions as evidenced in Lewis's Ransom Space trilogy and the Chronicles of Narnia, arguing effectively that Lewis's fiction is a powerful tool of pre-evangelism in an increasing post-Christian world. — **DON KING**, Professor of English at Montreat College and author of *C. S. Lewis, Poet: The Legacy of His Poetic Impulse* and *The Collected Poems of C. S. Lewis: A Critical Edition*

FOREWORD

In his book, *The God Who Is There*, Francis A. Schaeffer records an incident at Oxford University after giving a talk on communicating the gospel to those who had been captivated by the naturalistic thinking of the West. Schaeffer writes, "A student stood up and said, 'Sir, if we understand you correctly, you are saying that pre-evangelism must come before evangelism. If this is so, then we have been making a mistake at Oxford. The reason we have not been reaching many of these people is because we have not taken enough time with pre-evangelism.' I said that I totally agreed."[1] The student was not saying, nor was Schaeffer, that pre-evangelism is necessary in every evangelistic encounter. The point being made was that a growing number of people in the West committed to the worldview of naturalism dismissed the idea that reality consisted of more than the material. That is, the naturalistic worldview denies the existence of a reality beyond experience and affirms that all questions of life can be answered through a scientific examination of the physical world. The student understood that naturalism made people tone deaf to the gospel. Furthermore, naturalism not only defined the vocabulary of and categories for public discourse, but it also refocused the lens through which even humanity was to be understood.

Agreeing with both Schaeffer and the student, Jacques Ellul, speaking of evangelism in the last half of the 20th century, wrote, "We ought to have a very exact knowledge of the full reality of the situation before we can hope to win any response. The gospel no longer penetrates. We seem to be confronted by a blank wall. Now if we want to go further, either we must find a door, or we must break down the wall."[2] The situation has only deepened since Ellul penned these words and Schaeffer affirmed the Oxford student's observation. This, however, explains why it was (and is) so difficult to get a gospel response from modern man (as Schaeffer would say) or the post-Christian person. However, a survey of apologetic literature in Ellul's day reveals that little thought had been given to employing pre-evangelism. There were at least two exceptions, Francis Schaeffer and C. S. Lewis.

---

[1] Francis A. Schaeffer, *Complete Works of Francis A. Schaeffer: A Christian Worldview*, vol 1, "The God Who Is There" 2nd Edition, Westchester, IL: Crossway Books, 1985), 155.

[2] Jacques Ellul, *The Presence of The Kingdom*, trans by Olive Wyon (Colorado Springs, Co: Helmers & Howard, Publishers, Inc, 1989), 115. This was previously published by Seabury Press in 1967 one year before Schaeffer published *The God Who Is There*.

Brian M. Williams

The 21st century finds apologetics alive and well in many of the western countries, but I would say not in all. Still, unfortunately, there are only a few apologetic books highlighting the idea of pre-evangelism. I teach apologetics in different places in the world, and I am aware that in some places few have heard of pre-evangelism. In fact, I have just been asked to teach on pre-evangelism to a group of Christian leaders in Ghana. I find that when pre-evangelism is explained, there is an overwhelming receptivity and later testimonies of its effectiveness. As noted, the idea of pre-evangelism can be found in the apologetic literature of C. S. Lewis and Francis Schaeffer. What is interesting, at least to me, is that to the best of my research, they never corresponded, leading one to conclude each came to the concept independent of the other. Although Lewis and Schaeffer's pre-evangelism, in kind, may look somewhat different, both built their pre-evangelism on a shared vision of reality or what is known as metaphysical realism. That is, as affirmed by the Apostle Paul's claim, reality encompasses both the unseen which is eternal and the seen which is temporal or transient (2 Cor 4:18). The physical realm of creation is ordered after the ideas in the Mind of God. As Brian Williams argues, pre-evangelism as seen in Lewis's imaginative writings was bound by this vision of reality. Furthermore, Williams shows the universal and timeless importance of pre-evangelism as part of evangelism.

Williams provides a brilliant treatment of Lewis's pre-evangelism as seen particularly in Lewis's imaginative literature, mainly *The Chronicles of Narnia* and *The Space Trilogy*. He not only argues for the importance of pre-evangelism but gives concrete examples to demonstrate how Lewis did it. Williams skillfully sets the tone of his book by devoting space early on recording events that shaped Lewis the man and the progression of his intellectual journey, particularly with reference to his vision of reality.[3] Ultimately, this led Lewis to a sacramental vision for reality which proved essential to his understanding and use of imagination. Lewis's sacramental vision of reality was not in the salvific sense, but in the sense that it points to something beyond itself while at the same time, as Williams says, "pointing as a kind of participation with that to which it points."

One cannot overemphasize the importance of Williams's insightful discussion of Lewis's use of imagination in his pre-evangelism. This point is crucial to understanding Lewis's use of the imagination. What makes this crucial, in my mind, is that many who hear the word "imagination" instinctively think that it refers to an exercise in some kind of escapism or something totally unhooked from reality. Williams points out, however,

---

[3] Lewis tells of this journey in *The Pilgrim's Regress* (Grand Rapids: Wm. B. Eerdmans Publishing Co, 1943).

that nothing could be further from the truth. Lewis rightly understands that imagination is possible only because there is an objective reality. Imagination does not make something up outside of reality; rather, it re-arranges things taken from reality. It is the only way imagination can work, according to Lewis. As Williams points out, Lewis's use of imagination works hand in glove with his sacramental vision of reality. He explains how Lewis creates stories of "supposal" to arouse within the reader latent longings of desire which answer only to a reality deeper or higher than perceived by the senses. Of course, at the end, this longing can only be satisfied in Christ.

This book is well written and therefore a joy to read, but it is more than a joy; it is pleasantly instructive. Biographically, for those who have not read Lewis, this book will endear you to the man by his love for Christ, his desire to make the gospel known and his literary genius. Personally, for any already acquainted with Lewis, your appreciation will be deepened. Evangelistically, for those who agree with Ellul that today the gospel often seems to not penetrate, Williams shows us a door by way of Lewis's imaginative pre-evangelism which could open the tone-deaf ears to the gospel of Christ. Williams mines from the fertile imaginative writings of Lewis lessons on the unity of imagination, reality, and pre-evangelism. The reader who begins this book with anticipation will not be disappointed and will be encouraged in the work of making Christ known to the peoples of the world.

—Bruce A. Little, PhD

Brian M. Williams

INTRODUCTION

The seeds of what I have to say in this book began germinating as early as my 2nd grade year of elementary school. Near the end of each day, Mrs. Simpson would take her place on a tall chair in front of our class and read to us aloud from *The Lion, the Witch, and the Wardrobe*. This was my first introduction to the magical land of Narnia and to C. S. Lewis. I was normally a very fidgety and distracted boy, but whenever my teacher would read a few pages from Lewis's story, I would sit as still as a statue, completely enraptured by the story that was unfolding before me.

Whether it would be accurate to say that this common-place classroom underwent a transformation each day or that I embarked on a journey outside of it to a land of fauns, centaurs, a terrible witch, and a wonderful lion, is hard to know. Whatever the case, I know this much for certain. A potent spell was cast, and I would never be the same. This story captured my imagination and produced in my heart a longing so intense that I would have given anything in my possession to be granted real, rather than merely imaginary access through the wardrobe into Narnia. The longing was almost painful, sharp, and stabbing. And yet, it was somehow strangely delightful at the very same time.

As a boy who chiefly loved sports, physical activity, and all things "tough," I did not dare share with anyone what was happening inside of me. I assumed that I was alone in these feelings and therefore somewhat odd. Secretly, I waited each day with bottled-up gleeful anticipation for Mrs. Simpson to take us once more into Narnia. Looking back now, I realize that I was longing for the enchanted longing itself that the story produced in me. Throughout the years that followed, even to the present day, this story has occupied such a substantial space in my imagination that it would be hard to make sense of my own journey to Christ and now with Him, apart from its influence.

If memory serves me correctly, it was the following year that our school took a field trip to the Orpheum Theater in downtown Memphis, TN to see the play *The Nutcracker*. That morning, as we sat in our classrooms before loading up on the bus, we were given programs to the play. In each program were drawings accompanied by short descriptions of each of the main characters. I can remember vividly looking at the drawing of the mysterious Drosselmeyer with his silvery white hair, patch over one eye, and long black cape. Suddenly, the same sense of enchantment that Narnia had awakened began to stir once again.

C. S. LEWIS PRE-EVANGELISM FOR A POST-CHRISTIAN WORLD

At last, we arrived at the theater and sat waiting for the play to begin. The lights went down, and the room became dark and very quiet. The red velvet curtain remained closed. As I waited there in the silent darkness, wondering what I was about to see and hear, thinking of Drosselmeyer and a magical nutcracker, the sense of longing grew more pronounced. The curtain went up, and the play began. I thought to myself, "I've been here before." The story, characters, and scenery were all different from Narnia, but "here" was no different. It was the same enchantment, the same spell again, the same aching sense of desire that had gripped me in the past. I would not have used the word then, as I don't think I knew it yet, but it was as if the transcendent was breaking through the mundane and making the world wonderfully different for a short time. I remember wanting to stay in that "place" forever.

There would be more of these experiences throughout my childhood and into my young adult years, but these two accounts remain the most potent in my memory. It took me years to discover what they meant, why they were so intense, and how it was that an unfulfilled desire could itself be so desirable, even while the satisfaction of it remained elusive.

I would have to wait a number of years before finding these answers. I would not become a Christian until the age of twenty. Not long after my conversion, I got married, and my wife and I moved to Wake Forest, NC to begin attending seminary training. During one of our Christmas breaks, we were back in Memphis staying with my mother-in-law. While there, I began reading C. S. Lewis's autobiography *Surprised by Joy*. As I read, I discovered that Lewis had felt the same things that I had felt, only he had discovered their meaning. For the first time in my life, it occurred to me that I was not alone. Another man knew exactly what it was to experience this aching yet desirable longing. Lewis gave to me a vocabulary for understanding and for expressing these experiences. He referred to them as instances of "Joy." In the end, he realized, as I now do also, that they were pointing to something beyond the world. They were pointing to the One who created and sustains it, who is more present than we ever dared dream. Joy was calling me to Him who is absolute truth, goodness, and beauty, the fountain of all legitimate pleasure in whose presence alone our hearts find rest. This One is none other than Christ the Lord.

Given that my doctoral studies have focused in the area of philosophy and theology, I have sought to understand, both philosophically and theologically, why it is that a story like *The Lion, the Witch, and the Wardrobe* can do for young people, and maybe for older people who haven't completely lost their sense of wonder, what it did for me. I became convinced that I needed to ask the question, very simply, "What is it about the world in which we live and the imaginations we have been given, that make these sorts of 'visitations' possible?" Further, I wanted to know—convinced now that such experiences do point us to Christ—how we can make sense of that fact. And then finally, I saw that Lewis came to believe that this phenomenon could be a great help to us as we try to help other people come to know true Joy in the person of Christ. This book is my attempt—one motivated by things very near to and deep within my heart—both to answer these questions with Lewis's help and to encourage followers of Christ to write new stories that might awaken Joy in others, so that they too can come in the end to find their Joy satisfied in Christ.

CHAPTER 1

C. S. Lewis: The Man

Introduction

In this first chapter, we will take a biographical look at C. S. Lewis, the man, in order to set the stage for understanding his view of the relationship between reality and the human imagination, and how he came to embrace such a view. Lewis struggled to make sense of this relationship until his conversion to theism in general and soon after to Christianity in particular. In the first book he published after becoming a Christian, *The Pilgrim's Regress*, he presented an allegorical apology, that is, an explanatory defense, for his newly discovered understanding of the nature of reality and the imagination.[4] His philosophical and theological conclusions on these matters justify his strategy of employing the medium of imaginative fiction to introduce people to Christian ideas clothed in mythological garb. We can call such a strategy "*pre*-evangelism," because Lewis was doing the preparatory work to help people understand key concepts they would need in order to make sense of the good news that the story of Christianity presents to all of humanity.

In this book, I seek to make sense of the ideas behind Lewis's pre-evangelistic strategy. When we hear what Lewis had to say on these matters and then turn to consider the state of our present-day culture, we can see how desperate the hour has become to recapture these truths that have fallen out of favor in much of the western world. I am convinced that Lewis's approach, and the ideas that stand behind it, can serve as a fruitful example for the efforts of Christians today, as we seek to inform our world

---

[4] The original title for *The Pilgrim's Regress* was *Pseudo-Bunyan's Periplus: An Allegorical Apology for Christianity, Reason, and Romanticism*. The publishers talked Lewis into shortening the title to *The Pilgrim's Regress*, and it is first published in 1933, just a year or so after his conversion to Christianity. Regarding the date of his conversion to theism, Lewis himself dates it to "the Trinity Term of 1929." See C. S. Lewis, *Surprised by Joy: The Shape of My Early Life* (Orlando: Harcourt, 1955), 228. Alister McGrath disagrees with the dating of Lewis' conversion to theism in general and places it in 1930. See Alister McGrath, *C. S. Lewis— A Life: Eccentric Genius, Reluctant Prophet* (Carol Stream: Tyndale House Publishers, 2013), 142.

of the truth. In particular, I will argue that C. S. Lewis's understanding of both the nature of reality and of the human imagination informed and motivated his pre-evangelistic strategy.

I should say a word about a very particular term I have chosen to use throughout this book in order to avoid misunderstanding. The term is "sacramental," and I will use this term to describe Lewis's view of reality. I suspect some of us have heard this term before. I am not using it in any way related to matters of Christian salvation, of having one's sins forgiven, of growing more into the character of Christ, or of any particular religious rituals one might do as a member of this or that denomination. The term is sometimes used in that way, but that is not my intended meaning. I am using it solely to describe how Lewis understood the nature of reality. Explaining his own meaning of the term, Lewis writes:

> [I]t is almost the opposite of allegory, and which I would call sacramentalism or symbolism. If our passions, being immaterial, can be copied by material inventions, then it is possible that our material world in its turn is the copy of an invisible world. As the god Amor and his figurative garden are to the actual passions of men, so perhaps we ourselves and our 'real' world are to something else. The attempt to read that something else through its sensible imitations, to see the archetype in the copy, is what I mean by symbolism or sacramentalism…The difference between the two can hardly be exaggerated. The allegorist leaves the given—his own passions—to talk of that which is confessedly less real, which is a fiction. The symbolist leaves the given to find that which is more real."[5]

The basic idea is that the world in which we live and experience on a daily basis is itself pointing beyond to something more solid, more stable, and in a sense more "real." You might say that we are living in the land of shadows but longing for the land of solids. That is what I mean by the term "sacramental." We will consider this concept in depth in the next chapter.

NATURALISM AND THE IMPORTANCE OF HEARING LEWIS'S VOICE

One of the great values of studying C. S. Lewis's life and writings is that they provide a lens through which we can better understand the interplay between reality and the human imagination. The search to

---

[5] See C. S. Lewis, *The Allegory of Love: A Study in Medieval Tradition* (Cambridge: Cambridge University Press, 2016), 56–57.

understand how the things we might imagine relate to the real world stood at the very center of his journey to Christ, and this search impelled him to try to make sense of a world in which nature, literature, and music repeatedly evoked experiences of intense imaginative longing.[6] He writes, for example, in his journal on January 17, 1927, a few years prior to his conversion, the following entry:

> Was thinking about imagination and intellect and the unholy muddle I am in about them at present: undigested scraps of anthroposophy and psychoanalysis jostling with orthodox idealism over a background of good old Kirkian rationalism. Lord what a mess! And all the time (with me) there's the danger of falling back into most childish superstitions, or of running into dogmatic materialism to escape them. I hoped the "King of Drum" might write itself so as to clear things up–the way "Dymer" cleared up the Christina Dream business.[7]

---

[6] Alister McGrath, *C. S. Lewis–A Life: Eccentric Genius, Reluctant Prophet* (Carol Stream: Tyndale House Publishers, 2013), 19. McGrath agrees: "The quest for...Joy would become a central theme of Lewis's life and writing." Lewis calls these longings "joy" throughout his writings.

[7] C. S. Lewis, *All My Road Before Me: The Diary of C. S. Lewis 1922–1927.* Edited by Walter Hooper (San Diego: Harcourt Brace Jovanovich, 1991), 431–432. By "anthroposophy," Lewis is referring to a position that his close friend Owen Barfield adopts but that he himself never does. Barfield embraces many of the ideas of Rudolf Steiner, a major proponent of anthroposophy. Steiner, and later Barfield, held to the notion of the evolution of human consciousness realizing itself through participation in divine consciousness. By "psychoanalysis," Lewis is referring to the ideas of Sigmund Freud, which burst onto the academic scene in 1919, shortly after the Great War (1914–1918) with the publication of the *International Journal of Psycho-Analysis.* Freud's ideas became very influential in Oxford, where Lewis was studying at the time. See C. S. Lewis, *Surprised by Joy,* 203, where Lewis writes of his early post-war Oxford years, "Thirdly, the new Psychology was at that time sweeping through us all ... What we were most concerned about was 'Fantasy' or 'wishful thinking.'" See also Alister McGrath, *The Intellectual World of C. S. Lewis* (Oxford: Wiley-Blackwell, 2014), 43–44, where McGrath writes, "One of the most decisive influences on the shaping of western culture after the Great War was the new psychoanalytical view of Sigmund Freud (1856–1939) ... Freud's analysis of wish-fulfillment seemed especially destructive to Lewis." By "orthodox idealism," Lewis is referring to the brief philosophical move he makes prior to accepting theism. See C. S. Lewis, *Surprised by Joy,* 209, where Lewis writes, "I was therefore compelled to give up realism. I had been trying to defend it ever since I began reading philosophy ... Idealism was then the dominant philosophy at Oxford and I was by nature 'against Government.' But partly, too, realism satisfied an emotional need. I wanted Nature to be quite independent of our observation; something other, indifferent, self-existing ... But now, it seemed to me, I had to give that up. Unless I were to accept an unbelievable alternative, I must admit that mind was no later-come epiphenomenon; that the whole universe was, in the last resort, mental; that our logic was participation in a cosmic *Logos.*" "Kirkian rationalism" refers to his former tutor William T. Kirkpatrick ("the Great Knock"). Lewis expresses his being indebted to the Great Knock for helping him to think. He refers to

The very next day, he recounts:

> I went for a walk across the fields to Stowe Woods and home by road. Still puzzled about imagination etc. As I was crossing the big field into Barton on the way back, I suddenly found myself thinking "What I won't give up is the doctrine that what we get in imagination at its highest is real in some way, tho, at this stage one can't say how": and then my intellectual conscience smote me for having got to that last pitch of sentimentality—asserting what "I won't do" when I ought to be enquiring what I can know.[8]

Lewis detailed his search for an answer to this paradox in his autobiography *Surprised by Joy* and his allegorical tale, *The Pilgrim's Regress*. The conclusion on which he settled not only helped him to understand reality more fully; it also later informed his pre-evangelism strategy. He adopted his strategy in a conscious effort to penetrate the wall around peoples' minds and hearts that had been erected largely by the influence of naturalism. Naturalism is the view that there is no such person as God, no angels, no spirits, no miracles, and such. The world of our everyday experience that we perceive via our five sense is all that really exists, according to the naturalist.

For the Christian living in the modern western world today, Lewis' voice on these matters cannot be ignored when one considers two things. (1) The conclusions of naturalism, which stand in direct opposition to Lewis' views on reality and the human imagination, have become extremely influential and pervasive in the present culture.[9] (2) Lewis recognized this

---

him in C. S. Lewis, *Miracles: A Preliminary Study* (New York: HarperOne, 2001), 109–110, "The very man who taught me to think—a hard satirical atheist (ex-Presbyterian) who doted on the *Golden Bough* and filled his house with the products of the Rationalist Press Association ... His attitude to Christianity was for me the starting point of adult thinking; you may say it is bred in my bones." "Dymer" is an epic poem that Lewis writes and publishes under the name "Clive Hamilton." "King of Drum" refers to a character in a poem that Lewis writes over a twenty-year period from 1918 to 1938 entitled *The Queen of Drum*. In one section of the poem, the characters try to figure out if their dreams are real embodied experiences or just mere dreams. The first mention of "Christina Dreams" is found in Lewis' diary entitled *All My Road Before Me*. He writes on April 11, 1922, "I walked to the bus with him afterwards: we began on Christina Dreams, but, as always with him, ended on immortality," 20. See C. S. Lewis, *Dymer*. Originally published under the pseudonym: Clive Hamilton (UK: Crossreach Publications, 2016), 5, where Lewis writes, "The 'Christina Dream', as we called it (after Christina Pontifex in Butler's novel), was the hidden enemy whom we were all determined to unmask and defeat. My hero, therefore, had to be a mad who had succumbed to its allurements and finally got the better of them."

[8] Ibid., 432.

[9] For a detailed argument from Lewis against Naturalism's view of the "supernatural" and the "miraculous," see C. S. Lewis, *Miracles: A Preliminary Study* (New York: HarperOne,

growing pervasiveness in his own day, and he responded to it at length and strategized his evangelistic approach in light of it.

Due to the influence of naturalism and its various cultural manifestations in the present day, the Christian message often falls flat, even if it is given some level of an initial hearing from time to time. Lewis recognized this unfortunate situation in his day, which has only intensified since then. He writes, for example, to a group of Anglican priests and youth leaders in 1945:

> The difficulty we are up against is this. We can often make people attend to the Christian point of view for half an hour or so; but the moment they have gone away from the lecture or laid down our article, they are plunged back into a world where the opposite position is taken for granted. Every newspaper, film, novel and textbook undermines our work. As long as that situation exists, widespread success is simply impossible. We must attack the enemy's line of communication. What we want is not more little books about Christianity, but more little books by Christians on other subjects—with their Christianity latent.[10]

He writes similarly in the epilogue to his book *Miracles*:

2001). The Naturalist believes that nothing exists except nature. Therefore, reality is one-dimensional in a sense. What one sees is what one gets. From this perspective, nothing in the world of Nature, which is "the whole show," points to anything beyond itself. The word "beyond" is meaningless given Naturalism. Thus, imaginative longings which seem to Lewis and many others like "visitors from another world," to use Roger Scruton's phrase from his segment *Why Beauty Matters*, are anything but this. Along with this, free will must go as well. See Ibid. 8, where Lewis writes, "No thoroughgoing Naturalist believes in free will: for free will would mean that human beings have the power of independent action, the power of doing something more or other than what was involved by the total series of events." He goes on to argue that, given Naturalism, knowledge itself seems impossible. This would mean, of course, that the person who finds herself puzzled about the meaning of her imaginative longings can no more reach a reasonable conclusion than a box of cereal can understand "2 + 2 = 4." Reasoning is not the sort of thing that accidentally emerging and determined beings can do. See Ibid., 22, 27, where Lewis writes, "But Naturalism, even if it is not purely materialistic, seems to me to involve the same difficulty, though in a somewhat less obvious form. It discredits our processes of reasoning or at least reduces their credit to such a humble level that it can no longer support Naturalism itself ... Any thing which professes to explain our reasoning fully without introducing an act of knowing thus solely determined by what is known, is really a theory that there is no reasoning. But this, as it seems to me, is what Naturalism is bound to do. It offers what professes to be a full account of our mental behavior; but this account, on inspection, leaves no room for the acts of knowing or insights on which the whole value of our thinking, as a means to truth, depends."

[10] C. S. Lewis, *Undeceptions: Essays on Theology and Ethics* (London: Bles, 1971).

> We all have Naturalism in our bones and even conversion does not at once work the infection out of our system. Its assumptions rush back upon the mind the moment vigilance is relaxed ... Everythingism is congenial to our minds because it is the natural philosophy of a totalitarian, mass-producing, conscripted age. That is why we must be perpetually on our guard against it. And yet ... and yet ... It is that *and yet* which I fear more than any positive argument against miracles: that soft, tidal return of your habitual outlook as you close the book and the familiar four walls about you and the familiar noises from the street reassert themselves ... The moment rational thought ceases, imagination, mental habit, temperament, and the 'spirit of the age' take charge of you again. New thoughts, until they have themselves become habitual, will affect your consciousness as a whole only while you are actually thinking them ... the mere gravitation of the mind back to its habitual outlook must be discounted.[11]

The present situation is one in which naturalism, or at least the functional entailments of naturalism, are not so much argued *for* as they are assumed. They are, as Lewis says, "in our bones."[12] The naturalistic, rather than the supernaturalistic view of reality, lies latent nearly everywhere. Thinking and even feeling "naturalistically" has become almost as effortless as breathing. One does not think about doing it; one simply does it. This is even the case very often for those who would not want to sign up explicitly to this philosophy. Could anyone reasonably deny that much of life in the present culture is structured and carried out as if God is not really present?

Various authors describe the situation in similar terms. Charles Taylor, in his voluminous work, *A Secular Age,* tells the story of how this present situation has come to pass and attempts to analyze the ideas that currently shape it. His usage of the term "secular age" captures the notion of a society thoroughly saturated by naturalism. For Taylor, a society has become secularized when two general movements occur. First, the public spaces have been "allegedly emptied of God, or of any reference to ultimate reality."[13] This public secularity then leads to the second movement:

> [A] move from a society where belief in God is unchallenged and indeed, unproblematic, to one in which it is understood to be one option among others, and frequently not the easiest to

---

[11] C. S. Lewis, *Miracles,* 268–272.
[12] Ibid., 268.
[13] Charles Taylor, *A Secular Age* (Cambridge: Belknap Press, 2007), 2.

embrace ... one which takes us from a society in which it was virtually impossible not to believe in God, to one in which faith, even for the staunchest believer, is one human possibility among others.[14]

Ken Myers also describes this move toward an increasingly naturalistic presumption. Myers says:

Christian concern about popular culture should be as much about sensibilities it encourages as about its content. The convictions behind this claim have become harder to explain with the passage of time, because the sensibilities that I believe to be problematic have now become so dominant as to be imperceptible.[15]

By "sensibilities," Myers means "the orientation of the affections, the posture of the soul, the desires of the heart, the characteristic hungers and expectations."[16] To put it another way, the present spirit of the age has tuned modern man's heart to the naturalistic fork. Craig M. Gay argues along similar lines:

One of the most consequential ideas embedded in modern institutions and traditions and habits of thought is theological. Stated bluntly, it is the assumption that even if God exists he is largely irrelevant to the real business of life ... In short, one of the most insidious temptations fostered within contemporary secular society and culture, a temptation rendered uniquely plausible by the ideas and assumptions embedded within modern institutional life, is the temptation to *practical atheism*.[17]

Rod Dreher agrees with these assessments and also suggests, soberingly, that the church, in many ways, has inhaled the noxious gases of naturalism. He maintains:

Not only have we lost the public square, but the supposed high ground of our churches is no safe place either. Well, so what if those around us don't share our morality? We can still retain our faith and teaching within the walls of our churches, we may think, but that's placing unwarranted confidence in the health of our religious institutions. The changes that have overtaken the West

---

[14] Ibid., 3.

[15] Ken Myers, *All God's Children & Blue Suede Shoes* (Wheaton: Crossway, 2012), v.

[16] Ibid., vi.

[17] Craig M. Gay, *The (Way) of the Modern World, Or, Why It's Tempting to Live as if God Doesn't Exist* (Grand Rapids: Eerdmans, 1998), 2.

in modern times have revolutionized everything, even the church, which no longer forms souls but caters to selves. As conservative Anglican theologian Ephraim Radner has said, "There is no safe place in the world or in our churches within which to be a Christian. It is a new epoch."[18]

To invoke Lewis' language from *The Abolition of Man*, modern man finds himself in the precarious position of having long since abandoned "the Tao."[19] By this term, Lewis means the traditional and objective values that exist as part of the framework of reality to which one's beliefs and attitudes either correspond or with which they conflict.[20] Abandoning belief in objective truth and values is one of the unavoidable entailments of naturalism. Problematically, in spite of modern man's abandoning these, he makes all sorts of judgments regarding social issues, politics, education, and various other cultural spheres that depend on "the Tao" if they are to be objective. If his judgments are not grounded in "the Tao," they are merely subjective values with no objective basis in reality. They are nothing more than opinions, we might say. If he tries to persuade another through merely subjective judgments, he adopts "either a fool's or a villain's undertaking."[21]

The crucial point I am making here is that the more pervasive naturalism becomes, taking it of course to be false, the more important Lewis's thoughts will prove to be. It was already entrenched so firmly in the consciousness of Lewis's day that the common unsuspecting supernaturalist could find no sanctuary in reading even the modern theologians, the very ones whom one would expect to meet as allies in such a battle. Lewis warned his readers of this sad state of affairs in the epilogue to his book *Miracles,* wherein he offers a defense of the miraculous in the face of naturalism. He writes:

> And when you turn from the New Testament to modern scholars, remember that you go among them as sheep among wolves. Naturalistic assumptions, beggings of the question such as that which I noted on the first page of this book, will meet you on every side—even from the pens of clergymen. This does not mean (as I was once tempted to suspect) that these clergymen are

---

[18] Rod Dreher, *The Benedict Option: A Strategy for Christians in a Post-Christian Nation* (New York: Sentinel, 2017), 9.

[19] C. S. Lewis, *The Abolition of Man* (New York: HarperOne, 2001), 29.

[20] See Ibid., 18, where Lewis describes the Chinese notion of the Tao specifically as "the reality beyond all predicates." He uses the term "the Tao" to refer to " … the doctrine of objective value, the belief that certain attitudes are really true, and others really false, to the kind of thing the universe is and the kind of things we are."

[21] Ibid., 29.

disguised apostates who deliberately export the position and the livelihood given them by the Christian Church to undermine Christianity. It comes partly from what we may call a 'hangover'. We all have Naturalism in our bones and even conversion does not at once work the infection out of our system. Its assumptions rush back upon the mind the moment vigilance is relaxed.[22]

Naturalism entails the very opposite conclusion to Lewis's thoughts on the nature of reality and the human imagination.

Whereas he sees this world in some way pointing beyond itself to the transcendent, the naturalist concludes that this material world experienced by the senses is all that exists, or to use Lewis' words, he concludes that the material world is "the whole show."[23] It points to nothing beyond itself. Thus, regarding experiences of imaginative longing, which occur as a somewhat common human experience, there seem to be only three possible conclusions for the naturalist: (1) The object or experience that evokes the longing can *itself* satisfy. (2) Something else in the material world can satisfy–some other object or experience than the one that evoked the longing. It has yet to be found, but perhaps through more time given to the search, it will be. (3) Satisfaction for imaginative longings cannot be obtained in this world, and given that, for the naturalist, this material world is the sum total of reality, satisfaction cannot be had at all. I want to maintain that the naturalistic perspective is far from "the whole show," and that the supernaturalist perspective, to which C. S. Lewis holds, is the correct one. It is to C. S. Lewis the man, his story and context, that the present chapter now turns.

C. S. LEWIS, THE MAN: A BRIEF BIOGRAPHY

Referring to C. S. Lewis, J. R. R. Tolkien once said to an incoming student at Oxford, "You'll never get to the bottom of him."[24] That incoming student was George Sayer who read English under Lewis and later became his close friend. Reflecting on his friendship with Lewis, Sayer admits, "Tolkien was right...I never got to the bottom of him."[25] The present task of this first chapter is not to attempt what Tolkien thought

---

[22] C. S. Lewis, *Miracles: A Preliminary Study* (New York: HarperOne, 2001), 267–268.
[23] C. S. Lewis, *Miracles*, 6.
[24] George Sayer, *Jack: C. S. Lewis and His Times* (San Francisco: Harper & Row, 1988), xvii.
[25] Ibid., xvii.

impossible, but simply to set a context within which a later analysis of Lewis' thoughts might be better understood.

As will become clear through the telling of this story, "Joy," what Lewis described as "imaginative longing," stood at the very center of his life and thought.[26] He admitted that his own autobiography, which he appropriately titled *Surprised by Joy*, would interest its readers in direct proportion to the degree to which they have experienced this particular kind of longing.[27] Joy played a sort of muse-like role in Lewis's life, appearing from time to time and moving him to contemplate the nature of reality and the identity of the object or objects provoking his imaginative longings. He struggled for years to make sense of these experiences, yet he was unable to understand *what* they were and to *what* they pointed until at last he came to understand the true nature of reality, or more properly, of ultimate reality.[28] Colin Duriez notes, "The experience of joy or longing that the adult C. S. Lewis speaks about...ran like a thread through his life, helping his later return to belief in God and Christian faith from atheism in adulthood."[29] It is therefore fitting that any telling of Lewis's personal story should keep central what lies at the center of his life, as this chapter will attempt to do.

BECKONED BY JOY: HIS BOYHOOD TO YOUNG ADULTHOOD YEARS (1898—1926)

Clive Staples Lewis was born on November 29, 1898 in Belfast, Ireland. His father Albert and his mother Flora were both "bookish" people, although they lacked the romantic strain that infected Lewis from an early age.[30] They developed a habit of reading for several hours each night after dinner, a structure which Lewis would adopt from his Oxford years onward.[31] Albert James Lewis (1863-1929) enjoyed a successful career

---

[26] C. S. Lewis, *Surprised by Joy: The Shape of My Early Life* (Orlando: Harcourt, 1955), 175.

[27] Ibid., vii. See also where he says later, referring to his experiences of joy, "The reader who finds these three episodes of no interest need read this book no further, for in a sense the central story of my life is about nothing else" 17.

[28] Ibid., 221. Lewis refers to ultimate reality as "the Absolute" and "utter reality."

[29] Colin Duriez, *C. S. Lewis: A Biography of Friendship* (Oxford: Lion Books, 2013), 14.

[30] Ibid., 4–5, "What neither he nor my mother had the least taste for was that kind of literature to which my allegiance was given the moment I could choose books for myself. Neither had ever listened for the horns of elfland. There was no copy either of Keats or Shelley in the house, and the copy of Coleridge was never (to my knowledge) opened. If I am a romantic my parents bear no responsibility for it."

[31] George Sayer, *Jack: C. S. Lewis and His Times*, p. 11.

as a solicitor in his own practice in Belfast. His success came partly due to qualities, some of which would later find fruitful expression in his son, Clive as well. Sayer describes Albert as possessing "an excellent memory...a quickness of mind that included a gift for telling repartee, and a fine resonant voice...a real rhetorical gift. He spoke in admirably rhythmic sentences...and above all, had the gift of presenting a complex argument in convincingly simple terms."[32] A voracious reader, a characteristic noted in his obituary, Albert enjoyed political novels, some poetry, and most humorous authors such as Dickens.[33] His personality was the direct opposite of his wife's. While Albert possessed a passionate and emotionally mercurial disposition, Flora was "analytical and cool in her emotions."[34]

Florence ("Flora") Augusta Lewis (1862-1908) was a well-educated woman who managed the home and provided Lewis and his brother Warren[35], three years his elder, with love and structure. She had attended the Royal University of Ireland in Belfast and had studied Logic and Mathematics, earning First Class Honors in the former and Second Class Honors in the latter.[36] By the time that Lewis was one month old, Flora was managing five servants in the home. Of the five servants, Lizzie Endicott, the nursemaid, influenced him most significantly, particularly with respect to his developing imagination. Along with "good parents, good food, and a good garden...to play in," his nursemaid was one of two great blessings in his early years.[37] He writes of her that "even the exacting

---

[32] Ibid., pp. 3-4. See also Alister McGrath in *C. S. Lewis: A Life*, p. 7 for his helpful distinction between a solicitor and an barrister, of which Albert was the former: "The Supreme Court of Judicature (Ireland) Act of 1877 followed the English practice of making a clear distinction between the legal role of 'solicitors' and 'barristers,' so that aspiring Irish lawyers were required to decide which professional position they wished to pursue. Albert Lewis chose to become a solicitor, acting directly on behalf of clients, including representing them in lower courts. A barrister specialized in courtroom advocacy, and would be hired by a solicitor to represent a client in the higher courts."

[33] See *Belfast Telegraph*, September 28, 1929, which contains Albert's obituary and describes him as a "well read and erudite man," who "found his chief recreation away from the courts of law in reading." See also C. S. Lewis, *Surprised by Joy*, p. 4.

[34] Colin Duriez, *C. S. Lewis: A Biography of Friendship*, p. 13.

[35] Lewis calls his brother "Warnie" throughout their lives. From here forward, he will be referred to as "Warnie."

[36] J. W. Henderson, *Methodist College, Belfast, 1868-1938: A Survey and Retrospect*. 2 vols. (Belfast: Governors of Methodist College, 1939), vol. 1, pp. 120-130. Note that the school's name is now Queen's University, Belfast.

[37] C. S. Lewis, *Surprised by Joy*, p. 5.

memory of childhood can discover no flaw—nothing but kindness, gaiety, and good sense...Lizzie was, as nearly as a human can be, simply good."[38]

Though Flora taught him Latin and French from a young age, she left the reading and telling of stories largely to Lizzie.[39] When Lewis was just two and a half years of age, she read "The Three Bears" to him. Along with this story, she opened to him the world of "folk tales and fairy tales, of leprechauns and crocks of gold, fantastical worlds such as the Isle of Apples and the Land of Youth."[40] No doubt inspired by his nursemaid, he practiced his own efforts at storytelling whenever his cousin, Claire Lewis, would come to visit. He would convince Warnie and Claire to listen to his imaginative adventure stories while they all sat inside a "prophetic" piece of furniture—a large oak wardrobe that had been carved by his grandfather.

His young imagination was stirred not only by stories, but also by the scenery and sounds to which Belfast exposed him. Lewis spent the first six years of his life in a semi-detached house in Dundela Villas in a suburb of Belfast with a view overlooking Belfast Lough. Sayer writes of this scenery, "The surroundings were beautiful. The city was ringed by green hills, and, to the northwest, there were 'interminable summer sunsets behind the green ridges.'"[41]

The city of Belfast had begun to grow rapidly in the nineteenth century and would enjoy general prosperity until the end of the First World War. During its prosperous period, the harbor and port were developed further to accommodate the growing industrial production which was imported mainly from England. From their house, as the brothers looked down into Belfast Lough, they could see the sea and ships as well as the nearby shipyards full of machinery which especially fascinated Warnie. Lewis writes, "This was in the far off days when Britain was the world's carrier and the Lough was full of shipping; a delight to both us boys, but most to my brother. The sound of a steamer's horn at night still conjures up my whole boyhood."[42] The first toy Lewis asked for was a wooden train, and throughout the course of his life, the front carriage of a train would remain his preferred mode of transportation.[43]

---

[38] Ibid., p. 5.

[39] George Sayer, *Jack: C. S. Lewis and His Times* (San Francisco: Harper & Row, 1988), 10.

[40] Colin Duriez, *C. S. Lewis: A Biography of Friendship* (Oxford: Lion Hudson, 2014), 17.

[41] Ibid., 12.

[42] C. S. Lewis, *Surprised by Joy*, 11.

[43] See George Sayer, *Jack: C. S. Lewis and His Times*, 14.

In April of 1905, the family moved to Little Lea, a three story red brick house that Albert commissioned to be built a little further out into the country than the Dundela Villas. Lewis describes the impact of his new home upon his life:

> The New House is almost a major character in my story. I am a product of long corridors, empty sunlit rooms, upstairs indoor silences, attics explored in solitude, distant noises of gurgling cisterns and pipes, and the noise of wind under the tiles. Also, of endless books. My father bought all the books he read and never got rid of any of them. There were books in the study, books in the drawing room, books in the cloakroom, books (two deep) in the great bookcase on the landing, books in a bedroom, books piled as high as my shoulder in the cistern attic, books of all kind reflecting every transient stage of my parents' interest, books readable and unreadable, books suitable for a child and books most emphatically not. Nothing was forbidden me. In the seemingly endless rainy afternoons I took volume after volume from the shelves.[44]

In Little Lea, one detects the early inspiration for Polly's and Digory's attic exploring that commenced their adventures in the first chapter of *The Magician's Nephew*.[45]

From the nursery window of Little Lea, he and Warnie could view the Castlereagh Hills, or the "Green Hills" as they called them, which cinctured the city. It is of these hills that Lewis writes, "They taught me longing—*Sehnsucht*; made me for good or ill, and before I was six years old, a votary of the Blue Flower."[46] He offers little help in illuminating the meaning of the German word "Sehnsucht" and the reference to the "Blue Flower," other than to associate the German term with the notion of longing. Alister McGrath, in his recent biography on Lewis, offers a helpful explanation that sheds light on both concepts. He writes:

---

[44] C. S. Lewis, Surprised by Joy, 10.

[45] See C. S. Lewis, *The Magician's Nephew* (New York: Macmillan Publishing Company, 1970), 5. "It is wonderful how much exploring you can do with a stump of candle in a big house, or in a row of houses. Polly had discovered long ago that if you opened a certain little door in the box-room attic of her house you would find the cistern and a dark place behind it which you could get in to by a little careful climbing ... Polly had ... brought up bits of old packing cases and the seats of broken kitchen chairs, and things of that sort, and spread them across from rafter to rafter so as to make a bit of floor. Here she kept a cash-box containing various treasures, and a story she was writing, and usually a few apples."

[46] C. S. Lewis, *Surprised by Joy*, 7.

What does Lewis mean by *Sehnsucht*? The German word is rich with emotional and imaginative associations, famously described by the poet Matthew Arnold as a "wistful, soft tearful longing." And what of the "Blue Flower"? Leading German Romantic writers, such as Novalis (1772–1801) and Joseph von Eichendorff (1788–1857), used the image of a "Blue Flower" as a symbol of the wanderings and yearnings of the human soul, especially as this sense of longing is evoked–though not satisfied–by the natural world.[47]

In the first book that Lewis wrote after his conversion to Christianity, *The Pilgrim's Regress*, he tells the allegorical tale of his personal search for the object of his longing. Significantly, he chose an object from nature, namely an island, as the image which beckons the lead character, John, forward on his journey. When John arrives at his destination and at last discovers that for which his heart was yearning, he notices that his island had merged with a mountain range. The angel who guides him on the last bit of his journey explains to him, "They are not only the same shape. They are the same...The Island is the Mountains: or, if you will, the Island is the other side of the Mountains, and not, in truth, an Island at all."[48] Throughout his life, Lewis emphasized the importance of scenery and atmosphere to the quality of a story, and his own stories drew much of their inspiration from these boyhood sights and sounds afforded to him by Ireland's beautiful landscape.

The other great blessing he mentions from his earliest years was his older brother, Warnie, with whom he remained very close throughout his entire life. Warnie and he began writing and illustrating imaginative stories over the holidays whenever Warnie would return from boarding school. Warnie's early drawings and stories dealt more with actual places as well as the mechanized realities of the world at that time–trains, ships, wars, and India, for example. While Lewis also explored these realities in his early stories, he found his greatest pleasure in "dressed animals and knights in armor."[49] He drew Warnie into his imaginative world of sophisticated

---

[47] Alister McGrath, *C. S. Lewis–A Life: Eccentric Genius, Reluctant Prophet* (Carol Stream: Tyndale, 2013), 16. See also C. S. Lewis, *The Pilgrim's Regress*. Wade Annotated Edition, 212. Downing provides the following note in the margin: "the Blue Flower: A symbol of a nameless longing in the novel *Heinrich von Ofterdingen* (1802) by the German writer Novalis (Friedrich von Hardenberg, 1772–1802)."

[48] C. S. Lewis, *The Pilgrim's Regress*, Wade Annotated Edition, Edited by David C. Downing (Grand Rapids: Eerdmans, 2014), 177.

[49] C. S. Lewis, *Surprised by Joy*, 13. See also p. 14. Lewis mentions that Sir Arthur Conan Doyle's *Sir Nigel* first gave him the image of "knights in armor," and Sir John Tenniel stirred his imagination for "dressed animals." Tenniel worked for fifty years as the chief political

anthropomorphic animals who talked and carried on societal and political life, and the two brothers eventually co-created the world of "Animal-Land" or "Boxen."[50] Warnie writes of these early literary creations:

> We would gaze out of our nursery window at the slanting rain and the grey skies...and...would see the dim high line of the Castlereigh Hills—our world's limit, a distant land, strange and unattainable. But we always had pencils, paper, chalk and paint boxes, and this recurring imprisonment gave us occasion and stimulus to develop the habit of creative imagination. We learnt to draw: My brother made his first attempt at writing; together we devised the imaginary country of "Boxen"...and it may not be fanciful to see, in that childhood staring out to unattainable hills, some first beginnings of a vision and viewpoint that run through the work of his maturity.[51]

While one can see the makings of Narnia in these early stories, Lewis admitted that Animal-Land lacked the crucial quality of enchantment that characterized the land of Narnia. He clarifies, "For readers of my children's books, the best way of putting this would be to say that Animal-Land had nothing whatever in common with Narnia except the anthropomorphic beasts. Animal-Land, by its whole quality, excludes the least hint of wonder."[52] The brothers envisioned Animal-Land as an island "with its north coast running along the back of the Himalayas."[53] Despite the lack of wonder in Animal-Land, it is the image of an island joined with mountains, as has been noted previously, that served as the very same geographical

---

cartoonist for *Punch*, a British magazine which ran from 1841 to 1992. Lewis' father had collected many of these magazine which were at Lewis' disposal. Tenniel also illustrated Lewis Carroll's *Alice* stories.

[50] See Walter Hooper, *C. S. Lewis: Companion and Guide* (San Francisco: Harper Collins, 1996), p. 131, where he notes that Lewis began writing the Boxen stories after the family moved in April of 1905 to "Little Lea," their larger house in Belfast. He also notes that Warnie's India and Clive's Animal-Land combined to make Boxen. Lewis was around seven years old when he began writing these stories.

[51] W. H. Lewis, ed. *The Letters of C. S. Lewis* (London: Bles, 1966), WHL Memoir 1.

[52] C. S. Lewis, *Surprised by Joy*, p. 15 (see footnote). He also writes, "My invented world was full (for me) of interest, bustle, humor, and character; but there was no poetry, even no romance, in it. It was almost astonishingly prosaic," 15.

[53] Ibid., 14.

image that Lewis later chose to represent the object of his imaginative longing in *The Pilgrim's Regress*.[54]

In his autobiography, *Surprised by Joy*, Lewis describes three of the most formative experiences that shaped not only his younger years, but also the entirety of his life. He calls these experiences instances of "Joy." They occurred between the ages of six and eight. The first instance took place on a summer day while he was standing next to a flowering currant bush. Suddenly, a sensation almost too strong to convey with words came over him, awakened by a memory. The memory was of a previous day when Warnie had brought into the nursery a biscuit tin "with moss and...twigs and flowers so as to make it a toy garden or a toy forest."[55] This toy garden had first awakened him to nature being something "cool, dewy, fresh, exuberant," and is his very first experience of beauty.[56] Later, the memory of this experience arrested him. Lewis remembers:

> It was a sensation, of course, of desire; but desire for what? not, certainly, for a biscuit tin filled with moss, nor even (though that came into it) for my own past ... before I knew what I desired, the desire itself was gone, the whole glimpse withdrawn, the world turned commonplace again, or only stirred by a longing for the longing that had just ceased. It has taken only a moment of time; and in a certain sense everything else that had ever happened to me was insignificant in comparison.[57]

Later, while he was reading Beatrix Potter's *Squirrel Nutkin*, joy arrested him a second time. This time, the experience, which seemed to come from "another dimension," delightfully troubled him with what he calls "the Idea of Autumn."[58] Again, "intense desire" gripped him.[59] He reread the book in an attempt to re-awaken the desire because the very desire itself, though its object remained a mystery to him at this time, proved immensely desirable.

Lewis' third glimpse of "Joy" came as he was reading Henry Wadsworth Longfellow's *Saga of King Olaf*. He turned a page and his eyes

---

[54] C. S. Lewis, *The Pilgrim's Regress*, 176–177. "But the world is round," said the Guide, "and you have come nearly round it. The Island is the Mountains: or, if you will, the Island is the other side of the Mountains, and not, in truth, as Island at all."

[55] C. S. Lewis, *Surprised by Joy*, 7.

[56] Ibid., 7.

[57] Ibid. 16.

[58] Ibid., 17.

[59] Ibid., 17.

fell on Longfellow's translation of three lines from the Swedish poet Esaias Tegner's *Drapa* which says:

> *I heard a voice that cried,*
> *Balder the beautiful*
> *Is dead, is dead—*[60]

This time, he was drawn up into "huge regions of northern sky" and found himself longing "with almost sickening intensity" for something indescribable and unidentifiable.[61] Tragically once again, no sooner than the desire came, it began to flee, and he found himself wishing it would return. He writes of these three experiences of joy:

> I will only underline the quality common to the three experiences; it is that of an unsatisfied desire which is itself more desirable than any other satisfaction...anyone who has experienced it will want it again...I doubt whether anyone who has tasted it would ever, if both were in his power, exchange it for all the pleasures in the world.[62]

While Lewis' early years proved formative due to visitations from "Joy," tragic loss also shaped his young life. In early 1908, his mother Flora's health began to decline. She and Albert underwent a medical consolation in their home which brought the decision to proceed with major surgery. The surgery, which Albert describes as a "horrible operation,"[63] commenced at Little Lea on February 15, 1908 and brought the grim diagnosis–abdominal cancer.[64] Lewis recalls, "And then my father, in tears, came into my room and began to try to convey to my terrified mind things it had never conceived before. It was in fact cancer."[65]

In May, during Flora's convalescence after the surgery, she enjoyed one final trip with Lewis to a harbor town in north Belfast. The following month she wrote the last known letter to her other elder son Warnie, who was at that time away at boarding school. The letter was written on June 15, 1908, the day before Warnie's birthday. Flora writes, "I am sorry not to have been able to write to you regularly this term, but I find I am really

---

[60] C. S. Lewis, *Surprised by Joy*, p. 17.
[61] Ibid., p. 17.
[62] Ibid., pp. 17-18.
[63] Cited in Colin Duriez, *C. S. Lewis: A Biography of Friendship*, 24.
[64] George Sayer, *Jack: C. S. Lewis and His Times*, 22.
[65] C. S. Lewis, *Surprised by Joy*, 18.

not well enough to do so. I have been feeling very poorly lately and writing tires me very much. But I must write today to wish you a happy birthday."[66]

Warnie was called home soon thereafter from Wynyard School in Watford, north of London, in order to be with his mother during her final days. A well-known photograph taken just prior to Flora's death shows Lewis and Warnie standing with their bicycles in front of a neighbor's home. Knowing what is to come as one looks into the faces of the young brothers in this photograph, it is difficult not the feel a lump in one's throat rising. Lying in her bed one day, Flora looked up at Albert, who had been speaking to her about the goodness of God, and she uttered words that would haunt her husband, "What have we done for Him?"[67] On August 23rd, 1908, at 6:30am, Flora died. Lewis was devastated. He recalls, "With my mother's death all settled happiness, all that was tranquil and reliable, disappeared from my life. There was to be much fun, many pleasures, many stabs of Joy; but no more of the old security. It was sea and islands now; the great continent had sunk like Atlantis."[68]

In the following month of September, Albert sent the boys off to England to Wynyard School. Given his love of the beautiful green and mountainous Irish countryside, when he arrived in England for the first time and noticed the drastically different scenery, Lewis reacted with "immediate hatred."[69] He writes, "The flats of Lancashire in the early morning are in reality a dismal sight; to me they were like the banks of Styx."[70] He goes on to describe the area from Fleetwood to Euston thus: "The flatness! The interminableness! The miles and miles of featureless land, shutting one in from the sea, imprisoning, suffocating! Everything was wrong; wooden fences instead of stone walls and hedges, red brick farmhouses instead of white cottages, and fields too big, haystacks the wrong shape."[71]

As if the death of his mother and separation from the natural beauty of Ireland which he had come to love were not hard enough on him, Wynyard School proved for Lewis to be like a "concentration camp."[72] The headmaster, Rev. Robert Capron, whom the brothers called "Oldie," ruled with an erratic and cruel temperament. On one occasion, Capron brutally attacked a young boy with such severity that his parents took the

---

[66] Cited in Colin Duriez, *C. S. Lewis: A Biography of Friendship*, 25.
[67] Cited in George Sayer, *Jack: C. S. Lewis and His Times*, 22.
[68] C. S. Lewis, *Surprised by Joy*, 21.
[69] Ibid., 24.
[70] Ibid., 24.
[71] C. S. Lewis, *Surprised by Joy*, 24.
[72] Ibid., 22.

headmaster to high court, resulting in a settlement.[73] Capron gave up the school mid-year in 1910 and secured a church pastorate in June of that year. Following a violent outburst towards his parishioners, he was restrained, declared insane, and committed to an asylum where he later died on November of 1911.[74] Lewis writes to his father, at the end of his first month at Wynyard School, "Please may we not leave on Saturday? We simply *cannot* wait in this hole till the end of term."[75]

Whereas the brothers deeply needed comfort from their father Albert during such an unsteady and painful time, Albert withdrew, further alienating himself from his sons. As a result, Warnie and Lewis drew closer to one another. Lewis writes, "We were coming, my brother and I, to rely more and more exclusively on each other for all that made life bearable; to have confidence only in each other ... We drew daily closer together ... two frightened urchins huddled for warmth in a bleak world."[76] He leaned on Warnie as his protector from the bullying that took place at Wynyard School.[77] This protection, however, did not last for the entirety of his enrollment as Warnie left in April of the following year to begin attending Malvern College.

In Warnie's absence, Lewis learned "if not friendship, at least gregariousness."[78] He and his new friends found themselves allies against their common enemy, "Oldie." The notion of friendship through the shared alliance against a foe proved formative to him throughout his entire life, and one can detect the early sentiments that would characterize the Inklings meetings in his later years. Lewis writes:

> To this day the vision of the world which comes most naturally to me is one in which "we two" or "we few" (and in a sense "we happy few") stand together against something stronger and larger ... Hence while friendship has been by far the chief source of my happiness, acquaintance or general society has always meant little

---

[73] Colin Duriez, *C. S. Lewis: A Biography of Friendship*, 29.

[74] Ibid., 31.

[75] C. S. Lewis, *The Collected Letters of C. S. Lewis: Family Letters (1905–1931)* Edited by Walter Hooper. Vol. 1 (San Francisco: HarperCollins, 2004), 7. The letter is postmarked September 29, 1908.

[76] C. S. Lewis, *Surprised by Joy*, 19.

[77] Ibid., 31. Lewis calls Warnie's new school "Wyvern," but it is properly called "Malvern College."

[78] Ibid., 31.

to me, and I cannot quite understand why a man should wish to know more people than he can make real friends of.[79]

The most important development in Lewis' life at Wynyard was that he began to practice Christianity as an "effective believer."[80] He attended a high Anglo-Catholic church twice each Sunday where he heard Christian doctrine taught by men who really believed what they were teaching. He also began praying and reading his Bible regularly during this period. Sadly, these beliefs would topple soon thereafter as he would later become a committed atheist.

In August of 1910, Albert sent Lewis to Campbell College, a public school about a mile from Little Lea. He stayed for a half-term as Albert became dissatisfied with the school for reasons that Lewis never discovered. Before being sent next to Cherbourg House in England, which he refers to as "Chartes"[81] in his autobiography, he enjoyed a six-week reprieve at home with Albert while Warnie was still away at Malvern College. Over these six weeks, he found comfort during the dark hours of solitude by sleeping in his father's room. He recalls, "I remember no other time in my life of such untroubled affection; we were famously snug together."[82] More significantly, he delighted in his imaginative fantasies which came to him with near hallucinogenic potency during this time. He recalls:

> Curiously enough it is at this time, not in earlier childhood, that I chiefly remember delighting in fairy tales. I fell deeply under the spell of Dwarfs ... I visualized them so intensely that I came to the very frontiers of hallucination; once, walking in the garden, I was for a second not quite sure that a little man had not run past me into the shrubbery.[83]

In the following January, Lewis and Warnie both headed to Malvern where Warnie continued attending the College and Lewis began attending the preparatory school. The two and a half years that Lewis spent at Cherbourg House, a preparatory school in Malvern would be some of his most formative years. The most important development in his thinking at this time was the conclusion he reached about the nature of reality. He admits, "I ceased to be a Christian."[84]

---

[79] Ibid., 32–33.
[80] Ibid., 33.
[81] C. S. Lewis, *Surprised by Joy*, 56.
[82] Ibid., 54.
[83] Ibid., 54–55.
[84] Ibid., 58.

Three factors influenced this shift of belief. First, the Matron, Miss Cowie, of whom he writes with affectionate appreciation for the motherly role she played in his life at this time, unintentionally helped to dismantle his faith. Through her own spiritual searchings, she awakened in him a fascination for the Occult. He describes this fascination as "spiritual lust," a passion that likely "more even that the desire for power ... makes magicians."[85] Lewis continues: "I was soon (in the famous words) 'altering "I believe" to "one does feel."' And oh, the relief of it!"[86] Whereas he had been practicing, up to that time, Bible reading and saying his prayers, he found an excuse to get rid of these increasingly difficult burdens of which, he writes, "I longed with soul and body to escape."[87] The Occult was exciting and even comforting, and, henceforth, he would accept only that which excited and comforted him. Both prayer and Bible reading had to go.

Another significant factor that led to Lewis' atheistic turn came from his reading the classics, particularly the poet Virgil.[88] In reading and being taught Virgil, he encountered various religious ideas that no teachers took to be true nor described as prefiguring Christianity in any sense. All seemed to speak about these religions as being nonsense with Christianity being the exception. The truthfulness of Christianity, in light of the universally accepted falsity of the pagan religions, seemed implausible to him. One cannot miss the irony that paganism contributed something, at first, to Lewis' rejection of Christianity but later would aid in his return to it.[89] He would spend nearly the next eighteen years of life as an atheist.

Not only had he abandoned his faith, he also found that joy, "the stab, the pang, the inconsolable longing,"[90] had fled. He laments: "The authentic 'Joy' ... had vanished from my life: so completely that not even

---

[85] C. S. Lewis, *Surprised by Joy*, 60.

[86] Ibid., 60.

[87] Ibid., 60.

[88] See Alister McGrath, *C. S. Lewis—A Life*, where he argued that Lewis' reading of Virgil and the classics is likely the most significant influence leading to his turn to atheism because of "its lingering presence in his subsequent writings" 30.

[89] Lewis will later come to see paganism as a kind of praeparatio evangelica. See Roger Lancelyn Green and Walter Hooper, *C. S. Lewis: A Biography*. Revised edition (London: Harcourt Brace, 1994), 33, where they mention a lecture Lewis delivered in which "he described himself as one who loved Balder before he loved Christ." Lewis would also say of Christianity, "If ever a myth had become fact, had been incarnated, it would be just like this ... Here and here only in all time the myth must have become fact; the Word, flesh; God, Man. This is not 'a religion,' nor 'a philosophy.' It is the summing up and actuality of them all." See C. S. Lewis, *Surprised by Joy*, 236.

[90] C. S. Lewis, *Surprised by Joy*, 72.

the memory or the desire of it remained."[91] He describes this season of separation from joy as a "long winter."[92] Though "winter" had come, much to his surprise and delight, it would soon give way to "a landscape of grass and primroses and orchards in bloom, deafened with bird songs and astir with running water."[93] The picture of winter melting into spring features prominently in *The Lion, the Witch, and the Wardrobe* as Aslan's presence begins to diminish the White Witch's power and to break the dreaded curse. Lewis goes on to describe the experience at Chartres that would reawaken in him what had been lost. He recounts:

> I can lay my hand on the very moment; there is hardly any fact I know so well, thought I cannot date it. Someone must have left in the schoolroom a literary periodical: *The Bookman*, perhaps, or the *Times Literary Supplement*. My eye fell upon a headline and a picture, carelessly, expecting nothing. A moment later, as the poet says, "The sky had turned round." What I had read was the words *Siegfried and the Twilight of the Gods*. What I had seen was one of Arthur Rackham's illustrations to that volume. I had never heard of Wagner, nor of Siegfriend ... Pure "Northernness" engulfed me: a vision of huge, clear spaces hanging above the Atlantic in the endless twilight of Northern summer, remoteness, severity ... and almost at the same moment I knew that I had met this before, long, long ago ... in *Tegner's Drapa*, that Siegfried (whatever it might be) belonged to the same world as Balder and the sunward sailing cranes. And with that plunge back into my own past there arose at once, almost like heartbreak, the memory of Joy itself, the knowledge that I had once had what I had now lacked for years, that I was returning at last from exile and desert lands to my own country; and the distance of the Twilight of the Gods and the distance of my own past Joy, both unattainable, flowed together into a single, unendurable sense of desire and loss, which suddenly became one with the loss of the whole experience, which ... had already vanished ... And at once I knew ... that to "have it again" was the supreme and only important object of desire.[94]

Lewis devotes quite a bit of space in his autobiography to discussing this experience and its ramifications on the remainder of his life. What he calls "Northernness" gripped him so intensely that, mingled with the Norse

---

[91] C. S. Lewis, *Surprised by Joy*, 72.
[92] Ibid., 72.
[93] Ibid., 72.
[94] Ibid., 72–73.

gods and their mythological world, it became for him an object of worship. He explains:

> Northernness seemed then a bigger thing that my religion, that may partly have been because my attitude toward it contained elements which my religion ought to have contained and did not ... Sometimes I can almost think that I was sent back to the false gods there to acquire some capacity for worship against the day when the true God should recall me to Himself.[95]

Not only did Joy return to him through Norse mythology, but his view of nature was transformed also. He began looking to the external world of nature for scenes that might fit into the world of the Norse gods. In time, nature ceased to remind him of the imaginative books he loved and came to be "herself the medium of the real joy."[96] The life of the imagination, mediated at this point in his life through both books and nature, became more important for Lewis than ever before; and yet, he remained baffled as to *whether* or *where* joy's true satisfaction could be found. He admits:

> One caution must here be repeated. I have been describing a life in which, plainly, imagination of one sort or another played the dominant part. Remember that it never involved the least grain of belief; I never mistook imagination for reality. About the Northernness no such question could arise: it was essentially a desire and implied the absence of its object.[97]

In 1913, at the end of the Summer Term at Cherbourg House, he secured a classical entrance scholarship to Malvern College, which he called "Wyvern."[98] This was no small accomplishment, as he took the entrance examinations, which were given over several days, while sick with fever and bedridden. Warnie writes later, after his brother's death, of his success at these examinations, "I am inclined to rate his winning of a scholarship under these circumstances as the greatest academic triumph of his career."[99]

Though he triumphed in obtaining a spot at Malvern College, he generally hated his time there, largely due to the school games he was

---

[95] C. S. Lewis, *Surprised by Joy*, 76.
[96] Ibid., 77.
[97] Ibid., 82.
[98] Ibid., 82.
[99] Cited in Colin Duriez, *C. S. Lewis: A Biography of Friendship* (Oxford: Lion Hudson, 2013), 35.

forced to play along with the torment he frequently received from the Bloods, the name of the aristocracy who ruled the uninitiated student body largely via the "fagging system."[100] Under this "knight and squire" system, the Blood would shout at a younger boy whenever he "wanted his O.T.C. kit brushed and polished, or his boots cleaned, or his study 'done out,' or his tea made."[101] Lewis despised the harsh and shameful treatment from the Bloods. The ridicule that he received tilled the soil in his heart for pride to begin to grow as never before. Prior to Malvern College, he had not been aware of his literary and intellectual superiority to other boys. As often happens, ridicule leads to bitter comparison and retaliation toward one's tormentor(s). Lewis was no exception. He describes an encounter which contributed to his transition to vengeful snobbery:

> A prefect called Blugg or Glubb or some such name stood opposite me, belching in my face, giving me some order ... What pushed me over the edge into pure priggery was his face–the puffy bloated cheeks, the thick, moist, sagging lower lip, the yoked blend of drowsiness and cunning. 'The lout!' I thought. 'The clod! The dull, crass clown! For all his powers and privileges, I would not be he.' I had become a Prig, a High-brow.[102]

While Malvern College proved a loathsome school to him, it did not come without its blessings. One such blessing came in the form of a teacher, "a queer, but very nice old man"[103] named Smewgy.[104] Smewgy helped to deepen his love and appreciation for poetry. He writes of his teacher:

> He was honey-tongued. Every verse he read turned into music on his lips: something midway between speech and song. It is not the only good way of reading verse, but it is the way to enchant boys ... He first taught me the right sensuality of poetry, how it should be savored and mouthed in solitude ... to be in Smewgy's form was to be in a measure enabled. Amidst all the banal

---

[100] C. S. Lewis, *Surprised by Joy*, 94.

[101] C. S. Lewis, *Surprised by Joy*, 95.

[102] Ibid., 104.

[103] C. S. Lewis, *The Collected Letters of C. S. Lewis: Family Letters (1905–1931)* Edited by Walter Hooper. Vol. 1, 29.

[104] "Smewgy" was properly Harry Wakelyn Smith (1861–1918). The common spelling of his nickname at Malvern College was "Smugy." Throughout Lewis' letters, he spells his name "Smugie." In his autobiography, Lewis chooses the spelling "Smewgy" for reasons of producing proper pronunciation in his readers. See C. S. Lewis, *Surprised by Joy*, 110, where Lewis writes, " ... Smewgy as we called him. I spell the name so as to insure the right pronunciation–the first syllable should rhyme exactly with *Fugue*–though the Wyvernian spelling was "Smugy."

ambition and flashy splendors of school life he stood as a permanent reminder of things more gracious, more humane, larger and cooler. But his teaching, in the narrower sense, was equally good. He could enchant but he could also analyze. An idiom or a textual crux, once expounded by Smewgy, became clear as day. He made us feel that the scholar's demand for accuracy was not merely pedantic, still less an arbitrary moral discipline, but rather a niceness, a delicacy, to lack which argued 'a gross and swainish disposition.' I began to see that the reader who misses syntactical points in a poem is missing aesthetic points as well.[105]

One can already detect at this point in Lewis's life, the rational and the romantic strains developing side-by-side. The "honey-tongued" teacher at Malvern College was also a sharp and clear reasoner, and Lewis became the better thanks to Smewgy's influence.

It is of the Malvern College years that he writes, "I was at this time living, like so many Atheists or Antitheists, in a whirl of contradictions. I maintained that God did not exist. I was also very angry with God for not existing. I was equally angry with Him for creating a world."[106] He saw his inner and outer lives at this time as utterly unrelated to each other. The outer life was the life of misery he describes with all the bullying, the school games, the cruel hierarchy led by the Bloods. His inner life, in stark contrast, was "really a period of ecstasy,"[107] enchanted by myth, fairy tale, and the sublimity of nature that might rise up and arrest him at any turn. Lewis explains, "The sense ached. I was sick with desire; that sickness better than health ... at any moment ... [the curtain] might be drawn aside to reveal all the heavens I then knew."[108] Even so, the "heavens" of his enchanted imagination had no place in Lewis's then "real, hard, dirty ... modern world."[109]

Joy had returned to his life at Cherbourg House through Norse mythology two years prior to this time, and had remained, but it had brought with it a duality of life that would not submit to unity until his conversion to Christianity. Reason and imagination, fact and myth would

---

[105] C. S. Lewis, *Surprised by Joy*, 112.
[106] C. S. Lewis, *Surprised by Joy*, 115.
[107] Ibid., 118.
[108] Ibid., 118–119.
[109] C. S. Lewis, *The Collected Letters of C. S. Lewis: Family Letters (1905–1931)* Edited by Walter Hooper. Vol. 1, 95.

not be joined together in his mind. Puzzled by this duality, he found it "difficult to narrate."[110] Little did he know, Norse mythology would bring another welcome visitor into his life–his first true friend, Arthur Greeves. Arthur lived near Little Lea, and although Lewis was aware of him and had even attended Campbell College with him, they had never officially met. Just before his final term at Malvern College, he received a message that Arthur was at home sick. He decided, with no later recollection why, to make a visit to Arthur. Lewis describes his fateful meeting thus:

> I found Arthur sitting up in bed. On the table beside him lay a copy of *Myths of the Norsemen*. "Do *you* like that" said I. "Do *you* like that?" said he. Next moment the book was in our hands, our heads were bent close together, we were pointing, quoting, talking–soon almost shouting–discovering in a torrent of questions that we liked not only the same thing, but the same parts of it and in the same way; that both knew the stab of Joy and that, for both, the arrow was shot from the North. Many thousands of people have had the experience of finding the first friend, and it is none the less a wonder; as great a wonder … as first love, or even greater. I had been so far from thinking such a friend possible that I had never even longed for one; no more than I longed to be King of England. If I had found that Arthur had independently built up an exact replica of the Boxonian world I should not really have been much more surprised.[111]

The first recorded letter from Lewis to Arthur is dated June 5, 1914, though from the opening lines, one can discern that some written correspondence had taken place between them prior to this letter.[112] Nevertheless, this note roughly marks the beginning of a lifelong correspondence and companionship. Signifying the depth of their friendship throughout his life, of all of the letters collected from Lewis's pen, he wrote more letters to Arthur than to any other person.

Their early conversations consisted of Norse mythology, various books they had read such as Homer's *Iliad*, Malory's *Le Morte d'Arthur*, several works from William Morris and George MacDonald, among others. They evaluated musical pieces, perhaps the one area in which Arthur possessed the superior knowledge. Some of their conversation revolved

---

[110] C. S. Lewis, *Surprised by Joy*, 118.

[111] C. S. Lewis, *Surprised by Joy*, 130–131.

[112] See C. S. Lewis, *The Collected Letters of C. S. Lewis: Family Letters (1905–1931)* Edited by Walter Hooper. Vol. 1, 58. Lewis writes, "Dear Arthur, I really must apologize for having kept such a long and unjustifiable–silence. But the readiest means of mending that fault are those of writing fully and at once–which I now propose to do."

around the immaterial happenings in their lives and exhibited a light and playful tone, as evidenced by Lewis' referring to Arthur for a season as "My dear Galahad," from *Le Morte d'Arthur*.[113] The far greater part of their correspondence, however, involved their discussing ideas, analyzing literature, debating philosophies, religions, and the like. Lewis never developed a taste for small talk but preferred to discuss what he considered to be more interesting or weightier matters. In fact, a letter dated July 4, 1916, reveals Arthur's disappointment that their friendship consisted mostly in the sharing of ideas than of the goings-on in their lives. He writes to Arthur:

> So you feel hurt that I should think you worth talking to only about books, music, etc.: in other words that I keep my friendship with you only for the highest plane of life: that I leave to others all the sordid and uninteresting worries about so-called practical life, and share with you those joys and experiences which make that life desirable ... But seriously, what can you have been thinking about when you said 'only' books, music etc., just as if these weren't the real things! However, if I had thought for a moment that it would interest you, of course you are perfectly welcome to a full knowledge of my plans—such as they are.[114]

He mentions having rejected Christianity for the first time in a letter to Arthur, dated March 7, 1916. Lewis writes, "Perhaps one of these days you may even make a Christian of me."[115] Their religious debates strained their early friendship more than any other topic, and Arthur was saddened to learn of Lewis's atheism and his reasons for his position.[116] Realizing the tension, Lewis eventually writes, "Now let us take off our armour, hang up our swords and talk about things where there is no danger of coming to blows!"[117] The following month, he wrote another letter trying to repair

---

[113] See C. S. Lewis, *The Collected Letters of C. S. Lewis: Family Letters (1905–1931)* Edited by Walter Hooper. Vol. 1, 115. This is the first time Lewis refers to Arthur as "Dear Galahad." Galahad is son to Lancelot and Elaine whose character is pure and holy. The letter is dated May 4, 1915. The last instance of Lewis referring to Arthur in this way comes in his letter dated June, 17, 1918.

[114] C. S. Lewis, *The Collected Letters of C. S. Lewis: Family Letters (1905–1931)* Edited by Walter Hooper. Vol 1, 205.

[115] C. S. Lewis, *The Collected Letters of C. S. Lewis: Family Letters (1905–1931)* Edited by Walter Hooper. Vol 1, 171.

[116] See C. S. Lewis, *The Collected Letters of C. S. Lewis: Family Letters (1905–1931)* Edited by Walter Hooper. Vol 1, 230–231 (Letter dated October 12, 1916), 234–235 (Letter dated October 18, 2016).

[117] Ibid., 235 (Letter dated October 18, 2016).

the injured relationship. In this letter, one can sense Lewis's maturity and the value he placed at an early age on friendship. He writes to Arthur:

> Anyway, language such as I have just read is not pleasant, and I was on the point of writing a very rude letter. But I remembered, what I do hope you will remember old man, that real friendships are very, very rare and one doesn't want to endanger them by quarreling over trifles. We seem to be always sparring nowadays: I dare say it's largely my fault (tho' in this case I really don't know why you're so angry) but anyway do let us stop it. Perhaps my nerves are a bit on edge as I get nearer to this abominable exam, and that makes me irritable. But I'll try to do my best if you will.[118]

Reflecting years later on his deeply cherished friendship to Arthur, and referring to the religious debates, he writes:

> He remains the victor in that debate. It is I who have come round. The thing is symbolical of much in our joint history. He was not a clever boy, he was even a dull boy; I was a scholar. He had no "ideas." I bubbled over with them. It might seem that I had much to give him and that he had nothing to give me. But this is not the truth. I could give concepts, logic, facts, arguments, but he had feelings to offer, feelings which most mysteriously—for he was always very inarticulate—he taught me to share. Hence, in our commerce, I dealt in superficies, but he in solids. I learned charity from him but failed, for all my efforts, to teach him arrogance in return.[119]

Near the end of Lewis's Malvern College years, after much strained deliberation, Albert made a decision regarding his son's education that proved to be one of the most significantly formative ones in Lewis's life.[120] He decided to send him to study with his former headmaster and Warnie's former tutor.[121] On Saturday, September 19, 1914, young Lewis arrived by

---

[118] Ibid., 253 (Letter dated November 15, 1916).

[119] Cited in Roger Lancelyn Green and Walter Hooper, *C. S. Lewis: A Biography*. Revised ed. (London: Harcourt Brace, 1994), 98.

[120] See C. S. Lewis, *The Collected Letters of C. S. Lewis: Family Letters (1905–1931)* Edited by Walter Hooper. Vol 1, 52 (Letter dated March 29, 1914). Albert discusses with Warnie the possibility of sending Lewis to study with Kirkpatrick. He writes, "For a boy like Jacks to spend the next three of four years alone with an old man like Kirk is almost certain to strengthen the very faults that are strongest in his disposition. He will make no acquaintances. He will see few people and he will grow more into a hermit than ever. The position is a difficult one and gives me many anxious hours."

[121] See Ibid., 53 (Letter dated April 30, 1914). Kirkpatrick expresses to Albert his gratitude for being entrusted not only with Albert's education from the position of headmaster, but also of his two sons as tutor. He writes to Albert, "I hope I shall be ready ... to receive him in the

train in Bookham and was greeted by William T. Kirkpatrick (1848–1921), whom the family affectionately called "the Great Knock."[122]

Their initial meeting remained etched in his mind, and he recalls it with vivid detail in his autobiography. As the two were walking together away from the train station, Lewis commented that Surrey seemed "wilder" than he had expected it to look. Kirkpatrick responded, "Stop! ... What do you mean by wildness and what grounds had you for not expecting it?"[123] The Great Knock proceeded to dismantle Lewis's unfounded comment. He interrogated him at length in an attempt, not to snub him, but to discover what he believed and on what grounds he believed it. Proving to Lewis that he had little understanding of the meaning of "wildness," the Knock said to him, "Do you not see, then that your remark was meaningless?"[124] Lewis then assumed that the conversation was ended, and he began to sulk a bit. He writes of this assumption, "Never was I more mistaken in my life. Having analyzed my terms, Kirk was proceeding to deal with my proposition as a whole. On what had I based ... my expectations about the Flora and Geology of Surrey? Was it maps, or photographs, or books? I could produce none."[125] The Knock finally concluded, "Do you not see, then, that you had no right to have any opinion whatever on the subject?"[126]

Whereas some would have recoiled at such a conversation, Lewis came to enjoy it and to thrive under the constant combat. He recalls, "By this time our acquaintance had lasted about three and a half minutes; but the tone set by this first conversation was preserved without a single break during all the years I spent at Bookham ... to me it was red beef and strong beer."[127] His schooling began almost immediately upon arriving at the Knock's house, which was called Gastons. On the Monday after their initial Saturday meeting, the Knock opened up the Greek version of Homer's *Iliad*, translated roughly one hundred lines and then handed Lewis Crusius' *Lexicon*, instructing him to translate as much as he could. As daunting as

---

autumn, if you are still in the same mind then. And here let me say that I feel almost overwhelmed by the compliment to myself personally which your letter expresses. To have been the teacher of the father and his two sons is surely a unique experience." Kirkpatrick had been headmaster of Lurgan College, County Armagh, Northern Ireland from 1876–1899. Albert attended the school from 1877–1879.

[122] C. S. Lewis, *Surprised by Joy*, 133.
[123] C. S. Lewis, *Surprised by Joy*, 134.
[124] Ibid., 134.
[125] Ibid., 135.
[126] Ibid., 135.
[127] Ibid., 135–136.

such a method may seem, it proved effective for Lewis. He studied Demosthenes, Cicero, and Virgil with distaste, but devoured Lucretius, Catullus, Tacitus, Herodotus, and Dante with great delight. He developed proficiency in Greek, Latin, and French, but struggled a bit with German.

His education progressed with a settled daily routine that remained archetypical in his mind throughout his life.[128] He would eat breakfast at eight. At nine, he would read and write at his desk until one o'clock with "absolute freedom" given his self-disciplined work ethic, which the Knock discerned early in their studies together.[129] Around eleven o'clock, he would enjoy a cup of tea and would continue working until lunch at one o'clock. From two until a quarter past four, Lewis would take a walk, which he preferred to enjoy alone, and then would return for another cup of tea also enjoyed ideally in solitude. He resumed his academic work from five until seven after which he would enjoy dinner with the Knock and his wife. The evening would conclude with good conversation or light reading, after which he would into bed no later than eleven o'clock.[130]

Under the Knock's tutelage, Lewis excelled in his studies, meriting his master's deep admiration and confirming the wisdom of Albert's decision to send him to his former headmaster. In a letter to Albert dated April 7, 1916 in which he discusses Lewis' future educational prospects, the Knock praises Lewis' intellectual aptitude and preparedness:

> I notice that you feel adverse at present to let him enter the university at the close of next Autumn .. But as far as preparation is concerned it is difficult to conceive of any candidate who ought to be in better position to face the ordeal. He has read more classics than any boy I ever had—or indeed I might add than any I ever heard of, unless it be an Addison or Landor or Macaulay. There are people we read of, but I have never met any.[131]

On December 5th–9th, 1916, he sat for his examinations at Oriel College, Oxford, the result of which brought good news. On December 13, 1916, he received a letter from the Master of University College, Reginald W. Macan, notifying him that he had earned not only a Scholarship, but an Exhibition to University College, Oxford.[132] As Lewis prepared to take his leave after two years with the ruthless dialectician, the Knock wrote a letter

---

[128] Ibid., 141.
[129] Ibid., 144.
[130] C. S. Lewis, *Surprised by Joy*, 141–143.
[131] C. S. Lewis, *The Collected Letters of C. S. Lewis (1905–1931)* Vol 1, 178.
[132] Ibid., 263. An Exhibition brought an additional financial endowment to Lewis, on top of the Scholarship.

to Albert dated December 20, 1916, in which he expressed both his fondness for and high esteem of his pupil. He writes:

> The generosity of your heart has led you to express yourself in terms altogether too complimentary to me. I ask you, what could I have done with Clive if he had not been gifted with literary taste and the moral virtue of perseverance? Now to whom is Clive indebted for his brains? Beyond all question to his father and mother. And I hold that he is equally indebted to them for those moral qualities which though less obvious and striking that the intellectual, are equally necessary for the accomplishment of any great object in life–I mean fixity of purpose, determination of character, persevering energy. These are the qualities that carried him through. I did not create them, and if they had not been there, I could not have accomplished anything. All this is so perfectly obvious that it is hardly worth emphasizing ... As a dialectician, an intellectual disputant, I shall miss him, and he will have no successor. Clive can hold his own in any discussion, and the higher the range of the conversation, the more he feels himself at home.[133]

Many years later, after Lewis had become a Christian, he expressed his gratitude for the Knock's influence in his life.[134] Though he came to reject the Knock's atheism, he never abandoned the precise reasoning and clarity towards which his teacher continually pressed him. He remembers, "The very man who taught me to think–a hard, satirical atheist (ex-Presbyterian) who doted on the *Golden Bough* and filled his house with the products of the Rationalist Press Associations–thought in the same way; and he was a man as honest as the daylight, to whom I here willingly acknowledge an immense debt."[135]

Also significant during Lewis' time at Bookham under the Great Knock, which would last from 1914–1916, the Great War began. Warnie was sent off to serve in France. Lewis, not yet old enough to serve but already determined to enlist should the war continue, made what he called "a treaty with reality."[136] That is, he submitted to the reality that he would likely have to fight in the war at some point while resolving at the same

---

[133] Ibid., 263–264.

[134] C. S. Lewis, *Surprised by Joy*, 148. Lewis writes here of the Knock, "My debt to him is very great, my reverence to this day undiminished."

[135] C. S. Lewis, *Miracles*, 109–110.

[136] C. S. Lewis, *Surprised by Joy*, 158.

time to give his full attention to his studies with the aim of winning a scholarship. He refused to allow the war to distract him before he enlisted. He describes his stance thus: "I said to my country, in effect, 'You shall have me on a certain date, but not before ... You may have my body, but not my mind. I will take part in your battles, but not read about them'."[137]

He made good on his resolution and immersed himself in his studies. During the years leading up to his enlistment, unannounced, Joy visited him again. It came to him on one occasion much in the same way that it came in his very first encounter–through a memory. He had been trying with all of his imaginative might to make Joy return, but to no avail. He describes his effort thus:

> I had no lure to which the bird would come. And now, notice my blindness. At that very moment there arose the memory of a place and time at which I had tasted the lost Joy with unusual fullness. It had been a particular hill walk on a morning of white mist. The other volumes of the Ring (The Rheingold and The Valkyrie) had just arrived as a Christmas present from my father, and the thought of all the reading before me, mixed with the coldness and loneliness of the hillside, the drops of moisture on every branch, and the distant murmur of the concealed town, had produced a longing ... which had flowed over from the mind and seemed to involve the whole body. That walk I now remembered ... If only such a moment could return! But what I never realized was that it had returned–that the remembering of that walk was itself a new experience of just the same kind ... Thus, the very moment when I longed to be so stabbed again, was itself such a stabbing.[138]

It is worth stating again, because he makes the point himself several times, that Lewis lived through these years with a sharp duality in his mind between the rational and the imaginative. He could not seem to get the two to join together any more than a man can get oil and water to mix. Of this duality, he writes:

> Such, then, was the state of my imaginative life; over against it stood the life of my intellect. The two hemispheres of my mind were in the sharpest contrast. On the one side a many-islanded sea of poetry and myth; on the other a glib and shallow "rationalism." Nearly all that I loved, I believed to be imaginary; nearly all that I believed to be real I thought grim and meaningless

---
[137] C. S. Lewis, *Surprised by Joy*, 158.
[138] Ibid., 166.

> ... Such, then, was my position: to care for almost nothing but the gods and heroes, the garden of Hesperides, Launcelot and the Grail, and to believe in nothing but atoms and evolution and military service.[139]

He contemplated whether Joy might actually be sexual desire or fascination with the Occult. But time coupled with further experiences of Joy, when pressed up against reality, proved these possibilities to be false. He reasons:

> What I like about experience is that it is such an honest thing. You may take any number of wrong turnings; but keep your eyes open and you will not be allowed to go very far before the warning signs appear. You may have deceived yourself, but experience is not trying to deceive you. The universe rings true whenever you fairly test it.[140]

One of the most important imaginative experiences of his life occurred during the time that he was considering these false notions of Joy's true nature. This one experience convinced him that it was neither sexual desire nor Occult magic that had been beckoning him throughout his life; rather, it was something purer that he later identified as "Holiness."[141] When Joy visited him on this occasion, it left both him and the the world around him, in a sense, enchanted. While he was waiting on the platform for the train to arrive in Leatherhead station, he purchased a copy of George MacDonald's *Phantastes: A Fairie Romance*. He boarded the train, and as he began to read his new book, he found that "all was changed."[142]

He describes the effect as follows:

> Up till now each visitation of Joy had left the common world momentarily a desert–"The first touch of the earth went nigh to kill." Even when real clouds or trees had been the material of the vision, they had been so only by reminding me of another world; and I did not like the return to ours. But now I saw the bright shadow coming out of the book and into the real world and resting there, transforming all common things and yet itself unchanged. Or, more accurately, I saw the common things drawn into the bright shadow ... That night my imagination was, in a

---

[139] C. S. Lewis, *Surprised by Joy*, 170, 174.
[140] Ibid., 177.
[141] Ibid., 179.
[142] C. S. Lewis, *Surprised by Joy*, 179.

certain sense, baptized; the rest of me, not unnaturally, took longer. I had not the faintest idea of what I had let myself in for by buying *Phantastes.*[143]

Prior to this time, one might have accused Lewis, perhaps with some legitimacy, of escapism through his imaginative wanderings. After this experience, however, given the effect it had upon his imagination and his perception of the real world, such a charge would lack merit.

The notion of escapism will be explored in greater detail in chapter three, but it is worth mentioning briefly at this point so that Lewis's new posture towards the world of daily experience is neither overlooked nor misunderstood. Escapism means that one tries to get out of the real world and into an imaginary one because it seems more desirable than the real. Lewis had felt pulled in that direction before. He ceased trying to escape, however, after the real world came to take on so many of the desirable qualities of his imagined ones. Such became his new posture. This is not to suggest that the great mystery was solved at this point in his life. His perplexity about the relationship between reality and myth, between reason and imagination would continue for some years, but the light on his path began to shine brighter than ever before as a result of his newly "baptized" imagination.

Lewis began his studies at Oxford in 1917, but before the first term concluded, he enlisted and was soon assigned to E Company of No. 4 Officer Battalion. The Battalion was stationed to reside in the billets at Keble College, Oxford. While there, he became friends with five men: Thomas Kerrison Daway, Denis Howard de Pass, Martin Ashworth Somerville, Alexander Gordon Sutton, and one other young man whom he initially found to be "too childish for real companionship."[144] This "childish" lad soon became Lewis's roommate, and one of his closest friends. His name was Edward Francis Courtenay ("Paddy") Moore.

Paddy's mother, Mrs. Jane King Moore, lived close to Keble College in Wellington Square, and the group of friends made frequent visits to her home where her daughter and Paddy's younger sister, Maureen also lived. Lewis and Paddy developed such an intimate friendship during the time leading up to their deployment that they entered into a pact together that would impact the remainder of Lewis's life. Each man vowed that if the other should die during battle, the surviving friend would take care of the

---

[143] Ibid., 181.
[144] C. S. Lewis, *The Collected Letters of C. S. Lewis (1905–1931)* Vol I, 319.

fallen soldier's living parent. Little did Lewis know when he first made this pact, that his word would soon be tested.

When October of 1917 arrived, Paddy was sent to France with the Rifle Brigade. On November 29, 1917, his nineteenth birthday, Lewis arrived at the front-line trenches of France, near the border of Belgium. During the winter, he fell ill with trench fever and was sent to recover at the hospital in Le Treport. During his three-week recovery in the hospital, he read G. K. Chesterton for the first time. Though he disagreed with Chesterton's Christianity at that time, he found him a delight to read. His description of his first impression of reading Chesterton sheds light on an invaluable skill he developed very early, thanks in part to the influence of the Great Knock. Lewis developed the skill of clear thinking and conceptual clarification. For example, in writing of Chesterton's humor, which he especially appreciated, he explains:

> I was by now a sufficiently experienced reader to distinguish liking from agreement. I did not need to accept what Chesterton said in order to enjoy it. His humor was of the kind which I like best—not "jokes" imbedded in the page like currants in a cake, still less (what I cannot endure), a general tone of flippancy and jocularity, but the humor which is not in any way separable from the argument but is rather (as Aristotle would say) the "bloom" on dialectic itself ... in reading Chesterton, as in reading MacDonald, I did not know what I was letting myself in for. A young man who wishes to remain a sound Atheist cannot be too careful of his reading. There are traps everywhere ... God is, if I may say, very unscrupulous.[145]

Lewis soon recovered from his fever and was sent back into battle with his company. His battalion launched an attack upon the German-controlled village of Riez du Vinage which proved successful. Following this, the Germans responded with a retaliation upon the village. In the heat of the German response, Lewis was standing next to Sergeant Harry Ayers when a shell exploded next to them, killing Ayers and wounding Lewis. He found himself once again in a hospital.

Warnie's response upon hearing of his brother's injury fittingly characterizes their life-long close relationship. Warnie was stationed fifty miles from No. 6 British Red Cross Hospital where Lewis was recovering. He borrowed a motorbike and set out on the fifty-mile treacherous journey to learn of his condition. Upon his arrival, he was relieved the learn that,

---

[145] C. S. Lewis, *Surprised by Joy*, 190–191.

Brian M. Williams

in comparison to the brutal horrors suffered by many of their comrades in the Great War, his brother's wounds were minor. Though not life-threatening, they were serious enough for Lewis to be returned to England.

Unfortunately, not all of the friends from E Company of No. 4 Officer Battalion would be as fortunate. Of the six friends whose visits to the Moore home had been frequent, only Lewis and de Pass survived.[146] Around the time of his arrival back to England, he learned that his dear friend Paddy, still in France, was missing. Eventually, the worst possible news was confirmed–Paddy Moore had been killed in battle.[147]

After returning to England for the purpose of an extended recovery, he arrived in Oxford in January of 1919 to continue his academic pursuits at Oxford University, all the while remaining close to Mrs. Moore. Various biographers debate the nature of Lewis' relationship with Mrs. Moore, wondering whether it was maternal, romantic, or some mixture of both. I will leave off any attempt to answer this question and instead emphasize the reality that, whatever the complexity of Lewis's motives might have been, did uphold his end of the pact he had made with his friend, Paddy. Up to the very day of Mrs. Moore's death, Lewis remained a man of his word.

On the heels of the Great War came not only political changes, but intellectual ones as well. McGrath writes, "Many, like the Anglo-American poet T. S. Eliot, felt that the Great War marked the final collapse of the cultural heritage of the nineteenth century."[148] Prior to World War I, many people looked to "the Myth of Progress" and its promise of an increasingly better world to be an anchor for their soul.[149] War, some argued, belonged to more primitive times. To them it certainly had no place in the modern, scientifically and technologically advanced world. Science fiction author, H. G. Wells, was among those who embraced this myth. He writes, "I think that in the decades before 1914 not only I but most of my generation–in the British Empire, America, France, and indeed throughout most of the civilized world–thought that war was dying out. So it seemed to us."[150]

---

[146] Alister McGrath, *C. S. Lewis: A Life*, p. 406. See footnote #24.

[147] See K. J. Gilchrist, *A Morning After War: C. S. Lewis & WWI*, (New York: Peter Lang, 2005), 112–113, where Gilchrist notes that Mrs. Moore had been told that her son had died of a bullet wound through the head while he was receiving medical attention for his injured leg.

[148] Alister McGrath, *The Intellectual World of C. S. Lewis*, 32.

[149] See Richard Gamble,

[150] H. G. Wells, *The New World Order* (London: Secker and Warburg, 1940), 10.

Neville Coghill, who would become one of Lewis' closest friends, expressed the same optimism, writing with reference to Lewis:

> There was no reason why we should not have been happy; we had both just emerged safely from a war which (we then believed) had ended war forever ... The old order seemed not only restored but renewed ... we seemed to be experiencing what happened to Odin and his fellow-gods when they returned after their long twilight.[151]

Joseph Loconte describes how the Myth of Progress colored peoples' ideas about war even while the Great War was underway. Loconte writes, "Here, then, is one of the most striking effects of the Myth of Progress. Even war itself—a process inherently destructive to human life and human societies—was believed to have regenerative properties."[152] This war was supposed to usher in an epoch of worldwide peace. After it ended, President Woodrow Wilson shared his "Fourteen Points" and established the League of Nations that would ensure the moral stability of the world and prevent a further global war. Rather than President Wilson's dream of a utopian society capturing the hearts of most of the world, in the years that followed, a growing sense of meaninglessness began to spread. Loconte explains, "The watchword was *disillusionment:* a new cynicism about liberal democracy, capitalism, Christianity, and the achievements of Western Civilization."[153]

Along with widespread cynicism came the impetus to question the old traditional moorings of Western society. This lead to new developments in philosophy and psychology that proved influential to Lewis at the time. He writes in his autobiography of a certain intellectual viewpoint that swept through Oxford following the Great War and took him captive along with many others. He called this perspective a "New Look."[154] It may also be labeled properly "Oxford Realism," and is associated with such thinkers as G. E. Moore and Bertrand Russell. It involves the complete abandonment of the supernatural and the wonderful for the mundane. Lewis explains, "For some months ... the words 'ordinary' and 'humdrum' summed up everything that appeared to me most desirable."[155] He insisted and tried to

---

[151] Cited in Colin Duriez, *The Oxford Inklings: Lewis, Tolkien, and their Circle* (Oxford: Lion Books, 2015), 47.

[152] Joseph Loconte, *A Hobbit, a Wardrobe, and a Great War* (Nashville: Nelson Books, 2015), 46–47.

[153] Ibid., 105.

[154] C. S. Lewis, *Surprised by Joy*, 203.

[155] Ibid., 203.

ally his emotions to the idea that, contrary to the many provocations brought about by "Joy," the world was thoroughly disenchanted. Oxford Realism therefore means, quite plainly, that the world of the senses is "rock-bottom reality."[156] Lewis describes his determined mindset at that time thus: "No more Avalon, no more Hesperides. I had ... 'seen through' them. And I was never going to be taken in again."[157]

In addition to Oxford Realism, Sigmund Freud's psychoanalytical theory became intensely popular in academic institutions. Freud himself likened the importance of his views to those of Copernicus and Darwin.[158] Most troublesome for Lewis's many experiences of "Joy" were Freud's ideas about "wish-fulfillment." Freud believed that many of peoples' ideas were influenced by hidden psychological phenomenon that did not point to reality. He reasoned therefore that people embraced their religious beliefs because they "wished" their beliefs were really true. Lewis writes of his mindset after swallowing much of Freud's theories, "Now what, I asked myself, were all my delectable mountains and western gardens but sheer Fantasies? Had they not revealed their true nature by luring me, time and time again, into undisguisedly erotic reverie or the squalid nightmare of Magic?"[159]

By this time, Lewis had already met and had begun a friendship with Owen Barfield, but Barfield's own thoughts about the nature of reality and of human thought were shifting. He had become an Anthroposophist. The most important idea of Barfield's that helped to shock Lewis out of his materialistic view was the notion that the human mind participated in some way with a cosmic Logos, or a transcendent order, and this participation in turn explained why the world was intelligible.

Lewis describes two major shifts in his thinking that came about due to Barfield's influence, though he himself never entertains Anthroposophism very seriously. He admits, "In the first place, he made short work of what I have called my 'chronological snobbery,' the uncritical acceptance of the intellectual climate common to our own age and the assumption that whatever has gone out of date is on that account discredited."[160] Of the second major shift, Lewis writes:

---

[156] Ibid., 208.
[157] C. S. Lewis, *Surprised by Joy*, 204.
[158] See Sigmund Freud, "A Difficulty in the Path of Psycho-Analysis." *Complete Psychological Works*. London: Hogarth Press, 1955, vol. 17, 137–144.
[159] C. S. Lewis, *Surprised by Joy*, 203–204.
[160] Ibid., 207.

> In the second place he had convinced me that the positions we had hitherto held left no room for any satisfactory theory of knowledge. We had been, in the technical sense of the term, "realists"; that is, we accepted as rock-bottom reality the universe revealed by the senses. But at the same time we continued to make for certain phenomena of consciousness all the claims that really went with a theistic or idealistic view. We maintained that abstract thought (if obedient to logical rules) gave indisputable truth, that our moral judgment was "valid," and our aesthetic experience not merely pleasing but "valuable" ... Barfield convinced me that it was inconsistent ... I was therefore compelled to give up realism ... Unless I were to accept an unbelievable alternative, I must admit that mind was no late-come epiphenomenon; that the whole universe was, in the last resort, mental; that our logic was participation in a cosmic *Logos*.[161]

While Lewis was continuing his education at Oxford, Albert would send him money regularly to pay for his living expenses. Little did he know, Albert's support went not only to his son's financial sustenance, but also to Mrs. Moore's, whom Lewis visited regularly on most afternoons and evenings while living at Oxford.[162] Some time in 1919, Lewis went to live with Mrs. Moore in her newly acquired home in Headington, an arrangement that he kept mostly secretive from his father.

Resigning himself to the reality that he possessed little talent and promise outside of an academic vocation, Lewis crystalized his academic plans. He chose to study *Literae Humaniores,* a focus that immersed him into the language, literature, history, and philosophical thought of the ancient, or classical world. He also studied modern philosophy from Descartes onward.[163] Students in this track would complete four years of study along with two examinations, "Honours Moderations" taken midway through and the final examination on "Greats" taken at the end of the program. Students would earn either, first, second, third, or fourth class in each of the exams. The highest honor possible was securing a double first in both examinations. To his great relief, in August of 1922, Lewis received news that he had earned such an honor.

---

[161] Ibid., 208–209. Lewis calls this view "realism," but he is really describing materialism coupled with naive realism.

[162] Mrs. Moore was divorced at this time and would not remarry.

[163] Colin Duriez, *C. S. Lewis: A Biography of Friendship,* 77.

Despite his accomplishment, he struggled to find a teaching post. Both his philosophy tutor, Edgar Carritt, as well as the master of University College, Reginald Macan, encouraged him to study for another Honour School so that he might be more employable. Heeding their advice, he chose as his subject English Literature.[164] After an exhausting three years'-worth of study which he managed to cram into two, in July of 1923 Lewis received news that he had earned First Class Honours in English Literature, thus securing a Triple First Class BA degree.

Yet even still, he continued having difficulty for the next couple of years securing a permanent teaching post. As opportunity after opportunity fell through, it seemed as though his vocational aspirations might never come to fruition. Finally, in May of 1925, Magdalen College of Oxford announced the opening of an "Official Fellowship and tutorship in English." After two other promising candidates pulled out, Frank Wilson, his former English tutor, and Neville Coghill, his close friend, Lewis was at last elected to the position. The official announcement in the London *Times* read as follows:

> The President and Fellows of Magdalen College have elected to an official Fellowship in the College as Tutor in English Language and Literature, for five years as from next June 15, Mr. Clive Staples Lewis, M.A. (University College). Mr. Lewis was educated first at Malvern College. He won a scholarship in classics at University College in 1915, and (after war service) a first class in Classical Moderations in 1920, the Chancellor's Prize for an English essay in 1921, a first class in *Literae Humaniores* in 1922, and a first class in the Honour School of English Language and Literature in 1923.[165]

---

[164] Though English Literature was a subject of increasing interest, it was relatively new when Lewis began studying it formally at Oxford. It was not until 1894 that the first School of English is established at Oxford. See Alister McGrath, *C. S. Lewis: A Life*, 98–99, where he describes the controversy of this growing subject: "Some derided its introduction as a way of giving weaker students something easy and pointless to study. Others were alarmed at the danger of creating a new degree that would be seen as second-rate. Great were meaty and substantial; how could English be anything other than subjective reflections on novels and poems? How could 'mere chatter about Shelley' be taken with academic seriousness? It was impressionistic and superficial—not the sort of thing that Oxford University would wish to encourage."

[165] Cited in Alister McGrath, *C. S. Lewis: A Life*, 111–112. McGrath writes in the endnote to this citation, "There is an error in this report. As we saw in the previous chapter, Lewis actually won his scholarship to University College in 1916 (not 1915), and took up his place at the college in 1917. The ceremony which officially admitted Lewis to the Magdalen College fellowship took place in August of 1925 and he began his fellowship on October 1 of that same year.

FULFILLED BY JOY: HIS CONVERSION TO CHRISTIANITY (1926-1931)

When Lewis began his role at Magdalen College, he made two friends whose influence upon his view of reality would prove to be significant. The two men were Hugo Dyson and J. R. R. Tolkien, both Christians. A conversation over a fateful walk with them would lead to a major turning point in his life, as will be shown a bit later. By this time, he had already befriended Neville Coghill, who was also a Christian. He and Coghill had taken a course together in the English School. When Coghill first spoke up in the discussion time, Lewis found him to be "a man after my own heart."[166] He describes him as, "the most intelligent and best-informed man in that class ... a Christian and a thorough-going supernaturalist."[167] Throughout his final years as a student and into his early years as a teacher, he found himself confronted at nearly every turn by Christianity, both through the men whom he befriended as well as the authors he read. Having moved from materialism to idealism thanks in part to Barfield's influence, he now accepted that something like rationality, *logos*, or dare he entertain the thought, a mind, lay fundamentally behind all of the known world of his experience.[168] One can see the battlements in Lewis' atheism beginning to fall in succession. Several more would have to topple before he would admit "that God was God."[169]

Lewis met Tolkien for the first time on May 11, 1926, at a faculty meeting. Tolkien was at that time Rawlinson and Bosworth Professor of Anglo-Saxon at Oxford. After engaging in a group discussion on an ideal English syllabus, he and Tolkien talked privately for a bit. Lewis's first impression of his new acquaintance was that of "a smooth, pale, fluent, little chap ... [who] thinks all literature is written for the amusement of men between thirty and forty ... No harm in him: only needs a smack or so."[170]

Lewis's friend and late biographer, George Sayer, identifies the year 1926 as the beginning of Lewis's conversion. Sayer writes, "Jack's conversion to Christianity occurred over a period of several years—from 1926, the year *Dymer* was published, when he began to believe in a

---

[166] C. S. Lewis, *Surprised by Joy*, 212.
[167] Ibid., 212.
[168] See Colin Duriez, *C. S. Lewis: A Biography of Friendship*, 106, where he writes, "The young don was still locked into his atheism , though now believing that the origin of all things was in an impersonal Absolute Spirit, not in matter."
[169] C. S. Lewis, *Surprised by Joy*, 228.
[170] C. S. Lewis, *All My Road Before Me*, 393.

nebulous power outside himself, to 1931, when he became a believer in Christ."[171] Just a month after first meeting Tolkien, Lewis received yet another visitation from Joy. He recounts in his diary entry dated June 4, 1926, "A beautiful misty warm morning, the mist all transparent and luminous with concealed sunshine, wood pigeons making a noise in the grove, and a heavy dew. It suggested autumn and gave me a sudden whiff of what I used to call 'the real joy.'"[172]

Tolkien later invited Lewis to a reading and discussion group he had formed called the "Coalbiters," the purpose of which was "to explore the original Icelandic literature such as the *Poetic Edda*, which was full of tales of Norse gods and heroes, and a great dragon, Fafner, which had enchanted Lewis as a child."[173] Also a member of the group was Lewis' friend, Neville Coghill. Through these meetings, Lewis's friendship with Tolkien deepened, and the seeds were planted for another group that included some of the same members that would eventually begin meeting.

In his autobiography, Lewis likened God throughout those years to a master chess opponent who made four key "Moves" that persuaded him in time to become a theist. The first "Move" came as he read the *Hippolytus* of Euripides and found Joy returning with all of the intensity of his Bookham years. He recalls:

> In one chorus all that world's end imagery which I had rejected when I assumed my New Look rose before me. I liked, but did not yield; I tried to patronize it. But next day, I was overwhelmed. There was a transitional moment of delicious uneasiness, and then–instantaneously–the long inhibition was over, the dry desert lay behind, I was off once more into the land of longing, my heart at once broken and exalted ... There was nothing whatever to do about it; no question of returning to the desert. I had simply been ordered–or, rather, compelled–to "take that look off my face."[174]

Not insignificantly, the first "Move" was not an intellectual one, but an imaginative one. God had not targeted Lewis's reason initially, but his desires. In His second "Move," God took aim at his reason, which re-enforced the first "Move." He read Samuel Alexander's *Space, Time, and Deity*, which was first delivered at The Gifford Lectures at Glasgow from 1916–1918, and he was particularly struck by Alexander's distinction

---

[171] George Sayer, *Jack: C. S. Lewis and His Times*, 129.
[172] C. S. Lewis, *All My Road Before Me*, 406.
[173] Colin Duriez, *C. S. Lewis: A Biography of Friendship*, 112.
[174] C. S. Lewis, *Surprised by Joy*, 217.

between "Enjoyment" and "Contemplation." He unpacks the distinction as follows:

> When you see a table you "enjoy" the act of seeing and "contemplate" the table. Later, if you took up Optics and thought about Seeing itself, you would be contemplating the seeing and enjoying the thought … I accepted this distinction at once and have ever since regarded it as an indispensable tool of thought … It seemed to be self-evident that one essential property of love, hate, fear, hope, or desire was attention to their object. To cease thinking about or attending to the woman is, so far, to cease loving; to cease thinking about or attending to the dreaded this is, so far, to cease being afraid. But to attend to you own love or fear is to cease attending to the loved or dreaded object.[175]

When he applied this distinction to his experiences of Joy, he discovered that:

> [A]ll my waitings and watchings for Joy, all my vain hopes to find some mental content on which I could, so to speak, lay my finger and say, "This is it," had been a futile attempt to contemplate the enjoyed … for all images and sensations, if idolatrously mistaken for Joy itself, soon honestly confessed themselves inadequate. All said, in the last resort, "It is not I. I am only a reminder. Look! Look! What do I remind you of?" … But a desire is turned not to itself but to its object. Not only that, but it owes all its character to its object … Joy itself, considered, simply as an event in my own mind, turned out to be of no value at all. All the value lay in that of which Joy was the desiring … Joy proclaimed, "You want—I myself am your want of—something other, outside, not you nor any state of you."[176]

At this point in his thinking, he was still an idealist in the sense that he believed that ultimate reality was Absolute, something like a cosmic "Reason" in which all human reasoning participated. This explains how the third "Move" fit in with his thinking at that time. He made the connection between humans having "a root in the Absolute" and the experience of Joy. He came to believe that this "root" explained "why we experience

---

[175] Ibid., 217–218.
[176] C. S. Lewis, *Surprised by Joy*, 219–220.

Joy: we yearn, rightly, for that unity which we can never reach except by ceasing to be the separate phenomenal beings called 'we.'"[177]

Slowly but steadily, though unbeknownst to him at the time, reason and imagination were beginning to come together. The old foes were beginning to join as allies. He admits, "This new dovetailing of my desire-life with my philosophy foreshadowed the day, now fast approaching, when I should be forced to take my 'philosophy' more seriously than I ever intended. I did not foresee this. I was like a man who has lost 'merely a pawn' and never dreams that this ... means mate in a few moves."[178]

The fourth "Move" came while Lewis was teaching philosophy and English, and through his teaching was aiming to make things clear to his pupils. His Hegelian view of the Absolute proved impossibly murky, and by extension, nearly incommunicable. As a result, he moved to a more Berkeleyan view of the Absolute. He explains, "And didn't Berkeley's 'God' do all the same work as the Absolute, with the added advantage that we had at least some notion of what we meant by Him?"[179] Unlike Berkeley, however, Lewis still rejected "the God of popular religion," refusing to refer to the Absolute as "God" and maintaining that personal relations with the Absolute were out of the question.[180]

Around this time, he read G. K. Chesterton's *The Everlasting Man* and saw for the first time a helpful explanation of Christian history laid out before him. He found Chesterton's explanation "very sensible."[181] Soon after reading Chesterton, he found himself engaged in a conversation about history with T. D. Weldon, college lecturer in the Greats at Magdalen College. He describes Weldon as "the hardest boiled of all the atheists I ever knew."[182] To Lewis's utter surprise, Weldon began arguing that the historicity of the Gospel accounts seemed trustworthy. He remembers Weldon saying something to the effect of, "Rum thing ... All that stuff of Frazer's about the Dying God. Rum thing. It almost looks as if it had really happened once."[183] Hearing such an admission from a man so staunchly

---

[177] Ibid., 221–222.
[178] Ibid., 222.
[179] C. S. Lewis, *Surprised by Joy*, 223.
[180] C. S. Lewis, *Surprised by Joy*, 223.
[181] Ibid., 223.
[182] C. S. Lewis, *Surprised by Joy*, 223.
[183] Ibid., 223–224. See also C. S. Lewis, *All My Road Before Me*, 299, in the entry dated Saturday 8 March, 1924, where Lewis remembers, "I took Alexander's *Space, Time and Deity* out of the Union and went to Wadham where I sat and walked in the garden reading the introduction, enjoying the beauty of the place, and greatly interested by my author's truthful antithesis of enjoyment and contemplation." See also 379 on the entry dated Tuesday, 27

opposed to Christianity disturbed Lewis. It made him rethink his own position.

Regarding his initial conversion to theism, Lewis held two concepts together in unity that some find hard to reconcile—providence and human freedom. He writes, "The odd thing was that before God closed in on me, I was in fact offered what now appears a moment of wholly free choice ... I could open the door or keep it shut ... You could argue that I was not a free agent, but I am more inclined to think that this came nearer to being a perfectly free act than most that I have ever done."[184]

As Lewis's many influences begin to close in on him, "Plato, Dante, MacDonald, Herbert, Barfield, Tolkien, Dyson, Joy itself" as well as others, it was as if his impersonal Absolute "Spirit" came to him and said, "I am the Lord ... I am that I am."[185] Describing his conversion to theism, Lewis recounts:

> You must picture me alone in that room in Magdalen, night after night, feeling, whenever my mind lifted even for a second from my work, the stead, unrelenting approach of Him whom I so earnestly desired not to meet. That which I greatly feared had at last come upon me. In the Trinity Term of 1929 I gave in, and admitted that God was God, and knelt and prayed: perhaps, that night, the most dejected and reluctant convert in all England.[186]

He states emphatically that at that point, he was only a Theist and not yet a Christian. Regarding his search for Joy's true object, it still remained a mystery for him. Reason and imagination remained still separated by a chasm of conceptual confusion, but the chasm was steadily shrinking. He writes of his newfound belief in God and its relationship to Joy, "For all I knew, the total rejection of what I called Joy might be one of the demands, might be the very first demand, He would make upon me."[187] He began attending his parish church on Sundays and his college chapel on weekdays.

April 1926, where Lewis recounts the same conversation. He writes, "After tea back to College and went on with Seebohm till hall. In the evening looked up language and was just settling down to Skeat's introduction when Weldon came in. This meant whiskey and talk until 12.30, greatly to my disappointment. We somehow got on the historical truth of the Gospels, and agreed that there was a lot that could not be explained away."

[184] C. S. Lewis, *Surprised by Joy*, 224.

[185] Ibid., 225, 227.

[186] Ibid., 228–229. Alister McGrath dates Lewis' conversion to theism to March–June of 1930 rather than Lewis' own dating of April–June of 1929. See Alister McGrath, *C. S. Lewis: A Life*, 141–145.

[187] Ibid., 230.

Though still not yet a Christian, he did not view the vast number of religious options and pagan myths as a strong obstacle to the truth, as do some people. His question at that time was not, "Which is the true religion amidst all of the false ones?" It was rather, "Where has religion reached its true maturity? Where, if anywhere, have the hints of all Paganism been fulfilled?"[188]

His good friend and fellow lover of mythology was about to help him discover the answer to this important question. On September 19, 1931, Lewis invited J. R. R. Tolkien and Hugo Dyson to Magdalen College for dinner. At evening following the meal, they set out together along Addison's Walk[189], conversing on the nature of myth. Lewis admitted that though he enjoyed reading myths, he knew that they were not true. He saw them as "lies breathed through silver."[190] Tolkien objected to Lewis's view and suggested that myths contained pieces of truth while the Christian myth brought together all of the fragments into one historically true account. In other words, Christianity was the collective truth found in all the myths summed up in one place. Duriez summarizes Tolkien's point well, writing:

> God ... is the superlative story-maker, the proper master of all who tell stories. His real world story has a pattern shared with the best human stories ... Glimpses of truth that God in his grace gave to the human imagination in its myths are focused and fulfilled in the master story of the Gospels.[191]

McGrath explains further, "Tolkien held that the gospels contained a 'story of a larger kind,' which embraced what Lewis found good, true, and beautiful in the great myths of literature, expressing it as 'a far-off gleam or echo of *evangelium* in the real world'."[192] While Tolkien spoke to Lewis, "There came a mysterious rush of wind through the trees that Jack felt to be a message from the deity, although his reason told him not to be carried away."[193]

---

[188] Ibid., 235.

[189] Lewis often walked this path that was named after Joseph Addison, English essaying, poet, and playwright, who and enjoyed the walk himself in the 17th century.

[190] This is the phrase that Tolkien attributes to Lewis in the dedication of his poem "Mythopoeia." He writes, "To the one who said that myths were lies and therefore worthless, even though breathed through silver." See J. R. R. Tolkien, "Mythopoeia" in *Tree and Leaf* (New York City: Harper Collins), 2001.

[191] Colin Duriez, *The Oxford Inklings: Lewis, Tolkien and Their Circle* (Oxford: Lion Books, 2015), 120.

[192] Alister McGrath, *The Intellectual World of C. S. Lewis*, 62.

[193] George Sayer, *Jack*, 134.

C. S. LEWIS PRE-EVANGELISM FOR A POST-CHRISTIAN WORLD

Lewis recounts how, in time, he came to embrace Tolkien's viewpoint on both the nature of myth and the truthfulness of the gospel accounts:

> I was by now too experienced in literary criticism to regard the Gospels as myths. They had not the mythical taste. And yet the very matter which they set down in their artless, historical fashion—those narrow, unattractive Jews, too blind to the mythical wealth of the Pagan world around them—was precisely the matter of the great myths. If ever a myth had become fact, had been incarnated, it would be just like this ... Here and here only in all time the myth must have become fact; the Word, flesh; God, Man. This is not "a religion," nor "a philosophy." It is the summing up and actuality of them all.[194]

He realized that the myths that he had loved all of this life and that had often been the meditators of Joy had not been lying to him outright. They had been dropping clues here and there, eventually leading him to the summation of all myths, the true myth become fact.[195]

Lewis's conversion to Christianity finally came on September 28, 1931, while riding in the sidecar of a motorbike driven by Warnie as they made their way to Whipsnade Park Zoo. He recalls the simplicity of his conversion as follows:

> When we set out I did not believe that Jesus Christ is the Son of God, and when we reached the zoo I did. Yet I had not exactly spent the journey in thought. Nor in great emotion. "Emotional" is perhaps the last word we can apply to some of the most important events. It was more like when man, after long sleep, still lying motionless in bed, becomes aware that he is now awake.[196]

Joy, at long last, had served its intended purpose for Lewis. He came to understand its true nature. Its importance lies not in the experience itself, as desirable as it is, but only "as a pointer to something other and outer."[197]

---

[194] C. S. Lewis, *Surprised by Joy*, 236.

[195] Lewis was probably expressing something of this belief that myths contained truth in a conversation he had with Clyde Kilby in 1953. Kilby visited Lewis at Magdalen College, Oxford, and the conversation turned to the topic of Christianity and art. Kilby recounts, "I mentioned Jonathan Blanchard's assertion that a novel is at best a 'well-told lie.' As I expected, he disagreed completely with this claim, saying that one is far more likely to find the truth in a novel than in a newspaper." See Clyde S. Kilby, *A Well of Wonder*, 17–18.

[196] Ibid., 237.

[197] Ibid., 238.

It functions like a signpost to travelers who have lost their way. The destination to which the signposts had pointed all along was not what Lewis had once thought—a place; rather, it had always been a Person, namely the Person of Christ.[198] Like the character John in *The Pilgrim's Regress*, Lewis at last understood that reason and imagination were not enemies, but allies, as are myth and truth, in a sense. Near the end of Lewis's allegory, a voice speaks to John while he is in a cave and says:

> Child, if you will, it is mythology. It is truth, not fact: an image, not the very real ... But this is My inventing, this is the veil under which I have chosen to appear even from the first until now. For this end I made your senses and for this end your imagination, that you might see My face and live.[199]

Concluding his autobiography, though he had found Joy's true "object," Lewis admits, "Not, of course, that I don't often catch myself stopping to stare at roadside objects of even less importance."[200]

The last significant event worth mentioning from this period in Lewis's life was his purchase of The Kilns, a home in Headington Quarry about four miles from central Oxford. In October of 1930, he, Warnie, and Janie Moore purchased the home where Lewis would live until his death in 1963. The name of home came from the brick-making furnaces behind the house. Regarding his impression of the Kilns, Lewis writes to Arthur Greeves, "This house has a good night atmosphere about it: in the sense that I have never been in a place where one is less likely to get the creeps: a place less sinister. Good life must have been lived here before us. If it is haunted, it is haunted by good spirits, perhaps such things are the result of fantasy, yet the feelings are real."[201]

EMPLOYED BY JOY: PROFESSOR, AUTHOR, APOLOGIST (1931-1963)

Having become a Christian, and as a result, having at last reconciled his life-long conundrum regarding the nature of reality and the human imagination, every sphere of Lewis' life took on a new purpose. He began to see the world differently. So dramatic was his transformation and so profound his commitment to Christ, that Walter Hooper would later write,

---

[198] Ibid., 230.
[199] C. S. Lewis, *The Pilgrim's Regress*, 174–175.
[200] C. S. Lewis, *Surprised by Joy*, 238.
[201] Cited in Douglas Gilbert and Clyde S. Kilby, *C. S. Lewis: Images of His World* (Grand Rapids: Eerdmans, 2005), 58.

"Lewis's self-giving was the most radical I've witnessed, and as I've said before, he was the most converted man I ever met."[202] He had found true Joy, and he would spend the rest of his years ordering his life in accordance with his new understanding of the nature of reality and the human imagination. This understanding would influence his teaching, writing, and his pre-evangelistic and apologetic methodology.

From the years of 1925 to 1954, Lewis's primary vocation was English Language and Literature Fellow at Magdalen College, Oxford. Referring to Lewis' academic vocation, Walter Hooper perceptively notes, "The theological books of C. S. Lewis are so well known that it is easy to forget that he earned his living at something else."[203] His routine at Magdalen College consisted of tutoring, delivering lectures, teaching courses, attending to the business of his college, and producing his own literary works. The influence of the Great Knock is impossible to miss as one considers the various testimonies of Lewis's didactic style from his pupils. George Sayer, whom Lewis tutored, recalls his own experience under Lewis' tutelage:

> "What exactly do you mean by the word 'sentimental,' Mr. Sayer?" he might begin. Then he would present a summary of the ways in which the word had been used in the past, perhaps adding, "Well, Mr. Sayer, if you are not sure what that the word means or what you mean by it, wouldn't it be very much better if you ceased to use it at all?" ... He would often affect Socratic ignorance: "I am not quite sure what you mean by this term. Perhaps you would be so good as to translate it for me into plain English."[204]

As far as public lectures go, Lewis's popularity in the English school remained unmatched. Very often, the lecture hall would be filled to maximum capacity while he delivered lectures, some of which eventually would be published in the volume *The Discarded Image*. Sayer remembers, "Lewis ... had a growing reputation as a lecturer—in fact he was one of the only three lecturers in the Oxford English Schools whose lectures were, I

---

[202] Walter Hooper, "The Inklings," in *C. S. Lewis and His Circle*, 199. Walter Hooper came to live with Lewis in the final months of his life and became a close friend and his personal secretary. Hooper would go on to help much of Lewis's literary work get published. Perhaps a better term than "converted" for Hooper to use in his description of Lewis's character would have been "sanctified."

[203] Walter Hooper, *C. S. Lewis: Companion & Guide* (San Francisco: Harper Collins, 1996), 18.

[204] George Sayer, *Jack: C. S. Lewis and His Times*, 117–118.

think, worth going to."[205] Unlike other professors who simply read their lectures, an approach that he noticed put most of the attendees to sleep, Lewis spoke from a condensed outline which allowed him to remain engaged with the audience more fully. His lectures were so stimulating that it was not uncommon for students to sit through the same ones multiple times.

Along with his lecturing, he became one of the most prolific authors of his time. When one considers the enormity of his' literary output, coupled with the fact that he wrote all of his works with a dipped ink pen, it staggers the mind. Furthermore, the influence of his conversion to Christianity upon the volume of work he produced cannot be gainsaid. Hooper writes:

> Before his conversion he could write well, and he was more ambitious then than at any time in his life. But apart from two early volumes of verse, nothing happened. I believe the whole thing can be summed up in five words. *Lewis had nothing to say.* It really does appear than when Lewis cared more about God than being a writer, God *gave* him things to say.[206]

The first work that he published after becoming a Christian was a semi-autobiographical allegory called *The Pilgrim's Regress: An Allegorical Apology for Christianity, Reason and Romanticism* in 1933. The story centers around John, a young man who experiences various glimpses of Joy awakened by a vision of an island. He sets out on a journey to find the island only to discover in the end that the object of his longing is not an island at all, but a person, namely Christ. Describing his own personal journey, which roughly mirror his character John's, Lewis writes, "On the intellectual side my own progress had been from 'popular realism' (materialism) to Philosophical Idealism; from Idealism to Pantheism; from Pantheism to Theism; and from Theism to Christianity."[207]

His two most notable literary contributions to his personal academic field were *The Allegory of Love: A Study in Medieval Tradition*, published in 1936, and *English Literature in the Sixteenth Century Excluding Drama*, published in 1954. Though both volumes are considered among the top works of their kind to this day, they remain largely unknown to many of

---

[205] George Sayer, "Recollections of C. S. Lewis" in *C. S. Lewis & His Circle*, 175.
[206] Walter Hooper, "The Inklings" in *C. S. Lewis & His Circle*, 204.
[207] C. S. Lewis, *The Pilgrim's Regress*. Wade Annotated Edition (Grand Rapids: Eerdmans, 2014), 207.

C. S. LEWIS PRE-EVANGELISM FOR A POST-CHRISTIAN WORLD

Lewis's readers. His imaginative fiction and Christian apologetic works are far more familiar.

In 1938, Lewis published his first work of imaginative fiction through which he expressed aspects of his Christian worldview. The book was called *Out of the Silent Planet*. He was surprised to discover that the vast majority of his reviewers completely missed some of his most significant Christian allusions. He shared this surprise in a letter written to his friend, Sister Penelope. She had written previously to him, asking several questions about the book, one of which was whether or not she could expect a sequel. He responded, and in doing so made mention briefly of his imaginative evangelistic approach which will be examined in detail in chapter four:

> You will be both grieved and amused to learn that out of the 60 reviews, only 2 showed any knowledge that my idea of a fall of the Bent One was anything but a private invention of my own? But if there were someone with a richer talent and more leisure, I believe this great ignorance might be a help to the evangelisation of England: any amount of theology can now be smuggled into people's minds under cover of romance without their knowing it.[208]

Lewis went on to complete not only a sequel in 1943, *Perelandra*, but a third volume in 1945, *That Hideous Strength*. The series revolves around a Philologist of Cambridge University, Dr. Elwin Ransom, who finds himself entangled in far deeper matters than the plans of sinister Dr. Weston, who would pursue scientific and technological progress at any cost. Spiritual beings called "Oyarsa" inhabit the world and seek to influence the affairs of the universe, some for good and others for evil. The supremely evil Oyarsa, the "bent one," had already corrupted the earth and was aiming to wreak unspeakable havoc through the human beings that he and his servants were able to control. To stop him and ultimately deliver humanity, "Maleldil" comes to the earth and deals a blow to the bent one that will bring about his final defeat in the end. Having mixed together skillfully Christianity, medieval fantasy, and science fiction, Lewis concluded his series with the destruction of the demonically influenced National Institute of Co-ordinated Experiments (N.I.C.E.) thanks to the help of Merlin the wizard.

Lewis wrote these stories with a deeper aim than the mere entertainment of his readers. He wanted to awaken them to valuable truths that he feared were being discarded. He knew that unless the truths were

---

[208] C. S. Lewis, *The Collected Letters of C. S. Lewis: Family Letters (1931–1949)* Edited by Walter Hooper. Vol. 2 (San Francisco: HarperCollins, 2004), 262.

recovered, disastrous consequences lie over the near horizon. He shared this aim with his friend Roger Green, to whom he writes, "I like the whole interplanetary idea as a mythology and simply wished to conquer for my own (Christian) pt. of view what has always hitherto been used by the opposite side."[209] Perhaps the reviewer who captured the thrust of Lewis's strategy best was Leonard Bacon, who writes in *The Saturday Review of Literature:*

> When Mr. Lewis, harking back to the world of Merlin, says that the mysterious Land of Logres, or "Lancelot, or Pelleas, or Pellenore," far away in the beginning of time, is what keeps England from degenerating into Great Britain, he says what is fundamentally true and so magnificently full of important implications that it would take common clay a month to ferret out the full bearing of the observation.[210]

While he presented truth, goodness, and beauty in their proper light and revealed the darkness of falsehood and evil in his space trilogy, he did so imaginatively through the voices of his fictional characters. His first explicit *apologia* in his own voice came in 1940 under the title *The Problem of Pain*. In this volume, Lewis tackled the problem of evil and suffering by offering what he believed to be classic and time-tested answers. He followed this approach throughout his life, avoiding the impulse towards originality for the sake of truths that had been tested throughout time and history. One can detect the influence of Barfield here who had helped to rid Lewis of his once-held "chronological snobbery." Whereas the younger Lewis formerly prided himself on being a man who thought in alignment with the *en vogue* ideas of his day, he eventually grew suspicious of entirely new philosophies that had not undergone the tests of time, reflection, and debate. If one senses any originality in reading Lewis's apologetic works, it is not due to the ideas themselves, but to Lewis's way with words and images in expressing old ideas in new and vividly imaginative ways.[211]

Just two years after publishing *The Problem of Pain*, he began releasing a series of fictitious letters in *The Saturday Evening Post*, written from a high-ranking devil to a lesser one, which would be compiled eventually

---

[209] Ibid., 236–237.

[210] Cited in Walter Hooper, *C. S. Lewis: Companion & Guide*, 240.

[211] See C. S. Lewis, *The Problem of Pain*, xii, where he writes, "If any real theologian reads these pages, he will very easily see that they are the work of a layman and an amateur. Except in the last two chapters, parts of which are admittedly speculative, I have believed myself to be restating ancient and orthodox doctrines. If any parts of the book are 'original', in the sense of being novel or unorthodox, they are so against my will and as a result of my ignorance."

into one volume called *The Screwtape Letters*. Here again, he made accessible to people, via the imagination, truths about good and evil, the nature of reality filled with conscious unseen spirits, and the character of God, who is wholly good.

In 1941, after World War II had been underway for a couple of years, J. W. Welch, the Director of the BBC's Religious Broadcasting Department, began looking for someone to deliver radio talks on Christianity to British citizens. He remembered reading Lewis's *The Problem of Pain*. He had been impressed with his ability to present tightly reasoned arguments in a way that the common person could grasp, and he decided to employ Lewis to be the Christian voice to the nation. With some initial reluctance, Lewis agreed. On April 6, 1941, he delivered the first of his broadcast talks which he continued giving throughout the war. For many, Lewis's voice was more recognizable than even Winston Churchill's during this time. Between 1942 and 1944, the BBC talks were published in four separate sections. Finally, in 1952 they were edited and compiled into one volume and given the title *Mere Christianity*.

The written response from Lewis's listeners was overwhelming. By this time, he had already taken up the habit of answering letters in response to his books, a discipline he would keep up faithfully throughout his life. After the BBC talks, the letters multiplied exponentially. Multitudes of questions, some very serious and others trivial, came to him in response to his presentation of the Christian faith. Through his wartime talks, the Oxford don became a household name associated with the defense of the Christian faith.

He produced another apologetic work during the war years, namely, *The Abolition of Man*. In this book, he begins by discussing a certain English Grammar book that implicitly denies universals and traditional values. He believed such a denial would be destructive to the foundations of Western civilization. Though he charitably concealed the authors' names and the title of the volume, he took their viewpoints head-on and proceeded to make a thorough case for the reasonableness of transcendent and objective truth claims and sentiments while also showing the devastating entailments of his opponents' position. In a recent round-table discussion on Lewis at Biola University, Co-founder and Professor of Spiritual Theology at Regency College, James Houston, recounts a conversation he had with Lewis regarding the significance of *The Abolition of Man*. He says, "I asked him towards the end of my time with him what was the most important message that he had sought to articulate in all his works, and he says, 'It's all contained in my three lectures ... The Abolition of Man.'"[212] Clearly for Lewis, the reclamation of universals and objective truth stood as one of the greatest needs of modern civilization.

For his third explicitly apologetic work, Lewis published *Miracles: A Preliminary Study* in 1947. In it, he argues for a pre-modern view of reality that includes the supernatural as part of the total system. The book provoked a debate with philosopher Elisabeth Anscombe, at that time a Research Fellow of Somerville College, Oxford. At a Socratic Club meeting at Oxford on February 2, 1948, Anscombe presented a paper entitled "A Reply to Mr. C. S. Lewis's Argument That 'Naturalism' is Self-Refuting."[213] In response to some of her criticisms, he rewrote a portion of the third chapter, not because he believed his argument to have been flawed but rather, he realized he had not elucidated his argument as clearly as he had needed to. Remarking on Lewis's character, Anscombe writes in a reprinted copy of her article, "The fact that Lewis rewrote that chapter, and rewrote it so that it now has these qualities, shows his honesty and seriousness."[214]

This same humble honesty and desire for truth characterized Lewis's apologetic engagement with ideas at the Socratic Club meetings held at Oxford. The group was founded by Stella Aldwinckle, who aimed to provide a venue for thoughtful Christians and atheists to discuss important ideas. She describes Lewis's involvement thus:

> C. S. Lewis himself always came. He came to every meeting, eight meetings a term, unless he was actually ill or had to attend something in London. His support was simply wonderful. In meetings, he was never ever dogmatic or domineering. He would listen sympathetically to the other person's point of view and would comment helpfully, not antagonistically. Because, you see, we weren't debating. In a debating society you are out to score points and to win the votes. But we were Socratic, that is, we wanted to get to the truth of things, and to follow the argument in good faith and good temper wherever it went.[215]

---

[212] Complete footnote: link: https://www.youtube.com/watch?v=l_1h2grszL4 accessed on 9/10/18.

[214] Elisabeth Anscombe, *Collected Philosophical Papers, Vol 2: Metaphysics and the Philosophy of Mind* (University of Minnesota Press, 1981),

[215] Stella Aldwinckle, "Memories of the Socratic Club" in *C. S. & His Circle: Essays and Memoirs from the Oxford C. S. Lewis Society,* edited by Roger White, Judith Wolfe, and Brendan N. Wolfe (Oxford: Oxford University Press, 2015), 193.

C. S. LEWIS PRE-EVANGELISM FOR A POST-CHRISTIAN WORLD

Commenting on the significant of the Socratic Club, Aldwinckle shares further:

> I now that many people appreciated the Socratic Club very much. In fact, Professor Grensted, who was professor of Christian philosophy at Oriel, reckoned that the Socratic Club was the most important thing that happened in Oxford during the war. He judged it was so important to have tackled the issues: to bring out agnosticism and atheism instead of having a rather hush-hush attitude to it, as it had been before the war.[216]

The group continued meeting a while longer after Lewis had accepted the Professorship of Medieval and Renaissance Literature at Magdalene College, Cambridge in 1955. Basil Mitchell assumed the presidency in his absence, but soon the group fizzled, largely due to the gaping hole that was felt without Lewis's involvement.

In 1950, Lewis published the first book in a seven-volume series that is for many of his readers, his most beloved work. He returned to the genre of imaginative fiction through the publication of *The Lion, the Witch, and the Wardrobe*.[217] Though some readers casually refer to these books as Christian allegory, they are more properly classified as "supposals."[218] He imaginatively supposes what it would be like if Christ had come as a lion to redeem a world full of talking animals that had been taken captive by an evil witch masquerading as the rightful queen. Like his space trilogy

---

[216] Ibid., 193.

[217] The order in which Lewis' Narnia stories were published is as follows: *The Lion, the Witch and the Wardrobe* (1950); *Prince Caspian* (1951); *The Voyage of the 'Dawn Treader'* (1952); *The Silver Chair* (1953); *The Horse and His Boy* (1954); *The Magician's Nephew* (1955); *The Last Battle* (1956).

[218] See Lewis' letter to Mrs. Hook, written on December 29, 1958, cited in Walter Hooper, *C. S. Lewis: Companion & Guide*, 424–425, where Lewis identifies the Narnia stories as "supposals" and explains the difference between these and allegories. He writes, "If Aslan represented the immaterial Deity, he would be an allegorical figure. In reality however he is an invention giving an imaginary answer to the question, 'What might Christ become like if there really were a world like Narnia and He chose to be incarnate and die and rise again in *that* world as He actually has done in ours?' This is not allegory at all. So in *Perelandra*. This also works out a *supposition*. ('Suppose, even now, in some other planet there were a first couple undergoing the same that Adam and Eve underwent there, but successfully.') Allegory and such supposals differ because they mix the real and the unreal in different ways. Bunyan's picture of Giant Despair does not start from supposal at all. It is not a supposition but a *fact* that despair can capture and imprison a human soul. What is unreal (fictional) is the giant, the castle and the dungeon. The Incarnation of Christ in another world is mere supposal: but *granted* the supposition, He would really have been a physical object in that world as He was in Palestine, and His death on the Stone Table would have been a physical even no less than his death on Calvary."

published earlier, his ambitions in his Narnia books went beyond merely writing entertaining children's stories. He wanted his readers to breath the air of a Christian view of reality. In a sense, he extracted truth from fact, dressed it up in fiction, and invited his readers to suppose that truth had shown up wearing different clothes.[219] McGrath agrees with this assessment, writing:

> We can rightly see Narnia as the imaginative outworking of the core philosophical and theological ideas Lewis had been developing since the mid-1930s, expressed in narrative rather than rational manner. The Narnia novels express in the form of a story the same philosophical and theological arguments advanced in *Miracles*. Fiction becomes the means of allowing readers to see—more than that, to *enjoy*—the vision of reality Lewis had already set out in his more apologetic works.[220]

Just as in the historically true story of Christianity in which Christ stands as the central figure tying together the whole plot, Lewis's Aslan functions much in the same way in his Narnia stories. He writes:

> All my seven Narnian books, and my three science-fiction books, began with seeing pictures in my head. At first they were not a story, just pictures. The *Lion* all began with a picture of a Faun carrying an umbrella and parcels in a snowy wood. This picture had been in my mind since I was about sixteen. Then one day, when I was forty, I said to myself: "Let's try to make a story about it." At first I had very little idea how the story would go. But then suddenly Aslan came bounding into it. I think I had been having a good many dreams of lions about that time. Apart from that, I don't know where the Lion came from or why He came. But once He was there He pulled the whole story together, and soon He pulled the six other Narnian stories in after Him.[221]

No story of Lewis can be told well without mentioning the group of Christian thinkers known as the Inklings who met regularly from roughly 1930 to 1963, the year of Lewis' death. Though scholars differ regarding the precise date that the Inklings began meeting, it can be said with confidence that sometime in the early 1930s the first meeting took place.[222]

---

[219] Lewis' distinction between truth, fact, reality, and myth is examined in detail in chapter three.

[220] Alister McGrath, *C. S. Lewis: A Life*, 260.

[221] Complete footnote: "It All Began with a Picture" in *Letters to Children*.

[222] Walter Hooper writes, "My guess is that if you had fifty speakers lecturing on the origin of the Inklings, each would begin somewhere different. But in the end I think all fifty

C. S. LEWIS PRE-EVANGELISM FOR A POST-CHRISTIAN WORLD

The group was formed and named initially by an undergraduate of University College named Edward Lean, who was tutored by Lewis. Leans invited Tolkien and Lewis to the group, and the meetings were held in his room until he left the college in 1933. The purpose of the group was to read aloud unpublished works to be submitted to helpful critique. Upon Lean's departure, Lewis began hosting the meetings in his room at Magdalen College.

Other than Lewis himself, notable participants included his brother Warnie, J. R. R. Tolkien, Hugo Dyson, Colin Hardie, Owen Barfield, Adam Fox, Charles Williams, Nevill Coghill, and Christopher Tolkien.[223] The core of the group, at least in 1941, can be identified through a letter from Lewis to his friend Dom Bede Griffiths, wherein he writes:

> Williams, Dyson of Reading, & my brother (Anglicans) and Tolkien and my doctor, Havard (your Church) are the 'Inklings' to whom my *Problem of Pain* was dedicated. We meet on Friday evenings in my rooms: theoretically talk about literature, but in fact nearly always talk about something better. What I owe to them all is incalculable. Dyson and Tolkien were the immediate human causes of my own conversion. Is any pleasure on earth as great as a circle of Christian friends by a good fire?[224]

Eventually the group began meeting twice weekly, once in Lewis' room at Magdalen and once in a back room of The Eagle and Child pub. Tolkien tells of a fateful conversation with Lewis that would spur them on to produce some of the finest literature of the last century, from Tolkien's *The Lord of the Rings* to Lewis' *The Problem of Pain* and *The Chronicles of Narnia*. Tolkien recounts, "Lewis said to me one day; 'Tollers, there is too little of what we really like in stories. I am afraid we shall have to try to write some ourselves.' We agreed that he should try 'space-travel,' and I should try 'time-travel.'"[225]

---

would admit that the friendship of C. S. Lewis and J. R. R. Tolkien is at the very heart of that remarkable group, whose influence is being felt nearly everywhere on the planet." See Walter Hooper, "The Inklings" in *C. S. Lewis & His Circle*, 197.

[223] Colin Hardie was a Fellow of Magdalen College and Tutor of classics from 1936–1973. Adam Fox was Dean of Divinity at Magdalen College and Professor of Poetry from 1938–1942. Christopher Tolkien was J. R. R. Tolkien's third son and editor of many of his father's works.

[224] C. S. Lewis, *The Collected Letters of C. S. Lewis: Volume II*, 501.

[225] Letters to Charlotte and Denis Plimmer, 9 February 1967, in *The Letters of J. R. R. Tolkien*, edited by Humphrey Carpenter and Christopher Tolkien (London: Allen & Unwin, 1981), 378.

In 1949, the twice-weekly meetings ended largely due to how busy the participants had become, especially Lewis and Tolkien. Tolkien felt that he needed to be home more often to care for his wife whose arthritis had become more pronounced. Likewise, Lewis, who made good on his promise to Paddy Moore, found himself increasingly occupied with carrying for Mrs. Moore. In addition, his brother Warnie was plunging ever deeper in alcoholism, which caused Lewis great anxiety. The group began meeting on Tuesday mornings and eventually on Monday mornings due to Lewis' new post at Cambridge and changed new schedule. After his death in 1963, the Inklings continued to meet for a while, but it was evident to all that without Lewis, the group would never be the same. Hooper writes, "The epitaph was spoken by R. B. Macallum, Master of Pembroke College, who at a meeting in 1964 said, 'Let's face it. Without Jack we can't go on. When the sun goes out there's no more light in the solar system.'"[226] Thus, the meeting of the Inklings came to an end, though their influence most certainly did not.

In January of 1950, Lewis received a letter from an admiring fan from America, Helen Joy Davidman Gresham. Her own journey to faith in Christ had been not entirely unlike his own. She had embraced both atheism and communism during the 1930s. Sayer writes, "She rejected all morality and saw nothing to live for except pleasure, and yet she had supernatural or mystical experiences rather like Jack's own."[227] In 1942 at a Communist party meeting, she met fellow atheist and communist Bill Gresham. They were wed soon thereafter, but Bill proved to be an unstable and unfaithful man throughout their marriage. One day, Bill phoned Joy and told her that he was going insane and could not come home. He hung up the phone, leaving Joy stunned and all alone with their two young sons, David and Douglas. It was during this desperate season of her life in the late 1940s that God broke through to her. She recalls the moment this way: "All my defenses–the walls of arrogance and cocksureness and self-love behind which I had hid from God–went down momentarily. And God came in ... a person so real that all my previous life was by comparison merely shadow play."[228]

By this time, Lewis had become famous as a Christian apologist and author in America, and Joy turned to his books for help. She reached out to the leading American authority on Lewis, Chad Walsh, who suggested that she write to him. She took his advice, and what transpired after the

---

[226] Walter Hooper, "The Inklings" in *C. S. Lewis & His Circle*, 211.

[227] George Sayer, *Jack: C. S. Lewis and His Times*, 212.

[228] Joy Davidman, "The Longest Way Round," in *These Found the Way*, edited by D. W. Soper (Philadelphia: Westminster, 1951), 23.

first letter in January of 1950 was a regular written correspondence between the two. She visited him for the first time in 1952. Three years after this first meeting, she moved with David and Douglas into a home close to the Kilns. Finally, in 1956, partly in an effort to support a needy divorcee with two young boys, Lewis married Joy, though only civilly at first. A religious marriage ceremony would come later.

Little did Lewis know at the time; sad news would be waiting just around the corner. On October 18, 1956, Joy went to answer a phone call from Katharine Farrer and collapsed in pain during the process. The hospital x-rays confirmed that she had a broken femur. Worse than this, she was diagnosed with cancer in multiple locations. In spite of the expectation that she would live only a few more months, Lewis and Joy decided to seal their civil marriage with an ecclesiastical one. The ceremony was performed in Churchill Hospital, Oxford by Lewis's former student, Peter Bide, who had become an Anglican clergyman. In addition to his wedding services, Bide was beckoned by Lewis to pray for his wife's healing. With some reluctance, Bide agreed to offer such a prayer.

The following month in April, Joy returned home to the Kilns to live out what she believed would be her final weeks. To her and Lewis's wonderful surprise, she began recovering to the point that she was able to walk again in December of that same year of 1957. They enjoyed an official honeymoon in Ireland during June of 1958. It seemed as though all was well, until the tragic news came that Joy's cancer had returned. The news came not long before they departed for a trip to Greece with their friends Roger and June Lancelyn Green. On July 13, 1960, Lewis said goodbye to his wife. Green cites Lewis's recollection of one of his final conversations with Joy: "Two of the last things she said were, 'You have made me happy' and 'I am at peace with God.'"[229] At Joy's request, Lewis wrote the following poem that is cut into a marble plaque at Oxford Crematorium:

> Here the whole world (stars, water, air,
> And field, and forest, as they were
> Reflected in a single mind)
> Like cast-off clothes was left behind
> In ashes yet with hope that she,
> Re-born from holy poverty,
> In lenten lands, hereafter may
> Resume them on her Easter Day.[230]

---

[229] Cited in Roger Lancelyn Green and Walter Hooper, *C. S. Lewis: A Biography*, 277.
[230] Cited in Walter Hooper, *C. S. Lewis: Companion & Guide*, 100.

With Joy's death, he experienced for the second time the loss of the most important woman in his life. Like his mother before, losing Joy wounded him deeply. His stepson, Douglas Gresham, shares an intimate account of the depth of Lewis pain that he saw more clearly than others. He remembers:

It has been said that Jack's years at Cambridge after Mother's death were happy. That is not true. Jack, when in company with his friends and colleagues, was (after a while) again the jovial, witty intellectual they had known for years, but only Warnie and I knew what effort that cost him, and Warnie knew less than I, for Jack was careful with Warnie: I was more invisible. Jack's colleagues and friends never saw him as he turned from waving a cheery good-bye at the door of The Kilns and casting some pearls of parting witticism to a departing guest; they never watched him suddenly slump, his whole body shrinking like a slowly deflating balloon, his face losing the light of laughter and becoming grey, until he became once more a tired, sick and grieving man, old beyond his years. Even Warnie did not know, but boys are sometimes hard to see, and many times I watched Jack, unseen by him, as he walked, his mind clear, through the pain of his own Gethsemane.[231]

As a means of coping with his intense grief, he recorded his daily thoughts in a diary, a habit that he had given up in 1927. Through the encouragement of his friend Roger Green, Lewis eventually published these thoughts into a book. McGrath writes, "Here death unleashed a stream of thought which Lewis could not initially control … The result was one of his most distressing and disturbing books: *A Grief Observed*."[232] It represents Lewis' darkest writings as a Christian. Rather than presenting an intellectual argument to the problem of evil, which he had done previously in *The Problem of Pain*, *A Grief Observed* presents the inner turmoil and wrestlings of one suffering in the throes of profound emotional agony. Like the psalmist who laments God's seeming absence, Lewis wondered, "Where is God? … God to Him when your need is desperate, when all other help is vain, and what do you find? A door slammed in your face, and a sound of bolting and double bolting on the inside. After that, silence."[233] Though he raised similar sobering questions and doubts throughout his season of darkness, he emerged in the end faithfully committed to the truth of Christianity, having found deep solace in the reality of Christ's cross. He writes, "If only I could bear it, or the worst of it, of any of it, instead of her. It was allowed to One, we are told, and I find I can now believe again,

---

[231] Douglas H. Gresham, *Lenten Lands* (New York: Macmillan, 1988), 132–133.
[232] Alister McGrath, *C. S. Lewis: A Life*, 341.
[233] C. S. Lewis, *A Grief Observed*, 5–6.

that He has done vicariously whatever can be so done. He replies to our babble, 'You cannot and you dare not. I could and dared.'"[234]

In June of 1961, Lewis began to suffer his own health problems. He developed a chronic kidney infection which brought about toxemia. His doctor placed him on a low-calorie diet and instructed him to get plenty of rest while sitting upright. According to Sayer, who visited him often during his final years, "He never lost his sense of humor. Indeed the worse he became, the more he valued this quality as one of the greatest of God's gifts."[235] Fittingly, the beauty of nature that had arrested and delighted him with visits of Joy throughout his life, was his companion to his final days. Sayer shares of a walk he took with Lewis in April of the year of his death. He recalls:

> We walked, with some hesitation, along a narrow path through a wood and suddenly found ourselves in a glade surrounded by a number of miniature deer. Jack was entranced, "You now, while I was writing the Narnia books I never imagined anything as lovely as this," he said. We sat on a fallen tree trunk, and Jack gazed radiantly at the elegant little animals and adored the deity that had created them. "Pure white magic," he said when we had returned to the car.[236]

Sayer remembers another occasion a little later when Lewis had a similar reaction:

> One fine autumn afternoon, I drove him along the London Road, up Beacon Hill to the crest of the Chilterns, then along the crest past Christmas Common. The beech trees had colored marvelously, and although the sun was shining, there was that slight sharpness in the air that he loved and described in some of the most moving passages of his books. We stopped, opened the windows of the car, and he gazed, rapt. He was praying, praising God, and adoring nature's beauty.[237]

Having discovered the true nature of reality that in turn had helped him to grasp the proper role of the imagination, Lewis no longer asked, as he once did through the lips of his character Dymer, "What do you mean,

---

[234] C. S. Lewis, *A Grief Observed*, 44.
[235] George Sayer, *Jack*, 245.
[236] Ibid., 246.
[237] George Sayer, *Jack*, 250.

wild wood? What do you mean?"[238] He knew now both what they meant, to whom they pointed, and who had made them.

A few months later, on November 22, 1963, he and Warnie exchanged their final words. Warnie recounts in his diary:

> Finding him asleep in his armchair after lunch, I suggested that he would be more comfortable in bed. He agreed and went there. After four o'clock I took him in his tea and had a few words with him, finding him thick in his speech, very drowsy, but calm and cheerful. It was the last time we ever spoke to each other. At five thirty, I heard a crash in his bedroom, and running in, found him lying unconscious at the foot of the bed. He ceased to breathe some three or four minutes after. The following Friday would have been his sixty-fourth birthday.[239]

C. S. Lewis died the next day, on November 22, 1963. On this same day and at the same hour, President John F. Kennedy also died. Lewis's funeral was held at Headington Quarry Church on November 26. Sayer remembers his friends who came: Barfield, Harwood, Tolkien, Colin Hardie, Lawlor, Peter Bayley, Maureen and Leonard Blake, Douglas, David, the Millers, and Paxford. Due to his grief, Warnie could not bear to attend the funeral, but instead spent the day drunk in bed.

A memorial service was held for C. S. Lewis on December 7, 1963 in the chapel of Magdalen College. Remembering his life, his close friend Austin Farrer shared these very appropriate words:

> His characteristic attitude to people in general was one of consideration and respect. He did his best for them and he appreciated them. He paid you the compliment of attending to your words. He did not pretend to read your heart. He was endlessly generous. He gave without sting, to all who seemed to care for them, the riches of his mind and the effort of his wit: and where there was need, he gave his money ... I must not let myself be led into a panegyric, still less a critique, of his writings. You will estimate them, and are free to estimate them variously; and what another generation will say, who can guess?[240]

---

[238] C. S. Lewis, *Dymer*. Originally published under the pseudonym: Clive Hamilton (UK: Crossreach Publications, 2016) 7.

[239] Warren Hamilton Lewis, "C. S. Lewis: A Biography" unpublished typescript in the Wade Collection, Wheaton, 470.

[240] Cited in Walter Hooper, *C. S. Lewis: Companion & Guide*, 120.

C. S. LEWIS PRE-EVANGELISM FOR A POST-CHRISTIAN WORLD

Given the passage of over fifty years since his death, one need not wager such a guess. The enormous influence of Lewis's writings is undeniable. Lewis thought that he, like most writers, would be forgotten a few years after his death. Walter Hooper, who served as Lewis' personal secretary for the last year of his life and later as his literary executor, objected to his prediction. McGrath notes four reasons why Lewis's influence has grown since his death. First, thanks to Hooper, a great number of previously inaccessible works by Lewis have been published. Second, various societies have been formed in his honor. Third, numerous biographies have emerged introducing Lewis to a wide readership. Fourth, interest in Tolkien in the 1960s and 1970s led to interest in the group with which he was affiliated, the Inklings, which in turn kept Lewis on the radar.

McGrath concludes his biography of Lewis with his own prediction of how the coming generations will view him. He writes:

> Some will doubtless continue to accuse Lewis of writing disguised religious propaganda, crudely and cruelly dressed up as literature. Others will see him as a superb, even visionary, advocate and defender of the rationality of faith, whose powerful appeals to imagination and logic expose the shallowness of naturalism. Some will hold him to defend socially regressive viewpoints, based on the bygone world of England in the 1940s. Others will see him as a prophetic critic of cultural trends that were widely accepted at his time, but are now recognized as destructive, degrading, and damaging ... Most, however, will see Lewis simply as a gifted writer who brought immense pleasure to many and illumination to some—and who, above all, celebrated the classic era of good writing as a way of communicating ideas and expanding minds. For Lewis, the best art hinted at the deeper structures of reality, helping humanity in its perpetual quest for truth and significance.[241]

I am convinced that one of Lewis' most valuable contributions to the present day, in which the culture seems to have naturalism thoroughly "in [its] bones,"[242] is to help his readers to "see" reality through the imagination. In doing so, he is performing the very opposite act of the magician who deceives his audience by sleight-of-hand trickery. Lewis is no magician. He is an evangelist who leads his audience not into illusion, but rather into reality by casting truth in the light of imaginative fiction and

---

[241] Alister McGrath, *C. S. Lewis: A Life*, 378–379.
[242] C. S. Lewis, *Miracles*, 268.

metaphorical expression. Having considered the biographical context through which Lewis comes to understand the nature of reality, the human imagination, and the relationship between the two, the remainder of this book will explore his imaginative pre-evangelistic strategy that is undergirded by such understanding.

CHAPTER 2

C. S. Lewis's Sacramental View of Reality

Introduction

In the previous chapter, we considered how Lewis's understanding of reality drastically changed upon his conversion to theism in general and soon thereafter to Christianity in particular. His chief former difficulty lay in his attempt to reconcile reason with imagination, or to put it another way, to reconcile thought with desire.[243] His imaginative life was full of desire, and the various visitations of Joy seemed to beckon to him from another world. Yet, his reason, shaped as it had been by naturalism, denied the existence of this other world.[244] He had been influenced heavily by the Enlightenment assumption that intellectual history was the story of older superstitious thinking steadily giving way to new, and by unjustified extension, more true and concrete thinking. Such "chronological snobbery," along with a host of other beliefs examined in the previous chapter, prevented Lewis for many years from affirming any aspect of reality beyond his senses. After he became a Christian, however, he began to understand how his imaginative life fit with reality that existed independently from his mind. He came to see that viewing nature sacramentally from a specifically Christian perspective best helped to shed light on his various experiences of Joy.[245] In this second chapter, we will

---

[243] One might also speak of Lewis's attempt to reconcile myth with reality.

[244] The term "world" is used here in the sense of "realm" or "dimension" or "facet of reality," and not in the sense of "reality." The author affirms the existence of only one world, or reality.

[245] This is in no way suggesting that Lewis embraced a sacramental view of reality because it helped him to understand his various experiences of Joy. He came to embrace this view because he thought it was true to reality, and one of the attending benefits of it was that it in turn shed light on Joy. He admits in *Surprised by Joy* that he thought that one of the first things that he might have to give up upon embracing theism was the value he had placed on his imaginative experiences. See C. S. Lewis, *Surprised by Joy*, 230–231, "I had hoped that the heart of reality might be of such a kind that we can best symbolize it as a place; instead, I found it to be a Person. For all I knew, the total rejection of what I called Joy might be one of the demands, might be the very first demand, He would make upon me. There was no strain of music from within, no smell of eternal orchards at the threshold, when I was dragged through the doorway. No kind of desire was present at all."

look closely at Lewis's view of reality. Here, I will argue that Lewis understands creation to possess an essentially sacramental quality.

This chapter connects to the previous one in that it seeks to explain the nature of reality in an effort to make philosophical and theological sense of *why* Lewis experienced the stabs of Joy through diverse mediums. It connects with the chapter that follows in a similar way. As I will argue in chapter three, the imagination draws on reality for its content, regardless of how creatively one might "reshuffle the universals."[246] In this way, what is true of the world of the senses will have much in common with the world of the imagination. If the creation bears a sacramental quality, so will the world of imagination as it always has one foot planted in the created world.[247]

I will begin the present chapter by clarifying some key concepts. Next, I will describe three qualities of Lewis's medieval mindset that help to explain his ontology, which simply means his understanding of the nature of reality. I will then elaborate on Lewis's sacramental understanding of the Plato's concepts of three universals, namely, truth, goodness, and beauty. After this, I offer a brief comparison between Lewis's and Plato's thoughts regarding the nature of reality. Finally, I will conclude this chapter with a short description of the effects of abandoning the sacramental view for the present day.

CLARIFYING KEY CONCEPTS

Though he never produced a book dealing at length with the sacramental nature of reality specifically, a case for Lewis's view can be made by gathering the various things he has said in the various places in which he has said them. I must clarify here three key concepts in order for the argument that follows to remain as immune as possible to some potential ambiguities. First, I want to state again that I am not using the term "sacramental" in any sense to refer to issues of soteriology, that is, of salvation. Rather, I am using it with respect to creation solely. That is, it refers to the sense one gets from the concept "natural theology." The notion is one of *pointing to* something. To what does nature point? Or, what hints does the created world give to us about the unseen, and about God in particular? I want to state emphatically that creation's "pointing to

---

[246] See C. S. Lewis, "Image and Imagination" in *Image and Imagination*, 49, where Lewis uses this phrase to describes what one does when one employs the use of one's imagination.

[247] See C. S. Lewis, "Image and Imagination" in *Image and Imagination*, 45, where Lewis writes that "things in the imagination ... seem, in the most troublesome way, to be half in the imagination and half in the real world."

something" is not *merely* the kind of pointing that we find in a sign that points to an object. Lewis views creation's pointing as a kind of participation with that to which it points, which is far more than what a mere sign gives to us.

Allow me to explain. To borrow a metaphor from the Scriptures, the author of Hebrews likely had something like this in mind when he wrote of "shadows" and "true forms" (Heb. 10:1).[248] A shadow can only be cast when light hits an object solid enough to block it for shining on the surface behind or beneath it. The shadow gives to you and to me a clue that something more solid than it is present. Lewis's sacramental view of reality bears a close affinity to this "shadows-pointing-to-solids" phenomenon.[249] The created world of our daily experience is like the shadow that tells us that something more real must be above it.

Chris Armstrong offers a helpful description of "sacramentalism" in the sense that Lewis understood it. He writes, "Put another way, sacramentalism is a linked set of beliefs that (1) transcendent spiritual reality manifests itself in and through created material reality, that (2) all creation is in some sense a reflection of the Creator, and thus that (3) God is present in and through the world."[250] This is the proper sense in which the term "sacramental" should be understood throughout this book.

The second key point for us to keep in mind is that the term "reality" refers to things both seen and unseen. It signifies all that Lewis would include in what he calls "the whole show" in his book *Miracles*.[251] Third and finally, when I use the phrase, "Lewis's sacramental view of reality," "Lewis" refers to the man *after* his conversion to Christianity. Thus, the "sacramental view of reality" I am considering here is the one he comes to embrace as a result of his embracing Christianity. No further attention needs to be given to Lewis's journey *to* his sacramental view, as that has been

---

[248] See also Hebrews 9:23–24 where the author contrasts the "copies of the heavenly things" from "the heavenly things themselves," and "copies" from "true things."

[249] Lewis employs this very language of "shadows" and "solids" throughout his writings. See C. S. Lewis, "Dogma and the Universe" in *God in the Dock*, 34, for instance: "The elaborate world-pictures which accompany religion, and which look each so solid while they last, turn out to be only shadows. It is religion itself—prayer and sacrament and repentance and adoration—which is here, in the long run, our sole avenue to the real."

[250] Chris Armstrong, *Medieval Wisdom for Modern Christians: Finding Authentic Faith in a Forgotten Age with C. S. Lewis* (Grand Rapids: Brazos Press, 2016), 144.

[251] Lewis writes this book as a defense of *Miracles* largely in the face of the challenges presented by the materialist view of reality. "Reality" for Lewis, includes quite a bit more than the materialist can admit.

covered sufficiently in chapter one. It is the arrived-at view that concerns the present chapter.

LEWIS'S MEDIEVAL MINDSET: BOOKISH, UNIFYING, & SACRAMENTAL

Any attempt to understanding Lewis's sacramental view is helped by looking over one's shoulder first to the past, and in particular to the medieval age. Without question, Lewis was a man whose thoughts were thoroughly steeped in medievalism.[252] Demonstrating the truth of this statement is not difficult, though it may not be widely known among Lewis's popular readership.[253] Stephen Yandell perceptively notes:

> Surely no role of C. S. Lewis has been more overlooked by the general public than that of medievalist ... Lewis's readership in the twenty-first century is vast, and although many might be able to identify "medievalist" as Lewis's profession, very few are perhaps aware of what this profession entails, what Lewis's scholarship argues, or how Lewis's medieval identity ultimately shaped every form of writing he undertook.[254]

Many of Lewis's readers have not engaged his scholarly works. Far more familiar are his popular fiction and Christian apologetics books. As one begins, however, to read more widely, one discovers an unmistakable medievalism threaded throughout the Lewisian corpus. Two of his great academic achievements, *The Allegory of Love* and *The Discarded Image* are undeniably medieval in content. The former deals with the interplay between allegory and the concept of courtly love in medieval literature. The latter represents his attempt to reconstruct the medieval model of the universe, which has been discarded by the modern age. If one were to read these two books and immediately turn to read his Space Trilogy or the

---

[252] One who has read Lewis's autobiography cannot fail to see the irony here. Prior to his conversion to Christianity, he used the term "medieval" as a derogatory description of a time long ago when people, he thought, were not as enlightened as moderns. Referring to Steiner's and Barfield's Anthroposophy, He writes, "For here, apparently, were all the abominations; none more abominable than those which had once attracted me. Here were gods, spirits, afterlife and pre-existence, initiates, occult knowledge, meditation. 'Why—damn it—it's *medieval*,' I exclaimed; for I still had all the chronological snobbery of my period and used the names of earlier periods as terms of abuse," p. 206.

[253] Throughout this chapter, the term "medieval" is synonymous with the "Middle Ages," which span roughly the years 500 A.D. through 1500 A.D. In terms of historical events, one can associate the beginning of the medieval period with the fall of the Roman empire in the West and the end with Luther and the Reformation.

[254] Stephen Yandell, "*The Allegory of Love* and *The Discarded Image*: C. S. Lewis as Medievalist" in *C. S. Lewis: Life, Works, and Legacy*, Vol. 4, p. 117.

Chronicles of Narnia, any doubts of his entrenchment in medievalism would be alleviated completely.

It is quite rare to find a medievalist walking among modern people, and Lewis makes no effort to hide the fact that he is a "dinosaur" whom some thought would have fit better in a much earlier time.[255] Not only was he a medievalist in spirit, he was also one in vocation.[256] He studied and taught medieval literature as part of his curriculum during his Oxford years, and when he came to Cambridge, he took the position as Professor of Medieval and Renaissance Literature.

The terms "medieval" or "medievalism" are admittedly fluid and carry a range of meaning.[257] For some of us, they conjure up images of knights, dragons, and castles, and such. I want to draw our minds, however, to three qualities that I am intending to evoke by the usage of the term

---

[255] See C. S. Lewis, "De Descriptione Temporum: Inaugural Lecture from the Chair of Medieval and Renaissance Literature," (Cambridge University, 1954). Accessed on 3/2/19 - https://www.romanroadsmedia.com/old-western-culture-extras/DeDescriptioneTemporum-CS-Lewis.pdf . After admitting that he is an old dinosaur, he concludes his lecture with these words: "It is my settled conviction that in order to read Old Western literature aright you must suspend most of the responses and unlearn most of the habits you have acquired in reading modern literature. And because this is a judgement of a native, I claim that, even if the defense of my conviction is weak, the fact of my conviction is a historical *datum* to which you should give full weight. That way, where I fail as a critic, I may yet be useful as a specimen. I would even dare to go further. Speaking not only for myself but for all other Old Western men whom you may meet, I would say, use your specimens while you can. There are not going to be many more dinosaurs."

[256] See C. S. Lewis, *The Collected Letters,* Vol. II, 161. Lewis refers to his vocation with this terminology. In what must be one of the more concise updates given throughout his letters, he offers Leo Baker the following information: "My father is dead and my brother has retired from the army and now lives with us. I have deep regrets about all my relations with my father (but thank God they were best at the end). I am going bald. I am a Christian. Professionally I am chiefly a medievalist. I think that is all my news up to date."

[257] The term "medieval" is often used synonymously with "the Middle Ages." See Stephen Yandell, "The Allegory of Love and the Discarded Image," pp. 120–121 for a helpful explanation of these terms. He writes, "The term Middle Ages often required explanation for new students to the field. Coined by an Italian humanist in the fifteenth century, the term served as a condescending way to refer to the 1,000-year period (approximately 500–1500 A.D.) that represented a wasteland of ignorance between the Classical period of Greek and Roman literature and the Renaissance. The term period is defined as if by accident—that period considered to be of no learning or artistic worth: the Middle Ages (or the medieval period, a contraction of the Latin *medium aevum*, meaning middle epoch or age—a term that Enlightenment thinkers in the sixteenth century would have seen as derogatory. Because of these difficulties, and the stigma of being a default period between great periods of artistic creation and scholarship, the early Renaissance historian glorified all things Classical, and therefore the period that fell between their own enlightenment and the earlier age of learning was a period without a name at all, defined in opposition to the periods of worth."

"medieval," with particular focus given to the second and third qualities especially. Two of these come from Lewis's own pen—the "essentially bookish character" and the tendency towards unification, or the "tidying up" of ideas from various sources.[258] The third quality is the sacramental view of creation. In his primer or prolegomena to medieval literature, *The Discarded Image*, Lewis describes in some detail the medieval mindset, writing:

> What both examples illustrate is the overwhelmingly bookish or clerkly character of medieval culture ... Every writer, if he possibly can, bases himself on an earlier writer, follows an *actour*: preferably a Latin one ... the Middle Ages depended predominantly on books. Though literacy was of course far rarer than now, reading was in one way a more important ingredient of the total culture ... At his most characteristic, medieval man was not a dreamer or a wanderer. He was an organiser, a codifier, a builder of systems. He wanted a 'place for everything and everything in the right place'. Distinction, definition, tabulation were his delight ... Highly original and soaring philosophical speculation squeezes itself into a rigid dialectical pattern copied from Aristotle ... There was nothing which medieval people liked better, or did better, than sorting out and tidying up. Of all our modern inventions I suspect that they would most have admired the card index ... This impulse is equally at work in what seem to us ... their most sublime achievements ... we see the tranquil, indefatigable, exultant energy of passionately systematic minds bringing huge masses of heterogeneous material into unity. The perfect examples are the *Summa* of Aquinas and Dante's *Divine Comedy*; as unified and ordered as the Parthenon or the *Oedipus Rex*, as crowded and varied as a London terminus on a bank holiday. But there is a third work which we can, I think, set beside these two. This is the medieval synthesis itself, the whole organization of their theology, science, and history into a single, complex, harmonious mental Model of the Universe. The building of this Model is conditioned by two factors I have already mentioned: the essentially bookish character of their culture, and their intense love of system.[259]

---

[258] C. S. Lewis, *The Discarded Image*, 5, 10–11.

[259] C. S. Lewis, *The Discarded Image*, 5, 10–11. See also Chris R. Armstrong, *Medieval Wisdom for Modern Christians*, 49, where he affirms Lewis' bookish nature from a young age. He writes, "Books were Lewis's native element. That so many of the books he read were

C. S. LEWIS PRE-EVANGELISM FOR A POST-CHRISTIAN WORLD

Regarding the "bookish character" manifested in Lewis's life, this began to develop early in his childhood and only increased in intensity as he increased in age. As a young boy, he was surrounded by books, constantly reading, and even writing his own stories. His formidable tutor, the Great Knock, once said of Lewis in a letter to Albert, "He has read more classics than any boy I ever had–or indeed I might add than any I ever heard of, unless it be an Addison or Landor or Macaulay. There are people we read of, but I have never met any."[260] Later, when lecturing at Oxford on medieval literature, he addressed packed-out rooms as "a lover of literature who had read every text he mentioned, had enjoyed most of them, and was eager to share both his knowledge and his enthusiasm with anyone whom he could persuade to do so."[261] According to Walter Hooper's testimony, Lewis once said to him, "You can't get a cup of tea large enough or a book long enough to suit me."[262]

Along with his love of books, Lewis possessed a strong desire, much like the medieval person, to "tidy up" things. One can detect this desire both in his conception of reality and in his imaginative fiction. His pilgrimage to Christianity is really at bottom a search to find coherence between his imaginative longings and the world of everyday experience. This quest is conceptually similar to the search for unity in the face of diversity among the ancient philosophers. Lewis's medieval unifying aim, which is characteristic of his entire life, is an extension of the same unity and diversity he discovered to be true of ultimate reality.

In his imaginative fiction, he brings together various elements of Paganism, Christianity, classical philosophy, and modern life.[263] In his Chronicles of Narnia series, he places dryads, nymphs, fauns, English boys and girls, talking beasts, Father Christmas, Jinn, Christ, and references to logic and to Platonic metaphysics, all into the same world.[264] In his science-

---

ancient or medieval is certainly important, but that they were books, and that Lewis loved them and sought in them wisdom for living, shows him to be intuitively at one with medievalism. In other words, Lewis came early to that bedrock medieval presupposition: our best authorities for truth are the ancient, written authorities."

[260] C. S. Lewis, The Collected Letters of C. S. Lewis (1905–1931) Vol 1, 178.

[261] Walter Hooper, *C. S. Lewis: Companion & Guide*, 526.

[262] C. S. Lewis, *Of Other Worlds: Essays and Stories*, ed. by Walter Hooper (New York: Harcourt Brace Jovanovich, 1966), v.

[263] Interestingly, his friend J. R. R. Tolkien thought that Lewis might have been a bit too loose and overzealous in some of his "syncretizing." Tolkien did not like, for example, Lewis's inclusion of Father Christian in *The Lion, the Witch, and the Wardrobe*. He thought that he seemed out of place.

[264] For a helpful and concise summary of several medieval elements found throughout the Chronicles of Narnia books, see Stephen Yandell, "*The Allegory of Love* and *The Discarded*

fiction trilogy, we find space-ships, an advanced scientific institution aimed at prolonging human life indefinitely, alien life on other planets, angels and demons, talking beasts, and even Merlin the wizard placed into the same imaginative reality. Any writer could conceivably throw various subjects together from diverse sources in an arbitrary albeit interesting fashion. This is hardly what Lewis does. He is very purposeful in the selection of his content and characters, always aiming to present both a coherent story and atmosphere fitting with his sacramental ontology.[265]

Christopher Armstrong describes this same impulse to bring seemingly disparate parts together in the medieval age. He explains:

> As they created their compendia of knowledge for their readers, medievals syncretized gleefully. That is, they cared little whether great truths had first been discovered and expressed by Christians or by ancient pagans. Christianity always provided the framework for truth. But within that framework, one might fit all the best thought of the pagans, as Christian thinkers had been doing ever since Justin Martyr (100-165) and Clement of Alexandria (ca. 150-ca. 215).[266]

Lewis believed that one of the greatest examples of this from the medieval time, where the beauty of bringing the universals and particulars together in unparalleled achievement was found, lay in Dante's *Paradiso*. He also considered this work the height of poetry. Armstrong notes, "In a 1930 letter to his friend Arthur Greeves, he describes the *Paradiso* as 'feeling more important than any poetry I have ever read.' He found in Dante's crowning cantica a 'blend of complexity and beauty ... very like Catholic theology—wheel within wheel, but wheel of glory, and the One radiat[ing] through the Many'."[267]

Image: C. S. Lewis as Medievalist" in *C. S. Lewis: Life, Works, and Legacy: Scholar, Teacher, and Public Intellectual*, Vol. 4 (Westport: Praeger, 2007), p. 134–135.

[265] This will be explored more thoroughly in chapter four.

[266] Christopher Armstrong, *Medieval Wisdom for Modern Christians*, 38. Armstrong adds similarly later, "... medieval poets, jurists, moral teachers, romance writers, and theologians, who all created compendia of knowledge for their readers, were often gleefully syncretistic. Not that they didn't care whether the deepest truths of things was to be understood in Christian, Platonic, Stoic, or pagan terms. Christianity always provided the framework, the 'norming norm,' for truth. But within that framework one might fit all the best thoughts of the pagans, as Christian thinkers had been doing ever since Paul spoke to the Greeks at Mars Hill about their 'unknown god' (Acts 17:23), using the words of their own poets: 'In him we live and move and have our being' (Acts 17:28)," 61.

[267] Christopher Armstrong, *Medieval Wisdom for Modern Christians*, 41.

C. S. LEWIS PRE-EVANGELISM FOR A POST-CHRISTIAN WORLD

Lewis even saw the entirety of his written work in a sense as a unified corpus. In 1953, he wrote a letter to Professor William Kinter, in which he envisioned the entire body of his literary work as a beautiful and ornate cathedral with each work integrally connected to the whole. He writes, "It's fun laying out all my books as a cathedral. Personally, I'd make *Miracles* and the other 'treatises' the cathedral school: my children's stories are the real side chapels, each with its own little altar."[268]

Whereas similarities between Christianity and other myths and religions are viewed by some as a challenge to the truthfulness of Christianity, Lewis took the very opposite view.[269] His doing so is not surprising, given the medieval desire to unify[270] that he happily embraced. He writes:

> What light is really thrown on the truth or falsehood of Christian Theology by the occurrence of similar ideas in Pagan religion? I think the answer was very well given, a fortnight ago by Mr. Brown. Supposing, for purposes of argument, that Christianity is true; then it could avoid all coincidence with other religions only on the supposition that all other religions are one hundred percent erroneous. To which, you remember, Professor H. H. Price replied by agreeing with Mr. Brown and saying, "Yes. From these resemblances you may conclude not "so much the worse for the Christians" but "so much the better for the Pagans."[271]

---

[268] C. S. Lewis, *The Collected Letters of C. S. Lewis*, Vol. III (letter dated March 28, 1953).

[269] See W. E. Honeycutt, "True Myth in the Apologetics of C. S. Lewis" in *C. S. Lewis as Philosopher*, 105–127, for a helpful article that explores Lewis's understanding of ancient myths and preparations for the "true myth."

[270] This term sometimes connotes the bringing together of mutually exclusive concepts or ideas; however, it can simply mean the harmonization of differing, but not contradictory things. It is the non-contradictory connotation that is meant by the use of this term throughout this chapter.

[271] C. S. Lewis, "Is Theology Poetry?" in *The Weight of Glory*, 127–128. By the term "syncretize," one should not think of a mindless tossing together of truly contrary parts. Lewis's syncretism, like the medievals', was an attempt to bring together elements from various systems that *do* fit. It had as much of a sifting as it did a joining element to it. For example, see C. S. Lewis, *The Problem of Pain*, 15, where Lewis writes, "The story [Christian Incarnation] is strangely like many myths which have haunted religion from the first, and yet it is not like them. It is not transparent to the reason; we could not have invented it ourselves. It has not the suspicious *a priori* lucidity of Pantheism or of Newtonian physics. It has the seemingly arbitrary and idiosyncratic character which modern science is slowly teaching us to put up with in the willful universe, where energy is made up in little, tiny parcels of a quantity no one could predict, where speed is not unlimited, where irreversible entropy gives time a real direction and the cosmos, no longer static or cyclic, moves like a drama from a real beginning

McGrath likewise argues that, given the truth of Christianity, one ought to expect to find glimmers of truth scattered throughout the mythological and religious landscape of diverse peoples and ages. He writes, "In every respect, the Christian vision of reality affirms that echoes, hints, rumors, and anticipations of the gospel will be found outside the domain of the church."[272] Looking beyond the medieval age to the ancients, we see that Aristotle looked favorably upon mythology as a possible source of truth and wisdom. Referring to the earliest philosophers, he writes:

> For it is owing to their wonder that men both now begin and at first began for philosophize; they wondered originally at the obvious difficulties, the advanced little by little and states difficulties about the greater matters, e.g., about the phenomena of the moon and those of the sun and the stars, and about the genesis of the universe. And a man who is puzzled and wonders thinks himself ignorant (whence even the lover of myth is in a sense the lover of wisdom, for myth is composed of wonders).[273]

In his attitude towards ancient philosophy, mythology, and truth, Lewis found himself very much in agreement with many of the Patristic Christians, most notably, Justin Martyr, Athenagoras, Clement of Alexandria, and Eusebius of Caesarea. Borrowing Eusebius's term, Lewis referred to the pagan myths and to some ancient philosophies as *praeparatio evangelica*, or a preparation for the gospel.[274] He places the header "Even Pagan mythology contained a Divine call" at the top of a section in *The Pilgrim's Regress*, making this same point.[275] Along these lines, Frederick Copleston, in his excellent treatment of the history of philosophy writes, "Eusebius ... regarded Greek philosophy, especially Platonism, as a preparation of the heathen world for Christianity."[276] Lewis

---

to a real end. If any message from the core of reality ever were to reach us, we should expect to find it in just that unexpectedness, hat willful, dramatic anfractuosity which we find in the Christian faith. It has the master touch—the rough, male taste of reality, not made by us, or, indeed, for us, but hitting us in the face."

[272] Alister McGrath, *The Open Secret*, 250.

[273] Aristotle, "Metaphysics," in *The Complete Works of Aristotle*, Vol. 2, 1554.

[274] See C. S. Lewis, *The Pilgrim's Regress*, 214, where Lewis writes of "the real *praeparatio evangelica* inherent in certain immediately sub-Christian experiences." This phrase means "preparation for the gospel."

[275] See C. S. Lewis, *The Pilgrim's Regress*, 154. See also the side-note on this same page, where Lewis writes, "There is, in my opinion, a divine element in most mythologies."

[276] Frederick Copleston, S. J. *A History of Philosophy: Volume II: Medieval Philosophy: From Augustine to Duns Scotus* (New York: Image Books, 1993), 29. For a helpful summary of how the Patristics viewed Greek philosophy, see this volume, pp. 13–39.

goes so far as to suggest that God illuminated Plato's understanding of creation. He writes:

> We do of course find in Plato a clear Theology of Creation in the Judaic and Christian sense; the whole universe—the very conditions of time and space under which it exists—are produced by the will of a perfect, timeless, unconditioned God who is above all and outside all that He makes. But this is an amazing leap (though not made without the help of Him who is the Father of lights) by an overwhelming theological genius; it is not ordinary Pagan religion.[277]

Though not all agree with this position, it became the majority view of the early church and remained so through the Middle Ages.[278] With reference to Augustine, Hans Boersma writes, "Along with nearly all Christian theologians prior to modernity, he was convinced that the Christian faith is about heavenly participation and that this biblical insight allows for some kind of Platonist-Christian synthesis."[279]

Along with the bookish and systematically unifying qualities of the medieval mindset, of equal and perhaps greater significance was the medieval conception of creation. It was, in a word, "sacramental," and Lewis heartily embraced this viewpoint. Armstrong writes:

> C. S. Lewis's affection for the medieval era and the ways he absorbed its lessons will also help us to understand and benefit from medieval Christians' love affair with tradition and theological inquiry, their grounded and detailed moral code and

---

[277] C. S. Lewis, *Reflections on the Psalms* (New York: HarperCollins, 2017), 93.

[278] Copleston argues that it begins to wane during the Scholastic period. See Frederick Copleston, S. J. *A History of Philosophy: Vol II*, 31. Boersma argues similarly. See Hans Boersma, *Heavenly Participation*, p. 21, where he writes, "The argument of part I of this book is that until the later Middle Ages (say, the fourteenth and fifteenth centuries), people looked at the world as a mystery … 'Mystery' referred to realities behind the appearances that one could observe by means of the senses. That is to say, though our hands, eyes, ears, nose, and tongue are able to access reality, they cannot *fully* grasp this reality. They cannot *comprehend* it … Throughout the Great Tradition, when people spoke of the mysterious quality of the created order, what they meant was that this created order—along with all other temporary and provisional gifts of God—was a sacrament."

[279] Hans Boersma, *Heavenly Participation: The Weaving of a Sacramental Tapestry* (Grand Rapids: William B Eerdmans Publishing Company, 2011), 7. See the helpful disclaimer that Boersma gives in the footnote, "Throughout this book I use the phrase 'Platonist-Christian synthesis.' I do not mean to suggest with it that Platonism and Christianity merged to form an entity that was greater than either of the two. As will become clear, it is my conviction that the Christian faith judiciously appropriated certain elements of Platonic thought in the process of Christianizing the Hellenic world."

the compassionate ministry it underwrote, *their sacramental understanding of creation*, their emotion as they approached the divine, their sense of how the incarnation lifted up their own humanity, and the ways they disciplined that humanity to keep their hearts fixed on God.[280]

Lewis employed various terms in fleshing out his view of the created world. Significantly, he found the term "sacramental" to be the most fitting one.[281] He writes, for instance, in his essay "Transposition":

> The suns and lamps in pictures seem to shine only because real suns or lamps shine on them; that is, they seem to shine a great deal because they really shine a little in reflecting their archetypes. The sunlight in a picture is therefore not related to real sunlight simply as written words are to spoken. It is a sign, but also something more than a sign, and only a sign because it is also more than a sign, because in it the thing signified is really in a certain mode present. If I had to name the relation I should call it not symbolical but sacramental.[282]

Boersma helps illuminate the reason why Lewis likely thought "sacrament" a more fitting term than "symbol" in his attempt to convey the nature of reality. Drawing on the same distinction Lewis made between signs and sacraments, Boersma explains:

> What, then, is so distinct about the sacramental ontology that characterized much of the history of the church? Perhaps the best way to explain this is to distinguish between symbols and sacraments. A road sign with the silhouette of a deer symbolizes the presence of a deer in the area, and its purpose is to induce drives to slow down ... The former is a sign referring to the latter, but in no way do the two co-inhere. It is not as though the road sign carries a mysterious quality, participating somehow in the stags that roam the forests ... Things are different with sacraments. Unlike mere symbols, sacraments actually *participate* in the mysterious reality to which they point ... For Lewis, a

---

[280] Chris R. Armstrong, *Medieval Wisdom for Modern Christians* (Grand Rapids: Brazos Press, 2016), 42.

[281] Because Lewis holds that "sacramental" is the most fitting term, this essay employs the same term as a descriptor for his view of reality. He also uses at times the term "symbolism." See C. S. Lewis, *The Allegory of Love*, "The attempt to read that something else through its sensible imitations, to see the archetype in the copy, is what I mean by symbolism or sacramentalism," 56.

[282] C. S. Lewis, "Transposition" in *The Weight of Glory and Other Addresses*, 102.

sacramental relationship implies real presence. This understanding of sacramentality is part of a long lineage.[283]

Lewis also employed the term "transposition" to convey this participatory nature of reality. This terms holds before one's mind the idea of something being transferred onto another thing. For Lewis, the universal, or the unchanging form is transposed onto the particular, or the changing thing. He explains: "It is therefore, at the very least, not improbably that Transposition occurs whenever the higher reproduces itself in the lower."[284] By "higher," he means that which is archetypal, universal, and unchanging. By "lower" he means the copy, the particular, and the changing.

In *The Pilgrim's Regress*, he titles one section "Archetype and Ectype," which means "original and copy."[285] In this section of the allegory, John is talking with Father History about the objects that have provoked intense longing throughout his life. John admits, "Father, I am terribly afraid. I am afraid that the things the Landlord really intends for me may be utterly unlike the things he has taught me to desire."[286] Father History then responds, "They will be very unlike the things you imagine. But you already know that the objects which your desire imagines are always inadequate to that desire. Until you have it you will not know what you wanted."[287] The point he is making to John is that the "ectypes," the changing particulars, will never satisfy him. They were never meant to do so. Rather, they were meant to arouse deep longing so that John that might find his true satisfaction by looking upward to the "archetype[288]," and discovering its ultimate source.

---

[283] Hans Boersma, *Heavenly Participation*, 22–23.
[284] C. S. Lewis, "Transposition" in *The Weight of Glory and Other Addresses*, 103.
[285] C. S. Lewis, *The Pilgrim's Regress*, 161.
[286] C. S. Lewis, *The Pilgrim's Regress*, 161.
[287] C. S. Lewis, *The Pilgrim's Regress*, 162.
[288] See C. S. Lewis, *The Pilgrim's Regress*, 210–211. where Lewis helpfully explains this. Referring to his many failed attempts to find satisfaction in the particulars that aroused his longing, he writes, "But every one of these impressions is wrong. The sole merit I claim for this book is that it is written by one who has proved them all to be wrong. There is no room for vanity in the claim: I know them to be wrong not by intelligence but by experience, such experience as would not have one my way if my youth had been wise, more virtuous, and less self-centered than it was. For I myself have been deluded by every one of these false answers in turn, and have contemplated each of them earnestly enough to discover the cheat. To have embraced so many false Florimels is no matter for boasting: it is fools, they say, who learn by experience. But since they do at least learn, let a fool bring his experience into the common stock that wiser men profit by it."

Lewis shows his sacramentalist hand further in *The Last Battle*. After arriving in the "real Narnia," the characters express some confusion as to *where* exactly they have come as well as the nature of the place that looks so much like, yet in some ways different from, the old Narnia. The conversation ensues as follows:

> "The Eagle is right," said the Lord Digory. "Listen, Peter. When Aslan said you could never go back to Narnia, he meant the Narnia you were thinking of. But that was not the real Narnia. That had a beginning and an end. It was only a shadow or a copy of the real Narnia, which has always been here and always will be here: just as our own world, England and all, is only a shadow or copy of something in Aslan's real world. You need not mourn over Narnia, Lucy. All of the old Narnia that mattered, all the dear creatures, have been drawn into the real Narnia through the Door. And of course it is different; as different as a real thing is from a shadow or as waking life is from a dream." His voice stirred everyone like a trumpet as he spoke these words: but when he added under his breath "It's all in Plato, all in Plato: bless me, what *do* they teach them at these schools!" the older ones laughed.[289]

If this "transposition" proved epistemically valueless to humanity, it might not be worthy of our discussing it much at all. However, quite significantly for Lewis, he believed that it could convey knowledge, albeit a modest amount perhaps for some. He maintains:

> But who dares to be a spiritual man? In the full sense, none of us. And yet we are somehow aware that we approach from above, or from inside, at least some of those Transpositions which embody the Christian life in this world. With whatever sense of unworthiness, with whatever sense of audacity, we must affirm that we know a little of the higher system which is being transposed.[290]

This knowledge does not mean, of course, that every person rightly discerns the nature of the "higher system."[291] In Lewis's own case, it remained rather elusive to him for many years, to the point that he denied any higher system entirely. His protagonist in his early poem *Dymer*,

---

[289] C. S. Lewis, *The Last Battle*, 169–170.

[290] C. S. Lewis, "Transposition" in *The Weight of Glory and Other Addresses*, 105.

[291] C. S. Lewis, "Transposition" in *The Weight of Glory and Other Addresses*, 105. Nor do they necessarily discern the true nature of the "lower" either, as is evidenced in Lewis's own journey.

catches a whiff of this transposition, but he cannot understand it. After running out into the woods, where he encounters beauty, he shouts, "What do you mean, wild wood? What do you mean?"[292] Dymer never comes to a satisfactory answer.[293]

The problem with denying the "higher system," as was illustrated through Lewis's biography in chapter one, is that it can be extremely difficult to make sense of the world and of a number of experiences in life common to us all. On the other hand, when the upper story is admitted, many find that great explanatory power comes to their aid. Lewis suggests this in a letter written to Dom Bede Griffiths on May 10, 1945, wherein he writes:

> I'm working on a book on Miracles at present ... And here's the funny thing. To write a book on miracles, which are in a sense invasions of Nature, has made me realize Nature herself as I've never done before. You don't see Nature till you believe in the Supernatural: don't get the full, hot, salty tang of her except by contrast with the pure water from beyond the world. Those who mistake Nature for the All are just those who can never realize her as a particular creature with her own flawed, terrible, beautiful individuality.[294]

Lewis borrowed imagery from Plato's The Cave analogy in order to argue the same point in his article "Is Theology Poetry." He explains:

> I was taught at school, when I done a sum, to "prove my answer." The proof or verification of my Christian answer to the cosmic sum is this. When I accept Theology I may find difficulties, at this point or that, in harmonizing it with some particular truths which are indebted in the mythical cosmology derived from science. But I can get in, or allow for, science as a whole. Granted that Reason is prior to matter and that the light of that primal Reason illuminates finite minds, I can understand how men should come, by observation and inference, to know a lot about the universe they live in. If, on the other hand, I swallow the scientific cosmology as a whole, then not only can I not fit in Christianity, but I cannot even fit in science. If minds are wholly

---

[292] C. S. Lewis, *Dymer*. Originally published under the pseudonym: Clive Hamilton (UK: Crossreach Publications), 7.

[293] Dymer, his protagonist, never reaches a satisfactory answer because Lewis himself had not reached one yet at the time that he writes the poem. He is still an atheist when *Dymer* is published in 1926.

[294] C. S. Lewis, *The Collected Letters of C. S. Lewis*, Vol. II, 648.

dependent on brains, and brains on biochemistry, and biochemistry (in the long run) on the meaningless flux of the atoms, I cannot understand how they thought of those minds should have any more significance than the sound of the wind in the trees ... Christian theology can fit in science, art, morality, and the sub-Christian religions. The scientific point of view cannot fit in any of these things, not even science itself. I believe in Christianity as I believe that the Sun has risen, not only because I see it, but because by it I see everything else.[295]

Alister McGrath both agrees with and adopts Lewis's perspective as the starting point for his new vision of natural theology, which he sets forth in the book, *The Open Secret*. Rather than beginning with the particulars of creation and trying to construct an argument for God's existence, or some aspects of God's character, McGrath suggests admitting one's Christian perspectival framework at the outset. The test then becomes examining how much explanatory power one's framework lends to reality. McGrath writes of Lewis's understanding of Christianity's explanatory power:

> Yet when the full and true story is told, it is able to bring to fulfillment all that was right and wise in those fragmentary visions of things ... Seeing the full picture helps us make sense of previous hazy, fuzzy, confused, and fragmentary accounts of it, allowing these fragments to be colligated within a larger vision of things, which lent coherence to the individual parts that they lacked when considered on their own.[296]

In addition to "sacramental," "transposition," and "symbolism," Lewis uses the term "theophany," to convey nature's "pointing-to-something-higher" quality. He writes:

> I have tried ... to make every pleasure into a channel of adoration. I don't mean simply by giving thanks for it. One must of course give thanks, but I mean something different. How shall I put it? We can't—or I can't—hear the song of a bird simply as a sound. Its meaning or message ('That's a bird') comes with it inevitably—just as one can't see a familiar word in print as a merely visual pattern. The reading is as involuntary as the seeing. When the wind roars I don't just hear the roar; I 'hear the wind.' In the same way it is possible to 'read' as well as to 'have' a pleasure. Or not even 'as well as.' The distinction ought to

---

[295] C. S. Lewis, "Is Theology Poetry?" in *The Weight of Glory*, 138–140.
[296] Alister McGrath, *The Intellectual World of C. S. Lewis*, 66–67.

become, and sometimes is, impossible; to receive it and to recognise its divine source are a single experience. This heavenly fruit is instantly redolent of the orchard where it grew. This sweet air whispers of the country from whence it blows. It is a message. We know we are being touched by a finger of that right hand at which there are pleasures forevermore. There need be no question of thanks or praise as a separate event, something done afterwards. To experience the tiny theophany is itself to adore. Gratitude exclaims, very properly, 'How good of God to give me this.' Adoration says, 'What must be the quality of that Being whose far-off and momentary coruscations are like this!' One's mind runs back up the sunbeam to the sun.[297]

In his famous sermon entitled *The Weight of Glory*, he describes the human longing for the deeper reality to which nature points. He refers to this deeper reality as a "transtemporal, transfinite good" that he labels simply "the thing itself."[298] This good, he maintains, is the object of humanity's "real destiny."[299] He is describing, of course, not a "thing" but rather a person–*the* Person, which is God.

All other lesser goods are meant to serve as pointers to this ultimate good, like sign-posts on the road to humanity's true destination, or perhaps better, as shadows indicating the solids standing above them. If the lesser goods are mistaken for the ultimate good, they become idols, and like any idol, they corrupt rather than bless the worshipper. Referring to these lesser goods through which we experience a "desire for something that has never actually appeared in our experience,"[300] Lewis writes:

> The books or the music in which we thought the beauty was located will betray us if we trust to them; it was not *in* them, it only came *through* them, and what came through them was longing. These things—the beauty, the memory of our own past—are good images of what we really desire; but if they are mistaken for the thing itself, they turn into dumb idols, breaking the hearts of their worshippers. For they are not the thing itself; they are only the scent of a flower we have not found, the echo of a tune we have not heard, news from a country we have never visited. Do you think I am trying to weave a spell? Perhaps I am; but remember your fairy tales. Spells are used for breaking

---

[297] C. S. Lewis, *Letters to Malcolm*, 90.
[298] C. S. Lewis, *The Weight of Glory*, 29.
[299] Ibid., 29.
[300] Ibid., 30.

enchantments as well as for inducing them. And you and I have need of the strongest spell that can be found to wake us from the evil enchantment of worldliness which has been laid upon us for nearly a hundred years. Almost our whole education has been directed to silencing this shy, persistent, inner voice; almost all of our modern philosophies have been devised to convince us that the good of a man is to be found on this earth.[301]

In Lewis's *The Pilgrim's Regress*, the protagonist John perceives how all of reality was now speaking to him, leading him on to Christ. In hindsight, he realizes that it was actually Christ, *through these things*, compelling him to go forward. Lewis narrates:

> The blue sky above the cliffs was watching him: the cliffs themselves were imprisoning him: the rocks behind were cutting off his retreat: the path ahead was ordering him on. In one night the Landlord — call him by what name you would — had come back to the world, and filled the world, quite full without a cranny. His eyes stared and His hand pointed and His voice commanded in everything that could be heard or seen, even from this place where John sat, to the end of the world: and if you passed the end of the world He would be there too. All things were indeed one — more truly that Mr. Wisdom dreamed — and all things said one word: CAUGHT ... Above all it grew upon him that the return of the Landlord had blotted out the Island: for if there still were such a place he was no longer free to spend his soul in seeking it, but must follow whatever designs the Landlord had for him. And at the very best it now seemed that the last of things was at least more like a person than a place, so that the deepest thirst within him was not adapted to the deepest nature of the world.[302]

Let us sum things up to this point. Lewis viewed reality very much through the medieval lens. Being a bookish man, he overcame his chronological snobbery and placed great confidence in long-held ideas that had the privilege of being scrutinized by a large number of minds over a large number of years. He sought to understand the coherent meaning of reality and found eventually that apart from a sacramental view with Christ as the central figure of both reality and history, such meaning remained stubbornly evasive. Having found at last the one whom Chesterton calls

---

[301] C. S. Lewis, *The Weight of Glory*, 30–31.
[302] C. S. Lewis, *The Pilgrim's Regress*, 148–149.

the "Everlasting Man," the creator of sustainer of all things, Lewis was able to begin putting together the ontological pieces that point to him.

THE SACRAMENTAL NATURE OF UNIVERSALS "IN" THE PARTICULARS

We will now examine these ontological pieces in some detail, specifically focusing on Lewis's view of the universals–truth, goodness, and beauty, and their sacramental manifestation in the particulars.[303] Two claims undergird what I am saying in this section. First, Lewis held truth, goodness, beauty to be objective. This is a far cry from where our present culture stands today, sadly even among many of our modern theologians. Second, Lewis believed that these universals inhere sacramentally in the particulars.

He identifies the Platonic triad, affirming their objectivity as follows[304]:

> For if our minds are totally alien to reality then all our thoughts, including this thought, are worthless. We must, then, grant logic to the reality; we must, if we are to have any moral standards, grant it moral standards too. And there is really no reason why we should not do the same about standards of beauty. There is no reason why our reaction to a beautiful landscape should not be the response, however humanly blurred and partial, to a something that is really there.[305]

ON TRUTH: REASON THAT POINTS UPWARDS

The Objective Quality of Truth

Truth, for Lewis, is "always *about* something, but reality is that *about which* truth is."[306] He believes that truth, which man comprehends by way

---

[303] See Roger Scruton, *Beauty: A Very Short Introduction*, 2–4, where he writes, "There is an appealing idea about beauty which goes back to Plato and Plotinus, and which became incorporated by various routes into Christian theological thinking. According to this idea beauty is an ultimate value—something which we pursue for its own sake ... Aquinas regarded truth, goodness and unity as 'transcendentals'—features of reality possessed by all things, since they are aspects of being, ways in which the supreme gift of being is made manifest to the understanding. His views of beauty are more implied than stated; nevertheless, he wrote as though beauty too is such a transcendental ... He also thought that beauty and goodness are, in the end, identical, being separate ways in which a single positive reality is rationally apprehended."

[304] See Alister McGrath, *The Open Secret*, 291, where he writes of "the Platonic triad of truth, beauty, and goodness."

[305] C. S. Lewis, "De Futilitate" in *Christian Reflections*, 71.

[306] C. S. Lewis, "Myth Become Fact" in *God in the Dock*, 58.

of his reason, is universal and objective. This is not to say that man *holds* truth objectively, but that the truth which he does hold is itself objective. Put simply; the word "objective" is predicated not of *how* man knows but of *that which* he knows. Lewis knew well that man brings his presuppositions, influences, and entire character to the knowing process and that consequently, he gets it wrong at times.[307] Thankfully, it is also possible for him to get it right. This is to say that man can know reality in some measure as it truly is. Because none of us is God, we cannot know any part of reality exhaustively. We can, thankfully, know it sufficiently and truly. And I should say that, contrary to the views held widely throughout much of our present culture today, and even sadly held by many of our theologians, who will tell us about "the white perspective" or the "black perspective," the "male perspective" or the "female perspective," truth is no preferer of race or gender. It makes itself available to all human beings made in God's image who will look and listen.

The only way that a person can know reality is "as it truly is."[308] Knowledge, if it is to count as such, is "reality-bound" and will thus be "reality-shaped." In his helpful essay "De Futitilate," Lewis argues:

> A universe whose only claim to be believed in rests on the validity of inference must not start telling us that inference is invalid. That would be a bit too nonsensical. I conclude then that logic is a real insight into the way in which real things have to exist. In other words, the laws of thought are also the laws of things: of things in the remotest time and the remotest space.[309]

---

[307] Of course, the impact of one's character will impact different beliefs to different degrees. In some cases, there may be little to no impact. Hitler could do his sums as well as Mother Theresa, no doubt. Both a wicked tyrant and a humble saint would affirm the logical validity of "All men are mortals. Socrates is a man. Therefore, Socrates is a mortal." But on other matters, particularly those of metaphysics and meaning, morality, and value judgments, we find greater impact. See C. S. Lewis, "De Futilitate" in *Christian Reflections*, 68, where he writes, " ... nothing is more obvious than that we frequently make false inferences: from ignorance of some of the factors involved, from inattention, from inefficiencies in the system of symbols (linguistic or otherwise) which we are using, from the secret influence of our unconscious wishes or fears."

[308] The definition of truth affirmed here is "justified, true belief." In claiming that man can only "know" reality "as it truly is," the point is that "false knowledge" is no thing at all. He may hold "false beliefs" and think he has knowledge. But definitionally, if what he believes is false, it fails to count as knowledge. He can believe almost anything at all about reality, but he can only know truth about it. The author is aware of the challenges to this definition by Gettier-type problems and such but is not convinced that these present a legitimate problem to such a general conception of knowledge. Further, this general and classic definition should suffice to make the point here.

[309] C. S. Lewis, "De Futilitate" in *Christian Reflections*, 63.

C. S. LEWIS PRE-EVANGELISM FOR A POST-CHRISTIAN WORLD

Thus, Lewis maintained, in agreement with Aristotle, that thought, language, and reality all share a common structure. The importance of this statement cannot be emphasized enough, given the epistemological confusion that characterizes our present culture. The notion of thought, language, and reality sharing a common structure helps to explain the sense in which Lewis holds knowledge to be objective. Jerry Root offers a helpful explanation along these lines:

> Lewis believed, rather, that the subject, or the knower, must always surrender to the dictates of that which can be known. For Lewis, truth was not reality *per se*; truth was what people thought about reality when they thought accurately about it. For Lewis truth was found when there was coherence between reality and thought and that such a coherence was achievable, though this achievement would never be absolute, always approximate. One could have a sure word about some things but not necessarily a last word about anything. The sure word prevented Lewis from being a relativist; the inability to find a last word preserved Lewis from arrogance.[310]

While Lewis believed that man, by way of his reason, could arrive at truth, he was under no illusion that reason operated all by itself. Thus, it is possible that a person goes wrong in his reasoning process. It is also possible that he might go right but not want to follow where reason leads due to other factors. In fact, with respect to knowing God, Lewis points out that:

> [T]he instrument through which you see God is your whole self. And if a man's self is not kept clean and bright, his glimpse of God will be blurred—like the Moon seen through a dirty telescope. That is why horrible nations have horrible religions. They have been looking at God through a dirty lens.[311]

---

[310] Jerry Root, "C. S. Lewis, Objectivity, and Beauty" in *C. S. Lewis and the Arts: Creativity in the Shadowlands* (Baltimore: Square Halo Books, 2013), 63. Root is simply saying that one could take any idea or subject, and the depths could always be plumbed deeper or the examined from a different angle.

[311] C. S. Lewis, *Mere Christianity*, 164–165. See C. S. Lewis, *The Problem of Pain*, 149, where he makes a similar point. He writes, "Heaven offers nothing that a mercenary soul can desire. It is safe to tell the pure in heart that they shall see God, for only the pure in heart want to." See also A. G. Sertillanges, O. P., *The Intellectual Life*, 20, where he writes, "Do you believe that we think with the intelligence only? Are we merely a bundle of faculties among which for this or for that purpose we select the desired instrument? We think 'with our whole soul,' declared Plato. Presently, we shall go much farther, we shall say: with our whole being … it is not the mind that thinks but the man."

Lewis illustrates this truth in *The Magician's Nephew*. After Aslan has just finished singing Narnia into existence and giving to the various beasts the power of speech, nearly everyone is rejoicing and delighting in the song that is enchantingly beautiful to their ears. Meanwhile, Uncle Andrew stands hiding in a cluster of rhododendrons, bitterly sulking and complaining. Aslan's song has not pleased him, nor has he understood the meaning of the event he has witnessed. Referring to Uncle Andrew's skewed interpretation, Lewis explains, "For what you see and hear depends a good deal on where you are standing: it also depends on what sort of person you are."[312]

Lewis was affirming two truths in this scene. First, he is affirming that objective truth, even about God, can be had, and second, that man might also get it wrong. That is to say, again, that truth, which is by nature objective, is held "subjectively" by man.[313] This view is similar to that for which Michael Polanyi argues in *The Tacit Dimension* and *Personal Knowledge*. Bruce Reichenbach agrees with Lewis's and Polanyi's affinities regarding personally held knowledge. Reichenbach writes, "Lewis, like Polanyi, sees knowing as personal."[314] It follows that if there is a "blurred"

---

[312] C. S. Lewis, *The Magician's Nephew* (New York: Collier Books, 1970), 125.

[313] The concept "subjective" should not be confused with the concepts "relative" or "subjectivity." Affirming that man holds truth subjectively is merely admitting that he holds truth as a subject who sees things from a particular place in the world. He may get it right or he may get it wrong. He is not, however, helplessly locked into his subjective position such that he cannot arrive confidently at the truth. He has the aid of first principles, truths that he does not argue *for* but *from which* he must argue. One might think of the laws of logic and Kant's categories. Further, he possesses generally reliable rational faculties. If one wants to argue against the reliability of man's rational faculties, he must realize that in doing so he is using his own rational faculties that he either trusts or distrusts. If he distrusts them, he has no grounds for thinking his argument good. If he trusts them, he shows himself to be a hypocrite who does not apply the same test to his own position. Last, man has the intelligibility of reality itself by which he can test his viewpoints. These are not explicitly "theistic" affirmations, though the author's viewpoint is that theism best accounts for them. For instance, John Searle, who admittedly rejects theism, affirms these. He writes, " For a helpful explanation of how objective truth can be held subjectively, see Michael Polanyi, *The Tacit Dimension* (Chicago: University of Chicago Press, 2009). Polanyi argues for a Critical Realist position with which Lewis's view aligns.

[314] Bruce R. Reichenbach, "Knowledge, Truth, and Value in the Narnian Chronicles" in *C. S. Lewis as Philosopher: Truth, Goodness, and Beauty*, 2nd ed. Edited by David Baggett, Gary R. Habermas, and Jerry L. Walls (Lynchburg: Liberty University Press, 2017), 144. Reichenbach clarifies helpfully, "But does this not make knowing a subjective rather than an objective event? Polanyi argues that it does not, for there is an objective world that is given to us in our experience, whereas in complete subjectivity all meaning and understanding is contributed by the knower ... Thus, although all knowing is grounded in the knower, it can still be objective because both the paradigms with which one works and their associated gestalts are often public possessions of communities, subject to the challenge of potential

view to speak of, there must by distinction be a clear view as well.[315] Both are real possibilities for man. Given this, neither the radical skeptic nor the naive realist is correct.[316] The truth lies in between the two, which affirms that reality can be known to us as it truly is, though we must be careful that we are thinking rightly about it, as getting it wrong is always a possibility.

Lewis also affirmed what some philosophers had called first principles. These principles might be described as things not *about which* people think but *with which* they think. They are self-evident maxims, for Lewis. Along these lines, he maintains, "If nothing is self-evident, nothing can be proved."[317] A little later, he continues:

> But you cannot go on "explaining away" forever: you will find that you have explained explanation itself away. You cannot go on "seeing through" things forever. The whole point of seeing through something is to see something through it. It is good that the window should be transparent, because the street or garden beyond it is opaque. How if you saw through the garden too? It is no use trying to "see through" first principles. If you see through everything, then everything is transparent. But a wholly

---

defeaters. The objective component to knowledge is maintained in establishing contact with reality. Personal knowledge, then, fuses the personal and the objective," 144–146.

[315] See C. S. Lewis, "De Futilitate" in *Christian Reflections*, 62–63, where Lewis is arguing that some, certainly not all, human thoughts must be objective and true. He is responding to a context wherein scientific claims can be held to be objective and true whereas moral and metaphysical claims cannot. He writes, "I mean, the proper, distinction for our present purpose: that purpose being to find whether there is any class of thoughts which has objective value, which is not *merely* a fact about how the human cortex behaves ... for if logic is discredited science must go down with it. It therefore follows that all knowledge whatever depends on the validity of inference. If, in principle, the feeling of certainty we have when we say 'Because A is B therefore C must be D' is an illusion, if it reveals only how our cortex has to work and not how realities external to us must really be, then we can know nothing whatever. I say, 'in principle' because, of course, through inattention or fatigue we often make false inferences and while we make them feel as certain as the sound ones."

[316] The radical skeptic's position is self-defeating and unlivable. He must not be radically skeptical towards his radical skepticism, and even the radical skeptic stops and red lights and goes on greens. The naive realist's position is proved wrong by simple observation coupled with the laws of logic. Almost any example of a disagreement of viewpoints between two people will make the point–the umpire vs. the coach regarding the pitch called "strike," the student vs. the teacher who disagree over the answer to the math problem, or the husband and wife who argue over which day they saw Bob at the grocery store. Logic affirms that contradictory or conflicting statements cannot both be true. Either one or both parties in argument must be wrong. So naive realism is out.

[317] C. S. Lewis, *The Abolition of Man*, 40.

transparent world is an invisible world. To "see through" all things is the same as not to see.[318]

Therefore, he thought that humanity is not locked helplessly into an epistemological loop such that we cannot even begin the process of seeking to know. We must begin somewhere, and in doing so, we must either presuppose the validity of thinking or the objectivity of the things about which we aim to think.[319] Unless we make such a beginning and trust at least some of our thoughts as real insights into reality, truth will remain unattainable. Included in the unattainable truths would also be the truth that truth is unattainable. We can see how this quickly becomes an epistemological mess. Lewis soundly rejected such an epistemological stalemate and opted for the hopeful but tempered stance that affirms the following: Truth is objective. Man can know it accurately, though never exhaustively. He may get it wrong, but even when he does, he has reality itself to help him towards the truth.[320]

The Sacramental Quality of Truth

In holding truth to be objective, Lewis believed by extension that a statement's truthfulness is not dependent upon a person's consent. It reaches, and in a sense, *points*, much higher for that. Truths, wherever they may be found, are sacramental for Lewis. This is the point that A. G. Sertillanges makes when he writes, "Every truth is a reflection; behind the reflection, and giving it value, is the Light ... One might say a particular truth is only a symbol, a symbol that is real, a sacrament of the absolute ... Hence, for the fully awakened soul, every truth is a meeting-place; the sovereign Thought invites ours to the sublime meeting."[321]

Human reason, according to Lewis, is "the organ of truth."[322] This organ, however, cannot function autonomously on its own. It depends

---

[318] C. S. Lewis, *The Abolition of Man*, 81.

[319] See C. S. Lewis, The Abolition of Man, 48, where he argues earlier, "And open mind, in questions that are not ultimate, is useful. But an open mind about the ultimate foundations either of Theoretical or Practical Reason is idiocy. If a man's mind is open on these things, let his mouth at least be shut. He can so nothing to the purpose. Outside the *Tao* there is no ground for criticizing either the *Tao* or anything else."

[320] See C. S. Lewis, "De Futilitate" in *Christian Reflections*, 61, where Lewis again affirms first principles, writing, "However small the class, *some* class of thoughts must be regarded not as merely facts about the way human brains work, but as true insights, as the reflection of reality in human consciousness."

[321] A. G. Sertillanges, O. P., *The Intellectual Life: Its Spirit, Conditions, Methods*, translated by Mary Ryan (Washington: The Catholic University of America Press, 1998), 30–31.

[322] C. S. Lewis, "Bluspels and Flalansferes" in *Selected Literary Essays*, 265.

upon another, far higher source of "Reason." Lewis went so far as to envision human reason *participating* in this higher Reason. He explains:

> For him [the Theist], reason—the reason of God—is older than Nature, and from it the orderliness of Nature, which alone enables us to know her, is derived. For him, the human mind in the act of knowing is illuminated by the Divine reason. It is set free, in the measure required, from the huge nexus of non-rational causation; free from this to be determined by the truth known."[323]

Lewis believed that the reasoning process itself, if it is to be trusted as reliably pointing to truth, was unexplainable from the Naturalist's position. He argued that, given Naturalism, reason would be simply another mindlessly determined event that man would have little grounds for trusting to deliver truth. Given a purely materialistic explanation of the universe, human reason, at best, would arrive at truth by mere chance. To this point, Lewis argues, "If the value of our reasoning is in doubt, you cannot try to establish it by reasoning."[324]

He believed that a far better explanation, one that allows man to trust his reason, was to suggest that man's reason came not from a mindless process, but from another reason itself, a non-contingent source, in fact. He writes:

> It is only when you are asked to believe in Reason coming from non-reason that you must cry Halt, for, if you don't all thought is discredited. It is therefore obvious that sooner or later you must admit a Reason which exists absolutely on its own. The problem is whether you or I can be such a self-existent Reason.[325]

Lewis continues, much in line with Aristotle's argument from contingency, and later Aquinas's:

> I therefore cannot be that self-existence Reason which neither slumbers nor sleeps. Yet if any thought is valid, such a Reason must exist and must be the source of my own imperfect and intermittent rationality. Human minds, then ... come into Nature from Supernature: each has its tap-root in an eternal, self-existent

---

[323] C. S. Lewis, *Miracles*, 34–35.
[324] C. S. Lewis, *Miracles*, 33.
[325] C. S. Lewis, *Miracles*, 42.

rational Being, whom we call God. Each is an offshoot, or spearhead, or incursion of that Supernatural reality in Nature.[326]

It is this participatory imagery that helps one to see how Lewis viewed truth and the reasoning process itself as bearing a sacramental quality. In choosing to employ the metaphorical language of tap-roots connecting branches and spearheads that pierce through a surface, he is conveying a relationship far stronger than merely one thing *resembling* another thing. He is trying to get across the notion of something close to subsistence, of the greater being really present in the lesser.

Similar language is found in his autobiography as he recounted his pre-Christian contemplations about the nature of the universe. He writes:

> I was therefore compelled to give up realism ...Idealism was then the dominant philosophy at Oxford and I was by nature 'against Government' ... I wanted Nature to be quite independent of our observations; something other, indifferent, self-existing ... But now, it seemed to me, I had to give that up. Unless I were to accept an unbelievable alternative, I must admit that mind was no late-come epiphenomenon; that the whole universe was, in the last resort, mental; that our logic was participation in a cosmic *Logos*.[327]

Though he is describing his move to Idealism here, he understood it to be one step closer to Theism and eventually to Christianity. With each move that he made, while he corrected some matters, he never abandoned the belief that human reason shares in Divine Reason and that logic "down here" is tethered to ultimate Logic "up there." The important final move he made from Idealism to Theism was in his eventual realization that the Absolute is not the impersonal "Nobody-knows-what"[328] of Hegel, but the "Absolute Spirit."[329] He is in fact a "Person,"[330] *the* Person, God, whom Lewis calls "Reason itself."[331]

This importance of this point in Lewis's thinking cannot be gainsaid; that is, the sacramental nature of truth points not merely to some abstract

---

[326] C. S. Lewis, *Miracles*, 42–43.

[327] C. S. Lewis, *Surprised by Joy*, 209. When Lewis writes of "realism" here he is talking about the same thing that people mean when they speak of "materialism" today. Implicit in either term is that the whole of reality of material, and that nothing at all like mind, certainly not divine mind, exists.

[328] C. S. Lewis, *Surprised by Joy*, 222.

[329] C. S. Lewis, *Surprised by Joy*, 227.

[330] C. S. Lewis, *Surprised by Joy*, 230.

[331] C. S. Lewis, *Surprised by Joy*, 228.

C. S. LEWIS PRE-EVANGELISM FOR A POST-CHRISTIAN WORLD

Truth "up there"—wherever that might be—but to a Person. Ultimate Reality, the great Universal who unites all universals and particulars, is personal. This Person is the Christ, whom John happily equates with the Greek conception, the "Logos."[332] Lewis clarifies the Christian position thus: "I had hoped that the heart of reality might be of such a kind that we can best symbolize it as a place; instead, I found it to be a Person."[333]

Boersma agrees with Lewis along these lines. Writing of reality's "christological anchor,"[334] he argues:

> The Platonic connection allowed Christians to say that the eternal Logos—infinitely transcending the created order—provides the foundation and stability of the created order and of human history. The fragmentation of postmodernism witnesses to the fact that once we lost this christological foundation, natural realities end up drifting anchors in the raging waves of history. To put it differently, the loss of the christological thread undermines the unity of the sacramental tapestry. Culturally, therefore, we are more than ever in need of a philosophical position that allows us to maintain that universals are real, as well as a theological position that argues that they find their reality in the eternal Word of God.[335]

Entailed in this idea is the notion that *both* the reasoning process itself, *and* the truth which it apprehends, sacramentally point to Christ, the "Logos." Lewis elaborates:

---

[332] See John 1:1. See Craig Bernthal, *Tolkien's Sacramental Vision: Discerning the Holy in Middle Earth* (Kettering: Second Spring, 2014), 85–86, where Bernthal offers a helpful and brief historical survey of the concept "logos." He writes, "Heraclitus of Ephesus was the first known Greek philosopher to use the word logos as a philosophical term. For him, it is the eternal divine law, moral as well as natural. For the Stoics, the logos meant the principle of active reason that permeated and animated the universe and engaged in creation. They associated it with God, and in this context the word became influential in Jewish philosophy. Philo of Alexandria, a Jewish Platonist, saw the logos as an intermediary between God and man, the intermediary closest to God in a Platonic system that had a succession of intermediaries. Because it was the highest intermediary, Philo called it 'the first born of God,' and he associated it with the Angel of the Lord in the Old Testament ... He identified the Logos as the instrument through which God created the universe. Justin Martyr, one of the earliest Christian theologians, associated the Logos not only with Christ, but with the Angel of the Lord and Wisdom."

[333] C. S. Lewis, *Surprised by Joy*, 230.

[334] Hans Boersma, *Heavenly Participation*, 51.

[335] Hans Boersma, *Heavenly Participation*, 51.

It seems much more likely that human thought is not God's but God-kindled ... We are interested in man only because his rationality is the little tell-tale rift in Nature which shows that there is something beyond or behind her ... The supernatural Reason enters my natural being ... like a beam of light which illuminates or a principle of organisation which unifies and develops.[336]

McGrath makes a similar point, writing, "A Christian natural theology holds that the *logos* through which the world was created is embedded in the structures of the created order, above all the human person, and incarnated in Christ."[337] Referring to the human person as the example "above all" of a *logos*-structured reality, McGrath has in mind particularly man's reason. He explains further in the same chapter, writing of the "created correspondence between the world and the mind, reflecting the fact that both are the creation of the same God, expressing the same divine *logos*."[338]

ON GOODNESS: MORALITY THAT POINTS UPWARD

The Objective Quality of Goodness

In addition to truth, Lewis also maintained that goodness is both objective and sacramental in nature. The three books in which he laid out his most thorough arguments on morality are *The Problem of Pain*, *Mere Christianity*, and *The Abolition of Man*. In *Mere Christianity*, he begins by arguing for objective morality, or what used to be called the "Law of

---

[336] C. S. Lewis, *Miracles*, 44–45, 48.

[337] Alister McGrath, *The Open Secret*, 233. It is debated whether or not what McGrath calls "natural theology" is how the term should be understood. Admittedly, McGrath is not inferring *from* the particulars *to* a conclusion about the existence and/or nature of God. He takes issue with this approach as he believes it begins with a flawed assumption, namely that man comes to the evidence with no presuppositions or biases through which he reads the evidence. He equates this approach largely with the Enlightenment influence on reason, and opts instead to admit up front the belief grid through which he approaches the question of the meaning of the reality. He argues that all people come with such a grid. To pretend otherwise is naive and dishonest for McGrath. The particular nuance of McGrath's "natural theology" is that one should admit one's belief grid up front, lay it, as it were, on top of the evidence, and see if it makes the best sense of the evidence one observes. The idea is to see, in the end, which postulated grid has the most explanatory power of the observed data. McGrath believes that this is what Lewis had in mind with his famous line, "I believe in Christianity as I believe that the sun has risen, not only because I see it, but because by it I see all other things."

[338] Alister McGrath, *The Open Secret*, 247.

Nature," by which older thinkers really meant the "Law of Human Nature."[339] Lewis explains this Law thus:

> The idea was that, just as all bodies are governed by the law of gravitation, and organisms by biological laws, so the creature called man also had his law—with this great difference, that a body could not choose whether it obeyed the law of gravitation or not, but a man could choose either to obey the Law of Human Nature or to disobey it.[340]

He responds to two key objections, both of which allow him the opportunity to solidify his position in affirming the objective nature of the moral law. Some object that what Lewis calls the "Law of Nature" is more accurately "herd instinct."[341] Lewis responds by demonstrating that all people know what it is like to experience conflicting instincts and the corresponding decision that adjudicates between them. For example, when a person sees another drowning, two instincts arise – one for self-preservation and another for saving the drowning person. In these situations, a "third thing" emerges that encourages the fulfillment of one impulse over the other. This, Lewis argues, cannot itself be one of the impulses. If the Moral Law were identical with one of humanity's impulses, "we ought to be able to point to some one impulse inside us which was always what we call 'good,' always in agreement with the rule of right behavior. But you cannot."[342] He argues all impulses must be suppressed at certain times—the impulses for sex, patriotism, mother love, etc.

Further, when impulses are in conflict, something often tells the conflicted individual to obey the weaker impulse. Lewis explains, "You probably *want* to be safe much more than you want to help the man who is drowning: but the Moral Law tells you to help him all the same ... The thing which tells you which note on the piano needs to be played louder cannot itself be that note."[343] Delivering these talks over the BBC radio during World War II, Lewis makes the clever point:

> The moment you say that one set of moral ideas can be better than another, you are, in fact, measuring them both by a standard, saying that one of them confirms to that standard more nearly than any other. But the standard that measures two things

---

[339] C. S. Lewis, *Mere Christianity* (New York: Harper Collins, 2001), 4.
[340] C. S. Lewis, *Mere Christianity*, 4.
[341] C. S. Lewis, *Mere Christianity*, 9.
[342] C. S. Lewis, *Mere Christianity*, 11.
[343] C. S. Lewis, *Mere Christianity*, 10.

is something different from either. You are, in fact, comparing them both with some Real Morality, admitting that there is such a thing as real Right, independent of what people think, and that some people's ideas get nearer to that real Right than others. Or put it this way. If your moral ideas can be truer, and those of the Nazis less true, there must be something—some Real Morality—for them to be true about. The reason why your idea of New York can be truer or less true than mine is that New York is a real place, existing quite apart from what either of us thinks.[344]

Next, Lewis compares the "Laws of Nature" with the "Law of Human Nature." Regarding the laws of nature, Lewis observes that they are merely observations of "what Nature, in fact, does."[345] Stones and trees "obey" these "laws" in the sense that they do by nature what they cannot but help to do. Trees put down roots, grow upwards, sprout leaves, etc. Rocks fall back to the earth when tossed up into the air. The Law of Human Nature, by contrast, does not describe merely what humans do. Rather, it describes what we ought to do but fail very often to do. Lewis writes, "In other words, when you are dealing with humans, something else comes in above and beyond the facts."[346] What comes in is an objective universal standard that tells us how we ought to behave, whereas the fact of the matter is that we often behave in direct conflict with this standard.

Lewis completes the first part of his argument in Book I of *Mere Christianity* by arriving, not at the God of Christianity, but only "as far as a Somebody or Something behind the Moral Law."[347] He argues that this "Being behind the universe is intensely interested in right conduct—in fair play, unselfishness, courage, good faith, honesty, and truthfulness."[348] He insists again that, "we have not yet got as far as a personal God—only as far as a power, behind the Moral Law, and more like a mind than it is like anything else."[349]

With *Mere Christianity*, one can see plainly that Lewis holds that moral goodness is objective and that the Law, which helps to adjudicate the status of actions as either good or evil, stands above humanity. Armstrong clarifies, "In other words, Lewis believed that 'natural law is a metaphysical reality,' as the whole Western medieval tradition, from one end to the

---

[344] C. S. Lewis, *Mere Christianity*, 13–14.
[345] C. S. Lewis, *Mere Christianity*, 17.
[346] C. S. Lewis, *Mere Christianity*, 17.
[347] C. S. Lewis, *Mere Christianity*, 29.
[348] C. S. Lewis, *Mere Christianity*, 30.
[349] C. S. Lewis, *Mere Christianity*, 30.

other, had assumed. 'In the last essay he wrote for publication, Lewis said of natural law, "I hold this conception basic to all civilization."'[350]

The Sacramental Quality of Goodness

Not only is morality objective, but more goodness also participates sacramentally in God's nature, just as we saw with truth. Lewis writes, "[I]t is true to say that God's own nature is the sanction of His commands."[351] One entailment of this truth is that every commandment, every act of goodness that aligns with God's moral standards, is a pointer or a mirror to His character. On this point, Lewis stands in sharp contrast to the nominalists, such as Scotus and Ockham, who denied the link between God's commandments and His nature. Lewis argues:

> It has sometimes been asked whether God commands certain things because they are right, or whether certain things are right because God commands them. With Hooker, and against Dr. Johnson, I emphatically embrace the first alternative. The second might lead to the abominable conclusion (reached, I think, by Paley) that charity is good only because God arbitrarily commanded it — that He might equally well have commanded us to hate Him and one another and that hatred would then have been right. I believe, on the contrary, that 'they err who think that of the will of God to do this or that there is no reason besides His will'. God's will is determined by His wisdom which always perceives, and His goodness which always embraces, the intrinsically good. But when we have said that God commands things only because they are good, we must add that one of the things intrinsically good is that rational creatures should freely surrender themselves to their Creator in obedience.[352]

Even more strongly in *Reflections on the Psalms*, he writes, referring at first to the Psalmists who implicitly rooted the moral Law in God's nature:

> By this assurance they put themselves, implicitly, on the right side of a controversy which arose far later among Christians. There were in the eighteenth century terrible theologians who held that "God did not command certain things because they are right, but certain things are right because God commanded them." To make

---

[350] Chris R. Armstrong, *Medieval Wisdom for Modern Christians*, 51.
[351] C. S. Lewis, *Surprised by Joy*, 232.
[352] C. S. Lewis, *The Problem of Pain*, 99.

the position perfectly clear, one of them even said that though God has, as it happens, commanded us to love Him and one another, He might equally well have commanded us to hate Him and one another, and hatred would then have been right. It was apparently a mere toss-up which He decided on. Such a view in effect makes God a mere arbitrary tyrant. It would be better and less irreligious to have no ethics than to have such an ethics and such a theology as this.[353]

Still further, he writes, "God enjoins what is good because it is good, because He is good. Hence His laws have *emeth* 'truth', intrinsic validity, rock-bottom reality, being rooted in His own nature, and are therefore as solid as that Nature which He has created."[354] Lewis would rather a man deny morality altogether than deny the ontological connection between objective morality and God's nature.

Further, he is so emphatic on the point that humanity's idea of goodness must not be foreign to God's goodness that he says that apart from this, people could have no confidence in understanding good or bad. Neither could they rest assured that what God calls good today, he will not call evil tomorrow. He compares humanity's understanding of goodness related to God's perfect goodness with the analogy of knowing and being able to draw perfect circles. He reasons that while no one has ever drawn a perfect circle, people have some idea of it. In the same way, God's goodness differs from humanity's, not like two unrelated things differ, but like an imperfect circle differs from a perfect one.[355]

Not only does Lewis employ reason to argue for the participatory quality of goodness rooted in God's nature, but he also describes various experiences of goodness through which he feels the sacramental pull towards God. One such pull comes from his reading of George MacDonald's fairy tale *Phantastes*. This is the book that Lewis claims "baptized"[356] his imagination. In the preface to *George MacDonald: An Anthology*, he explains in particular what gripped him through MacDonald's story. He recalls:

> The quality which had enchanted me in his imaginative works turned out to be the quality of the real universe, the divine,

---

[353] C. S. Lewis, *Reflections on the Psalms*, 70–71.

[354] C. S. Lewis, *Reflections on the Psalms*, 71.

[355] See C. S. Lewis, *The Problem of Pain*, 30, where he writes, "The Divine 'goodness' differs from ours, but it is not sheerly different: it differs from ours not as white from black but as a perfect circle from a child's first attempt to draw a wheel."

[356] C. S. Lewis, *Surprised by Joy*, 181.

magical, terrifying, ecstatic reality in which we all live. I should have been shocked in my teens if anyone had told me that what I learned to love in *Phantastes* was goodness. But now that I know, I see there was no deception. The deception is all the other way round—in that prosaic moralism which confines goodness to the region of Law and Duty, which never lets us feel in our face the sweet air blowing from "the land of righteousness," never reveals that elusive Form which if once seen must inevitably be desired with all but sensuous desire—the thing (in Sappho's phrase) "more gold than gold."[357]

Lewis realized that it was moral goodness that beckoned to him as if from another world when he read *Phantastes*. The experience proved so profound that his view of reality was deeply impacted long after the Joy had vanished. He reflects:

Up till now each visitation of Joy had left the common world momentarily a desert—'The first touch of the earth went nigh to kill.' Even when real clouds or trees had been the material of the vision, they had been so only by reminding me of another world; and I did not like the return to ours. But now I saw the bright shadow coming out of the book into the real world and resting there, transforming all common things and yet itself unchanged. Or, more accurately, I saw the common things drawn into the bright shadow.[358]

This experience has sometimes been referred to as an encounter with moral beauty. Lewis experienced it again years later during an Inklings Meeting. Tolkien was reading to him the two chapters "Shelob's Lair" and "The Choice of Master Samwise." He was so deeply moved by Samwise's courage and sense of loyalty to his friend Frodo, that he was brought to tears.[359]

---

[357] C. S. Lewis, *George MacDonald: An Anthology*, xxxviii.
[358] C. S. Lewis, *Surprised by Joy*, 181.
[359] See J. R. R. Tolkien, "Letter to Christopher Tolkien," 31 May 1944, in *The Letters of J. R. R. Tolkien*, 83. "The Inklings meeting was very enjoyable ... The rest of my time ... has been occupied by the desperate attempt to bring 'The Ring' to a suitable pause, the capture of Frodo by the Orcs in the passes of Mordor, before I am obliged to break off by examining. By sitting up all hours, I managed it: and read the last 2 chapters (*Shelob's Lair* and *The Choice of Master Samwise*) to C.S.L. on Monday morning. He approved with unusual fervor, and was actually affected to tears by the last chapter, so it seems to be keeping up.".

In his *Reflections on the Psalms*, Lewis describes the affective power of "moral beauty"[360] as he considers Psalm 119, which chiefly concerns the moral law. He writes, "This is not priggery nor even scrupulosity; it is the language of a man ravished by moral beauty. If we cannot at all share his experience, we shall be the losers."[361] Importantly, when he and his close friend and colleague Tolkien began their literary careers as authors of imaginative fiction, it was moral goodness that they held up before their readers in the hopes that they might taste and eventually find Him to be good, who is in fact ultimate Goodness. Loconte writes:

> In the worlds of Middle-earth and Narnia, evil is a perversion of goodness, which is the ultimate reality. Although Lewis is much more explicit in naming God as the source of everything good in the world, Tolkien shares his Christian belief that evil represents a rejection of God and the joy and beauty and virtue that originate in him.[362]

In *The Problem of Pain*, Lewis argues that humanity's recognition of the moral law points to God. He argues:

> ... the consciousness not merely of a moral law, but of a moral law at once approved and disobeyed. This consciousness is neither a logical, nor an illogical, inference from the facts of experience; if we did not bring it to our experience we could not find it there. It is either inexplicable illusion, or else revelation ... And if revelation, then it is most really and truly in Abraham that all people shall be blessed, for it was the Jews who fully and unambiguously identified the awful Presence haunting black mountain-tops and thunderclouds with "the righteous Lord" who "loveth righteousness."[363]

Later, he equates goodness with God, which is to say that God is not merely good, but is goodness itself, and therefore the fountain from which all instances of goodness in the world flow. It follows that every instance of goodness found here below is in some way an expression of God's nature. It is a sunbeam to be followed up to the sun, to use Lewis's famed expression.[364] Referring to goodness, Plato argued similarly that the world

---

[360] C. S. Lewis, *Reflections on the Psalms*, 69.

[361] C. S. Lewis, *Reflections on the Psalms*, 69.

[362] Joseph Loconte, *A Hobbit, a Wardrobe, and a Great War*, 148.

[363] C. S. Lewis, *The Problem of Pain*, 11, 13.

[364] This concept of following the sunbeam up to the sun is consistent with what James writes in James 1:17, which says, "Every good and perfect gift is from above, coming down from the Father of lights, with whom there is no variation or shadow due to change." If one

bears an affinity to the nature of God. He writes of the craftsman who fashioned the world:[365]

> Now why did he who framed this whole universe of becoming frame it? Let us state the reason why: He was good, and one who is good can never become jealous of anything. And so, being free of jealousy, he wanted everything to become as much like himself as was possible.[366]

One can see the hierarchy present in Plato's thought, which is consistent with Lewis's. Goodness "down below" is derivative of ultimate Goodness, which is identified with God. Lewis clarifies, "But God's love, far from being caused by goodness in the object, caused all the goodness which the object has, loving it first into existence and then into real, thought derivative, lovability. God is Goodness … he eternally has, and is, all goodness."[367] He stands in agreement with the psalmists who "call the directions or 'rulings' of Jahweh 'true'"[368] because "they are based on the very nature of things and the very nature of God."[369] In Lewis's view, it is possible for one both to see and to feel the sacramental quality of goodness. He knew both well.

ON BEAUTY: DESIRE THAT POINTS UPWARD

The Objective Quality of Beauty

It would not be difficult to find today individuals who affirm the objective nature of both truth and goodness, yet who remain unconvinced of the same with respect to beauty.[370] Lewis is most assuredly not one of

---

follows the good and perfect gift upwards, one will eventually come to the divine Giver, who is God. This is the sense in which Lewis thought that almost anything could be a theophany.

[365] Some readers of Plato will be more familiar with the term "Demiurge." The notion is that of a divine agent who carries out the work of creating the universe based on a changeless model. See Plato, "Timaeus" in *Complete Works* edited by John M. Cooper (Indianapolis: Hacket Publishing Company, 1997), 1234. See Cooper's helpful footnote: "Greek demiourgos, also sometimes translated below as 'maker' … or 'fashioner' … whence the divine 'Demiurge' one reads about in account of the *Timaeus*."

[366] Plato, "Timaeus" in *Complete Works* edited by John M. Cooper (Indianapolis: Hacket Publishing Company, 1997), 1236.

[367] C. S. Lewis, *The Problem of Pain*, 43–44.

[368] C. S. Lewis, *Reflections on the Psalms*, 70.

[369] C. S. Lewis, *Reflections on the Psalms*, 70.

[370] See Roger Scruton, *Beauty: A Very Short Introduction* (Oxford: Oxford University Press, 2011), xi–xii, where he writes, "That familiar relativism has led some people to dismiss judgements of beauty as purely 'subjective'. No tastes can be criticized, they argue, since to

these individuals. Root writes, "C. S. Lewis's view of beauty and the arts cannot be separated from his view of truth and objectivity."[371] Few suggestions offend the modern person so easily as the suggestion that one's tastes might be bad—that is, that what one calls beautiful might actually be ugly, that what one finds merely interesting might be more deserving of humble reverence, and such. On the topic of objective beauty, Lewis walks like a dinosaur among modern people as throughout his writings, he affirms both the objective and the sacramental qualities of beauty.[372]

He begins his argument in *The Abolition of Man* with the story of Coleridge at the waterfall.[373] As the story goes, two tourists were present with Coleridge. One called the waterfall "sublime" whereas the other called it merely "pretty." Coleridge sided with the first tourist and was repulsed by the second one's comment. This story, first told by Coleridge, is recounted by two men who had written an English textbook within which they make implicit, though monumentally significant points about values, truth, and beauty. They conclude, "When this man said *This is sublime*, he appeared to be making a remark about the waterfall ... Actually ... he was not making a remark about the waterfall, but a remark about this own

---

criticize one taste is simply to give voice to another; hence there is nothing to learn or to teach that could conceivably deserve the name of 'criticism' ... When each year the Turner prize, founded in memory of England's greatest painter, is awarded to yet another bundle of facetious ephemera, is this not proof that there are no standards, that fashion alone dictates who will and who will not be rewarded, and that it is pointless to look for objective principles of taste or public conception of the beautiful? ... I suggest that such skeptical thoughts about beauty are unjustified. Beauty, I argue, is a real and universal value, one anchored in our rational nature, and the sense of beauty has an indispensable part to play in shaping the human world."

[371] Jerry Root, "C. S. Lewis, Objectivity, and Beauty" in *C. S. Lewis and the Arts*, 63.

[372] See C. S. Lewis, *The Abolition of Man*, 14–15, where Lewis writes, "Until quite modern times all teachers and even all men believed the universe to be such that certain emotional reactions on our part could be either congruous or incongruous to it—believed, in fact, that objects did not merely receive, but could *merit,* our approval or disapproval, our reverence or our contempt. The reason why Coleridge agreed with the tourist who called the cataract sublime and disagreed with the one who called it pretty was of course that he believed inanimate nature to be such that certain responses could be more 'just' or 'ordinate' or 'appropriate' to it than others. And he believed (correctly) that the tourists thought the same." As he looks back throughout history, Lewis sees the doctrine of objective values being affirmed in various times and places. He calls this doctrine, "the *Tao.*" He writes further, "This conception in all its forms, Platonic, Aristotelian, Stoic, Christian, and Oriental alike, I shall henceforth refer to for brevity simply as 'the *Tao*'" 18.

[373] See Jerry Root, "C. S. Lewis, Beauty, and Objectivity," in *C. S. Lewis and the Arts*, 64, where he writes, "Lewis's response to *The Green Book* is chronicled in *The Abolition of Man* and it is there he sets forth, in detail, his objectivist values and underscores his thoughts about objectivity; and, it must be remembered, it is these that guide him in making judgments in matters of beauty and art."

feelings."[374] Lewis proceeds to take this view apart and to offer his own argument for the reality of objective values, which he extends to the realm of the beautiful.[375] He argues that the objects themselves, or to speak in the broadest sense, *reality* itself, determines which responses are most fitting.[376]

Because Lewis accepts Plato's tripartite explanation of the soul, as well as the Platonic and Aristotelian view of education, a pre-modern of beauty and the entailments thereof can hardly be overemphasized. A brief explanation will be helpful here. Plato held that the human soul is made up of three separate parts, or powers—reason, sentiment/emotions, and appetites. He likened reason to the head, sentiment/emotions to the chest, and appetites to the belly.[377] Further, he extended the analogy also to three

---

[374] C. S. Lewis, *The Abolition of Man*, 2.

[375] Scruton agrees with Lewis's approach to beauty. See Roger Scruton, *Beauty: A Very Short Introduction*, 6, where he writes, "With beauty matters are otherwise. Here the judgement focuses on the *object judged*, not the subject who judges." He also writes later, "When I describe something as beautiful I am describing *it*, not my feelings towards it—I am making a claim, and that seems to imply others, if they see things aright, would agree with me," 26–27.

[376] See Roger Scruton, *Beauty: A Very Short Introduction*, 61, where Scruton refers to Edmund Burke's *On the Sublime and Beautiful*. Drawing on Burke, Scruton offers a helpful distinction between beauty and sublimity and offers an illustration that demonstrates the which term is more fitting given two scenarios. Scruton writes, "In the aesthetic context words have a tendency to slip and slide, behaving more like metaphors than literal descriptions. And the reason for this is plain. We are not, in aesthetic judgement, simply describing some object in the world. We are giving voice to an *encounter*, a meeting of subject and object, in which the response of the first is every bit as important as the qualities of the second ... Burke discerned two radically distinct responses to beauty in general, and to natural beauty in particular: one originating in love, the other in fear. When we are attracted by the harmony, order and serenity of nature, so as to feel at home in it and confirmed by it, then we speak of its beauty; when, however, on some wind-blown mountain crag, we experience the vastness, the power, and threatening majesty of the natural world, and feel our own littleness in the face of it, then we should speak of the sublime."

[377] See Plato, *Republic* in *Plato: Complete Works*, 1067–1077 for his description of the tripartite soul. *Republic* stands as Plato's argument for the true nature of justice, which is necessary to having good citizens, who are therefore necessary for having a good republic. He begins his argument by seeking justice in the city. He reasons that justice will be more easily perceptible in the city than in the individual as the city is larger. This is analogous to one's being able to see more easily with one's eyes something large rather than something small. He argues that justice, in the city, is each person doing his share, or carrying out his proper task. He writes, "Moreover, we've heard many people and have often said ourselves that justice is doing one's own work and not meddling with what isn't one's own ... Then, it turns out that this doing one's own work—provided that it comes to be in a certain way—is justice," 1064–1065. He lists the three classes in the republic as the guardians, soldiers, and craftsmen. Corresponding analogously to these three classes, he then applies his reasoning to the individual in order to locate justice in the smaller "place." He writes, "But a city was thought to be just when each of the three natural classes within it did its own work, and it was thought to be moderate, courageous, and wise because of certain other conditions and states of theirs

roles in a civilization: reason (the guardian), sentiments (the soldiers/military), and desires (the craftsmen). He argued that reason should lead as guardian. Sentiment was then to lend support to reason as a soldier, and the two working together were to bring the appetites, the craftsmen, into submission to their direction. Plato understood the power of the "chest" (sentiments) to influence the person. When allied to reason, it can be a great help towards the virtuous life. On the other hand, when allied to appetites, which so often are contrary to reason, great harm can result to the individual. Drawing on this tripartite conception of the soul from Plato, Lewis writes in *The Abolition of Man*:

> It still remains true that no justification of virtue will enable a man to be virtuous. Without the aid of trained emotions the intellect is powerless against the animal organism ... We were told it all long ago by Plato. As the king governs by his executive, so Reason in man must rule the mere appetites by means of the "spirited element". The head rules the belly through the chest ... The Chest-Magnanimity-Sentiment—these are the indispensable liaison officers between cerebral man and visceral man. It may even be said that it is by this middle element that man is man: for by his intellect he is mere spirit and by his appetite mere animal.[378]

... Then, if an individual has these same three parts in his soul, we will expect him to be correctly called by the same names as the city if he has the same conditions in them," 1066–1066. Plato equates the guardians with wisdom/reason, which corresponds to the head. He equates next the soldiers with courage/sentiments, which correspond to the chest. Finally, he equates the craftsmen with moderation/appetites, which correspond with the belly. Therefore, the head (reason) rules. The chest (sentiment) is supposed to come to the aid of the head and help to bring the belly (appetite) into submission to both. He explains this relationship as follows, "Therefore, isn't it appropriate for the rational part to rule, since it is really wise and exercises foresight on behalf of the whole soul, and for the spirited part to obey it and be its ally? ... And isn't it, as we were saying, a mixture of music and poetry, on the one hand, and physical training, on the other, that makes the two parts harmonious, stretching and nurturing the rational part with fine words and learning, relaxing the other part through soothing stories, and making it gentle by means of harmony and rhythm? ... And these two, having been nurtured this way, and having truly learned their roles and been educated in them, will govern the appetitive part, which is the largest part in each person's soul and is by nature the most insatiable for money. They'll watch over it to see that it isn't filled with the so-called pleasures of the body and that it doesn't become so big and strong that it no longer does its own work but attempts to enslave and rule over the classes it isn't fitted to rule, thereby overturning everyone's whole life," 1073. Injustice in the individual, then, is one of the parts "meddling" with the job of the other part. If the sentiments or the appetites rule, rather than reason, the individual will be corrupted.

[378] C. S. Lewis, *The Abolition of Man*, 24–25. Richard Weaver agrees with this. See Richard Weaver, *Ideas Have Consequences*, 19, where he writes, "When we affirm that philosophy begins with wonder, we are affirming in effect that sentiment is anterior to reason. We do not undertake to reason about anything until we have been drawn to it by an affective

The danger that Lewis saw in the denial of objective values, which includes the denial of objective beauty, is that man's "chest" will inevitably grow deformed. Doing so will not come to the aid of reason to help steer the individual towards truth. It cannot possibly due so once the conclusion has been reached that there is no truth, but only opinion to speak of regarding beauty. Without the chest as ally, the head will not be able to keep the individual on the right course. Lewis makes this very point when referring to the proper use of rhetoric. He reasons, "The proper use is lawful and necessary because, as Aristotle points out, intellect of itself 'moves nothing': the transition from thinking to doing, in nearly all men at nearly all moments, needs to be assisted by appropriate states of feeling."[379] He argues the same in *The Abolition of Man* thus:

> ... a persevering devotion to truth, a nice sense of intellectual honor, cannot be long maintained without the aid of a sentiment which Gaius and Titius could debunk as easily as any other. It is not excess of thought but defect of fertile and generous emotion that marks them out. Their heads are no bigger than the ordinary: it is the atrophy of the chest beneath that makes them seem so.[380]

With this in mind, we can now see the serious entailments of the denial of objective beauty with respect to the education process, which Lewis set forth for his readers.[381] He held that the purpose of education was not simply to train people for vocations, but to aid in producing *good* people. He extends "good" to the whole person—intellect, sentiments, and appetites. Referring to Aristotle and Milton, he explains:

> Neither of them would dispute the purpose of education is to produce the good man and the good citizen, though it must be remembered that we are not here using the word "good" in a narrowly ethical sense. The "good man" here means the man of good taste and good feeling, the interesting and interested man, and almost the happy man.[382]

---

interest ... how frequently it is brought to our attention that nothing good can be done if the will is wrong! Reason alone fails to justify itself."

[379] C. S. Lewis, *A Preface to Paradise Lost*, 53.

[380] C. S. Lewis, *The Abolition of Man*, 25.

[381] Again, he holds that the

[382] C. S. Lewis, "Our English Syllabus" in *Image and Imagination*, 22. In fact, Lewis distinguishes education from training. He is referring to making good citizens with the former term. With the latter, he is referring to making skilled citizens, fit for their respective vocations.

Lewis holds that beauty, when justly affirmed and enjoyed, will come to aid man's reason, as the true and the beautiful aim at the same ultimate end. He adopts this view from Plato, who had argued this convincingly in the *Republic*. Lewis recalls Plato's argument thus:

> In the *Republic*, the well-nurtured youth is one "who would see most clearly whatever was amiss in ill-made works of or ill-grown works of nature, and with a just distaste would blame and hate the ugly even from his earliest years and would give delighted praise to beauty, receiving it into his soul and being nourished by it, so that he becomes a man of gentle heart. All this before he is of an age to reason; so that when Reason at length comes to him, then, bred as he has been, he will hold out his hands in welcome and recognize her because of the affinity he bears to her."[383]

Plato gave temporal priority to the development of the chest over the head, and Lewis agreed. If a young person's sentiments are marred from a young age, he will find it painfully difficult to follow reason's lead when the age for reasoning arrives. He will be like a man whose torso has been twisted backward, pulling him in one direction while his head tries to steer him in another. Plato's point is that the torso will not likely turn and right itself; rather, the head will likely twist backward to join the torso's distortion. This sheds some light for us on why propaganda is immensely powerful and sadly is so often used manipulatively for evil ends. It also helps us to understand why reasoned argumentation tends to fall flat when confronting falsehood in the present culture. We must remember that at many times we are engaging people whose chests have been thoroughly shaped by the spirit of the age, thanks in large part to the media and the television and movie industries.

Pre-modern education was as much about rightly trained sentiments as it was about getting right information and right reasoning into the student's head. Lewis recalls, "Aristotle says that the aim of education is to make the pupil like and dislike what he ought."[384] Training one to like what deserves to be liked and vice versa is part of training in virtue. Lewis states further, "St. Augustine defines virtue as *ordo amoris*, the ordinate condition of the affections in which every object is accorded that kind of degree of love which is appropriate to it."[385] Here again, Lewis is affirming that reality dictates the right response from the observer.

---

[383] C. S. Lewis, *The Abolition of Man*, 16–17.
[384] C. S. Lewis, *The Abolition of Man*, 16.
[385] C. S. Lewis, *The Abolition of Man*, 16.

C. S. LEWIS PRE-EVANGELISM FOR A POST-CHRISTIAN WORLD

Very seriously, Lewis believed that a society that has rejected objective values, which prevents one from making any objective claims regarding beauty, is headed towards disaster.[386] With no objective truth to be known and no objective beauty to be enjoyed and affirmed as such, both chest and head lie at the mercy of the ever-changing winds of the spirit of the age. Lewis feared that such a turn would produce those who hate education but obsess overtraining, or to put it another way, those who neglect to learn how to live and focus solely on how to make livings. Thus Lewis warns, " ... if education is beaten by training, civilization dies.[387]

The Sacramental Quality of Beauty

Just as every truth and every instance of goodness down below points upwards to God, the same is true of beauty for Lewis. Again, this pointing is the functional entailment of the ontological reality of beauty's participation in God. Kallistos Ware, formerly a student at Magdalen College during Lewis' professorial years there, recalls his frequent greetings with Lewis along Addison's Walk, and he offers some insight into Lewis's sacramental view of beauty. He writes:

> He [Lewis] would go for a walk through the grounds of the college, along Addison's Walk and round by the Magdalen "Water Walks," and I liked to do that too, and I used to meet him on those occasions ... Now I find it appropriate that I should most often have seen C. S. Lewis in a place of remarkable natural beauty, because Lewis was in fact very sensitive to the beauty of the world around us ... But while Lewis was sensitive to the beauty of the natural world, what mattered to him was not merely the external aesthetic appearance around us. What mattered to him was that the world of nature has sacramental value ... We might say that for Lewis the world of nature was

---

[386] C. S. Lewis, *The Abolition of Man*, 27. Richard Weaver also believed the the loss of universals was the first and greatest step towards Western civilization's demise. See Richard Weaver, *Ideas Have Consequences*, 21, "It must be apparent that logic depends upon the dream, and not the dream upon it. We must admit this when we realize that logical processes rest ultimately on classification, that classification is by identification, and that identification is intuitive. It follows then that a waning of the dream results in confusion of counsel, such as we behold on all sides in our time. Whether we describe this as decay of religion or loss of interest in metaphysics, the result is the same; for both are centers with power to integrate, and, if they give way, there begins a dispersion which never ends until the culture lies in fragments."

[387] Again, by "education" Lewis means rightly trained heads, chests, and bellies. By "training," he means skills useful for one's vocation. See C. S. Lewis, "Our English Syllabus," 22.

both solid and transparent. It was solid: he valued the "is-ness" of material things, and he conveyed this distinctive character very effectively in his writing. But while he valued the material world around us in and for itself, he valued it still more because of its transparency, because of the way in which the material world brings us to an apprehension of God.[388]

Lewis believed that man could apprehend God in the world because God was present in it. He writes of God's presence *in* creation as follows: "In Pantheism God is all. But the whole point of creation surely is that He was not content to be all. He intends to be 'all *in* all ...'"[389] A little later in the same work, he writes, "He is so brim-full of existence that He can give existence away, can cause things to be, and to be really other than Himself, can make it untrue to say that He is everything."[390] Roger Scruton employs similar language in his discussion of beauty. He explains, "What is revealed to me in the experience of beauty is a fundamental truth about being—the truth that being is a gift, and receiving it is a task. This is a truth of theology that demands expositions as such."[391] This explanation leads us to the fact that every gift must have a giver. And if the gift that is created is beautiful, how much more he who created it?

If God is ultimate Beauty, this means, of course, that He far surpasses everything else that participates in His beauty, as the brightness of the sun surpasses everything else that is illuminated in its light. Lewis tries to capture this notion in the book that concludes The Chronicles of Narnia. Emeth, a Tarkaan and formerly a worshiper of the false god Tash, recounts his meeting with the lion Aslan as follows:

> So I went over much grass and many flowers and among all kinds of wholesome and delectable trees till lo! in a narrow place

---

[388] Kallistos Ware, "Sacramentalism in C. S. Lewis and Charles Williams," in *C. S. Lewis & His Circle: Essays and Memoirs from the Oxford C. S. Lewis Society*, edited by Roger White, Judith Wolfe, and Brendan N. Wolfe (Oxford: Oxford University Press, 2015), 53.

[389] C. S. Lewis, *Letters to Malcolm*, 70. Lewis understands God to be "in" nature not as the panentheist does. The panentheist understands God to interpenetrate the universe. Lewis is emphasizing that everything that creation has must be given to it from God. In the portion quoted here, Lewis is pulling in pre-modern theology implicitly along with this statement. In his premodern view, and contrary to what the nominalists taught, God must act consistent to his nature. Therefore, what God does will be an expression of his nature. Lewis maintains that God exists necessarily, by virtue of his essence. Therefore, when he causes anything to exist, it is true, in a sense, that that thing is sharing in something that has come from God's essence. A constant dependence relationship exists between created things and the creator, in all sorts of ways, most fundamentally in terms of mere existence. Lewis does not express himself throughout his writings in a panentheistic sense.

[390] C. S. Lewis, *Letters to Malcolm*, 141.

[391] Roger Scruton, *The Face of God*, 151–152.

between two rocks there came to meet me a great Lion. The speed of him was like the ostrich, and his size was an elephant's; his hair was like pure gold and the brightness of his eyes, like gold that is liquid in the furnace. He was more terrible than the Flaming Mountain of Lagour, and in beauty he surpassed all that is in the world, even as the rose in bloom surpasses the dust of the desert.[392]

Lewis's lengthiest description of beauty's sacramental quality comes in his sermon *The Weigh of Glory*. He writes:

The books or the music in which we thought the beauty was located will betray us if we trust to them; it was not *in* them, it only came *through* them, and what came through them was longing. These things—the beauty, the memory of our own past—are good images of what we really desire; but if they are mistaken for the thing itself, they turn into dumb idols, breaking the hearts of their worshippers. For they are not the thing itself; they are only the scent of a flower we have not found, the echo of a tune we have not heard, news from a country we have never yet visited.[393]

He goes on to describe the longing for this beauty that is mediated through the particulars in the world. Lewis explains:

In one way, of course, God has given us the Morning Star already: you can go and enjoy the gift on many fine mornings if you get up early enough. What more, you may ask, do we want? Ah, but we want so much more—something the books on aesthetics take little notice of. But the poets and mythologies know all about it. We do not want merely to *see* beauty, though, God knows, even that is bounty enough. We want something else which can hardly be put into words—to be united with the beauty we see, to pass into it, to receive it into ourselves, to bathe in it, to become part of it. That is why we have peopled the air and earth and water with gods and goddesses and nymphs and elves—that, though we cannot, yet these projections can enjoy in themselves that beauty, grace, and power of which Nature is the image ... At present we are on the outside of the world, the wrong side of the door. We discern the freshness and purity of morning, but they do not make us fresh and pure. We cannot

---

[392] C. S. Lewis, *The Last Battle*, 164.
[393] C. S. Lewis, *The Weight of Glory*, 30–31.

mingle with the splendours we see. But all the leaves of the New Testament are rustling with the rumor that it will not always be so. Some day, God willing, we shall get *in*.[394]

Lewis's sacramental view of beauty that he embraces as a result of his belief in Christianity begins to explain *why* humanity longs "to be united with the beauty" that is seen in the world, whether it be mediated through nature, art, another person, a sacrificial act, or any number of mediums. Two truths form this explanation—This beauty coming through these things has its source in God, *and*, humanity was made for God, as Augustine has perceptively remarked.[395] The beauty of God is *tasted* through various experiences of it. This tasting produces longing for humanity's true end, or destination, though many fail to discern it, as Lewis had for many years. This helps to explain why even those who do not affirm God's existence often cannot help but describing their encounters with beauty as encounters with the transcendent.[396]

---

[394] C. S. Lewis, *The Weight of Glory*, 42–43. Lewis clarifies that he is not at all describing the eastern view of man becoming undifferentiated oneness with nature. He explains, "For you must not think that I am putting forward any heathen fancy of being absorbed into Nature. Nature is mortal; we shall outlive her. When all the suns and nebulae have passed away, each one of you will still be alive. Nature is only the image, the symbol; but it is the symbol Scripture invites me to use. We are summoned to pass in through Nature, beyond her, into that splendour which she fitfully reflects," 43–44. Scruton seems to have something like this in mind with his distinction between "aesthetic" and "utilitarian" interests in beauty. Applying Scruton's definition, Lewis is describing in the above paragraph "aesthetic" interest. See Roger Scruton, *Beauty: A Very Short Introduction*, 16, where he writes, "Wanting something for its beauty is wanting *it*, not wanting to do something with it … But wanting it for its beauty is not wanting to inspect it: it is wanting to contemplate it—and this is something more than a search for information or an expression of appetite." See Louis Markos, *Restoring Beauty: The Good, the True, and the Beautiful in the Writings of C. S. Lewis* (Downers Grove: InterVarsity Press, 2010), 29–30, where Markos describes the desire for Narnia's beauty in similar terms. He writes, "Does not every reader of the Chronicles (young or old) yearn to visit a land like Narnia, a land where animals can speak and stars come down in human form, where fauns and centaurs gambol on the green grass, and where the woods and the rivers are alive? Narnia shimmers with beauty, but it is a beauty that surpasses the pretty line drawings that accompany the text. It is a *felt* beauty, rich and wild and all-pervading. We want more than merely to gaze on it; we want to enter it, embrace it, become one with it."

[395] See Augustine, *Confessions* 2nd edition, translated by F. J. Sheed (Indianapolis: Hackett Publishing Company, 2006), 3, where he writes, "For Thou has made us for Thyself and our hearts are restless until they rest in Thee."

[396] See Timothy Keller, *Making Sense of God: An Invitation to the Skeptical* (New York: Viking, 2016), 16–19, where cites several examples of non-believers admitting that their experiences of beauty seemed to come from somewhere transcendent. He writes, "Julian Barnes, for example, finds himself moved deeply by certain works of art that he realizes should not really do so. Mozart's *Requiem* relies on the Christian understanding of death, judgment, and afterlife for its stunning grandeur. With his objective reason Barnes rejects these ideas. He believes there is nothing after death but extinction. Nevertheless, the *Requiem* moves him—and not merely the sounds but the words. 'It is one of the haunting hypotheticals for the

Scruton helps us understand this phenomenon from a related angle. He compares the encounter with the beauty in the world to an encounter with the sacred, such as a temple or a memorialized piece of land. He writes, "In the aesthetic experience we have something like a face-to-face encounter with the world itself, and with the things that it contains, just as we have in the experience of sacred things and places."[397] Whether one calls her experience an encounter with the sacred, the transcendent, or the holy, the words all hint at the same thing. This meeting with beauty that moves stirs the human heart to look not merely at something, but to contemplate it, and perhaps to contemplate even one's own life and purpose, is a meeting in some sense with Him who is Beauty itself.

So we see that truth, goodness, and beauty are objective for Lewis, and they explain why the particulars possess a sacramental quality. The universals that inhere in the particulars of the created world hint that something higher stands as the ultimate explanation for both the objective and the participatory qualities. Even for those who lack the vocabulary or the philosophical and theological understanding of such things, it is very likely that they have felt these things deeply. If one follows the particulars

---

nonbeliever,' he writes. 'What would it be like if [the *Requiem*] were true?' ... Leonard Bernstein famously admitted that when he heard great music and great beauty he sensed 'Heaven,' some order behind things. '[Beethoven] has the real goods, the stuff from Heaven, the power to make you feel at the finish: something is right in the world. There is something that checks throughout, that follows its own law consistently: something we can trust, that will never let us down' ... A classic example of this is what happened to Lord Kenneth Clark, one of Great Britain's most prominent art historians and authors, and the producer of the BBC television series *Civilization*. In an autobiographical account, Clark writes that when he was living in a villa in France, he had a curious episode. 'I had a religious experience. It took place in the church of San Lorenzo but did not seem to be connected with the harmonious beauty of the architecture. I can only say that for a few minutes, my whole being was radiated by a kind of heavenly joy, far more intense than anything I had ever experienced before ... gradually the effect wore off and I made no effort to retain it. I think I was right. I was too deeply embedded in the world to change course. But I had 'felt the finger of God' I am quite sure an, although the memory of this experience has faded, it still helps me to understand the joy of the saints."

[397] Roger Scruton, *The Face of God*, 132. Throughout this chapter, Scruton describes the earth as a gift, which presupposes a giver and a receiver, an "I" and a "Thou." It follows from the mere fact of creation being a gift from God, even before any consideration is given to beauty, that humanity stands every second in contact with the sacred. In fact, the notion of being itself, applied both to oneself and to creation, is most rightly understood as a gift. Scruton writes, "Gifts involve conscious reflection on self and other, on rights and duties, on ownership and its transcendence. Hence they can only be offered I to I, and gifts are acknowledgements between persons, in which each recognizes the freedom of the other ... His [the religious person's] need to give thanks is not circumstantial but metaphysical. It is rooted in the experience of being itself, in his way of understanding what it is to be. Being, for the religious person, is a gift, not a fact," 170-171.

up to the universals and these upward to their ultimate source, one is led not to a philosophical abstraction but to a Person. We are led to Christ, just as Lewis was.[398]

A BRIEF COMPARISON & CONTRAST WITH PLATO

Given the influence of Plato on Lewis's thinking on these matters, it will be helpful for us to consider a brief comparison and contrast between the two. Lewis writes, "To lose what I owe to Plato and Aristotle would be like the amputation of a limb."[399] Those familiar with Plato's philosophy of the Forms will detect quite easily his influence in Lewis's thinking throughout the entirety of his works, whether his imaginative literature, his Christian apologetics, or even his literary criticism.[400] Lewis maintains "that all things, in their way, reflect heavenly truth."[401] He also affirms, "All that was best in Judaism and Platonism survives in Christianity."[402] The ideas of Plato that he embraces are not what he thinks *about* from time to time as much as they are what he thinks *with* all of the time. This notion harkens back to an important lesson that Lewis learned during a discussion with Dom Bede Griffiths and Owen Barfield over lunch in his room at Magdalen College. Lewis had referred to philosophy as a "subject." Upon hearing this, Barfield instantly corrected him, saying, "It wasn't a *subject* to Plato. It was a way."[403] Thus for Lewis, philosophy, and quite a bit of Plato's philosophy in particular, became a way.

---

[399] C. S. Lewis, "The Idea of an 'English School'" in *Image and Imagination*, 8.

[400] Lewis's entire literary critical method depends on his view of real universal values. See C. S. Lewis, *Christian Reflections*, 7, where he states clearly, "Our criticism would therefore from the beginning group itself with me existing theories of poetry against others. It would have affinities with the primitive or Homeric theory in which the poet is the mere prisoner of the Muse. It would have affinities with the Platonic doctrine of a transcendent Form partly imitable on earth." He admits this also in his back-and-forth exchange with Professor Tillyard on the meaning of poetry and literature. See C. S. Lewis, *The Personal Heresy*, 62, where he writes, "I do not intend to relate my views to any 'vaguely mystical or Platonic notion (common enough in the late nineteenth century)'. I will indeed confess that some desultory investigation of the problem of the Universal has left me with a certain respect for the solution (I would hardly call it vague) which Plato inclined to in the dialogues of his middle period; and my respect is not diminished by the popularity which Plato enjoyed in the nineteenth century any more than by that which he enjoyed in the seventeenth, sixteenth, fifteenth, third, second, or first. But I base nothing on Plato. If there is anything Platonic in my position, I trust I shall argue to it and act from it." Lewis is simply admitting that while he agrees with Plato, he is not going to assume that his opponent does.

[401] C. S. Lewis, *Surprised by Joy*, 167.

[402] C. S. Lewis, "Christian Apologetics," in *God in the Dock*, 102.

[403] C. S. Lewis, *Surprised by Joy*, 225.

C. S. LEWIS PRE-EVANGELISM FOR A POST-CHRISTIAN WORLD

Lewis agrees with Plato that this world is in some way a copy of a higher pattern.[404] Lewis writes, "And this view must *in a certain sense* be accepted by all Theists: in the sense that the world was modeled on an *idea* existing in God's mind, that God *invented* matter."[405] As previously noted, this comes through in *The Last Battle* when Lord Digory insists that everyone who has come into new Narnia would understand its nature better if they had read and remembered Plato. Like Plato, Lewis was a metaphysical realist. That is to say; he believed that reality consisted of real things that lay "beyond" the things we can all see. Paul Tyson agrees with this assessment, writing, "The metaphysical vision that Lewis and Tolkien were imaginatively clothing was, in fact, Christian Platonism. This means that if you have read and enjoyed the stories of Narnia and Middle Earth you already know a lot about Christian Platonism."[406] Michael Muth analyzes Lewis's metaphysical vision in *The Chronicles of Narnia*, writing:

> It is my contention that Lewis's Narnia exerts its attractive force because it is a literary instantiation of a certain kind of metaphysics: a metaphysics of participation, of superfluity of being, of sacrament, in which beauty plays a central role. Lewis refers to this metaphysics as Platonic, though it is really Neo-Platonism as transformed by the Christians thinkers of the Middle Ages, with all of their sacramental, trinitarian and incarnations commitments.[407]

Again, Lewis embraced, as has been argued throughout the present chapter, universals, or what Plato calls "the Forms."[408] These are the non-physical realities that account for the unity in the created world of

---

[404] See Plato, "Timaeus," in *Complete Works*, 1235, where Plato writes, "Which of the two models did the marker use when he fashioned it? Was it the one that does not change and stays the same, or the one that has come to be? Well, if this world of ours is beautiful and its craftsman good, then clearly he looked at the eternal model."

[405] C. S. Lewis, *A Preface to Paradise Lost*, 89.

[406] Paul Tyson, *Returning to Reality: Christian Platonism for Our Times* (Portland: Cascade Books, 2014), 23.

[407] Michael Muth "Beastly Metaphysics: The Beasts of Narnia and Lewis's Reclamation of Medieval Sacramental Metaphysics" in *C. S. Lewis as Philosopher: Truth, Goodness, and Beauty,"* 229. While Muth is correct to equate Lewis's metaphysics with Plato, and with the Neo-Platonists to some degree, it is not the case that Lewis holds creation to be any kind of emanation from God, as this would make it an extension of His being, and *part* of Him. If God is a necessary being, as the ancients held, then the world, which is an emanation from Him, is also necessary. The unfortunate entailment at this point is that God is not free to create, but necessarily does so. Lewis held neither to the former emanation view nor its entailment.

[408] See Plato, "Timaeus" in *Complete Works*, 1254.

particulars. As Plato sets out to describe the creation of the universe, he distinguishes the Forms from the particulars in the following way:

> As I see it, then, we must begin by making the following distinction: What is that which always is and has no becoming, and what is that which becomes but never is? The former is grasped by understanding, which involves a reasoned account. It is unchanging. The latter is grasped by opinion, which involves unreasoned sense perception. It comes to be and passes away, but never really is.[409]

To be clear, Lewis both adopted and emended Plato's Forms, embracing the same clarification that Augustine made due to his commitment to Christianity. Plato was right to detect the unchanging aspects of reality.[410] His difficulty lay in where to locate the Forms.[411] Augustine located them in the mind of God and in particular the Logos, as did Lewis. The universals discussed in this chapter come from the very being of God. This is part of what Lewis has in mind when he writes, "He is so brim-full of existence that He can give existence away, can cause things to be, and to be really other than Himself, can make it untrue to say that He is everything."[412] When God gives existence away, He cannot give contrary

---

[409] Plato, "Timaeus" in *Complete Works*, 1234.

[410] Lewis happily found an alley in Plato for objective morality as well. See Frederick Copleston, S. J. *A History of Philosophy: Volume 1: Greece and Rome*, p. 111. where he writes, "Greek ethics were predominantly eudaemonological in character (cf. Aristotle's ethical system), and though, we believe, they need to be completed by Theism, and see against the background of Theism, in order to attain their true development, they remain, even in their incomplete state, a perennial story of Greek philosophy. Human nature is constant and so ethical values are constant, and it is Socrates' undying fame that he realized the constancy of these values and sought to fix them in universal definitions which could be taken as a guide and norm in human conduct."

[411] Aristotle clarifies that Plato holds to "participation" rather than mere "imitation," though he admits that Plato never elaborates satisfactorily on *how* the particulars participate in the Forms. Aristotle, "Metaphysics," in *The Complete Works of Aristotle*, Vol. 2, p. 1561, where he writes, "Plato ... held that the problem applied not to any sensible thing but to entities of another kind—for this reason, that the common definition could not be a definition of any sensible thing, as they were always changing. Things of this other sort, then, he called Ideas, and sensible things, he said, were apart from these, and were all called after these; for the multitude of things which have the same name as the Form exist by participation in it. Only the name 'participation' was new; for the Pythagoreans say that things exist by imitation of numbers, and Plato says they exist by participation, changing the name. But what the participation or the imitation of the Forms could be they left an open question."

[412] C. S. Lewis, *Letters to Malcolm*, 141.

to His nature.[413] He is, as has been said earlier, truth, goodness, and beauty. His giving will always bring to pass good, true, and beautiful results.[414]

While Lewis was a Platonist in some ways, he did not embrace all of Plato's ideas, and the points at which he departed are significant. First, Lewis had a much higher regard for the material world, particularly the body, than did Plato.[415] In *The Pilgrim's Regress*, Virtue is conversing with the Guide, and he asks, "Is it wholly wrong to be ashamed of being in this body?" The Guide responds, "The Landlord's Son was not. You know the verses — 'When thou tookest upon thee to deliver man'."[416] The Landlord, in Lewis's analogy is God the Father and his Son is Jesus. Jesus was not ashamed to take on a human body because it was intrinsically valuable, having been not only created by God, but made in his image, as the Scriptures teach. Lewis argues in *Mere Christianity*, "God never meant man to be a purely spiritual creature. That is why He uses material things like bread and wine to put new life into us. We may think this rather crude and unspiritual. God does not: He invented eating. He likes matter. He invented it."[417]

In contrast to this view, Plato described the body as a hindrance to truth that one should want to cast off in order to gain true knowledge. In *Phaedo*, Socrates asks Simmias:

---

[413] This notion is the basis for Lewis's argument against the nominalists who held that God could have made goodness bad and badness good. Lewis held that because of God's nature, goodness would be good, and evil bad in every possible world.

[414] Lewis bases part of his answer to the problem of evil on Augustine's view that evil has no existence but is parasitic. Thus, it is possible that goodness exist without evil but not evil without goodness. See C. S. Lewis, *Preface to Paradise Lost*, "

[415] See Diogenes Allen, *Philosophy for Understanding Theology*, 19, where he gives a helpful and nuanced explanation of Plato's view of the material world. He writes, "Clearly, for Plato this world is good, even though it is not perfect ... But equally clearly, the disorderly element of blind necessity is never completely mastered by the mind which designed the world, and the world soul which governs its motions in the heavens. So the evils and imperfections of the physical world are the result of matter. (The Bible, on other hand, affirms the goodness of the *material* world). That matter is evil does not take on really serious proportions, however, until we introduce Plato's understanding of the nature and destiny of the soul. The soul has fallen into a sensible world, and it must return to the suppressible world if it is to attain its proper destiny ... But as far as the physical universe itself is concerned, matter's resistance to being reduced to perfect order does not prevent the world from being fair and beautiful ... Plato's view is by no means that of Genesis, but it is not the total rejection of the world by the Gnostics and Manichaeans. We should not confuse Plato's attitude to the physical universe, however much he stresses the need to transcend it and the body, with views which totally reject it, as superficial Christian writers so often do."

[416] C. S. Lewis, *The Pilgrim's Regress*, 189.

[417] C. S. Lewis, *Mere Christianity*.

And indeed the soul reasons best when none of these senses troubles it, neither hearing nor sight, nor pain nor pleasure, but when it is most by itself, taking leave of the body and as far as possible having no contact or association with it in its search for reality ... And it is then that the soul of the philosopher most disdains the body, flees from it and seeks to be by itself?[418]

Socrates continues a bit later:

It really has been shown to us that, if we are ever to have pure knowledge, we must escape from the body and observe things in themselves with the soul by itself ... While we live, we shall be closest to knowledge if we refrain as much as possible from association with the body and do not join with it more than we must.[419]

Lewis admitted his break with Plato along these lines further in *The Problem of Pain*. He explains, "Again, where other systems expose our total nature to death (as in Buddhist renunciation) Christianity demands only that we set right a *misdirection* of our nature, and has no quarrel, like Plato, with the body as such, nor with the psychical elements in our make-up."[420] In his essay on Edmund Spenser, Lewis further fleshed out some of the similarities and differences between Christianity and Platonism. Significantly, he explained that Platonism views the created world as somehow deficient, as a "merely apparent" and "confused" reality. Christianity, in contrast, presents the creation in a much more positive light. Lewis writes:

Spenser wrote primarily as a (Protestant) Christian and secondarily as a Platonist. Both systems are united with one another and cut off from some—not all—modern thought by their conviction that Nature, the totality of phenomena in space and time, is not the only thing that exists: is, indeed, the least important thing. Christians and Platonists both believe in an "other" world. They differ, at least in emphasis, when they describe the relations between that other world and Nature. For a Platonist the contrast is usually that between an original and a copy, between the real and the merely apparent, between the clear and the confused: for a Christian, between the eternal and the temporary, or the perfect and the partially spoiled, The essential attitude of Platonism is appropriation or longing: the

---

[418] Plato, *Complete Works*, 57.
[419] Plato, *Complete Works*, 58.
[420] C. S. Lewis, *The Problem of Pain*, 103–104.

human soul, imprisoned in the shadowy, unreal world of Nature, stretches out its hands and struggles towards the beauty and reality of that which lies (as Plato says) "on the other side of existence." Shelley's phrase "the desire of the moth for the star" sums it up. In Christianity, however, the human soul is not the seeker but the sought: it is God who seeks, who descends from the other world to find and heal Man; the parable about the Good Shepherd looking for and finding the lost sheep sums it up.[421]

Boersma also affirms Christianity's higher regard for the body over Platonism's. He maintains that "Christians had a much higher regard for matter than did the Platonists. Platonists could not possibly see matter as inherently good."[422] Contrary to Plato, Lewis held that matter, and the entire universe, is inherently good. The present disorder is accidental rather than essential. It is, for Lewis, a good thing gone bad.[423]

The doctrine of the Incarnation of the Son of God stands, for Lewis, as *the* profound historical moment that demonstrates clearly Christianity's

---

[421] C. S. Lewis, "Edmund Spenser, 1552-99" in *Studies in Medieval and Renaissance Literature*, 144.

[422] Hans Boersma, *Heavenly Participation*, 33.

[423] See Hans Boersma, *Heavenly Participation*, 33-35, where Boersma gives three distinctions between Platonism and Christianity. He writes, "First, and most importantly, the Christian faith inherited from the Old Testament and from Judaism the belief that God did not have to create but was free to create. For Christians, the Creation was not an automatic or necessary emanation flowing from the being of God without an intervening act of his will. Creation was not simply an excretion from preexisting matter or spirit. Rather, God created the world free — ex nihilo (how of nothing). While creating the world was certainly a fitting or congruous thing for God to do, it was not a necessary act. Creation did not simply emanate from the being of God. Second, Christians had a much higher regard for matter than did the Platonists. Platonists could not possibly see matter as inherently good ... Third, both of these first two principles — creation as a free act ex nihilo and the acceptance of the goodness of creation — were based on a different understanding of the divine. The Neo-Platonic doctrine of emanation implied a hierarchy of being that posited at the top of the hierarchy the perfection of a simple moat, followed by various divine *Forms* or *Ideas*, which in turn led to the lowest realm, the imperfect world of multiplicity and matter — a world mirroring the realm of Forms or Ideas. In other words, Neo-Platonism functioned on the basis of a principle of absolute oneness: the one was the perfect, the many were the imperfect. Christians clashed sharply with the Platonic tradition on this point. They agreed that Scriptures reflects the principle of hierarchy; thus were they ready to ally themselves with Neo-Platonism on that point. But they did not accept that the one implied perfection while the many implied imperfection."

break with Platonism regarding the nature of the physical.[424] Through this "grand miracle", God pronounced the essential goodness of materiality, and in particular, of the human body.[425] For that in which the divine nature was pleased to dwell could not be less than good. Further, Lewis makes clear that the Christian's hope is not in the slugging off of one's body-prison, as one finds in Platonism. Rather, the Christian's hope entails remaking the body and the dwelling inside that new body in a restored physical world.[426] Lewis writes of Christ's incarnation:

> That is why I think this Grand Miracle is the missing chapter in this novel ... that is why I believe that God really dived down into the bottom of creation, and has come up bringing the whole redeemed nature on His shoulder ... Christ has risen, and so we shall rise ... the day will come when there will be a re-made universe.[427]

The final point worth mentioning at which Lewis parts from Plato is the doctrine of creation. Whereas Plato envisions the craftsman (also called "the demiurge") ordering and shaping preexistent material, Lewis holds to creation *ex nihilo* (meaning simply "creation from nothing"). For example, Plato writes, "There are being, space, and becoming, three distinct things which existed even before the universe came to be."[428] Referring to Plato's account of creation in *Timaeus*, Diogenes Allen writes, "It is clear that in this creation story there is no creation *ex nihilo*. It is a story of order being brought to preexistent matter."[429] Contrary to this view, Lewis maintained that God "created space-time, which is to the universe as the meter is to a poem or the key is to music."[430] God alone exists necessarily, for Lewis. He

---

[424] Of course, Plato formulated his views hundreds of years before Christ came into the world. The point here though is *what* Christ's coming illustrates regarding the value of the physical, and in particular, the human body.

[425] See C. S. Lewis, "The Grand Miracle," in *God in the Dock*, 76–85.

[426] See C. S. Lewis, *Miracles*, 126, where he writes, "Man when redeemed, and recalled to new life (which will in some undefined sense, be a bodily life) in the midst of a more organize and more fully obedience Nature, will be immune from it [death] again."

[427] C. S. Lewis, "The Grand Miracle," in *God in the Dock*, 85. See also C. S. Lewis, *Miracles*, 123, where Lewis affirms both the essential goodness of Nature as well as its soon-to-come glorification accomplished by Christ's incarnation, "God never undoes anything but evil, never does good to undo it again. The union between God and Nature in the Person of Christ admits no divorce. He will not *go out* of Nature again and she must be glorified in all ways which this miraculous union demands."

[428] Plato, "Timaeus," in *Complete Works*, 1255. By "being," Plato means the Forms. By "space," he means the receptacle of the material things. It has no characteristics. By "becoming" he means the physical objects.

[429] Diogenes Allen, *Philosophy for Understanding Theology*, 18.

[430] C. S. Lewis, "The Seeing Eye," in *Christian Reflections*, 167.

is "*the* Absolute Being—in the sense that He alone exists in His own right." Lewis writes of "the orthodox teaching that God made the material universe 'out of nothing,' i.e. not out of any pre-existing raw material."[431]

A DISENCHANTED WORLD

Sadly, our present culture has largely rejected this sacramental view of reality. It is actually more accurate to say that we have been handed the rejection from generations prior to ours. It might do some of us well to think on the fact that much of what seems "common sense" to people today would have been very uncommon a few centuries ago. Progress has been made in places for sure, but I do not believe we have progressed in our understanding of reality's fundamental nature.

Lewis thought the same, and he was aware of this rejection in his day. He feared that the ramifications would prove devastating to modern society. In *The Abolition of Man*, he argued that the loss of the objective would most certainly in time result in "the destruction of the society which accepts it."[432] The present situation has become increasingly that which Lewis feared. An obsession with progress, conceived in terms of the material, scientific, technological, political, and economic, spurs society "onward" at an alarming rate. Left in its wake are the things that Lewis valued most; that is, the things that are *objectively* deserving of highest esteem—truth, goodness, beauty, the like, and above all God.

Lewis's concern along these lines is impossible to miss if one reads his space trilogy. It provides a frightening and sobering imaginative account of where he envisioned the culture heading. He states this explicitly in the foreword to the final book in the trilogy, *That Hideous Strength*. He writes,

---

[431] C. S. Lewis, *A Preface to Paradise Lost*, 89.

[432] C. S. Lewis, *The Abolition of Man*, 27. Richard Weaver also believed the loss of universals was the first and greatest step towards Western civilization's demise. See Richard Weaver, *Ideas Have Consequences*, 21, "It must be apparent that logic depends upon the dream, and not the dream upon it. We must admit this when we realize that logical processes rest ultimately on classification, that classification is by identification, and that identification is intuitive. It follows then that a waning of the dream results in confusion of counsel, such as we behold on all sides in our time. Whether we describe this as decay of religion or loss of interest in metaphysics, the result is the same; for both are centers with power to integrate, and, if they give way, there begins a dispersion which never ends until the culture lies in fragments."

"This is a 'tall story' about devilry, though it has behind it a serious 'point' which I have tried to make in my *Abolition of Man*."[433]

In Lewis's mind, the ever-increasing gulf between the Christian and the modern-day naturalist was wider than many realized. In his inaugural lecture at Cambridge, he argued that the Pagan—who knew something of enchantment through the world, believed in spiritual reality, and was a moral objectivist—had more in common with the Christian than does the modern-day naturalist. He argues:

> But roughly speaking we may say that whereas all history was for our ancestors divided into two periods, the pre-Christian and the Christian, and two only, for us it falls into three—the pre-Christian, the Christian, and what may reasonably be called the post-Christian. This surely must make a momentous difference ... I am considering them simply as cultural changes. When I do that, it appears to me that the second change is even more radical than the first. Christians and Pagans had much more in common with each other than either has with a post-Christian. The gap between those who worship different gods is not so wide as that between those who worship and those who do not.[434]

Lewis also demonstrated how modern-day language reflects this unfortunate towards disenchantment. He calls this turn "the greatest change in the history of Western Man."[435] For example, the realm of the stars and planets is simply called "space," as if nothing more were to be said than that black distance exists between the various heavenly bodies. Given Lewis's sentiments on this point, one can understand why he put into the mind of his protagonist in *Out of the Silent Planet* the following thought:

---

[433] Others have raised similar alarms. See, for example, Richard Weaver's *Visions of Order: The Cultural Crisis of Our Time* (Wilmington: Intercollegiate Studies Institute, 1995), 4, where Weaver writes, "The nature and proper end of man are central to any discussion not only of whether a certain culture is weakening, but also of whether such a culture is worth preserving." He later argues that the "present course of our culture is not occasion for complacency but for criticism and possible reconstruction," 6. He warns of democracy as not merely a political concept, but a comprehensive perspective that denies any universal perspective and "produces an envious hatred not only of all distinction but even of all difference," 15.

[434] C. S. Lewis, "De Descriptione Temporum: Inaugural Lecture from the Chair of Medieval and Renaissance Literature," (Cambridge University, 1954). Accessed on 3/2/19 - https://www.romanroadsmedia.com/old-western-culture-extras/DeDescriptioneTemporum-CS-Lewis.pdf

[435] C. S. Lewis, "De Descriptione Temporum." He especially had in mind the loss of a sense of guilt that he believes attends the loss of a sense of the divine.

> He had read of "Space": at the back of his thinking for years had lurked the dismal fancy of the black, cold vacuity, the utter deadness, which was supposed to separate the world. He had not known how much it affected him till now—now that the very name "Space" seemed a blasphemous libel for this empyrean ocean of radiance in which they swam ... No: space was the wrong name. Older thinkers had been wiser when they named it simply the heavens—the heavens which declared the glory.[436]

In his Cambridge lecture, he also noted another important shift in language and thought resulting from the rejection of universals. This shift further illustrates the obsession with progress that Lewis associated with "the birth of the machines."[437] He was referring largely to the Industrial Revolution. He writes:

> How has it come about that we use the highly emotive word "stagnation," with all its malodorous and malarial overtones, for what other ages would have called "permanence"? Why does the word at once suggest to us clumsiness, inefficiency, barbarity? ... Why does "latest" in advertisements mean "best"? ... I submit that what has imposed this climate of opinion so firmly on the human mind is a new archetypal image. It is the image of old machines superseded by new and better ones. For in the world of machines the new most often really is better and the primitive really is the clumsy. And this image, potent in our minds, reigns almost without rival in the minds of the uneducated.[438]

With no signs of slowing down, the present-day obsession with progress starts to make Lewis look like something of a modern-day prophet. More accurately, he was merely a man who understood his times and who was keen enough to track the logical entailments of the thoughts and sentiments of the spirit of the age. Others have done the same, though their warnings have yet to be heeded sufficiently. My hope is that Christians will find courage to return to truths that, though no longer "hip" or "fashionable," are nevertheless true, and therefore worth the effort and the suffering that may come through our efforts of recovery. A return to the belief in universals and the sacramental nature of reality that attends this belief is perhaps the most important reclamation we must make in our day. Lewis is a great help to us in this endeavor.

---

[436] C. S. Lewis, *Out of the Silent Planet* (New York: Scribner, 2003), 34.
[437] C. S. Lewis, "De Descriptione Temporum."
[438] C. S. Lewis, "De Descriptione Temporum."

CONCLUSION

In this chapter, I have sought to explain Lewis's sacramental ontology. We have considered together his medieval mindset, focusing on three aspects: the bookish nature, the desire for organization or unification, and a sacramental view of reality. The last of these three have received the greatest attention. In fleshing out his sacramental view, we have considered truth, goodness, and beauty by consulting Lewis's thoughts. I have argued two points with respect this these universals, and that is that Lewis affirms both their objective reality *and* the sacramental quality of the particulars in which they inhere. Next, a brief comparison and contrast with Plato's thoughts, specifically his ontology, has been offered. Finally, we have entertained the entailments of the rejection of a sacramental ontology like that which Lewis affirms. The result is what many have called disenchantment. We feel this disenchantment as we lose our sense of wonder and awe towards the creation and towards that to which it points.

It would be difficult to exaggerate the importance that Lewis places on a true view of reality. Not only does it help to unite his reason with his desire and thus explain the nature of the various visitations of Joy that led him eventually to Christ. He also believed that the recovery of a true vision of reality was necessary for the restoration and preservation of Western society. Highlighting this importance, Armstrong writes of the Inklings, "Together they launched a holy war on their era's scientific materialism and the spiritual declension that accompanied it. Each lifted up in their writings a rich, world-embracing Christian vision against the gray deadness of modern secular[izing] society. For each, this was a life-and-death battle, with the future of the Western world hanging in the balance."[439]

Lewis took up his pen and began doing his part to try to bring about some level of recovery of objective values, a sacramental view of reality, and a sense of re-enchantment towards creation. He sought the medium of imaginative literature in particular in order to try to gain a hearing. For example, he concluded his book *Perelandra* with fictional correspondences between him and Dr. Ransom based on an imagined week-long visit he spent with him, during which time he learned the details of his journey to the planet Malacandra.

During this fictitious visit, Lewis recounts a conversation in which Dr. Ransom says, "Anyway ... what we need for the moment is not so much a body of belief as a body of people familiarized with certain ideas. If we could even effect in one per cent of our readers a change-over from the

---

[439] Chris R. Armstrong, *Medieval Wisdom for Modern Christians*, 30.

conception of Space to the conception of Heaven, we should have made a beginning."[440] Though this correspondence was imaginary, Dr. Ransom's aim was in reality Lewis's own. He labored to this end with great diligence and thoughtfulness. He hoped that if he could help re-awaken desire for truth, goodness, and beauty in the imaginations of his readers, it might weaken their defenses so that the gospel might gain an eventual fair hearing.[441] The question that arises for us at this point is why Lewis's view of reality is so crucial to his understanding of the human imagination. It is this key question that we will explore together in the following chapter.

---

[440] C. S. Lewis, *Out of the Silent Planet*, 152.

[441] This is in no way suggesting that Lewis was asking people to stop thinking rationally in order to embrace Christianity. He believed Christianity was not only thoroughly rational but that it could be rationally defended very effectively. The point made here is that Lewis had little hope that those whose reason has been warped according to post-Enlightenment thinking would be persuaded at first by rational argument.

CHAPTER 3

C. S. Lewis's Romantic View of the Human Imagination

Introduction

To this point, we have walked with Lewis through his own story as he sought to reconcile his reason with his imagination. We noted that most crucial to his journey were his various experiences of Joy mediated through nature, story, and song. He denied the "other world" from which these experiences seemed to beckon to him because his view of reality was too shallow for a long time. After becoming a Christian, Lewis understands why the world was a far more enchanted place than he had previously supposed. In the truest sense, Lewis was not encountering any *other* world; rather, he was encountering the *true* world the meaning of which went deeper than he had yet admitted. All of the mythologies, the songs, and the beauty of nature that had delighted him and transported him to regions of awe, had in fact, been patches of Godlight,[442] coruscations of God's presence made mysteriously manifest to him.[443] These were God's gracious means of drawing Lewis to himself until at last he would come to "believe that Jesus is the Son of God."[444]

In the last chapter, we examined in greater philosophical and theological detail the nature of this reality. I argued that key to understanding Lewis's view of reality is the pre-modern, medieval mindset. The most important characteristics of this mindset are two: the tendency to systematize and organize as well as the tendency to view creation sacramentally. We saw that Lewis adopted a sacramental ontology that was influenced heavily by Platonic philosophy. For him, truth, goodness, and beauty stand as objective universals that participate in the particulars of the created world. These universals are grounded ultimately in God's being,

---

[442] C. S. Lewis, *Letters to Malcolm*, 91.

[443] See C. S. Lewis, *Letters to Malcolm*, 75, where Lewis writes, "We may ignore, but we can nowhere evade, the presence of God. The world is crowded with Him. He walks everywhere *incognito*. And the *incognito* is not always hard to penetrate. The real labour is to remember, to attend. In fact, to come awake. Still more, to remain awake."

[444] C. S. Lewis, *Surprised by Joy*, 236.

and therefore their presence in creation serves as a participatory pointer to God. Further, the world of everyday experience is in some sense a copy of a higher, truer reality—the "ectype" pointing to the "archetype."[445] This phenomenon sheds light on *why* Lewis felt drawn to the transcendent through his many experiences of Joy.

In this chapter, we will build on what has been said up to this point and focus specifically on Lewis's romantic view of the human imagination. Suppose creation is of such a nature that it is sacramentally "shot through" with the presence of God. In that case, we are compelled to ask - What must be the power and function of the human imagination that God has given to humanity as a part of this same creation? How might it help us to apprehend God? Further, if the imagination depends in some way upon creation for its *material*—and I will be argued emphatically in this chapter that it does—might this begin to make sense in a deeper way of why Lewis felt a sacramental pull both through the physical as well as through the imaginary world?

We will try to achieve great clarity in this chapter with the answers to these questions. In one of his essays, Lewis admits in which he describes the role of imagination and particularly of metaphorical language, "And so, admittedly, the view I have taken has metaphysical implications."[446] Again, the word metaphysical is simply referring to the nature of reality that lies behind or beyond the material. With a view to these implications, I make the case in this chapter that Lewis's view of the romantic imagination, consistent with and dependent upon his sacramental ontology, possesses a two-fold mediating capacity between humanity and God, helping us both to desire and to apprehend God to some degree.[447]

This chapter's argument will progress along the following lines. First, we will explore a detailed investigation into Lewis's romantic understanding of the human imagination. Next, we will consult two books that Lewis encouraged his readers to consider. These two works will help us to comprehend more fully Lewis's understanding of both reality and the

---

[445] C. S. Lewis, *The Pilgrim's Regress*, 161.

[446] C. S. Lewis, "Buspels and Flalansferes: A Semantic Nightmare," in *Selected Literary Essays*, edited by Walter Hooper (Cambridge: Cambridge University Press, 2013), 265.

[447] As will become clear as this chapter unfolds, regarding this two-fold function of the imagination, arousing desire is meant to lead to knowledge. Thus, the former serves the latter. Desire will have missed its mark if it does not yield knowledge in the end. Many a person has followed this desire only to seek its fulfillment in the wrong places, and therefore never attaining the knowledge of God towards which the desire is meant to motivate man. That said, desire is significant in its penultimate role in serving as a motivator to set man out on his search for ultimate satisfaction.

human imagination. Following this, we will analyze the interplay between both imagination and nature as well as between imagination and story, as these are the two mediums through which joy chiefly was aroused in Lewis. I make the claim that we can be helped, by way of our imagination, both to desire and to apprehend God *through* the mediums of nature and story.

WHAT IS THE IMAGINATION? THE ORGAN OF MEANING

This first section aims to provide both a definition and an explanation, to the degree to which Lewis's writings will afford, of the human imagination. Similar to his sacramental ontology, he produced no single work dedicated to this topic. Rather, one finds short sections here and there in various books and articles specifically on the imagination as well as topical off-shoots that either imply or entail his conclusions on the matter. At this point, the task is to present these pieces together so that a fuller picture than one finds in any single work by Lewis may be painted all in one place.

In a rather obscurely titled essay, "Bluspels and Flalansferes: A Semantic Nightmare," Lewis gives a brief definition of the human imagination, albeit with minimal elucidation. He writes:

> But it must not be supposed that I am in any sense putting forward the imagination as the organ of truth. We are not talking of truth, but of meaning: meaning which is the antecedent condition both of truth and falsehood, whose antithesis is not error but nonsense. I am a rationalist. For me, reason is the natural organ of truth; but imagination is the organ of meaning. Imagination, producing new metaphors or revivifying old, is not the cause of truth, but its condition.[448]

This definition is commonly quoted by authors mentioning Lewis's view of the imagination. Justifiably, some of them lament the fact that he only offers an appetizer-sized treatment of this topic at the very end of this essay. The reader is left wanting more, wondering what Lewis might have said had he written several more pages.

Thankfully, the curious reader discovers that Lewis did write more and also pointed to two key works by other writers that heavily influenced his thinking along these lines. The two books, which we will examine in detail later in this chapter, are *Poetic Diction* by Owen Barfield and *Symbolism*

---

[448] C. S. Lewis, "Buspels and Flalansferes: A Semantic Nightmare," 265.

and Belief by Edwyn Bevan. Through consulting these two books and the other works of Lewis that touch on this topic, we can begin to understand more thoroughly the gist of what Lewis likely would have said if he had had more time and space to say it in a single work.[449]

In the above-quoted portion, Lewis makes two crucial points. The first focuses on the imagination's relationship to meaning. The second centers on meaning's logical relationship to truth, meaning being the "antecedent condition."[450] Lewis referred to the imagination "the organ of meaning."[451] That is, he held that the imagination's proper function was to produce or to discern meaning. He does not elaborate on *how* this function operates, nor does he explain in what sense it relates to reality in this same essay. For such an elaboration, the reader shall have to look elsewhere, to a far lesser known essay entitled "Image and Imagination," that first became available to the wider public in 2013, thanks largely to Walter Hooper. A thorough treatment of this nearly lost essay in which Lewis fleshes out the meaning behind the imagination as "the organ of meaning" will occupy the early part of the present chapter.[452]

Regarding the second point, that of meaning being the antecedent, or prior condition to truth, Lewis argues that before a statement or concept can rise to the level of being judged as true or false, it must first "mean." For example, the statement, "Red three not Sally temperament," cannot be judged reasonably as either true or false. This is because it is sheer nonsense. If someone asks, "Is it true?" the only reasonable response would be: "I have no judgement on the matter as I have no idea what in the world it means." Further, the terms "bluspel" and "flalansfere" are concepts that cannot be said to correspond to or stand at odds with, reality unless one knows what these terms mean. One would have to be given the explanation of these metaphorical terms, which would require the employment of one's imagination, before they can be judged as concepts that are true or false.

---

[449] No one may rightly suppose that Lewis's productivity as a writer was due to his being single for most of his life. Anyone who has read a few biographies will discover very quickly the enormous amount of responsibility that rested on his shoulders, from the daily burden of taking care of Ms. Moore, to lecturing, grading papers, and tutoring students, to answering the thousands of letters he received, to hosting the Socratic Club meetings at Oxford, to his many speaking and preaching engagements, and on and on. The subjunctive phrase, "if he had had more time," is a reasonable allowance to make here.

[450] C. S. Lewis, "Bluspels and Flalansferes," 265.

[451] C. S. Lewis, "Bluspels and Flalansferes," 265.

[452] C. S. Lewis, "Bluspels and Flalansferes," 265.

Brian M. Williams

A "ROMANTIC" IMAGINATION

The notion of a "romantic" view of the human imagination will help us to understand meaning's relationship to truth. Let us now consider the sense in which Lewis used the term "romantic." His most thorough explanation is found in the afterword to the third edition of *The Pilgrim's Regress*. In this afterword, Lewis admitted to having assigned an "(unintentionally) 'private' meaning"[453] to the word "Romanticism."[454] For as will be seen in a bit, this is the very same word he chose as his adjectival descriptor for the imagination in a later essay. After listing seven possible meanings of the word "romantic," Lewis explains:

> But what I meant by 'Romanticism' when I wrote the *Pilgrim's Regress*—and what I would still be taken to mean on the title page of the book—was ... a particular recurrent experience which dominated my childhood and adolescence and which I hastily called "Romantic" because inanimate nature and marvelous literature were among the things that evoked it ... The experience is one of intense longing. It is distinguishable from other longing by two things. In the first place, though the sense of want is acute and even painful, yet the mere wanting is felt to be somehow a delight ... This hunger is better than any other fullness; this poverty better than all other wealth ... For this sweet Desire cuts across our ordinary distinctions between wanting and having. To have it is, by definition, a want: to want it, we find, is to have it. In the second place, there is a peculiar mystery about the object of this Desire. In experienced people (and inattention leaves some inexperienced all their lives) suppose, when they feel it, that they know what they are desiring.[455]

In choosing to label Lewis's understanding of the human imagination as "romantic," I am in no way attempting to be original or clever. I am simply taking the term from Lewis's own pen in a couple of places. Given Lewis's definition of romanticism, when this adjective is predicated of the imagination, we can see that it refers specifically to the imagination's function. Specifically, the romantic imagination is a faculty that is meant to aid the person by stirring up longing so that he might follow this longing to its intended end, who is God.[456] In using the words "is meant to," the

---

[453] C. S. Lewis, *The Pilgrim's Regress*, 207.

[454] C. S. Lewis, *The Pilgrim's Regress*, 207.

[455] C. S. Lewis, *The Pilgrim's Regress*, 209–210.

[456] See also Chad Walsh, *C. S. Lewis: Apostle to the Skeptics* (Eugene: Wipf & Stock, 1949), 116, where Walsh explains Lewis's usage of the term "Romanticism." Walsh writes,

cat is out of the bag that we have introduced the notion of purpose, of *telos*. And where there is purpose, there must be a purpose-Giver.

Thus, "romantic" is the most fitting adjective for understanding Lewis on the human imagination.[457] In a letter written to T. S. Eliot in June of 1931, Lewis described an essay he was writing on the imagination. He explains in his letter:

> The essay ... does, as you have divined, form the first of a series of which I have all the materials in hand ... The whole, when completed, would form a frontal attack on Crocean aesthetics and state a neo-Aristotelian theory of literature (not of Art, about which I say nothing) which inter alia will re-affirm the romantic doctrine of imagination as a truth-bearing faculty, though not quite as the romantics understood it.[458]

The essay to which Lewis referred in this letter contains a section in which he set apart his romantic view of the imagination from Benedetto Croce's view. He also emphasized what he believed to be its key function. In this point of emphasis, Lewis offered a more nuanced definition of the

---

"Romanticism, as he uses the word, is an experience of intense longing, which differs from other desires in two ways: the yearning itself is in itself a sort of delight, and a peculiar mystery envelops the object of desire."

[457] It must be admitted that Lewis himself comes to object to the use of the word "romantic," but not because it is not a good word. He objects because the term comes to have so many varied meanings that it often causes more confusion than it brings help. See C. S. Lewis, *The Pilgrim's Regress*, 207–208, where Lewis writes, "

[458] C. S. Lewis, "Image and Imagination" in *Image and Imagination: Essays and Reviews*, edited by Walter Hooper (Cambridge: Cambridge University Press, 2013), 34. This letter refers, in part, to an essay that Walter Hooper found in a "ruled school-notebook of the sort that Lewis typically used for his drafts." Hooper chose the title "Image and Imagination" for the essay, and had it published for Lewis posthumously in 2013. By "Crocean aesthetics," Lewis is referring to the philosophy of Benedetto Croce (1860–1952), who made contributions to philosophy, aesthetics, and literary criticism. Croce holds to "Absolute Idealism," that is, the view that all that exists is Mind. Lewis takes issue not only with his metaphysics, but particularly with how he extends his metaphysics to his philosophy of art. Croce maintains that art is solely mental. Gary Kemp explains, "For our purposes, it is simplest to regard Croce as an idealist, for whom there is nothing besides mind. So in that sense, the work of art is an ideal or mental object along with everything else; no surprise there, but no interest either. But he still maintains the ordinary commonplace distinction between mental things—thoughts, hopes and dreams—and physical things—tables and trees. And on *this* divide, the work of art, for Croce, is *still* a mental thing. In other words, the work of art is *doubly* ideal; to put it another way, *even if Croce were a dualist*—or a physicalist with some means of reconstructing the physical-mental distinction—the work of art would remain mental." See Gary Kemp, "Croce's Aesthetics" in the Stanford Encyclopedia of Philosophy, https://plato.stanford.edu/entries/croce-aesthetics/ (accessed April 5th, 2019).

imagination than what we commonly would find in other works on the subject.

If we were to look for a standard definition of the imagination, we would discover that, most often, the definitional emphasis is placed on the faculty's function of producing mental images. This sounds reasonable enough at first. But as we will see, it falls woefully short of its truer and deeper function. For example, Charles Taliaferro writes, "A commonplace ... fairly uncontroversial definition of imagination can be put succinctly: *Imagination is the power to create or form images in the mind.* Or, with a slight modification: *It is the power to create or form mental images.*"[459] If we were to take this definition and then read Lewis's thoughts on the matter, it would become unmistakably clear that, while he agrees that the forming of mental images is *part* of the role of the imagination, he views this power as subordinate to a greater role. He argues that the greater role is to lead one *through* the image or the concept *to* the meaning. In other words, the imagination's supreme task is, for Lewis, the conveyance of meaning.[460] I cannot emphasize the importance of this distinction strongly enough.

Lewis described himself as an "extreme visualist,"[461] meaning that he recognized his ability to produce mental images with dynamic clarity. We might expect Lewis to celebrate this ability, but he does just the opposite. Surprisingly, he spoke of it in a negative light and underemphasized its importance.[462] He writes, " ... this unruly power—in truth not the ally of

---

[459] Charles Taliaferro and Jill Evans, *The Image in Mind: Naturalism, Theism, and the Imagination* (New York: Bloomsbury, 2013), 12.

[460] Through the conveyance of meaning, desire is often aroused, which is extremely important for Lewis also. Imaginative desire is meant to lead one to God, as Lewis discovered in his own journey. See Stratford Caldecott, "Speaking the Truths Only the Imagination May Grasp: Myth and 'Real Life,'" in *The Pilgrim's Guide: C. S. Lewis and the Art of Witness*, edited by David Mills (Grand Rapids: William B. Eerdmans Publishing Company, 1998), 86, where Caldecott defines the imagination far more in keeping with Lewis's view. He writes of, "Their imagination (by which I mean that faculty by which they view the world and try to make sense of it) ..."

[461] C. S. Lewis, *Image and Imagination*, 45.

[462] To be fair, Lewis employs this ability for great good. Most, if not all, of his fantasy stories began with vivid images in his mind. See C. S. Lewis, "It All Began with a Picture ..." in *On Stories*, 79, where he writes, "One thing I am sure of. All my seven Narnian books, and my three science-fiction books, began with seeing pictures in my head. At first they were not a story, just pictures. The *Lion* all began with a picture of a Faun carrying an umbrella and parcels in a snowy wood. This picture had been in my mind since I was about sixteen. Then one day, when I was about forty, I said to myself: 'Let's try to make a story about it.'"

imagination, but a mere nuisance to it—must be corrected and restrained in dealing with literature."[463]

He writes similarly in *The Personal Heresy*:

I am speaking of *what is imagined*, not of the *image* or *mental picture*. That the two are distinct is proved by the fact that very adequate, or even fine, imagining may go with very inadequate images. We all enjoy *Hero and Leander*, and this implies that we all succeed in *imagining* beautiful human bodies; but only extreme visualizers, and, among them, only persons of considerable artistic training, have *images* of the human body which would stand examination. Those who share with the present writer a lively visualizing power can testify that this unruly faculty is as often the enemy as the servant of imagination; just as elaborate and 'realistic' toys hinder rather than help children in their play. The poet may give all his readers a common *imaginatum*: he is not to aim at giving them identical *imagines*."[464]

Clearly, for Lewis, the thing imagined bears far more significance than the image when it comes to the imagination.

Turning now to his essay, "Image and Imagination," we will look at a helpful example at some length, in order to demonstrate Lewis's point that the image is not of ultimate importance in the imaginative experience. I should offer fair warning that this part of the argument may be the most difficult to grasp. It may be helpful to read this section twice in order to comprehend clearly precisely what Lewis is saying. He argues in this article that one image, found in different contexts but "seen" as identical in each, can conjure up in one's mind very different meanings and aesthetic sentiments. He employs the image of a tower. Let us imagine reading two different stories, both including towers. In one story, the tower might be the same as a tower in the real world—a structure built of stacked stone reaching high up into the sky with a room at the top. If a character in this story walked into the tower by accident, it would resist him just as would any solid structure such as a stone wall. To gain entrance, he would have

---

[463] C. S. Lewis, *Image and Imagination*, 45.
[464] C. S. Lewis, *The Personal Heresy*, 23, footnote #9. See also C. S. Lewis, *Miracles*, 107–127, where Lewis argues the following three points: "(1) That thought is distinct from the imagination which accompanies it. (2) That thought may be in the main sound even when the false images that accompany it are mistaken by the thinker for true ones. (3) That anyone who talks about things that cannot be seen, or touched, or heard, or the like, must inevitably talk as *if they could be seen* or touched or heard."

to open the door and walk inside. We can imagine that in another story, the tower might be different from actual towers in the real world in the following sense. It might be a phantom tower that, although it might appear identical to its real solid counterpart, it would be in fact a mere apparition. If the same character walked into this tower, he would go right through it and come out on the other side.[465]

It is perfectly conceivable that these two towers, though very different in terms of their material/immaterial constitution, might produce one and the same image in the mind of the reader. Further, if the reader were to draw both towers on a sheet of paper, he might draw each exactly the same way. Thus, in terms of mere visual *imaginata*, we can discern no difference whatsoever. Yet, it is also clear that we would take them to be very different towers. Lewis, therefore, reasons that "images are not enough: for the way in which they affect us depends, not on their content as images, but on what they are taken to be."[466]

When the same image is taken to be different things in two different stories such as in the example Lewis gives, it becomes clear that both the meaning of the image as well as the associated sentiments that it produces in the "chest" of the reader will be very different. Lewis explains further:

> And, perhaps, now that we have raised the question of the visuals, you will admit that the images actually present to the reader matter very little to his appreciation. In fact, the image is not what counts ... The attempt to do without a context for the *imaginata* collapses. Take away from the imagined tower all its implications and it ceases to be an imagined thing and becomes merely an image.[467]

For Lewis, the ability to form a mental image was only important in the service of another more important end—that of delivering meaning. The images which one conjures up in the mind are, in this way, servants to a higher master. The master is the meaning itself, which includes not only some apprehension of the essence of the thing, but also the associations and sentiments that accompany it.

A word of clarity is needed at this point. By "apprehension of the essence of a thing," I mean to suggest that one perceives, and to some degree understands, something of the "whatness" of the thing. For instance, one can imagine a variety of towers, all different in terms of their particular

---

[465] C. S. Lewis, *Image and Imagination*, 44.
[466] C. S. Lewis, *Image and Imagination*, 44.
[467] C. S. Lewis, *Image and Imagination*, 44.

shapes, colors, sizes, locations, material constitutions, and such. Yet, they still know that each remains properly a tower. Lewis has the essence or universal in mind when he writes, "Mention a tower, or a king, or a dog, in a poem or tale, and they come to us not in the nakedness of pictures form and color, but with all the associations of towerhood, kinghood, and doghood."[468]

Further situating properly the status of the image beneath that of the meaning that it mediates, Lewis writes, "What sort of blotch or blur is my 'image' of the dark tower to which Roland came? I hardly know. I only know that it is different every time I read the line and that there is a no proportional difference in my poetical experience."[469] He likened an excessively visual imagination like his own to overly realistic and expensive children's toys. Both the extremely vivid image and the realistic toy can hinder the imagination's true purpose—the production or recognition of meaning. This is what he means when he writes, "It is not the children with the costly toys who play best: or if they do, they do it in spite of the toys."[470]

Once we understand that the imagination's supreme task is to help the imaginer grasp meaning, we can now move to consider the role that context plays in the process. Lewis demonstrated how the imagination necessarily depends upon a context. Importantly, the context upon which the image unavoidably must depend cannot be supplied entirely by the imagination. Rather, it must be supplied by the real world. It will take some time and a good bit of concentration for us to understand how this phenomenon works. Moreover, the importance of this move in Lewis's argument cannot be overstated, either for his present argument or for the overall argument of this book. Therefore, we will treat it here at some length.

Lewis anticipates a likely objection, writing:

You cannot have even a fairy tale unless the reader and writer understand what a castle, or a stepmother, or a giant *is.* Now I have used the word "is" advisedly. To read the fairy-tale we must know what a castle is; and that would seem to be a bit of knowledge about the real world. It will be objected, of course, that you may also need to know what a fairy "is"; and this does not seem to be equally a bit of knowledge about the real world.

---

[468] C. S. Lewis, *Image and Imagination*, 44.
[469] C. S. Lewis, *Image and Imagination*, 45.
[470] C. S. Lewis, *Image and Imagination*, 45.

It would, therefore, seem safer to emend "know what a castle is" and say "know what the author means by a castle." That is (apparently), we do not need to know about things: we need only know of what imaginations in the author's mind each word is the name.[471]

While this objection to the imagined story's dependence upon the knowledge of real things might seem reasonable at first, Lewis proceeds to dismantle it. He argues that apart from the real world, the imagined one would have no content with which to work at all.

Lewis carries out his argument by engaging in a fictional debate with an imaginary narrator of a story. His opponent begins his story thus: "Once upon a time there was a princess, who lived in a tower."[472] Lewis asks him, "What is a tower?"[473] Not one to be fooled too easily, the narrator responds, "You are not going to catch me that way. The tower *is* not anything *in rerum natura*,[474] it is only the name of something in my imagination."[475] Lewis presses to know of what thing in the narrator's imagination his tower is the name. The narrator describes it thus: "Oh, a tall kind of building, you know, with five or six stories and battlements on the top ... I mean a thing made out of some hard substance,—stones or brick or wood—with empty spaces inside, where people live."[476]

Pressing for clarity, Lewis inquires, "Dear me, this gets more and more difficult. We have now a whole host of things: stones, brick, wood and people, not to mention 'substance.' Are these the names of realities, or of things in your imagination?"[477] The narrator insists that they are things only in his imagination. Lewis asks if the material in his imagination has color and shape, and whether or not it is solid like matter in the real world. His opponent answers in the affirmative. He then asks if the matter has an inside, where one would find something like "discrete atoms, or forces."[478] Lewis continues, "And this is all present in your imagination?"[479] The narrator responds that he is not sure. Lewis then asks whether or not his tower occupies space such that if one were to look a little left or right, or

---

[471] C. S. Lewis, *Image and Imagination*, 38.
[472] C. S. Lewis, *Image and Imagination*, 38.
[473] C. S. Lewis, *Image and Imagination*, 38.
[474] This phrase means, "In the nature of things" or "In the realm of the material world."
[475] C. S. Lewis, *Image and Imagination*, 38.
[476] C. S. Lewis, *Image and Imagination*, 39.
[477] C. S. Lewis, *Image and Imagination*, 39.
[478] C. S. Lewis, *Image and Imagination*, 39.
[479] C. S. Lewis, *Image and Imagination*, 39.

above or below a particular bit of space, one would find more space. His opponent answers, "Naturally."[480]

Following this line of thinking, Lewis questions whether this space ends or goes on forever, to which the narrator affirms that it goes on forever. He asks him if he, therefore, holds an infinite space in his imagination. Again, his opponent admits, "I don't know."[481] This line of questioning continues with respect to the princess and her parents, grandparents, distant ancestry, and even to the beginning of organic life. He asks if all of this is held in the narrator's imagination. In proper Socratic fashion, Lewis reasons:

> For if the words in your story are really the names of things in your imagination, it will follow that in every sentence, and more than once in every sentence, a complete universe in all its detail must be present to your imagination. But that is impossible ... If the words used in literature name only *imaginata*, then, since any one object implies an infinite series both in time and space, every single *imaginatum* implies an infinite imagined series. For the *imaginata* are not in the same position as real objects. A real object, no doubt, demands a context reaching away on every side to infinity: but just because it is an object in the real world that context is provided for. It is there, *in fact*, whether we think of it or not. But the whole contention about literature was that it referred to objects existing only in imagination; and imagination cannot provide (as reality can) the necessary context. It is clear, therefore, that we shall have to allow some sort of interplay, or overlapping, between the imagined and the real, for only in the real can *imaginata* find the context they need ... To get a single blade of grass growing in that imaginary world you must make it a world indeed—a real universe, self-sufficing in space and time. But only one author can do that sort of stage-set. On this view only God can tell stories.[482]

Lewis anticipates another objection at this point. One might complain that it is impossible to imagine an infinite number of things. Lewis readily agrees with this and then asks, "But does that mean that we can dispense with it? For, of course, if we need it, and yet do not imagine it, the

---

[480] C. S. Lewis, *Image and Imagination*, 39.
[481] C. S. Lewis, *Image and Imagination*, 39.
[482] C. S. Lewis, *Image and Imagination*, 40–41.

conclusion will be that we are using the *real* world to provide a context for our imaginary tower."[483]

He proceeds to take on another possible objection. His opponent insists that all he had in mind were *mere* images all along, and not any context that would draw in the real world with it. Lewis responds to this line of thought by asking whether he might be able to imagine two different stories—one in which a wanderer keeps meeting phantasmal appearances of towers and another where he encounters solid towers. The narrator concedes that each story would produce a different aesthetic experience in the mind of the reader although the images might look exactly the same. The result of this concession allows Lewis to demonstrate rather strongly that in literature, it is not the image that really matters, but what the image is "taken to be."[484]

With this reasoning set forth, we now can see precisely *why* Lewis argues that the imagination's greater task is not the production of an image, but the conveyance of meaning *through* the image. We have seen how the very same image can affect us differently given the context in which it is placed and what it is taken to be. Thus, a fitting definition of the imagination will have to say more than the standard one that was given at the beginning of this chapter.[485]

This same phenomenon of the same image conveying different things holds true in the real world as well. For instance, those present at Jesus's crucifixion all saw the same scene before them. They differed, significantly, however, regarding the meaning they assigned to what they saw. Some *saw* a charlatan and blasphemer receiving the punishment he deserved. Others *saw* the Son of God, who, although guiltless, was suffering a criminal's punishment. Some jeered. Others wept. The difference cannot be explained by a description of what was seen. It can only be explained by what the whole scene was taken to be.[486]

---

[483] C. S. Lewis, *Image and Imagination*, 41.

[484] C. S. Lewis, *Image and Imagination*, 43.

[485] The definition cited earlier is this: "A commonplace ... fairly uncontroversial definition of imagination can be put succinctly: *Imagination is the power to create or form images in the mind.* Or, with a slight modification: *It is the power to create or form mental images.*" See Charles Taliaferro and Jill Evans, *The Image in Mind*, 12.

[486] The difference, of course, between this example and the instances in imaginative literature where similar *imaginata* are taken to be two different things, is that at Jesus's crucifixion, only one event is taking place. People interpret this one event differently, though only one interpretation is correct. In the example given of two different towers, one phantasmal and one solid, the difference lies in there being two different actual contexts. The point made by citing an historical event is merely to show that one visual scene can convey different things depending upon the context that people assign to it, whether true or false.

To return to the crucial point in our argument at this stage, we can affirm that only the real world can furnish the entire context for any *thing* that one sees. The problem with the mind of any finite imaginer, compared to the real world, is that the mind can never provide the entire context that is needed for the *imaginata* to be coherent and meaningful. The questions that Lewis asks the narrator about "hard substances," "discrete atoms," "space," "princesses" and "ancestors" substantiate this point.[487]

With reference to this particular point, Lewis writes:

We now know that the words which occur in literature are not the names of mere images; and if they are the names of things, then these things demand a context which the imagination cannot supply, and therefore these things are not, in any unequivocal sense, 'things in the imagination'. They seem, in the most troublesome way, to be half in the imagination and half in the real world; and this, however troublesome, is precisely the view we shall have to come to.[488]

Next, Lewis describes the role of the imagination in perception in order then to apply it analogously to the role of the imagination in literature. Others have analyzed the imagination's role in the perceptive process as well. According to Charles Taliaferro and Jil Evans, Hume, for example, argued that it is via the imagination that the observer completes the picture of what he actually sees by filling in the context based off of past experiences.[489] They likewise mention Kant's description of this same power and his point that while the observer rarely sees the entire surface of the perceived object, he is able to complete the picture by use of the imagination. Taliaferro and Evans note Kant's two categories: reproductive imagination and productive imagination. Of Kant's reproductive imagination, they write:

Arguably, you cannot (strictly speaking) see at any one time a full, dense three-dimensional object; one only sees the object's surface or curvature. Imagination is what enables us perceptually

---

Thus, in the real world as well as in the imaginary one, what matters most is not what one "sees," but how one understands the meaning of what one sees. The solider who remarked, "Truly, this man was the Son of God," understood the meaning of Jesus's crucifixion far better than the men who wagged their tongues at Jesus, though technically, they all saw the same visual scene.

[487] C. S. Lewis, *Image and Imagination*, 39–40.
[488] C. S. Lewis, *Image and Imagination*, 45.
[489] Charles Taliaferro and Jil Evans, *The Image in Mind*, 16.

to think of ourselves as perceiving baseballs rather than only being able to claim to perceive the surface of a baseball and infer that there is more to the object than its surface.[490]

They comment next on Kant's productive imagination thus:

> The productive imagination then works to synthesize our experiences, allowing us to apprehend the world as a unified subject, seeing objects whole or as unities. Kant described this power as "transcendental" insofar as it was an operation that is prior to or it is a foundation for our understanding of the world and ourselves.[491]

The reason for citing these examples, and Kant in particular, is that Lewis draws upon both of the imaginative roles that Kant describes in order to set up his analogy. Lewis argues:

> In ordinary life we never see a 'tower.' We see a colored shape, which we take to be a tower, because we believe that it has another side, and is solid, and hollow, and fulfills all the other conditions of towerhood, which, however, are not given in the experience of seeing it. In other words, we turn a mere sense-datum into a tower by attributing to it a context. We link up the present experience with other actual and inferred experiences in one determinate way, and this fixes the present experience as a 'tower': if we had linked it up differently, or failed to link it up at all, it would not be a tower. In the case of the sense data, then, in taking any sense datum as a 'thing', we assert categorically certain connections between it and the rest of our real world.[492]

The predicament that Lewis aimed to solve is this. In the real world, the entire context of any "thing" is supplied by reality itself. While engaging with the real world, the imagination allows one to see a sense datum and interpret it as what it actually is, a baseball or a tower, with the whole

---

[490] Charles Taliaferro and Jill Evans, *The Image in Mind*, 16. See also Gregory Basham, "Lewis and Tolkien on the Power of the Imagination," in C. S. Lewis as Philosopher: Truth, Goodness, and Beauty, 2nd ed. Edited by David Baggett, Gary R. Habermas, and Jerry L. Walls (Lynchburg: Liberty University Press, 2017), 299–300, where Basham writes, "Following Kant, it has been customary to distinguish two types of (imagistic) imagination: reproductive and productive. Reproductive imagination is the power of reproducing mental 'copies' of objects that have previously been perceived (e.g., recalling what one's fourth-grade classroom looked like). Productive imagination, by contrast, is explicitly creative and constructive. This is the faculty of 'fancy,' the power of recombining perceived originals into new and sometimes fantastical combinations, such as a winged horse or a golden mountain."

[491] Charles Taliaferro and Jill Evans, *The Image in Mind*, 16.

[492] C. S. Lewis, *Image and Imagination*, 45–46.

context supplied for it by reality. With this procedure in mind, Lewis sought to explain how, in the imaginative realm, one "takes a mere image as an imagined 'thing'"[493] Something must be present in order to take this important step. This step requires a context that, as it has been demonstrated, presses one to the edge of infinity. This, of course, asks far too much of any finite imagination, and yet, people still take their images to be imagined things.[494]

Lewis elaborates on how this works, writing:

> If you mention the Parthenon, I cannot furnish its context in my own mind: but then the real Acropolis and the Balkan Peninsula and the solar system *can*. But if you speak of Valhalla, and I cannot furnish the context, and without the context it is a mere image, who or what comes to our aid?[495]

He argues that this context is in some way "assumed" but not "implicit."[496] He explains the important distinction between "assumed" and "implied" as follows. The assumed imaginative context is unlike the unstated but implied steps in a chain of reasoning. In the realm of reason, each statement, if followed logically, either rests necessarily on another statement or necessarily entails another.

In contrast to the realm of reasoning, in the imaginative story, many of the unstated elements are not implied in this way. To illustrate, Lewis compares a mirror to a painting. In a mirror, one can discover where the lines that lie outside the frame go because one can turn around and look at the real world that is wider and bigger than that which the mirror can contain. This is akin to the realm of reason or logical deduction. The lines go neither anywhere they please nor wherever one might imagine. Where they go is fixed by reality. If, on the other hand, we look at a painting and asks where the road in the background goes once it disappears, we cannot tell in the way that we can with a mirror. Referring to a road in a painting, Lewis maintains that one "can only reply either that it does not exist, and therefore goes nowhere, or that it may go anywhere: for it might turn sharply the moment it was out of sight."[497]

---

[493] C. S. Lewis, *Image and Imagination*, 46.

[494] Whether they admit that they take them to be imagined things, as Lewis's imaginary narrator was reluctant to do, they implicitly take them to be such. Otherwise, all meaning collapses and they remain mere images.

[495] C. S. Lewis, *Image and Imagination*, 46.

[496] C. S. Lewis, *Image and Imagination*, 47.

[497] C. S. Lewis, *Image and Imagination*, 47.

Again, Lewis is trying to explain by way of illustration how one's understanding of the real world funds one's understanding of the imagined one. The illustration of looking into a mirror is analogous to one's view of the real world whereas the illustration of looking at a painting is analogous to one's view of the imaginary world. His aim is to try to bring clarity to how we gain knowledge of unseen things in the real world versus how we gain the same of unseen things in a work of fiction. We can also look at a mirror and discover what the rest of the room looks like that we do not immediately see, we can simply lean one way or another way to see more. But whichever way we lean, we will see only that which is actually present. It is not the same in a work of fiction. We can only examine what we are given. There is no sense in which we can "lean" this way or that within the imagined story to see more, any more than one can do this with a painting that shows a road terminating at the edge of the border. But then Lewis's whole point is that when we read an imagined story, we fill in, in some sense, these unseen, unstated elements. The question to be answered is how we do this, from what source we are drawing.

To say that the unimagined data in a work of fiction exist only in the imagination does not satisfy Lewis. In the imagination, one will only ever find *imaginata*. That is the proper and only "stuff" present in that realm. And we have already seen the problem that arose with supplying context in this realm that pushed us to the edge of infinity. Yet, it is the unimagined material that, when pressed, one must rely on eventually in order to turn mere images into imagined things with a meaningful context, as has been argued. As this section is perhaps the most difficult to grasp in Lewis's argument, it is worth repeating that the pressing question is *where*, or perhaps, *how* to find this unimagined material, if not in the imaginary realm. Returning to his tower example, Lewis concludes:

> There remains only one possible explanation. If we asked the teller what he meant by a tower, he would, after the tortures to which he has been submitted, reply: "I was imagining the sort of thing which you *could* walk all round, in which you *could* find stones and mortar, which would have foundations, etc.—which *would* in short fit into a whole spatio-temporal system in one way and not in another."[498]

In answering this way, it becomes clear that the context needed, the unimagined material which to this point in the argument has remained troublingly elusive, is *hypothetical*, and the hypothetical is in some sense, reality-dependent. Lewis explains:

---

[498] C. S. Lewis, *Image and Imagination*, 48.

But all hypothesis rests on some actuality ... "I could do this" means "I could do this if I liked." We must therefore find the hidden protasis in the sentence: "I was imagining the sort of thing which you could walk all round." Clearly the protasis "If you liked" will not serve. For, short of direct spatio-temporal inconsistency, you could do anything you chose in imagination: and to enumerate one or two of the myriad incompatible possibilities, therefore, will not determine your imagined thinking. It remains, then, to supply the only protasis which is left, namely "If it were real."[499]

With this point, the argument which began in the imaginary realm has led us at last back to reality. To return to Kant's notions of the productive and reproductive imagination, more than what is seen with the eye must be supplied in order to perceive what is seen as a real thing. The real world readily supplies this, and because it does, it is by way of one's imagination which draws on the real world, that the unseen details can be added. In the imaginary realm, again, unless one can grasp infinity, this can never be supplied solely by the imagination sufficiently. Thus, imaginary things end up showing themselves to be just as dependent upon reality as real things. Helpfully, Lewis elucidates:

But in the imagination, *either* there *is* no more than meets the eye, *or* if there is, we do not know what it may be and therefore cannot assume it. Therefore imagination cannot yield the "something more." Therefore reality must yield it. But since reality does not actually give it, it must be given hypothetically. That is, what is really implicit in the imagination is *hypothetical assertion*: and all hypothetical assertion is about reality. The statement "I am imagining that, if it were real, would have the properties X Y Z" is a statement concerned just as much with the real world as with imagination; for it can be easily converted to the form "The universals X Y Z, in the circumstances P Q R, would yield the appearance which I am imagining." What we do when we imagine, then, is to suppose ... a reshuffling of universals taken from the actual world.[500]

Lewis offers the example of Britomart from Spenser's *The Fairie Queene* to demonstrate how the imaginary realm relies necessarily upon the real world. Britomart is a female knight who epitomizes chastity. The point Lewis makes with this example is to show that the ideas of female and medieval knight, which are combined in the imaginary creation of

---

[499] C. S. Lewis, *Image and Imagination*, 48.
[500] C. S. Lewis, *Image and Imagination*, 49.

Britomart are "not imaginations: they are summarized knowledge of the real."[501] He argues further that in order to appreciate poetry, which is always tossing together real things into various imaginative combinations, one must possess knowledge of real things which, of course requires knowledge of the real world. Lewis aptly writes, "Always the real world is the bank on which the poet draws his cheques."[502]

He puts the conclusion of his argument to the test by altering various real elements in the story of Roland.[503] Lewis envisions Roland approaching his dark tower while the bells of the tower begin to ring. For illustrative purposes, Lewis alters the bell sounds and replaces them with birds. The result of this alteration demonstrates that the reader will be affected differently by this version of the story precisely because he knows what both bell sounds and birds are in the real world, and in some way he will associate the birds with the sounds. If the birds were changed to bats, the meaning and atmosphere of the scene would change still more. This felt change would transpire whether or not the reader visualized bats or birds vividly. Again, we have said that it is not the image of birds or bats in the sky, which might look largely indistinguishable in one's imagination, especially from a distance, that explains the important distinction between the scenes. Rather, it is the reader's knowledge of birds and bats in the real world, and all of the associations attending them that he can recall, that make the crucial difference.

Lewis extends the fantastical elements further, writing, "Let these bell-born birds be no common birds but the souls of dead men whose blood was used to temper the bells: and let them fly out singing with human voice *Justorum animae*."[504] In order for us to understand and to appreciate this scene, we must have knowledge from the real world of "death, and blood, and Christianity."[505] Lewis concludes his article with the following claim:

> Poetry imitates the universal, and when we read poetry we are engaged in knowing. Thus said Aristotle, thus the Neo-Platonists

---

[501] C. S. Lewis, *Image and Imagination*, 49.
[502] C. S. Lewis, *Image and Imagination*, 49.
[503] Roland is the military leader who served under Charlemagne.
[504] C. S. Lewis, *Image and Imagination*, 50. Justorum animae means "the souls of the just."
[505] C. S. Lewis, *Image and Imagination*, 51.

... This is the same orthodoxy to which Wordsworth returned ... It is not the romantics, but the Croceans, who are the heretics.[506]

Once again, we see that reality remains inescapable.

To wrap up Lewis's argument, which began with the question of whether or not the narrator's imaginary items were items solely in his imagination, we can see now how reality has proven to be inescapable. Imaginary things, if they are to be "things" indeed, which means that they are meaningfully embedded within a context, must rely eventually upon the real world. It is true that they do not share the same *mode* of existence as real things do. Their existence is, in a way, hypothetical. That is to say, while they exist "in the mind" of the imaginer, what they "are," really means hypothetically, "what they would be like if they existed."

To make a similar point along these lines, it is clear that no one can think an entirely original thought. If a person thinks he can achieve this by imagining unreal things such as centaurs or fairies, or by imagining water inhabiting the sky region above and conversely the sky inhabiting the water region below, one is not being as original perhaps as he supposes. In the case of the centaur for example, he is taking the knowledge he has received of both man and horse from the real world, and combining elements from each into one creature. Likewise, in turning the world upside down, he is taking his knowledge of sky, water, and spatial dimension, and reordering things.

The important point to recognize is that in none of these examples, or in any that one could imagine, is the imaginer thinking a purely original thought. He is like the artist who is handed a palette with various globs of color put onto it. The artist is free to paint whatever he likes or even to mix colors to make new colors. In doing this, however, he does not make paint itself. He takes the paint he is given and works with it. Similarly, the imaginer's "paint" comes from the real world, which he had no hand in making. He is free, like the artist, to mix the elements he has received from the real world, but what he will never do no matter how desperately he tries, is to introduce a new idea that is not some rearrangement or combination of some actual things that reside first of all in the real world.

This conclusion reached in this chapter is relevant to what we have said in the previous chapter on Lewis's sacramental ontology. If the real

---

[506] C. S. Lewis, *Image and Imagination*, 53. Again, the Crocean heresy is for Lewis, the denial of the vital connection between the imagination and reality, that is external to the mind.

world bears a sacramental quality that points beyond itself ultimately to God, and if the imaginary world draws necessarily upon the things in the real world for its own construction, it follows that the imaginary world itself can share this same quality.[507] It was the recognition of this truth that in part inspired Lewis to use imaginative fiction in order to convey truth about the real world that otherwise might not have been given a hearing were it to be presented in the form of rational argumentation. I am not suggesting for one second, nor did Lewis ever suggest, that we should not utilize rational argumentation. Far from it. I have been using it myself throughout the entirely of this book. I am suggesting that when a person has stubbornly closed to this approach, we have another door we can knock on, namely the person's imagination. Having surveyed Lewis's most thorough treatment on the imagination, the two books that heavily influenced his thoughts on this subject will now be examined in detail.

2 RECOMMENDED BOOKS FOR THINKING CLEARLY ABOUT REALITY AND IMAGINATION

Even considering what we have to this point, it will be difficult for us to adequately understand Lewis's views on the imagination if we remain ignorant of two books that shaped his thinking profoundly.[508] Of these two books, Lewis writes:

> In order to explain this I must now touch on a subject which has an importance quite apart from our present purpose and of

---

[507] It will do this to varying degrees of success depending upon how the world is presented. It certainly does convey truth with equal potency in all imaginative stories. In fact, some may deceive far more than they enlighten. This phenomenon will be examined in the next chapter.

[508] See C. S. Lewis, *Miracles*, 107–127. Lewis's purpose in referring the Bevan's and Barfield's books is to bolster his argument for the historical factuality of Christian miracles in the face of some common and unfortunately unhelpful responses from Christians. Lewis understands that Christians claim many things that seem "savage" or "primitive," to which scientific advances refutes. Inevitably, Christians "turn round and explain that they didn't men what they said, that they were using a poetic metaphor or constructing an allegory, and that all that really was intended was some harmless moral platitude," p. 110. Lewis has little sympathy for this response, and argues instead, "In one sense I am going to do just what the skeptic thinks I am going to do: that is, I am going to distinguish what I regard as the 'core' or 'real meaning' of the doctrines from that in their expression which I regard as inessential and possibly even capable of being changed without damage. But then, what will drop away from the 'real meaning' under my treatment will precisely *not* be the miraculous. It is the core itself, the core scraped as clean of inessentials as we can scrape it, which remains for me entirely miraculous, supernatural—nay, if you will, 'primitive' and even 'magical.'" In an effort to bring clarity to this defense, he proceeds to explain some of the ideas present in Bevan's and Barfield's books and suggests that his readers consult them further.

which everyone who wishes to think clearly should make himself master as soon as he possibly can. And he ought to begin by reading Mr. Owen Barfield's *Poetic Diction* and Mr. Edwyn Bevan's *Symbolism and Belief*.[509]

Barfield's and Bevan's books help us to fill in aspects of Lewis's view of the human imagination that are crucial for demonstrating the relationship between his sacramental ontology and the imaginary realm. This relationship bears heavily upon his pre-evangelistic strategy through the medium of imaginative fiction, which we will delve into in the next chapter.

Poetic Diction by Owen Barfield

Owen Barfield was a close friend to both Lewis and Tolkien. His book *Poetic Diction* influenced both men's thoughts on reality, imagination, metaphor, and myth. Three concepts in particular stand out as particularly relevant to this chapter's treatment of Lewis's understanding of the human imagination. The first is Barfield's description of what he calls "aesthetic imagination."[510] The second is his argument that a good metaphor is ontologically connected to the thing it symbolizes. The third is his distinction between "poetry as the cause of immediate pleasure" and "poetry as a possession."[511] Each of these ideas gives helpful nuance to Lewis's emphasis on the imagination's chief function being the conveyance of meaning.

With regard to his notion of the aesthetic imagination, Barfield writes, "Imagination is recognizable as aesthetic, when it produces pleasure merely by its proper activity."[512] He elaborates a bit later:

> When I try to describe in more detail than by the phrase "aesthetic imagination" what experience it is to which at some time or other I have been led, and at any time may be led again, by all of these examples, I find myself obliged to define it as a "felt change of consciousness," where "consciousness" embraces all my awareness of my surroundings at any given moment, and "surroundings" includes my own feelings. By "felt" I mean to signify that the change itself is noticed, or attended to ... when I, as a European adult, actually observe or visualize a three-masted

---

[509] C. S. Lewis, *Miracles*, 111.
[510] Owen Barfield, *Poetic Diction*, 33.
[511] Owen Barfield, *Poetic Diction*, 47.
[512] Owen Barfield, *Poetic Diction*, 33.

screw steamer with two funnels, the manner in which I immediately experience my surroundings, the *meaning* which they have for me, is determined by the various concepts which I have learnt, since my childhood, to unite with the percept, or complex of percepts, underlying the phenomenon in question. By "percept" I mean that element in my experience, which in no way depends on my own mental activity, present or past—the pure sense-datum. The concepts likely to be operative in this case are reflected in such English words as "mast," "mechanical propulsion", "steam", "coal", "smoke", "chimney for smoke to escape by", etc., all of which are summed up and, as it were, fused in my own peculiar and habitual idea of "steamer." It is this idea which determines for me the quality, or meaning, of my immediate experience in observation.[513]

Much can be gleaned from Barfield's "aesthetic imagination" that also shows up throughout Lewis's works. When Barfield describes his interaction with the percept "steamer," he emphasizes the meaning, rather than the image, just as Lewis does in his treatment of the imagination. The qualities that the percept raises in his consciousness are what really matter. The "mast," "steam," "coal," and "smoke" are what produce his "felt" change of consciousness as he engages with the steamer. These are the qualities that help one understand what a steamer is taken to be. The image in the mind may be helpful, but unless it conjures up the qualities and associations of a real steamer, it does not benefit the imagination very much. Lewis expresses the same ideas in his writings.

Further, as we saw in the first chapter through Lewis's story, the notion of aesthetic pleasure via the imaginative experience was central to Lewis's entire life and thought. Significantly, these experiences are untamable like the wind in that they "blow where they will" and refuse to be captured and possessed by the one who wishes to prolong their visitations. Like Lewis, Barfield writes of being "led," rather than leading, in the above-cited portion. One pictures him as the sought rather than the seeker in these imaginative transactions. More, though such experiences fade rather quickly after arriving, they leave something of themselves behind. They mark their host with a "felt change of consciousness."[514]

These same qualities are found in Lewis's descriptions of his own imaginative experiences. One remembers from the first chapter the many

---

[513] Owen Barfield, *Poetic Diction: A Study in Meaning* (Oxford: Barfield Press, 2010), 40.

[514] Owen Barfield, *Poetic Diction*, 44.

encounters with joy that arrested him without warning. Sometimes they came through a memory of a toy garden. Other times they came through children's literature, such as Beatrix Potter's *Squirrel Nutkin*. Still at other times they came through a poetic line announcing the death of "Balder the beautiful."[515]

Though the mediums through which these qualities might greet us may vary, they can all be categorized fittingly into Barfield's aesthetic imaginative experiences. For instance, Lewis felt that the pleasure came upon him apart from either his planning or his consent with each experience. He simply found himself arrested and enraptured. He was the led, rather than the leader. Further, he desperately longed for the sweet "stab"[516] to linger, only to find that the moment he began to attend to it, it had left him. Lewis remembers:

> It was a sensation, of course, of desire … before I knew what I desired, the desire itself was gone, the whole glimpse withdrawn, the world turned commonplace again … It had taken only a moment of time; and in a certain sense everything else that had ever happened to me was insignificant in comparison.[517]

When he tried to conjure it up again, he found that he could produce no such spell. He could not *stab* himself. Rather, he could only *be stabbed*. Barfield describes such experiences in the same vein, writing:

> So it is with the poetic mood, which, like the dreams to which it has so often been compared, is kindled by the passage from one plane of consciousness to another. It lives during that moment of transition and then dies, and if it is to be repeated, some means must be found of renewing the transition itself.[518]

He describes a bit later the desire to "renew the thrill," admitting that failure in "the wistful quest" is very common.[519] As did Lewis, Barfield

---

[515] C. S. Lewis, *Surprised by Joy*, 17.
[516] C. S. Lewis, *Surprised by Joy*, 72.
[517] C. S. Lewis, *Surprised by Joy*, 72
[518] C. S. Lewis, *Surprised by Joy*, 16.
[519] Owen Barfield, *Poetic Diction*, 45–46. Barfield quotes George Santayana, who describes this same rare yet profound phenomenon thus: "Men are habitually insensible to beauty. Tomes of aesthetic criticism hang on a few moments of real delight and intuition. It is in rare and scattered instants that beauty smiles even on her adorers, who are reduced for habitual comfort to remembering her past favors. An aesthetic glow may pervade experience, but that circumstance is seldom remarked; it figures only as an influence working subterraneously on thoughts and judgements which in themselves take a cognitive or practical direction. Only when the aesthetic ingredient becomes predominant do we exclaim, How

recognized that the imagination is a faculty through which intense, unannounced, and fleeting pleasure can come. Such is the bounty of the aesthetic imagination.

The second concept relevant to Lewis's thought is what Barfield calls the "true metaphor."[520] The true metaphor is the one that captures fittingly a relation between itself and the thing it symbolizes.[521] Most important to

---

beautiful! Ordinary the pleasures which formal perception gives remain an undistinguished part of our comfort or curiosity. Taste is formed in those moments when aesthetic emotion is massive and distinct; preferences then grow conscious, judgements then put into words will reverberate through calmer hours; they will constitute prejudices, habits of apperception, secret standards for all other beauties. A period of life in which such intuitions have been frequent may amass tastes and ideals sufficient for the rest of our days. Youth in these matters governs maturity, and while men may develop their early impressions more systematically and find confirmations of them in various quarters, they will seldom look at the world afresh or use new categories in deciphering it. Half our standards come from our first masters, and the other half from our first loves. Never being so deeply stirred again, we remain persuaded that no objects save those we then discovered can have a true sublimity ... Thus the volume and intensity of some appreciations, especially when nothing of the kind has preceded, makes them authoritative over our subsequent judgements. On those warm moments hand our old systematic opinions; and while the latter fill our days and shape our careers it is only the former that are crucial and alive."

[520] Owen Barfield, *Poetic Diction*, 79. See also Appendix III, 198–200, where Barfield distinguishes between the "accidental" or "false metaphor" and true, writing, "That, in the post-logical period, accidental metaphors have found their way into the current meanings of words, if anything, more easily than the true is apparent from etymology. Nor is this surprising. For from what has been said ... we can very easily see that this kind of metaphor is based on *a synthesis of ideas*, rather than on immediate cognition of reality. And since all words are, as we have seen, obliged to express general notions, the false metaphor is naturally more adapted to the dictionary meaning of a word than the true ... The distinction between true and false metaphor corresponds to the distinction between Myth and Allegory, allegory being a more or less conscious hypostatization of *ideas* (Appendix II, 6), followed by a synthesis of them, and myth the true child of Meaning, begotten on imagination. There is no doubt that, from a very early date, the Greek poets began to mix false metaphor with their original myths, just as the Greek philosophers began to contaminate them with allegory; so that in this case the form in which the myths have come down to us is itself dual. The modern poet has created a new myth or made a true use of an old one, according as the myth in question is the direct embodiment of concrete experience and not of his *idea* of that experience—in which case he has only invented an allegory, or made an allegorical use of a myth, as the case may be."

[521] Obviously, given that a metaphor is a kind of symbol for the thing itself, and therefore not the thing itself, its relational fittingness will never be a one-to-one kind of perfection. It will be, rather, an approximation of the truth. To speak of true metaphors and false ones, while oversimplified in a sense, should be sufficiently instructive for the purposes of this chapter. If one wanted to aim for more precision, which is beyond the scope of this chapter, one could speak of "more fitting" or "less fitting" metaphors and attempt to demonstrate the precise points at which the metaphor aligns with or departs from the thing in itself. When speaking of a "real ontological relation" between the metaphor and the thing itself, one need not press this to mean that every facet of the metaphor relates perfectly to the thing. For instance, the phrase, "The Lord is my fortress," which would count as a true metaphor, is helpful in conveying the real relations of protection, strength, security, surrounding, and such that are fitting when speaking of the Lord's protection of His people.

this concept is Barfield's attempt to answer the question of "why this direct perception should in itself have value as a cause of wisdom."[522] By "direct perception," he is referring to the recognition of a real ontological connection between the thing itself and the metaphor. The reason that true metaphors "work," according to Barfield, is that they reveal a real metaphysical linkage between the symbol and the symbolized. He argues, therefore that wisdom is the value present in the perception of these relations.[523] Barfield explains:

> [T]hese poetic, and *apparently* metaphorical values were latent in meaning from the beginning ... Then what is the true metaphor? In the same essay of Shelley's, from which I have already quoted, he cites a fine passage from Bacon's *Advancement of Learning:* "Neither are these only similarities, as men of narrow observation may conceive them to be, but the same footsteps of nature, treading or printing upon several subjects or matters." This is the answer. It is these "footsteps of nature" whose noise we hear alike in primitive language and in the finest metaphors of poets. Men do not *invent* those mysterious relations between separate external objects, and between objects and feelings or ideas, which is the function of poetry to reveal. These relations exist independently, not indeed of Thought, but of any individual thinker ... The language of

---

The metaphor need not be pressed too far to include other possible relations, which would of course be false, such as "possibly penetrable," "made by human hands," and such. See C. S. Lewis, "Bluspels and Flalansferes," 253–255, where Lewis admits that perceiving real relations between the metaphor and thing itself will still only yield a piece of truth, and even in the best metaphors, error in thinking will creep in if pressed too far. He writes, "When we are trying to explain, to someone younger or less instructed than ourselves, a matter which is already perfectly clear in our minds, we may deliberately, and even painfully, pitch about for the metaphor that is likely to help him. Now when this happens, it is quite plain that our thought, our power of meaning, is not much helped or hindered by the metaphor that we use. On the contrary, we are often acutely aware of the discrepancy between our meaning and our image. We know that our metaphor is in some respects misleading; and probably, if we have acquired the tutorial shuffle, we warn our audience that it is 'not to be pressed' ... For all of us there are things which we cannot fully understand at all, but of which we can get a faint inkling by means of metaphor ... What truth we can attain in such a situation depends rigidly on three conditions. First, that the imagery should be originally well chosen; secondly that we should apprehend the exact imagery; and thirdly that we should know that the metaphor is a metaphor."

[522] Owen Barfield, *Poetic Diction*, 77.

[523] See Owen Barfield, *Poetic Diction*, 77, where he writes, "It is important to recollect that ... these values are not merely poetic in the sense of causing pleasure, but also in the true, creative sense, as causing wisdom ... for we are still left asking *why* this direct perception should in itself have value as cause of wisdom."

primitive men reports them as direct perceptual experience. The speaker has observed a unit, and is not therefore himself conscious of *relation*. But we, in the development of consciousness, have lost the power to see this one as one. Our sophistication, like Odin's, has cost us an eye; and now it is the language of poets, in so far as they create true metaphors, which must *restore* this unity conceptually, after it has been lost from perception. Thus, the "before-apprehended" relationships of which Shelley spoke, are in a sense "forgotten" relationships. For though they were never yet apprehended, they were at one time seen. And imagination can see them again.[524]

Thus, for Barfield, the metaphor and the thing itself remain ontologically linked.

Therefore, Wisdom seems to be, for Barfield, the perception of real meaning in the world. It is *seeing* things as they truly are, through two sets of eyes—the physical and the imaginative. Looking through these two sets of eyes, the wise person sees three things—the thing itself, the metaphor, and the essential qualitative connections between the two.[525] The important similarity between Barfield and Lewis at this point must be highlighted. Both men emphasized the imagination's supreme role of perceiving and conveying meaning over the shallower but oft-emphasized power of mental image-making. It will be remembered that Lewis calls the imagination "the organ of meaning." Were he to have followed the more common understanding of the imagination, he might well have called it "the organ of images." He does not, because meaning-making *through* image-making is the real task of the imagination.

Barfield elaborates further along these lines:

Considered subjectively, it observes the resemblances between things, whereas the first principle marks the differences, is interested in knowing what things *are*, whereas the first discerns

---

[524] Owen Barfield, *Poetic Diction*, 77–79. While by the word "Thought" Barfield likely has in mind an anthroposophic view of reality, one need not adopt this view to detect the helpful ring of truth present in his statement. One can understand "Thought" to be simply God's thoughts, within which there are no imperfections or limitations, other than that which falsehood and logical absurdity would "limit." God, possessing maximum possible knowledge, certainly knows all of these relations, and they are all true whether or not man ever recognizes them or not.

[525] See Owen Barfield, *Poetic Diction*, 48, where he defines knowledge and wisdom as follows, "This ability to recognize significant resemblances and analogies, considered as in action, I shall call *knowledge*. considered as a *state*, and apart from the effort by which it is imparted and acquired, I shall call it *wisdom.*"

what they are not. Accordingly, at a later stage in the evolution of consciousness, we find it operative in individual poets, enabling them ... to intuit relationship which their fellows have forgotten—relationships which they must *now* express as metaphor. Reality, once self-evident, and therefore not conceptually experienced, but which can *now* only be reached by an effort of the individual mind—this is what is contained in a true poetic metaphor; and every metaphor is "true" only in so far as it contains such a reality, or hints at it.[526]

Thus, the true metaphor brings reality before the mind. Lewis agreed with Barfield and maintained further that if a real ontological connection between a good metaphor and the thing itself did not exist, then metaphorical language would not be false, but rather nonsensical. Again, before a statement could be regarded as true or false for Lewis, it must first "mean." Lewis argues:

> I said at the outset that the truth we won by metaphor would not be greater than the truth of the metaphor itself; and we have seen since that all our truth, or all but a few fragments, is won by metaphor. And thence, I confess, it does follow that if our thinking is ever true, then the metaphors by which we think must have been good metaphors. It does follow that if those original equations, between good and light, or evil and dark, between breath and soul and all the others, were from the beginning arbitrary and fanciful—if there is not, in fact, a kind of psycho-physical parallelism (or more) in the universe—then all our thinking is nonsensical. And so, admittedly, the view I have taken has metaphysical implications. But so has every view.[527]

Both men emphasized the imagination's power to see *through* the image *to* the meaning of the image, which includes the various associated concepts and attendant feelings. The notion of truly associated concepts and attendant feelings formed the basis of much of Lewis's literary criticism. He found at times, for example, authors using metaphors that conjured up associations that seemed to him not to fit well with the atmosphere or even the plot of a particular scene. In fact, the primary reason why Lewis decided to craft his own mythological story of Cupid and Psyche stemmed from his insistence that words, metaphors, plot, and atmosphere should all work to form a coherent and meaningful story. Implied in all of this is the notion

---

[526] Owen Barfield, *Poetic Diction*, 80.
[527] C. S. Lewis, "Bluspels and Flalansferes," 265.

that some metaphors are more fitting than others, which was precisely Barfield's point about "good" and "bad" metaphors. Lewis emphatically agreed with him on this point.

An example from Lewis's imaginative fiction through which he applied this principle will help to elucidate the point. Lewis wrote *Till We Have Faces*, out of a long-held burden to correct one crucial scene by adding an element to it that was, for him, unpardonably absent. The element that he added was the numinous, which was Rudolf Otto's term for a mysterious sense of the divine, or even the uncanny. As the myth is commonly told, Cupid's castle is visible, just as any other castle is. Lewis thought that it should not have been visible to Pysche's sisters, but only to Psyche. If one reads Lewis's version, this scene unmistakable achieves the numinous atmosphere for which he aimed. It is uncanny, mysterious, troubling, and enchanting all at the same time. It certainly coheres well with the rest of the story.

Allow me to recall for you Lewis's point regarding the imagination's chief role in his essay "Image and Imagination." The point he made, again, in his imaginary argument with the writer, was that the real difference in the imaginative experience was not the *imaginata*, but what the *imaginata* is taken to be. Whereas in "Image and Imagination," he made his point with a tower, in *Till We Have Faces*, he applied the principle via a castle. Both Lewis and Barfield stressed that the image is not supreme. Rather, the meaning is. It should be clear by this point that the common definition of the imagination as an image-making faculty is not only too shallow, but likely misleading. We see now how a proper understanding and definition of the imagination relates to Barfield's notion of the true metaphor.

The third helpful concept in Barfield's books is the distinction he makes between "poetry as the cause of immediate pleasure" and "poetry as a possession." The important quality unique to "poetry as a possession" is the expansion of one's consciousness with the effect that one comes to view the world differently as a result of the metaphors becoming part of one's thinking and even feeling. While in Barfield's "poetry as the cause of immediate pleasure," one is changed permanently by delight and the longing for the delight to return, one may not necessarily progress to the next stage of viewing the world forevermore in a sense, *through* the metaphor. This is the crucial step taken when one progresses from being delighted by the metaphor to possessing it. Barfield explains:

> What, then, is meant by poetry as a possession? To some extent in all the examples ... I am impressed not merely by the *difference* between my consciousness and the consciousness of which they are the expression, but by something more. I find that, in addition

to the moment or moments of aesthetic pleasure in appreciation, I gain from them a more permanent boon. It is as though my own consciousness had actually been expanded. In V(a), for example, the image contains so much truth and beauty that henceforth the eyes with which I behold real boats and waves and swans, the ears with which in the right mood I listen to a song, are actually somewhat different ... and the absorption of this metaphor into my imagination has enabled me to bring more than I could before. It has created something in me, a faculty or a part of a faculty, enabling me to observe what I could not hitherto observe. This ability to recognize significant resemblances and analogies, considered as in action, I shall call *knowledge*. Considered as a *state*, and apart from the effort by which it is imparted and acquired, I shall call it *wisdom* ... A little reflection shows that all *meaning*—even of the most primitive kind—is dependent on the possession of some measure of this power.[528]

This expansion of consciousness, which refers to the grasping of more and of deeper levels of relations between metaphors and the things in themselves, which again, are real ontological relations, will be deeply important to Lewis's pre-evangelistic strategy that we will examine closely in the next chapter. As we will see, in Lewis's imaginative fiction stories, he does not display Christianity overtly. Instead, he chooses various metaphorical and symbolic means of conveying Christian truths under cover of myth. One might say that his aim is first to expand his reader's consciousness to the truths about reality before stating explicitly the one true myth that makes sense of all of these truths and brings them together into one coherent and historically true account.

Another way of putting this would be to say that Lewis wanted to baptize the reader's imagination, just as his had been by Macdonald's *Phantastes*, in order that the "rest" of the reader might take the plunge in time after encountering the explicit gospel. The similarity between Barfield's "poetry as a possession" and Lewis's imagination being baptized is striking. Lewis recounts his experience of reading MacDonald's *Phantastes*:

Up till now each visitation of Joy had left the common world momentarily a desert–"The first touch of the earth went nigh to kill." Even when real clouds or trees had been the material of the vision, they had been so only by reminding me of another world;

---

[528] Owen Barfield, *Poetic Diction*, 47–48.

and I did not like the return to ours. But now I saw the bright shadow coming out of the book and into the real world and resting there, transforming all common things and yet itself unchanged. Or, more accurately, I saw the common things drawn into the bright shadow ... That night my imagination was, in a certain sense, baptized; the rest of me, not unnaturally, took longer. I had not the faintest idea of what I had let myself in for by buying *Phantastes*.[529]

It is worth quoting a piece from the earlier portion from Barfield again, in order to highlight the similarity between his and Lewis's thoughts. Barfield writes:

The image contains so much truth and beauty that henceforth the eyes with which I behold real boats and waves and swans, the ears with which in the right mood I listen to a song, are actually somewhat different ... and the absorption of this metaphor into my imagination has enabled me to bring more than I could before.[530]

The wise person is the one who sees more, via the imagination, than he could before. This wisdom does not change the world in a Kantian sense, where the internal world of the mind adjusts the external world; rather, one's perspective is transformed to align more closely with the nature of reality as it truly is. This is the value of a good, or true metaphor. It aids the imagination and in turn conveys reality to us so that we might know it with increasing clarity.

Symbolism and Belief by Edwyn Bevan

The second book that Lewis tells his readers is indispensable to thinking rightly about matters pertaining to the imagination is Edwyn Bevan's volume, *Symbolism and Belief.* Just as is the case with Barfield's book, if one wants to understand Lewis's view on the imagination better, Bevan's book cannot be avoided. The following are concepts drawn from Bevan that help to illuminate how Lewis thinks about the relationship between reality and imagination.

Bevan begins by distinguishing between two kinds of symbols. The first, less important kind, at least for the purposes of this chapter, are those that signify but that do not resemble the things themselves. Moreover, they do not they give any new information about the things they symbolize. An example of this kind of symbol would be a nation's flag or a company's

---

[529] C. S. Lewis, *Surprised by Joy*, 181.
[530] Owen Barfield, *Poetic Diction*, 47–48.

logo. The second kind of symbols, which are far more relevant to Lewis's thoughts, are "those which purpose to give information about the nature of something not otherwise known" in which "resemblance is essential."[531] He gives the example of a blind man being told that the color red is like the sound of a trumpet.[532]

In this second kind of symbolism, while one must be familiar with the symbol in order for the enchantment to work, one need not be acquainted with the thing symbolized. If the thing itself happens to be known in some capacity, one will learn something deeper about the thing itself through the symbol. If one possesses no knowledge of the thing itself whatsoever, one still will learn something of it through the symbol. An example that Bevan gives of this kind of symbolism is a weeping willow conveying unhappy love through its posture which is like a "drooping head and hanging hands."[533]

This distinction between two kinds of symbols is important because it begins to illuminate the key reason Lewis insisted that he preferred the term "sacramentalism" to "symbolism" when describing the equivalent of Bevan's second kind of symbol. Lewis writes:

> The suns and lamps in pictures seem to shine only because real suns or lamps shine on them; that is, they seem to shine a great deal because they really shine a little in reflecting their archetypes. The sunlight in a picture is therefore not related to real sunlight simply as written words are to spoken. It is a sign, but also something more than a sign, and only a sign because it is also more than a sign, because in it the thing signified is really in a certain mode present. If I had to name the relation I should call it not symbolical but sacramental.[534]

Again, Bevan argues that the resemblance between the symbol and the symbolized is essential in this kind of symbolism.[535] That is to say that something of the essence, the "whatness" of the symbolized, resides, or is made manifest *in* the symbol. For Lewis, when one encounters the symbol,

---

[531] Edwyn Bevan, *Symbolism and Belief* (London: George Allen and Unwin LTD, 1938), 13.

[532] Edwyn Bevan, *Symbolism and Belief*, 12.

[533] Edwyn Bevan, *Symbolism and Belief*, 13.

[534] C. S. Lewis, "Transposition" in *The Weight of Glory and Other Addresses*, 102.

[535] See Edwyn Bevan, *Symbolism and Belief*, 15, where he writes further, "But our time will be given to a consideration of the other kind of symbols, those which purport to give information about the unseen world, those in which resemblance of some sort between the symbol and the thing symbolized is essential."

one also encounters, in some capacity, the archetype after which it is patterned. Humanity thus *possesses*, thanks largely to the imagination, this marvelous power of "seeing" the unseen in this way. Because of the symbol, one sees perhaps only through a glass darkly, yet *still sees something of the truth even so.*

Bevan demonstrates how these kinds of sacramental symbols convey knowledge about the unseen—namely, about God. This phenomenon interested Lewis greatly, and he applied it in principle throughout his imaginative literature, perhaps most clearly in *The Chronicles of Narnia* within which he dressed up truth in mythological clothing. We will examine this in the next chapter.

The five concepts that Bevan explores are: height, time, light, spirit, and wrath. He finds each to be a metaphor that conveys truth about God, and he explains how each serves this end. For example, Bevan demonstrates the essential resemblance between God and height, arguing that:

> Although it is, perhaps, not impossible that all races of mankind everywhere might by an accident have lighted upon one and the same fancy which was wholly baseless, it would certainly be very odd. And if one believes that man's thought about God was in any way guided by God Himself, it is all the more difficult to suppose that an imagination as universal as that which connects the Divine with height was not in some sense veridical. As I said in my last lecture, it is not conceivable that such a feeling meant an intellectual apprehension of truth as we should express it to-day, but it does seem possible that it was something we may call a feeling of appropriateness which outran intellectual understanding … There seems to be nothing monstrous in supposing such a feeling of appropriateness in minds still very backward in knowledge of the universe and in logical thought. For even in the psychology of modern man a feeling of appropriateness, a sense, a *flair*, often outruns clear established knowledge, often even the possibility of rational justification. Yet it may turn out—in poets especially—when clear established knowledge comes, to have been veridical. No doubt such feelings may also turn out to have been false lights, *igneous fatui*: it is only when looked back upon from the standpoint of larger knowledge, from the ultimate practical result, that true and false feelings of appropriateness can be distinguished. Yet we certainly believe that some truths, before they are grasped by the intellect, do throw by anticipation a veridical image of themselves upon

the feelings—whatever the psychological or philosophical explanation of that may be—and we pronounce afterwards that the men who followed such feelings did right.[536]

We can make three observations from this paragraph that sounds eerily "Lewisian." First, Bevan is hinting at an essential connection between the symbol and the symbolized. This is crucial to his and to Lewis's understanding of symbolism and metaphor. Referring to the association of height with divinity, Bevan writes, "The universality of this idea amongst mankind may, I think, give us pause if we are inclined to say that it is nothing but fancy."[537] The reason that the association seems fitting universally throughout human history is that a real, ontological connection exists between the concepts "spatially high," "greatness," "divinity," and ultimately "God."

Second, when Bevan writes of "a feeling of appropriateness which outran intellectual understanding," he is hitting very closely on a phenomenon that Lewis perceived and which he eventually exploited in order to pre-evangelize his audience through imaginative fiction. Lewis asked his readers simply to taste at first. He invited them to delight in the symbol before grasping that which it symbolized. Along these lines, Lewis, writes:

> But in fact all good allegory exists not to hide but to reveal ... For when allegory is at its best, it approaches myth, which must be grasped with the imagination, not with the intellect ... It is the sort of thing you cannot learn from definition: you must rather get to know if as you get to know a smell or a taste, the "atmosphere" of a family or a country town, or the personality of an individual.[538]

All the while, he hoped that through tasting, delight would arise that would lead his readers to ask the question, "Is there truth here?" This, of course, is the same journey that Lewis took through which he came at last to Christ.

Third, as I argued in the previous chapter, given that Lewis believed that all human reason was in some sense participation in divine Reason, *and* given that the world of everyday experience points sacramentally beyond itself to the more real archetype, it follows that those who are

---

[536] Edwyn Bevan, *Symbolism and Belief,* 58.
[537] Edwyn Bevan, *Symbolism and Belief,* 57.
[538] C. S. Lewis, *The Pilgrim's Regress,* 215–216.

"very backward in knowledge" can still apprehend this "feeling of appropriateness" and find it to be true to reality.[539] Clearly, neither Bevan nor Lewis believed that human feelings, reason, and imagination were so corrupted by the fall that they could not grasp some measure of truth via natural revelation.

Along with height, light commonly has been associated with the divine throughout various ages, cultures, and religions. Neither can this association be dismissed easily as mere coincidence. Bevan explains:

> In all great religions of antiquity the chief gods are characterized by their connexion with light. In Egypt, this led to the chief god being identified with the sun—the Ra or Re of Heliopolis combined at Thebes with the local god *Amen.* If Osiris, the special god of the dead, was originally a god of the dark lower world, the belief came to prevail that he rose again into the light-world and carried the pious dead with him in his boat ... When the sense of the numinous in primitive Aryna religion, Rudolf Otto says, took the form of a visionary hallucination, it was regularly the vision of something shining, burning, just as in the Old Testament the presence of the Divine is revealed to Moses by the appearance of a burning bush. Both the very early general terms for numinous forms, *vast* and *deva,* connote in their root meaning, brilliance, radiancy. The numinous is essentially the luminous. It is Zoroastrianism which most signally among religions gives prominence to the idea of light as representing the Divine in contrast to darkness representing the Evil Power, which sets the light creation of Ahuramazda against the dark creation of Angramainyus ... If we find the light-symbol play a greater part in the religious and theosophical literature of the Graeco-Roman world at the beginning of the Christian era, in the Hermetic literature, in magical papyri, and in Gnosticism, this may no doubt have been to some extend due to the influence of Zoroastrianism. In Manichaeism, a religion itself partially Persian in origin, the identification of the good with light is fundamental. In the New Testament too, light is prominent as a religious symbol.[540]

---

[539] Edwyn Bevan, *Symbolism and Belief,* 58.

[540] Edwyn Bevan, *Symbolism and Belief,* 129–133. Bevan writes further, "Take, for instance, the familiar language in a book of the New Testament. 'God is light, and in him is no darkness at all. If we say that we have fellowship with him and walk in darkness, we lie and do not the truth. But if we walk in the light as he is in the light, we have fellowship one with another.' Is it the chief idea that apprehension of God means true knowledge of the

C. S. LEWIS PRE-EVANGELISM FOR A POST-CHRISTIAN WORLD

Lewis's genius, owing something to Bevan, lies largely in recognizing this essential connection between the metaphor and the thing or quality itself and employing this recognition through his fantasy stories. He imaginatively conveyed reality in such a way that sneaks past a post-Christian culture's naturalistically-shaped defenses and helps them to encounter truth dressed in mythological or fantastical garb.

Bevan makes much of the symbol's power to produce feelings associated with the reality in which the symbols participate. These feelings are something like the combination of both sensations and emotions. One might call them sensate-emotive apprehensions.[541] Something more than feelings but less than clear intellectual comprehension is present. Bevan explains, writing of:

> [T]he way in the normal life of men certain things seem to stand for some vague vast reality characterized only by the emotion it produces. There are three main kinds of emotion called forth in this way by visible objects—the feeling of the beautiful, the sexual feeling, and the germinal feeling of religious awe, what Rudolf Otto has made it the fashion to call the numinous … If we analyse the feeling called up by intense admiration for the beautiful it certainly contains something besides mere pleasant sensation. It contains something akin to intellectual apprehension; you seem to take knowledge of some world of reality there behind the object, or spreading out like a halo from the object. But it is not intellectual apprehension; you have no definite concept what the beautiful object stands for: you only know that it means something, means something real and wonderful, introduces you into a fairyland.[542]

---

universe, so that the man who has it can order his conduct aright? Or that in God supreme goodness is found with no admixture of evil? Or that a peculiar kind of wonder, exhilaration and fear is created by the disclosure of God? Probably all these ideas run together. One could not translate the phrase 'God is light' into a statement of any one of these ideas singly without robbing it of its power, because it involves all those ideas together and yet presents the imagination with something which has apparent unity and simplicity. We feel that we know best what is meant by the declaration that 'God is light' when no attempt is made to explain it. We have come almost to lose the sense that light is only a symbol; we almost feel it to be a literal statement of recognized truth. But light may produce another emotional effect beside joy, a peculiar kind of admiration. It is the diffused light, the light of day, which produces joy: it is concentrated light, looked at directly in a blaze or in a shining surface, which produces admiration," 140–141.

[541] Bevan does not use this term, but it seems like a helpful term rather than writing of "feelings" or "sensations" repeatedly, as these words might be misleading.

[542] Edwyn Bevan, *Symbolism and Belief,* 275–276.

In this way, the imagination is more connected with the emotional and sensate dimensions than is the reason. Propositions and dry syllogisms convey truth in a certain, often very helpful, way. However, they do not tend to arouse the emotions, or the sense of the thing itself, in the way that symbols and metaphors do. Lewis describes this power, latent in images and metaphors, as follows:

> Yet mental images play an important part in my prayers. I doubt if any act of will or thought or emotion occurs in me without them. But they seem to help me most when they are most fugitive and fragmentary—rising and bursting like bubbles in champagne or wheeling like rooks in a windy sky: contradicting one another (in logic) as the crowded metaphors of a swift poet may do. Fix on any one, and it goes dead. You must do as Blake would do with a joy; kiss it as it flies. And then, in their total effect, they do mediate to me something very important. It is always something more qualitative—more like an adjective that a noun. That, for me, gives it the impact of reality. For I think we respect nouns (and what we think they stand for) too much. All my deepest, and certainly all my earliest, experiences seem to be of sheer quality ... Plato was not so silly as the Moderns think when he elevated abstract nouns—that is, adjectives disguised as nouns—into the supreme realities—the Forms.[543]

Lewis demonstrated this power further, comparing several statements in a helpful essay entitled, "The Language of Religion."[544] He writes:

(I) It was very cold

(II) There were 13 degrees of frost

(III) 'Ah, bitter chill it was! The owl, for all his feathers was a-cold; The hare limped trembling through the frozen grass, And silent was the flock in woolly fold: Numb'd were the Beadsman's fingers.[545]

While the above statements all communicates truth, each does so in a different way. Lewis calls the first statement an example of "ordinary

---

[543] C. S. Lewis, *Letters to Malcolm*, 86.

[544] See C. S. Lewis, "The Language of Religion," in *Christian Reflections*, 129.

[545] C. S. Lewis, "The Language of Religion," 129. A careful reading of Lewis's essay justifies the application of what he has to say about "poetic language" to the imagination generally and to his imaginative fiction specifically. He clarifies, "It must be remembered that I have been speaking simply of Poetic language and not of poetry." Both poetic language and his imaginative stories share the use of symbolism and metaphor abundantly in order to convey real things to which these symbols and metaphors point.

C. S. LEWIS PRE-EVANGELISM FOR A POST-CHRISTIAN WORLD

language," the second "scientific," and the third "poetic."[546] The first and second are easily understandable, though the second is far more precise in terms of quantifying the coldness with a testable measurement. While the scientific statement excels in quantifiable precision, Lewis points out that:

> On the other hand it does not, of itself, give us any information about the quality of a cold night, does not tell us what we shall be feeling if we go out of doors. If, having lived all our lives in the tropics, we didn't know what a hard frost was like, the thermometer reading would not of itself inform us.[547]

While helpful in communicating aspects of truth, scientific language cannot convey all that is to be known truly of reality.

This begins to reveal what differentiates the poetic from the ordinary, and especially from the scientific. It is its capacity to "express an experience which is not accessible to us in normal life at all, an experience which the poet himself may have imagined and not, in the ordinary sense, 'had.'"[548] We remember that this is one of the qualities of the kind of symbolism that Bevan describes. Through the imagination, one can apprehend something true of things that have yet to be known by experience. Again, as we have seen, this apprehension is more than mere emotion but less than what one gets through physical sensate experience and rational argumentation. The term "sensate-emotive apprehensions" seems fitting to capture the nature of these experiences. Lewis explains further:

> I think that Poetic language often expresses emotion not for its own sake but in order to inform us about the object which aroused the emotion. Certainly it seems to me to give us such information. Burns tells us that a woman is like a red, red rose, and Wordsworth that another woman is like a violet by a mossy stone half hidden from the eye. Now of course the one woman resembles a rose, and the other a half-hidden violet, not in size, weight, shape, colour, anatomy, or intelligence, but by arousing emotions in some way analogous to those which the flowers would arouse ... This is the most remarkable of the powers of Poetic language: to convey to us the quality of experiences which we have not had or perhaps can never have, to use factors within our experience so that they become pointers to something outside our experience—as two or more roads on a map show

---

[546] C. S. Lewis, "The Language of Religion," 129.
[547] C. S. Lewis, "The Language of Religion," 130.
[548] C. S. Lewis, "The Language of Religion," 133.

us where a town that is off the map must lie ... My conclusion is that such language is by no means merely an expression, nor a stimulant, or emotion, but a real medium of information.[549]

The importance of recognizing the imagination's power to arouse sensate-emotive apprehension far more effectively than dry propositions or scientific language cannot be gainsaid when we consider the following. The culture's defenses, both in Lewis's and our own, tend to be erected in protection of the rational far more than the imaginative and sensate-emotional. In other words, people will reject more readily clear statements of truth and arguments in support of Christianity than they will qualities and feelings that attend some Christian ideas when those ideas are dressed up in imaginative language and symbols.

For instance, an atheist who may find herself deeply moved by Aslan's death on the stone table and his return to life a short time after likely will be repulsed if one speaks to her of Christ's death and resurrection. Yet, the very feelings she experiences towards Aslan are the same ones she ought to feel towards Christ. This gives the Christian an open door or a place to begin, with those whose rational defenses are heavily fortified. This phenomenon can be exploited, of course, in service of falsehood just as readily as it can in the service of truth, but this is true of all good things— they can be twisted. People can be duped, quite easily, it seems, into associating feelings with ideas, people, and things that are not the proper feelings one ought to have towards them. In going awry in this way, truth that comes to such people via rational argumentation does not often gain much of a hearing. This is what Lewis has in mind when he writes, through the mouth of the demon Screwtape:

> It sounds as if you supposed that *argument* was the way to keep him out of the Enemy's clutches. That might have been so if he had lived a few centuries earlier. At that time the humans still knew pretty well when a thing was proved and when it was a not; and if it was proved they really believed it. They still connected thinking with doing and were prepared to alter their way of life as the result of a chain of reasoning. But what with the weekly press and other such weapons we have largely altered that. Your man has been accustomed, ever since he was a boy, to have a dozen incompatible philosophies dancing about together inside his head. He doesn't think of doctrines as primarily "true" or "false," but as "academic" or "practical," "outworn" or "contemporary," "conventional" or "ruthless." Jargon, not

---

[549] C. S. Lewis, "The Language of Religion," 132–134.

argument, is your best ally in keeping him from the Church. Don't waste time trying to make him think that materialism is *true*! Make him think it is strong, or stark, or courageous—that it is the philosophy of the future. That's the sort of thing he cares about.[550]

Hopefully, it is becoming clearer why Barfield, Bevan, and Lewis held the imagination in particularly high esteem. Their esteem had little to do with the power to picture images vividly in one's imagination. Extreme visualizers are not the best imaginers according to their views. Rather, those who can detect most effectively the real "information," the true meaning, and the fitting sensate-emotive apprehensions mediated through the imaginative realm are those whose imaginations are working best.[551]

To revisit the previously quoted portion from Lewis on Barfield's and Bevan's books that have been surveyed briefly in this chapter, Lewis insists that "everyone who wishes to think clearly should make himself master as soon as he possibly can. And he ought to begin by reading Mr. Owen Barfield's *Poetic Diction* and Mr. Edwyn Bevan's *Symbolism and Belief*."[552] The most important ideas with respect to the human imagination have been sifted from these books and explained to illuminate Lewis's own view further. It is to the relationship between nature and human imagination that the present chapter now turns.

IMAGINATION AND NATURE

Nature and story have been chosen here in particular because they are the two realms through which Lewis's romantic imagination was most stirred. He writes of "a particular recurrent experience which dominated my childhood and adolescence and which I hastily called 'Romantic' because inanimate nature and marvellous literature were among the things that evoked it."[553] While nature and story aroused *Sehnsucht* in Lewis, he readily admitted that for other people, different mediums may do the job

---

[550] C. S. Lewis, *The Screwtape Letters*, 3–4.

[551] See C. S. Lewis, *Letters to Malcolm*, 85, where he writes, "I conclude that there were people whose visual imagination was weak and needed to be stimulated. But the trouble with people like ourselves is the exact reverse. We can say this one another because, in our mouths, it is not a boast but a confession. We are agreed that the power—indeed, the compulsion—to visualise is not the "Imagination" in the higher sense, not the Imagination which makes a man either a great author of a sensitive reader. Ridden on a *very* tight rein, this visualising power can sometimes serve true Imagination; very often it merely gets in the way."

[552] C. S. Lewis, *Miracles*, 111.

[553] C. S. Lewis, *The Pilgrim's Regress*, 209.

with equal effectiveness.[554] As we will see, in both nature and in story, we can experience both a kind of desiring and a kind of seeing, just as Lewis did.

Desiring Through Nature

Chapter one explored in part the role that the beauty of nature played in Lewis's life. Significantly, his first encounter with beauty came through nature, as his older brother Warnie brought in a toy garden that he had constructed inside a biscuit tin. Likewise, his first encounter with joy came as he remembered the day that Warnie brought his garden into the nursery. Nature continued to stab him throughout his life, even to the very end. Sayer recounts a trip he took with Lewis in the year that Lewis died:

> One fine autumn afternoon, I drove him along the London Road, up Beacon Hill to the crest of the Chilterns, then along the crest past Christmas Common. The beech trees had colored marvelously, and although the sun was shining, there was that slight sharpness in the air that he loved and described in some of the most moving passages of his books. We stopped, opened the windows of the car, and he gazed, rapt. He was praying, praising God, and adoring nature's beauty.[555]

Given that we have explored many of Lewis's experiences with nature to this point, it is not necessary to go through them again. The purpose at this stage of the argument is to distinguish, with the role of the imagination in mind, the difference between "*desiring* through nature" and "*seeing* through nature." For Lewis, and perhaps for a great many others, desire came before sight. To state it another way, imaginative longing often precedes intellectual understanding. This is no small insight considering the pre-evangelistic strategy Lewis eventually employed.

In the previous chapter, we explored Lewis's sacramental understanding of reality. We saw that nature participates in some way in God's being such that God can be seen *through* nature. Lewis understood this participation to be more significant than God's merely being of cause of nature, or his sustaining it. He understood nature below to be a copy of something above; that is, he envisioned the shifting shadows below to point to the unchanging substance above them. Lewis called these

---

[554] See C. S. Lewis, *The Pilgrim's Regress*, 209, where Lewis writes, "I still believe that the experience is common, commonly misunderstood, and of immense importance: but I know now that in other minds it arises under other *stimuli* and is entangled with other irrelevancies and that to bring it into the forefront of consciousness is not so easy as I once supposed."

[555] George Sayer, *Jack*, 250.

respectively the "ectype" and the "archetype."[556] He believed that nature conveys something of God's character *and* that the human heart only finds its true satisfaction in following these inklings to their ultimate aim—union with God. A significant entailment follows from this insight. Nature often arouses desire that it cannot ultimately satisfy. We can understanding, especially if Lewis is correct in his ontology, why some people mistakenly worship nature. If, on the other hand, nature is seen for what it truly is, we find ourselves invited to enjoy it, but not as the thing for which we ultimately long. We will enjoy it as a man enjoys a photograph of his wife. The photograph reminds him of her, though it is not her. Further, as anyone knows who has been far away from his wife for some time, the photograph intensifies his desire to return to her.

Nature is like the photograph that is meant to intensify humanity's longing for the true and ultimate goal of desire, which is God. This is what I am trying to capture by the notion of "desiring *through* nature." Nature is not merely to be desired and enjoyed. It is to be the medium through which the ultimate desire is awakened so that ultimate enjoyment in God can be had.[557] Lewis maintained that if one mistakenly follows the desire in the hopes of finding satisfaction *in* the thing which aroused it, he will always come to disappointment in the end. If, on the other hand, one follows the desire such that he looks not *to* nature but *through* it, he may come in the end to God. He writes:

> It appeared to me therefore that if a man diligently followed this desire, pursuing the false objects until their falsity appeared and resolutely abandoning them, he must come out at last into the clear knowledge that the human soul was made to enjoy some object that is never fully given—nay, cannot even be imagined as given—in our present mode of subjective and spatio-temporal experience ... The dialectic of Desire, faithfully followed, would retrieve all mistakes, head you off from all false paths, and force you not to propound, but to live through, a sort of ontological proof.[558]

---

[556] C. S. Lewis, *The Pilgrim's Regress*, 59.

[557] The word "merely" is used here, because nature is good, and therefore is rightly desirable in so far as the desire is fitting. Every good object, James suggests, is properly desirable. The point is to do more than merely enjoy the object. It is to do two things—to enjoy it *and* to look through it to the One the enjoyment of whom far surpasses all other good things.

[558] C. S. Lewis, *The Pilgrim's Regress*, 212.

In his allegory The Pilgrim's Regress, it is not surprising that the character John first experiences this strong desire that Lewis calls "joy" through an encounter with nature, namely a far-off island. John's entire journey serves as an allegorical depiction of the point Lewis makes in the above-cited paragraph. While desire stabs John immediately, understanding comes quite late in his journey. He follows the desire, though mistaking it consistently in terms of that to which it points him until at last, he comes to see that the proper response is to allow the desire to pull him *through* nature. In other words, the imagination, working with the material supplied to it by nature via the senses, is designed to lead man to God. This is the precise point that Lewis makes when God finally speaks to John, saying, "For this end I made your senses and for this end your imagination, that you might see My face and live."[559]

Desire, which motivates man's search, is meant to result in sight, or knowledge of the One behind nature's pull. This, again, is part of what Lewis had in mind when he employed the term "romanticism." The experience may seem helplessly vague at first to the one who encounters it. If left to itself and not brought together with reason, the desire that is awakened will prove to be little help in the end. Referring to this phenomenon in Lewis's thoughts, Chad Walsh writes:

> The concept of "Romanticism" makes it possible for the individual better to understand a strange variety of experiences which seem at first glance so subjective that they cannot be communicated to others. "Romanticism" is a clue to their meaning, and the key to unlocking the hidden meaning of much that is otherwise bewildering and almost meaningless ... The process of "growing up" is often misunderstood. It does not consist of ridiculing and forsaking what was most deeply significant in childhood. Rather, it means understanding the truths that were once perceived in flashes, and fitting the fragments of truth together. A phrase of music, the sight of birds flying high overhead, the lonely tulip poplar standing golden on a distant autumn hill—these are clues to mysteries that the proud adult neglects at the risk of drying up into something less than fully human.[560]

The truly mature person whose childlike wonder and adult rationality have grown up together is the one who comes to understand those aspects of reality that stirred his longing. In fact, in the final chapter, I will argue that it is unlikely that a person would ever undertake with very much

---

[559] C. S. Lewis, *The Pilgrim's Regress*, 175.
[560] Chad Walsh, *C. S. Lewis: Apostle to the Skeptics*, 119.

seriousness that he does not first find interesting. The imagination helps to awaken such interest.

According to Lewis, God's design is that while we should remain children in one sense, we must grow up into adults in another. To remain a child while never growing up at all means never progressing to the next stage of "seeing through nature," which involves disciplined reason. To become an adult while leaving the valuable childlike part behind is to abandon sweet desire, to jettison "joy' which comes to our aid on the journey. Lewis juxtaposes these two extremes in *The Pilgrim's Regress* by the North and the South regions—the North representing cold reason to the neglect of desire and emotion and the South representing strong desire and emotion to the neglect of reason.[561] We need the best of both the North and South without the extremes of either, and so now we must look briefly to the "North," where we learn that the point is not merely to desire but to see.

Seeing Through Nature

Long before Lewis learned to see through nature, he began asking the right questions. In fact, he put one such question into the mouth of the protagonist in his pre-conversion epic poem *Dymer*. We have already mentioned this scene, but it will be helpful to turn to it once again. While Dymer is sitting in class, receiving instruction based on a very rigid and heavily "Northern" view of reality, a bird appears on the window. Drawn

---

[561] See C. S. Lewis, *The Pilgrim's Regress*, 213–214, where Lewis explains, "The things I have symbolized by North and South, which are to me equal and opposite evils, each continually strengthened and made plausible by its critique of the other, enter our experience on many different levels. In agriculture we have to fear both the barren soil and the soil which is irresistibly fertile. In the animal kingdom, the crustacean and the jellyfish represent two low solutions of the problem of existence. In our eating, the palate revolts both from excessive bitter and excessive sweet. In art, we find on the one hand, purists and doctrinaires, who would rather ... lost a hundred beauties than admit a single fault, and who cannot believe anything to be good if the unlearned spontaneously enjoy it: on the other hand, we find the uncritical and slovenly artists who will spoil the whole work rather than deny themselves any indulgence of sentiment or humor or sensationalism. Everyone can pick out among his own acquaintance the Northern and the Southern types—the high noses, compressed lips, pale complexions, dryness and taciturnity of the one, the open mouths, the facile laughter and tears, the garrulity and (so to speak) general greasiness of the others. The Northerners are the men of rigid systems whether skeptical or dogmatic, Aristocrats, Stoics, Pharisees, Rigorists, signed and sealed members of highly organized 'Parties.' The Southerners are by their very nature less definable; boneless souls whose doors stand open day and night to almost every visitant, but always with readiest welcome for those ... who offer intoxication. The delicious tang of the forbidden and the unknown draws them on with fatal attraction; the smudging of all frontiers, the relaxation of all resistances, dream, opium, darkness, death, and the return to the womb. Every feeling is justified by the mere fact that it is felt: for a Northerner, every feeling on the same ground is suspect."

by painful desire, he steals out of the room and runs into the woods where he cries out, "What do you mean, wild wood? What do you mean?"[562] Significantly, Dymer only asks this question with such passion because his desire had been awakened.

Lewis's understanding of the two-fold function of the imagination proves relevant at this point. Again, the imagination serves both to arouse desire *and* to help one grasp meaning. In order to achieve this end, it will have to receive help from another faculty, namely human reason. Thus, for Lewis, reason and imagination, far from standing at odds with one another, are allies in the same cause. This is precisely what Lewis tried convey in his allegory *The Pilgrim's Regress*, which significantly, was originally titled *Pseudo-Bunyan's Periplus: An Allegorical Apology for Christianity, Reason, and Romanticism*.[563]

When reason works together with the imagination in response to joy, we are beginning to go beyond mere longing to looking. We are beginning to ask, "What does all of this mean?" We may not see clearly at first, but we must look if we are ever to perceive. Like Lewis, we may begin to sense that far more meaning than what we noticed at first is calling to us through nature. Robert Sloan Lee tries to capture this phenomenon, writing, "The experience of the inconsolable longing creates the sense that everything is itself, yet, something more than itself."[564] It is this "something more" that we are meant to see by following our awakened desires to their true end.[565]

The beauty and even the very being of nature, set on display before the eyes of humanity, hints of the One who is not simply one more beautiful existing thing, but very beauty and very existence Himself. Commenting along these lines regarding the Creator-creature distinction, Lewis writes:

---

[562] C. S. Lewis, *Dymer*. Originally published under the pseudonym: Clive Hamilton (UK: Crossreach Publications, 2016) 7.

[563] See the footnote on the title page in C. S. Lewis, *The Pilgrim's Regress*, where editor David Downing writes, "Lewis's original full title was *The Pilgrim's Regress, or Pseudo-Bunyan's Periplus: An Allegorical Apology for Christianity, Reason, and Romanticism*. Though his publishers convinced him to shorten it, that long original title, with its arcane vocabulary, suggests that Lewis was writing less for a popular audience than for the intellectual elite of his generation. *Pseudo-Bunyan* indicates that he intends to update Bunyan's *Pilgrim's Progress* for modern readers. *Periplus* means "sailing around," taking the long way to get to one's destination."

[564] Robert Sloan Lee, "As if Swallowing Light Itself: C. S. Lewis's Argument from Desire, Part I," in *C. S. Lewis as Philosopher*, 320.

[565] Again, various mediums can arouse the inconsolable longing. This sections only deals with nature.

C. S. LEWIS PRE-EVANGELISM FOR A POST-CHRISTIAN WORLD

All creatures, from the angel to the atom, are other than God; with an otherness to which there is no parallel: incommensurable. The very words "to be" cannot be applied to Him and to them in exactly the same sense. But also, no creature is other than He in the same way in which it is other than all the rest. He is in it as they can never be in one another. In each of them as the ground and root and continual supply of reality ... One is always fighting on at least two fronts. When one is among Pantheists one must emphasize the distinctness, and relative independence, of the creatures. Among Deists ... one must emphasize the divine presence in my neighbor, my dog, my cabbage-patch.[566]

Every instance of beauty in nature is an instance of something having received beauty from the infinite fountain. Likewise, everything that exists depends upon God, who necessarily exists, in order to be and to continuing "be-ing."

The logic at this point is a lesser-to-greater argument. If humanity is naturally drawn to beauty, which seems indisputable, and if the beauty in created things produces some limited amount of pleasure and satisfaction, how much more pleasure and satisfaction will we find if we come to the infinite Source itself? More strongly, if the desire that nature arouses is meant to be satisfied, the only place we can find this satisfaction is in the One whose perfect beauty and being are communicated through the things that have been made. He is the only fountain that will never dry on us.

In Lewis's understanding, we do not begin truly to see until we see *through* nature in this way to the One who created and who upholds it, the One whose beauty shines forth in some capacity through it. Naturally, as things look different depending upon which angle one approaches them from, nature looks very different when one at last sees it from the angle of Christianity.[567] In *The Pilgrim's Regress*, after John has become a Christian, and as he is preparing to take his regressive journey through the places he has just visited, his Guide says to him, "Come ... if you are ready let us start East again. But I should warn you of one thing—the country will look very different on the return home."[568] Fittingly, the very next page heading that begins Book Ten, the final section of Lewis's allegory, contains the following summary: "John now first sees the real shape of the world we

---

[566] C. S. Lewis, *Letters to Malcolm*, 73–74.
[567] In particular, the medieval Christian perspective which Lewis held is referred to here.
[568] C. S. Lewis, *The Pilgrim's Regress*, 177.

live in."[569] Lewis conveys this same idea when he writes, "I believe in Christianity as I believe that the Sun has risen, not only because I see it, but because by it I see everything else."[570] Luc Ferry, in his book *A Brief History of Thought*, also affirms this notion. He writes:

> You will recall that *theoria* always comprises two aspects: on the one hand an unveiling of the sensual structure of the universe (the divine); on the other hand the instruments of knowledge which it employs to arrive at this understanding (the vision or contemplation). Now it is not simply the divine, the *theion*, which is utterly changed here by becoming an individual being; but also the *orao*, the fashion of seeing, or act of contemplating, understanding and approaching reality that is transformed.[571]

Thus, how one sees should be informed by what one sees. If nature is sacramental, one must learn not only to look *at*, but also to look *through*.

To summarize what we have considered in this section on "desiring through nature" and "seeing through nature," I am making the case that given the sacramental nature of reality and the two-fold function of the imagination,[572] some people might be helped in coming to know God in the following way. First, as they encounter the beauty of nature, they may experience what Lewis, and a great many others, have experienced—immortal longings. If one then follows these desires in the hope of finding lasting satisfaction in the created objects that provoke them, one will discover that the objects are unable to deliver what one seeks. Lewis's words will prove true: "Every one of these supposed *objects* for the Desire is inadequate to it."[573]

If one continues this journey and finds, or rather is found, by Christ, he will see that all of his deep longings were pointing him *through* the objects *to* the Maker and Sustainer of them all. Looking then at the world out of newly acquired Christian eyes, particularly those that view reality sacramentally as Lewis does, one will find the depth and coherence of meaning that hitherto had remained elusive. Put simply, he will begin to see the world increasingly for what it truly is. McGrath argues similarly:

---

[569] C. S. Lewis, *The Pilgrim's Regress*, 181.

[570] C. S. Lewis, "Is Theology Poetry?" in *The Weight of Glory*, 140.

[571] Luc Ferry, *A Brief History of Thought: A Philosophical Guide to Living*, translated by Theo Cuff (New York: HarperCollins, 2011), 62–63.

[572] This two-fold desire of the imagination, mentioned above, is to arouse desire and to aid one in grasping meaning.

[573] C. S. Lewis, *The Pilgrim's Regress*, 211.

C. S. LEWIS PRE-EVANGELISM FOR A POST-CHRISTIAN WORLD

One of the most persistent things in contemporary aesthetic reflection is that the appreciation of nature depends on an understanding of *what nature actually is* ... An ontology of nature—an understanding of what nature actually is—can thus be argued to play a critical role in shaping and guiding human aesthetic responses to the natural world ... From a Christian perspective, an appreciation of the beauty of nature can be interpreted as a transitory intuition of what is eternal, the experience *signifying* yet not *delivering* something of immense and transformative importance, and creating a sense of absence, a feeling of longing, within the human soul.[574]

Seeing through nature in this way serves both on the front end and the back end, as McGrath notes. He calls the appreciation of beauty an intuition in the sense that it gives the observer a clue to the transcendent. Once the individual connects the dots and looks at reality from the Christian perspective, his newfound perspective further justifies what he originally intuited. His first *seeing*, prior to conversion, is more like a confirmation of his former suspicion.

Lewis describes this kind of desiring and seeing as a discipline to be cultivated. For Lewis, we are meant to grow in the disciplines of desiring and seeing through nature. He writes most clearly about this discipline in his book *Letters to Malcolm*. While Lewis recognized that ultimate satisfaction could never be had through the objects of nature, he did not prescribe a habitually ascetic response to them. That is, he did not try to diminish the importance of nature or dull enjoyment of it. Rather, he encouraged people to seek consistently to derive pleasure from the things in the world commensurate with their being what they are, but also—and this is the most important part—to take the next step of looking through them to the God to whom they point. In fact, he aimed to discipline himself to the point that the pleasure and the felt recognition of God's goodness through nature became one and the same operation. He writes:

> Yet you were not—or so it seemed to me—telling me that "Nature," or "the beauties of Nature," manifest the glory. No such abstraction as "Nature" comes into it. I was learning the far more secret doctrine that *pleasures* are shafts of the glory as it strikes our sensibilities. As it impinges on our will or our understanding, we give it different names—goodness or truth or the like. But its flashes upon our senses and mood is pleasure ... I

---

[574] Alister McGrath, *The Open Secret*, 280–282.

have tried ... to make every pleasure into a channel of adoration. I don't mean simply by giving thanks for it. One must of course give thanks, but I mean something different. How shall I put it? We can't—or I can't—hear the song of a bird simply as a sound. Its meaning or message ("That's a bird") comes with it inevitably—just as one can't see a familiar word in print as a merely visual pattern. The reading is as involuntary as the seeing. When the wind roars I don't just hear the roar; I "hear the wind." In the same way it is possible to "read" as well as to "have" a pleasure. Or not even "as well as." The distinction ought to become, and sometimes is, impossible; to receive it and to recognise its divine source are a single experience. This heavenly fruit is instantly redolent of the orchard where it grew. This sweet air whispers of the country from whence it blows. It is a message. We know we are being touched by a finger of that right hand at which there are pleasures forevermore. There need be no question of thanks or praise as a separate event, something done afterwards. To experience the tiny theophany is itself to adore.[575]

Lewis sought to make the step from deriving pleasure to enjoying it as a gift from God instant and involuntary. To the degree that success in the operation is achieved, our imagination becomes a medium for repeated instances of joy; both enjoyed and understood.

IMAGINATION AND STORY

Lewis tells us that the two mediums which stirred his desires by stimulating his imagination were chiefly nature and story. A fantastical tale just as easily as a distant green mountain range could awaken longing in him. Given the dependence relationship between story and nature that we have already established, much of what has been said about "desiring through nature" and "seeing through nature" will be closely analogous to what will be said in this final section, which turns now to story.

Desiring Through Story

Imaginative fiction played a pivotal role in Lewis's life, both in terms of aiding him along in his journey towards becoming a Christian and in helping him thereafter to try to stir up the same longing in the hearts of his readership through his own stories. Just as desire can be awakened through encountering nature, the same can occur through stories, whether fictional

---

[575] C. S. Lewis, *Letters to Malcolm*, 89–90.

C. S. LEWIS PRE-EVANGELISM FOR A POST-CHRISTIAN WORLD

or non-fictional.[576] The reason for this has already been explored at some length in this chapter, but it may serve well to connect the dots again, with respect to the analysis given of Lewis's essay "Image and Imagination" as well as the Bevan's and Barfield's books.

In his essay "Image and Imagination," we remember that Lewis discerned that the imaginative realm depends upon the real for its "building materials." Thus, what we find in an imaginative story will always be the real-world elements, altered or rearranged to some degree. For example, we might find purple waters, centaurs, wraiths, and such. The color purple which we find on flowers and in the sky on certain evenings can be removed from its flower and/or sky location and transported to the waters via the imagination. Likewise, we can join half of a horse and half of a man, combining the two to make a new creature. With the wraith, we combine the notion of a human with that of a transparent object, or perhaps with something like organized mist through which one can see.

This capacity to reshuffle creatively such things as humans, mist, and such, in new combinations not found in the real world is intriguing and seems suspiciously to suggest the reality of universals. It shows that the human mind can do more with these bits and pieces than that which the senses perceive. Further, people can communicate such things to one another meaningfully even if they have never experienced them. This suggests a capacity to know universals in some way. Even if a person has only ever seen the color red present in a ball and has only ever seen green trees, that same person can still comprehend a red tree with no measure of "ballness" brought into the conception.

If the real world bears a sacramental nature, as I have argued, it follows that if the materials are moved from that realm to the imaginary one, something of their sacramental quality may survive the journey. In fact, it seems that this quality must survive given that even in the physical world, one only knows the meaning of its objects by the aid of one's imagination. In other words, one's imagination is, in a sense, no less engaged when one encounters the real world than it is when one encounters the imaginary one. Therefore, the imaginative operation that one employs in story bears strong resemblance to that which one employs when interacting with the real world. It follows that if inconsolable longing can be awakened in the real world precisely because of its sacramental quality in light of humanity's true end, namely to know God to love God,

---

[576] For the purposes of this essay, the focus shall remain on fictional stories.

then the same enchantment lies waiting for us in the imaginative realm of story as well.

The reality of this enchantment is borne out by experience both in Lewis's and Tolkien's lives, respectively, as well as in the lives of a great many others for whom stories have delivered the sweet stab. Scott Calhoun writes of Lewis and Tolkien:

> Both Oxford Dons received inspiration from the languages of pre-Renaissance worlds, and sought to write stories that would inspire others by captivating the imagination and illuminating the human heart ... Essentially, Lewis and Tolkien discovered in their youth that mythologies had a certain power over them. Later in life, they discovered that they were not alone in the depth of their love for myth. Their belief in myth's ability to convey facts, and truth, about the world solidified their friendship. A study of Lewis and Tolkien as friends, readers, and storytellers, is really the study of how two people, each enchanted the realm of myth and the mythopoeic enterprise.[577]

Calhoun continues, describing the particular quality of story that Lewis and Tolkien found especially delightful—the sense of the numinous, or the uncanny. He writes:

> Myth also brought its readers in touch with the numinous, or that which is awe-inspiring, "other," and existing in a sort of spiritual dimension beyond human reality. For Lewis and Tolkien, it was the otherness of Northernness that they enjoyed so much that myth frequently brought them in touch with.[578]

The numinous is one of the key qualities of myth that can enchant and awaken longing. This quality will be further discussed in the next two chapters.

Lewis and Tolkien both realized that desire can be awakened through story as potently as it can through nature. Whether one encounters the numinous, the beautiful, or the heroic, one can feel oneself pulled in the direction of the fountain from which these qualities flow. The desire can be, as Lewis describes it, almost sickening in terms of its intensity. As was clear in Lewis's own journey, he did not discern rightly the nature of his own longings for quite some time. Nevertheless, they proved valuable in that they set him on the path of seeking the true end to which they were

---

[577] Scott Calhoun, "C. S. Lewis and J. R. R. Tolkien: Friends and Mutual Mentors," in *C. S. Lewis: Life, Works, and Legacy*, Vol. 1, 250–251.

[578] Scott Calhoun, "C. S. Lewis and J. R. R. Tolkien: Friends and Mutual Mentors," 258.

leading him all along. This is part of the enchantment of story—its power to awaken desire.

Seeing Through Story

When Lewis read Beatrix Potter's *Squirrel Nutkin* and was arrested by the idea of Autumn, and when he later read Longfellow's translation of *Drapa*, and his eyes fell upon the words "Balder the beautiful is dead...is dead!", and he found himself enchanted by northernness, he had desire but not sight. He supposed *that* these stories meant something likely profound, but he could not discern yet *what* they meant on this deeper level. This deeper level that seemed to peek its head out again and again through stories continued to tantalize and elude his understanding.

If one individual is to be credited with helping Lewis most significantly to "see through story," the honor rightly falls to Tolkien. On a fateful night as they strolled together along Addison's Walk, Tolkien began to explain to Lewis the true nature of myth. He helped him to see that all of the mythologies that he cherished so deeply and that had awakened in him sweet desire, had brought before his eyes glimmers of truth and reality. Whether the story was about a dying god coming back to life, or about a young mistreated girl suddenly falling in love and gaining a happy ending through the fitting of a magic slipper, deep truths were shining through the pages. It is part of the true story of reality that a god really did die and come back to life, *the* God, in fact. Further, the true historical plot structure is copied closely by the common fairy-tale structure. A happy situation takes a tragic turn. At the precise point when all hope seems abandoned, a sudden turn takes place that brings resolution, or the happy ending, setting the wrong things right again. Tolkien calls this the *eucatastrophe* (literally, "the good catastrophe), or more explicitly, the *evangelium* (literally, "the good news") in the fairy tale.[579] Of course, this structure was true in the real world long before it was ever true in fairy land. We will look at this in far greater detail in the next chapter, but it is worth mentioning if only briefly at this point.

Stratford Caldecott notes how children growing up in the modern age live very detached from nature. As a result, their imaginations are shaped largely by technology rather than the world of sky, trees, birds, butterflies, rivers, mountains, moon and stars. Given the sacramental nature of reality to which Lewis holds, we can understand why Caldecott writes, "A life lived

---

[579] J. R. R. Tolkien, "On Fairy Stories," in *Tree and Leaf*, 77.

close to the earth, to nature in all its forms ... helps to create in a child the possibility of religious awakening."[580]

Perceptively, Caldecott recognizes that it is not only the realm of nature that can accomplish this wonderful illumination in the individual's mind. He maintains that it can also occur in the realm of story. He writes:

> For those children estranged from nature, the early influence of good literature can have the same salutary effect. Traditional folk and fairy tales, heroic stories, and legends can help prepare someone for what C. S. Lewis referred to as the "baptism" of the imagination; something that for him, albeit not for everyone, was an important preparatory step for receiving the gospel of Christ as Saving Truth.[581]

Because we may "see" in a story, no matter how fantastical it might be, elements of reality presented in their true light, the imaginary realm may help to acquaint us quite effectively with reality as it truly is. In Tolkien's *The Lord of the Rings* stories, for example, sacrifice in friendship is cast in its true light. One would betray a heart of stone who could read of Samwise's risking his own life to recover what he believes is the dead body of his beloved friend Frodo from Shelob's lair and not feel deeply moved and painfully desirous of such a friendship himself.

Further mirroring reality, evil is not an impersonal force in Tolkien's Middle Earth. Neither is it a necessary element of reality, the antithesis of the good meant somehow to balance nature. Still more, it is certainly not up for grabs whether or not the evil shadow that has passed over the land is truly evil or not. Moral relativism has no place in this story. Evil is personified in the character of Sauron, who is evil beyond question, and who above all desires power. He would have all creatures enslaved to his will by his cunning allurement through magic rings that promised strength while hiding their true diabolical ensnarement that awaited those who wielded them.

Where one finds beauty, heroism, evil, or friendship in the realm of story, if these are cast in their proper light, one is being shown reality. That is, one is invited to see *through* the story *to* the reality that undergirds it and gives it its ring of truth. Caldecott cites Tolkien along these lines who

---

[580] Stratford Caldecott, "Speaking the Truth Only the Imagination May Grasp: Myth and 'Real Life,'" in *The Pilgrim's Guide: C. S. Lewis and the Art of Witness*, 86.

[581] Statford Caldecott, "Speaking the Truth Only the Imagination May Grasp: Myth and 'Real Life,'" in *The Pilgrim's Guide: C. S. Lewis and the Art of Witness*, 86–87.

C. S. LEWIS PRE-EVANGELISM FOR A POST-CHRISTIAN WORLD

writes, "Legends and myths are largely made of 'truth,' and indeed present aspects of it that can only be received in this mode."[582]

No matter how much one "sees" through story, one will not see all that one should until one sees Christ as the logos, the One in whom all things hold together. The imaginary realm can take us only so far. It this sense, it cannot evangelize. Most properly, it can only "pre-evangelize," which was the very aim for which Lewis employed the medium.

CONCLUSION

In this chapter, I have attempted to bring clarity to Lewis's understanding of the relationship between reality and the human imagination. I have argued, in agreement with Lewis, that the imagination depends upon reality for its content. This entails the idea that even in the imaginative realm of a fantastical story, one cannot escape reality. The importance of this realization for the present chapter is that the same sacramental quality characteristic of the real world can be found in the imaginative one as well. This then explains why Lewis was stirred with inconsolable longing through the mediums of both nature and imaginative story. This also demonstrates that his reliance upon imaginative stories to pre-evangelize his readership was not simply a pragmatic strategy that seemed to "work"; rather, it was rooted in the nature of reality itself, upon which the imaginary realm necessarily depends. Precisely how Lewis carried out this strategy will be our focus in the next chapter.

---

[582] Stratford Caldecott, "Speaking the Truth Only the Imagination May Grasp: Myth and 'Real Life,'" in *The Pilgrim's Guide: C. S. Lewis and the Art of Witness*, 87.

Brian M. Williams

CHAPTER 4

C. S. Lewis's Use of Fiction as Pre-Evangelism: Exploring The Space Trilogy and The Chronicles of Narnia

Introduction

In the last two chapters, I have set forth C. S. Lewis's view of the nature of reality and of the human imagination, and I have argued for an inseparable linkage between the two. As we saw, Lewis came to view nature sacramentally. He understood the imagination to serve as the "organ of meaning" through which one is enabled both to desire and comprehend to some degree truth about reality that lies deeper than merely what the senses perceive. Desire is only ultimately satisfied, and *the* Truth that makes sense of all other truths is only found, in Christ. Like John in his allegorical tale The Pilgrim's Regress, Lewis eventually reached this conclusion in his own journey.

We have seen how, along with nature, the realm of imaginative story can awaken inconsolable longings. In order to make sense both of how and why this works, we delved into the notions of symbolism and metaphor. Along with Barfield and Bevan, Lewis helped us see that good symbols and metaphors bear an ontological connection with the things they symbolize. Further, just as the stuff of nature participates in God's being and in a way points to him, the stuff of the imaginative realm is nothing but nature's material, transported, reshuffled, and recast into imaginary contexts. Therefore, the same sacramental quality present in the real world can be found in a fictional story. Because this is the case, an imaginative story can produce the same "stab" in the heart of both the reader of story and the wanderer in nature. In this present chapter, I will attempt to explain Lewis's pre-evangelistic strategy that he carried out through his imaginative fiction. In doing so, I make the case that Lewis's pre-evangelistic strategy is a consistent application of his view of reality and the human imagination, one that is born out of his having soundly discerned the spirit of the age in his own context, and strategized his approached in light of it.

In order to sustain this argument, the present chapter will proceed as follows. First, some preliminary disclaimers will be given, which help to

C. S. LEWIS PRE-EVANGELISM FOR A POST-CHRISTIAN WORLD

distinguish Lewis's pre-evangelism from explicit evangelism. We will then consider Lewis's understanding of the concepts: myth, reality, and truth. Next, we will examine Lewis's notion of "supposal," as opposed to allegory, in detail. Finally, we will analyze his imaginative fiction works in order to illuminate how he carried out his pre-evangelistic aim through them. The works we will survey are *The Space Trilogy* and *The Chronicles of Narnia*.

LEWIS'S PRE-EVANGELISM AS DISTINCT FROM EXPLICIT EVANGELISM

A bit of hedging is in order at the outset to not present Lewis's pre-evangelistic strategy as promising more than it reasonably can deliver. His strategy has strong merit, and this merit is the impetus for my writing this book. That being the case, it is only part of a bigger strategy, namely, the strategy of evangelism at large. In the previous chapter, I concluded by making the crucial point that while both nature and story are meant to awaken desire and impart knowledge, this phenomenon is best categorized not as evangelism but as *pre*-evangelism. The distinction is important. Evangelism is the explicit communication of the good news that Jesus, the Christ, has come into the world and died for sinners, was raised on the third day, and offers to impart forgiveness and eternal life to all who will repent and call upon his name by faith. This explicit message, and none other, is "the power of God for salvation to everyone who believes" (Rom 1:16, ESV). Pre-evangelism, conceptually distinct from, yet most certainly harmonious with evangelism, is the attempt to remove obstacles, both felt and thought, and to awaken desire for the transcendent so that the gospel might be given a fair hearing and an interested hearing. We might think of pre-evangelism as the power of God working to predispose a person towards being receptive of the gospel.[583] The term often used for mediums and strategies which do such a thing is *praeparatio evangelica*, which simply means "preparation for the gospel."[584]

Lewis was well aware, and we must be also, that unless a person is given the explicit gospel, romantic longings alone will not secure the *ultimate* good of helping this person come to know Christ. In fact, Lewis admitted that one might quite easily misunderstand such longings, as he did

---

[583] See C. S. Lewis, "Christianity and Culture," in *Christian Reflections*, 23, where Lewis writes of the power of imaginative literature to "predispose to conversion."
[584] This Latin term means "preparation for the gospel."

for many years, resulting in the pursuit of destructive ends. In his essay entitled "Christianity and Culture," Lewis warns:

> The dangers of romantic *Sehnsucht* are very great. Eroticism and even occultism lie in wait for it. On this subject I can only give my own experience for what it is worth. When we are first converted I suppose we think mostly of our recent sins; but as we go on, more and more of the terrible past comes under review. In this process I have not (or not yet) reached a point at which I can honestly repent of my early experiences of romantic *Sehnsucht*. That they were occasions to much that I do repent, is clear; but I still cannot help thinking that this was my abuse of them, and that the experiences themselves contained, from the very first, a wholly good element. Without them my conversion would have been more difficult.[585]

While we are wise to heed such a warning, we must also consider the other side of the coin, which Lewis emphasized repeatedly throughout his writings, namely that *Sehnsucht* can also serve as a preparatory help to one's salvation. With a tempered tone, Lewis explains further:

> My general case may be stated in Ricardian terms—that culture is a storehouse of the best (sub-Christian) values. These values are in themselves of the soul, not the spirit. But God created the soul. Its values may be expected, therefore, to contain some reflection or antipasto of the spiritual values. They will save no man. They resemble the regenerate life only as affection resembles charity, or honor resembles virtue, or the moon the sun. But though "like is not the same," it is better than unlike. Imitation may pass into initiation. For some it is a good beginning. For others it is not; culture is not everyone's road into Jerusalem, and for some it is a road out ... I conclude that culture has a distinct part to play in bringing certain souls to Christ. Not all souls—there is a shorter, and safer, way which has always been followed by thousands of simple affectionate natures who begin, where we hope to end, with devotion to the person of Christ.[586]

By "culture," Lewis was referring to "intellectual and aesthetic activity," which he admitted is a helpful path for some to take, though not for all, in journeying to Christ.[587]

---

[585] C. S. Lewis, "Christianity and Culture," in *Christian Reflections*, 22–23.
[586] C. S. Lewis, "Christianity and Culture," in *Christian Reflections*, 23–24.
[587] C. S. Lewis, "Christianity and Culture," in *Christian Reflections*, 12.

C. S. LEWIS PRE-EVANGELISM FOR A POST-CHRISTIAN WORLD

Lewis recognized that a pre-evangelistic strategy can have great value for some people, especially given the pervasiveness of naturalism in his day that made Christianity appear implausible. In putting into practice such a strategy, he set out to write his imaginative fiction works in an attempt to circumvent the barricades of reason that had been erected in the minds of a large portion of the population in his day. Many people had become disillusioned, especially after two world wars, towards traditional morality and Christianity. These were viewed as tried-but-found-wanting doctrines of an unenlightened age, as shackles from the past that needed to be broken off if society at large was to make real progress.[588] The challenge for overt evangelism in Lewis's day was that, for many a hearer, once he caught a whiff of the "old religion," he immediately closed himself off to any consideration of the possibility of its truthfulness. In the rare event that one did give Christianity a decent hearing, the individual would be set loose immediately to reenter a world that had been brought under the grip of naturalism at almost every turn.

Lewis describes this unfortunate situation as follows:

The difficulty we are up against is this. We can make people (often) attend to the Christian point of view for half an hour or so; but the moment they have gone away from our lecture or laid down our article, they are plunged back into a world where

---

[588] The notion of progress implies, of course, some destination towards which one means to head. Lewis understood the desired destination of the spirit of the age in his day to be largely the perpetuation of the human race. It was a very naturalistic view of life where means were sought chiefly to improve life here and now, and to ensure the same would continue for the generations to come. See C. S. Lewis, "A Reply to Professor Haldane," in *On Stories: And Other Essays on Literature* (New York: HarperOne, 2017), 109, where Lewis admits to his squabble with scientism, the aim of which was to improve and prolong human life. Responding to Professor Haldane's criticism of *That Hideous Strength*, Lewis writes, "If any of my romances could be plausibly accused of being a libel on scientists it would be *Out of the Silent Planet*. It certainly is an attack, if not on scientists, yet on something which might be called *scientism*—a certain outlook on the world which is casually connected with the popularisation of the sciences, though it is much less common among real scientists than among their readers. It is, in a word, the belief that the supreme moral end is the perpetuation of our own species, and that this is to be pursued even if, in the process of being fitted for survival, our species has to be stripped of all those things for which we value it—of pity, of happiness, and of freedom." See C. S. Lewis, *The Collected Letters of C. S. Lewis*, Vol. II, p. 262, where Lewis expresses this same concern in a letter written to Sister Penelope dated August 9, 1939. Referring to his motivation for writing *Out of the Silent Planet*, Lewis writes, "What set me about writing the book was the discovery that a pupil of mine took all that dream of interplanetary colonisation quite seriously, and the realization that thousands of people, in one form or another depends some hope of perpetuating and improving the human species for the whole meaning of the universe—that a 'scientific' hope of defeating death is a real rival to Christianity."

> the opposite position is taken for granted. As long as that situation exists, widespread success is simply impossible. We must attack the enemy's line of communication. What we want is not more little books about Christianity, but more little books by Christians on other subjects—with their Christianity *latent.* You can see this most easily if you look at it the other way round. Our Faith is not very likely to be shaken by any book on Hinduism. But if whenever we read an elementary book on Geology, Botany, Politics, or Astronomy, we found that its implications were Hindu, that would shake us. It is not the books written in direct defense of Materialism that make the modern man a materialist; it is the materialistic assumptions in all the other books. In the same way, it is not books on Christianity that will really trouble him. But he would be troubled if, whenever he wanted a cheap popular introduction to some science, the best work on the market was always by a Christian. The first step to the re-conversion of this country is a series, produced by Christians, which can beat the *Penguin* and the *Thinkers Library* on their own ground. Its Christianity would have to be latent, not explicit: and of course, its science perfectly honest. Science *twisted* in the interest of apologetics would be sin and folly.[589]

He realized that rational argumentation, while necessary at times, was not *always* a particularly effective as an entry point to engage the common person in conversation about Christian truths in his day. After writing the first volume *Out of the Silent Planet* in his space trilogy, he became further convinced of the power of imaginative fiction to do what argument alone could not. He expressed this confidence in a letter written to his friend, Sister Penelope, in response to one she had written to him a few days prior. He writes:

> You will be both grieved and amused to learn that out of about 60 reviews, only 2 showed any knowledge that my idea of a fall of the Bent One was anything but a private invention of my own? But if only there were someone with a richer talent and more leisure, I believe this great ignorance might be a help to the evangelization of England: any amount of theology can now be smuggled into people's minds under cover of romance without their knowing it.[590]

---

[589] C. S. Lewis, "Christian Apologetics," in *God in the Dock*, 90–91.
[590] C. S. Lewis, *The Collected Letters of C. S. Lewis*, Vol. II, 262.

C. S. LEWIS PRE-EVANGELISM FOR A POST-CHRISTIAN WORLD

By "romance," Lewis likely meant roughly what he described in the afterword to the third edition of *The Pilgrim's Regress*. He says that the term refers to:

> Stories about dangerous adventure—particularly dangerous adventures in the past or in remote places ... The marvelous is "romantic", provided it does not make part of the believed religion. Thus magicians, ghosts, fairies, witches, dragons, nymphs, and dwarfs are "romantic"; angels less so.[591]

Importantly, when he writes that romance might serve as "a help to the evangelisation of England,"[592] he seems to choose his words carefully. He does *not* say that through romance one *is* evangelizing. Rather, he says that one is *helping* the task of evangelizing. This help to which he refers is called, most properly, pre-evangelism. While he saw both tasks as important, he made no qualms about affirming the superiority of explicit evangelism. He viewed his own work with modest esteem, as a servant to a higher master. In his essay "The Decline of Religion," he argues:

> Conversion requires an alteration of the will, and an alteration which, in the last resort, does not occur without the intervention of the supernatural. I do not in the least agree with those who therefore conclude that the spread of an intellectual (and imaginative) climate favorable to Christianity is useless. You do not prove munition workers useless by showing that they cannot themselves win battles, however proper this reminder would be if they attempted to claim the honor due to fighting men. If the intellectual climate is such that, when a man comes to the crisis at which he must either accept or reject Christ, his reason and imagination are not on the wrong side, then his conflict will be fought under favorable conditions. Those who help to produce and spread such a climate are therefore doing useful work: and yet no such great matter after all. Their share is a modest one; and it is always possible that nothing—nothing whatsoever—may come of it. Far higher than they stands that character whom, to the best of my knowledge, the present Christian movement has not yet produced—the *Preacher* in the full sense, the Evangelist, the man on fire, the man who infects. The propagandist, the apologist, only represents John the Baptist: the Preacher represents the Lord Himself. He will be sent—or else he will not.

---

[591] C. S. Lewis, *The Pilgrim's Regress*, 209.
[592] C. S. Lewis, *The Collected Letters of C. S. Lewis*, Vol. II, 262.

But unless he comes we mere Christian intellectuals will not effect very much. That does not mean we should down tools.[593]

Thankfully, while Lewis understood his task to be of a lesser importance to the evangelist's, he did not "down his tools." Rather, he took up his pen and did what he could do for the great cause of evangelism. The result of his efforts has given the world some of the most beloved stories for both adult and child alike. We will examine some of these in detail in the final sections of this chapter.

KEY CONCEPTS: ON MYTH, REALITY, AND TRUTH

We turn now to consider some important concepts that Lewis employs that relate to the genre of imaginative fiction. Understanding these concepts will shed further light of us on the nature of his pre-evangelistic strategy. The concepts to be considered along these lines are myth, reality, and truth.

The nature of reality has already been discussed at length in the second chapter. Therefore, this section will not repeat what has already been said; rather, it will treat the concept of reality solely with reference to Lewis's imaginative fiction. It might seem strange at first glance to consider reality somehow being present in a story that is not actually factual—that is, that did not actually take place in history. After all, children are taught from a young age that a synonym for the word "fiction" is the word "fake." Therefore, the attempt to find reality in a "fake" story looks preliminarily like a fool's undertaking. Hopefully, given what we have looked at together in the previous chapter, we know better now.

Reality, for Lewis, is simply that which *is*. With respect to his imaginative fiction, reality is what the reader experiences while reading. This will take some explaining to unpack and to avoid what might easily be a misunderstanding. This experience of reality comes prior to his attempting to extract principles or truths. The moment the reader moves from enjoying the story to extracting principles, he begins to move away from reality and closer to truth.[594] The distinction is synonymous with one that Lewis admitted in his autobiography to learning early in his life. He came to differentiate enjoyment from contemplation. Enjoyment relates to reality whereas contemplation relates to truth. He explain the distinction this way:

---

[593] C. S. Lewis, "The Decline of Religion," in *God in the Dock*, 241.

[594] The point here is not that truth and reality stand at odds with one another. In fact, the contrary is true. The point is that the concepts "reality" and "truth" are distinct, as Lewis demonstrates.

C. S. LEWIS PRE-EVANGELISM FOR A POST-CHRISTIAN WORLD

When you see a table you "enjoy" the act of seeing and "contemplate" the table. Later, if you took up Optics and thought about Seeing itself, you would be contemplating the seeing and enjoying the thought ... I accepted this distinction at once and have ever since regarded it as an indispensable tool of thought ... It seemed to be self-evident that one essential property of love, hate, fear, hope, or desire was attention to their object. To cease thinking about or attending to the woman is, so far, to cease loving; to cease thinking about or attending to the dreaded this is, so far, to cease being afraid. But to attend to you own love or fear is to cease attending to the loved or dreaded object.[595]

Lewis maintains that one cannot perform both operations at exactly the same time. In the moment, one must either enjoy *or* contemplate. In a similar way, when reading a myth, one must either enjoy reality or contemplate truth. Lewis explains this distinction in a helpful article entitled "Myth Became Fact." He writes:

In the enjoyment of a great myth we come nearest to experiencing as a concrete what can otherwise be understood only as an abstraction. At this moment, for example, I am trying to understand something very abstract indeed—the fading, vanishing of tasted reality as we try to grasp it with the discursive reason ... [In reading myth] You were not knowing, but tasting; but what you were tasting turns out to be a universal principle. The moment we state this principle we are admittedly back in the world of abstraction. It is only while receiving the myth as a story that you experience the principle concretely. When we translate we get abstraction—or rather, dozens of abstractions. What flows into you from the myth is not truth but reality (truth is always *about* something, but reality is that *about which* truth is), and, therefore, every myth becomes the father of innumerable truths on the abstract level. Myth is the mountain whence all the difference streams arise which becomes down here in the valley ... Or, if you prefer, myth is the isthmus which connects the peninsular world of thought with that vast continent we really belong to. It is not, like truth, abstract; nor is it, like direct experience, bound to the particular.[596]

---

[595] C. S. Lewis, *Surprised by Joy*, 217–218.
[596] C. S. Lewis, "Myth Became Fact," 57–58.

Thus, myth bridges a gap between the abstract, which is propositional truth, and the concrete, which is experience. Through myth, Lewis believed that a person could experience concretely that which is abstract. In this way, it could provide something of a solution to the apparent chasm between enjoyment and contemplation in the sense that something that one might contemplate can be enjoyed while inside the mythological world.

The metaphor that Lewis chooses for myth and truth is, respectively, that of father and child. Myth is the father which begets truth. In this conception, the latter depends upon the former and thus follows after it logically. In the same way, one's evaluation of one's experience comes after the experience itself. At this point, we might be confused with the claim that a myth, which is not historically true, can convey reality to us. But we must keep our concepts clear and distinct - reality is what "is," and truth is a statement about what "is." We must also remember what we established in the last two chapters regarding universals and particulars, particularly about how the universals participate in the particulars. We said this phenomenon can also take place in a fictional story just as it can in the created world. With this in mind, let us consider that a myth is a narrative vehicle full of symbols, and we have said that symbols bear an ontological connection with the real things they symbolize. In this way, we can understand how myth points to reality, or even contains it. If this is still a little murky in our minds at this point, I trust that as we evaluate Lewis's stories later in this chapter, clarity will come.

Referring to imaginative tales that convey reality successfully such as *The Hobbit* and *Oedipus Rex*, Lewis writes, "The story does what no theorem can quite do. It may not be 'like real life' in the superficial sense: but it sets before us an image of what reality may well be like at some more central region."[597] Myth therefore *contains* bits of truth that one can contemplate—truths about the nature of truth itself as objective, the same regarding morality, expressions of beauty, and glimmers of theological truths that we will explore in Lewis's space trilogy and the Chronicles of Narnia later in this chapter. Caldecott summarizes Lewis's view of myth helpfully as follows:

> But what is a myth designed to express? It concerns not merely the world around us, but the world within us; not so much the surface appearance of the world, but its inner form. For myth is a way of describing the rules by which the world is made, the rules that govern our lives; whether or not we know them or obey them ... Stories composed by an individual, such as Hans

---

[597] C. S. Lewis, "On Stories," 21.

C. S. LEWIS PRE-EVANGELISM FOR A POST-CHRISTIAN WORLD

Christian Andersen's *Snow Queen*, Tolkien's *The Lord of the Rings*, or Lewis's *Chronicles of Narnia*, seem sometimes to touch on the same level of archetypal truth as the myths of a people, and they achieve enormous and lasting popularity as a result.[598]

Referring to fairy tales, Lewis writes:

For Jung, fairy tale liberates Archetypes which dwell in the collective unconscious, and when we read a good fairy tale we are obeying the old precept "Know thyself." I would venture to add to this my own theory, not indeed of the Kind as a whole but of one feature in it: I mean, the presence of beings other than human which yet behave, in varying degrees, humanly: the giants and dwarfs and talking beasts. I believe these to be at least (for they may have many other sources of power and beauty) an admirable hieroglyphic which conveys psychology, types of character, more briefly than novelistic presentation and to readers whom novelistic presentation could not reach.[599]

The notion to be stressed here is the quality of myth to convey reality in just this sense—of "liberating Archetypes,"[600] or of giving universal truths an imaginative particular instantiation, not in the form of an abstracted proposition, but rather in the form of a story and it various elements.

In the previous chapter, I argued that certain kinds of symbols can help to acquaint us not only with things seen, but also with the unseen. For Lewis, the greatest wonder of myth is that ultimate reality itself can be conveyed in this particular way through it. Hein explains:

The emanations of this higher, essential reality that reach to earth, the very atmosphere of glory which is the inevitable concomitant of all supernatural manifestations of the Real, was what Lewis called myth ... With Lewis, myth was a vehicle by which supernatural reality communicates to man."[601]

It is important to repeat that for Lewis, reality contains far more than what the senses perceive. In fact, what Hein calls "the Real" refers to

---

[598] Stephen Caldecott, "Speaking the Truths Only the Imagination May Grasp: Myth and 'Real Life'" in *The Pilgrim's Guide: C. S. Lewis and the Art of Witness* (Grand Rapids: William B. Eerdmans Publishing Company, 1998), 88.
[599] C. S. Lewis, "On Three Ways of Writing For Children," 53.
[600] C. S. Lewis, "On Three Ways of Writing For Children," 53.
[601] Roland Hein, *Christian Mythmakers*, 219–220.

universals, or archetypes. Lewis believed that people could apprehend these to some degree through myth.

Importantly, we must clarify that for the myth to convey reality successfully in this way, not just any symbols will do. They must be "good metaphors," as we have noted. In agreement with Bevan's notion of the "true metaphor" bearing a direct connection with reality, Lewis writes of a "psycho-physical" parallelism between the metaphor and the thing itself, when one employs the use of a "good metaphor."[602] Edward Uszynski points out both the power and the danger of metaphor, given how it impacts one's view of reality. Responding to Lewis's notion of the "good metaphor," he writes:

> Herein lies both the inherent strength and paradoxical weakness of metaphorical language: it may produce conceptual images and relations for the mind to "see" and understand, but the mind is completely dependent on what may be horribly inaccurate images and semantic connections. In Lewis's view, what choice do we have? Either we translate into metaphor or we speak nonsense, but no middle ground is offered. With the subjectivity of the reader a constant given, the author of metaphors seeks to create images and conceptual tensions that best represent the realities toward which they point.[603]

As we said in the previous chapter, the imaginary world can deceive just as easily as it can illuminate. The result depends largely upon whether one uses good or bad metaphors, fitting or unfitting symbols with the respect to the real things one wants to convey.

Given that metaphors can get adopted into our consciousness and can color how we view the world, a bad metaphor can distort our view of reality just as easily as a good one can illuminate our view of the same. In this sense, the word "imaginative" should not be viewed as inherently positive any more than the world "spiritual" should. Just as there are both good spirits and bad ones, the same is true of the stuff of imagination. Lewis sought to provide his readers with good metaphors and myths that would not obscure, but would rather elucidate the nature of reality. In doing so, he was aiming to set before his readership favorable conditions within which they could hear the gospel and respond appropriately. Uszynski explains further:

---

[602] Edward Uszynski, "C. S. Lewis as Scholar of Metaphor, Narrative, and Myth," in *C. S. Lewis: Life, Works, and Legacy*, Vol. IV, 238.

[603] Edward Uszynski, "C. S. Lewis as Scholar of Metaphor, Narrative, and Myth," in *C. S. Lewis: Life, Works, and Legacy*, Vol. IV, 238-239.

C. S. LEWIS PRE-EVANGELISM FOR A POST-CHRISTIAN WORLD

Obviously, Lewis believed that metaphor would not merely aid the bearer in shaping a "personal" reality, but that one's personal reality could be brought into conformity with "Real Reality" if metaphors were shaped, communicated, and received clearly. The glory of metaphor properly pursued lies in its ability to "innovate," to create new meaning based on uncommon associations ... Because Lewis believes ultimate reality exists objectively outside the individual, deriving its nature and essence from the Christian God, he does not argue in abstractions. Instead, he pursues developing metaphors that come so close to reflecting the actual thing described that the receiver is moved to reconsider previously held beliefs. He asks them to replace one set of imaginings concerning reality for another, to renew their mind with metaphorical images that approximate, whether they acknowledge it or not, "Real Reality."[604]

Fittingly, Lewis defines myth elsewhere as "a real though unfocused gleam of divine truth falling on human imagination."[605]

Having considered the concept of truth related to the imaginative realm to a point, we can look at this still from another angle, which compliments what has already been said. J. R. R. Tolkien, who influenced profoundly Lewis's understanding of the relationship between reality, myth, and truth, helps to shed light these matters. In his published lecture *On Fairy Stories*,[606] Tolkien writes:

Children are capable, of course, of *literary belief*, when the story-maker's art is good enough to produce it. The state of mind has been called "willing suspension of disbelief." But this does not seem to me a good description of what happens. What really happens is that the story-maker proves a successful "sub-creator." He makes a Secondary World which your mind can enter. Inside it, what he relates is "true": it accords with the laws of that world. You therefore believe it, while you are, as it were, inside. The moment disbelief arises, the spell is broken; the magic, or rather art, has failed. You are then out in the Primary World again, looking at the little abortive Secondary World from outside. If

---

[604] Edward Uszynski, "C. S. Lewis as Scholar of Metaphor, Narrative, and Myth," in *C. S. Lewis: Life, Works, and Legacy*, Vol. IV, 239–240.

[605] C. S. Lewis, *Miracles*, 218.

[606] See C. S. Lewis, "On Three Ways of Writing for Children," 52, where Lewis praises Tolkien's essay writing, "I hope everyone has read Tolkien's essay on fairy tales, which is perhaps the most important contribution to the subject that anyone has yet made."

you are obliged, by kindliness or circumstance, to stay, then disbelief must be suspended (or stifled), otherwise listening and looking would become intolerable. But this suspension of disbelief is a substitute for the genuine thing, a subterfuge we use when condescending to games or make-believe, or when trying (more of less willingly) to find what virtue we can in the work of an art that has for us failed.[607]

Tolkien offers some important qualifications for truthfulness within myth. First, he distinguishes the experience of successful sub-creation from the "willing suspension of disbelief." When one suspends disbelief by an act of the will while reading an imaginary tale, one exerts effort to pretend as though the story were true, though always remaining keenly aware that he is reading a mere tale. The thrill of the story, the enchantment that the atmosphere casts on the reader, remains absent during such exertion. One is neither drawn in to, nor delighted by the tale. One remains on the outside, as it were. In the sense in which Tolkien uses the term, Truth eludes the reader during the exercise of willing suspension of disbelief.

On the other hand, when one is drawn into the story, when the enchantment proves effective, and delight takes hold, this experience Tolkien describes as getting "inside" the story.[608] In order to get inside, one must, very simply, enjoy the story. This phenomenon depends upon the successful work of the sub-creator. Only while one engages the story from the inside does the concept of truth pertain in this sense. Thus, truth is that which "accords with the laws of that world" while one is "inside" the imaginary realm.[609] One need not suspend disbelief by an act of the will; rather, the tale simply strikes one as believable on its own terms. If the reader does not enjoy the story, he will not experience truth in the sense that Tolkien has in mind.

In addition to the absence of enjoyment, there is a second way that the tale may fail Tolkien's test of truth. If the same internal coherence present in the real world is lacking in the imaginary realm, the spell will be broken. For instance, if one detects internal incoherence, either in terms of how the plot unfolds or how a certain character behaves, given how he is portrayed elsewhere throughout the tale, it will not prove true for the reader. Thus, in this way also, truth can elude the reader.

It may be that many a story written by modern-day well-meaning Christians fails not for this second reason but for the first. Though the story

---

[607] J. R. R. Tolkien, "On Fairy-Stories" in *Tree and Leaf*, 37.
[608] J. R. R. Tolkien, "On Fairy-Stories" in *Tree and Leaf*, 37.
[609] J. R. R. Tolkien, "On Fairy-Stories" in *Tree and Leaf*, 37.

C. S. LEWIS PRE-EVANGELISM FOR A POST-CHRISTIAN WORLD

passes the test of internal coherence, it fails because it is utterly unenjoyable. Try as we might, we simply cannot "get inside" of it. Willing suspension of disbelief is our only option, and the experience becomes one of painful drudgery as we try in vain to enjoy it. In these instances, the author has failed as sub-creator.[610]

Many of Lewis's readers have found his works to be truthful in the sense in which Tolkien uses the term. His books have passed both tests for these individuals—the test of delight and internal coherence. Though this chapter will not explore Tolkien's concept further beyond this point, the importance of what Tolkien offers along these lines is desperately needed in the present day. The well-meaning Christian who presents a story while lacking the skill, the imaginative ability, and the wisdom to keep much of the Christianity latent though still present, may end up despite his best efforts, serving to make Christianity seem more even unbelievable and perhaps even dull. A deeper consideration of these matters by those more skilled than I in the art of story-telling might prove worthwhile.

WHY MYTHOLOGY IS NOT ESCAPISM BUT ENCHANTMENT

The charge is sometimes raised against imaginative writers such as Lewis and Tolkien that their works, far from helping readers to understand reality more truly and deeply, represents rather an attempt to escape from it, almost like the drug that the addict takes to dull his senses and to mask the painful feelings from which he hopes to hide. Both Lewis and Tolkien saw their works as doing the very opposite. Rather than taking the reader further away from reality, they aimed to bring him closer to it. Enchantment, and not escapism, was their goal.

Lewis took up this charge that has been aimed especially at children's fantasies. He admitted that such stories are often accused of giving young people a "false impression of the world they live in," to which he responds, "I think no literature that children could read gives them less of a false

---

[610] It could be also that the reader simply does not like imaginary stories. Tolkien and Lewis both allow for this possibility. See J. R. R. Tolkien, "On Fairy-Stories" in *Tree and Leaf*, 35, where referring to fairy stories, Tolkien writes, "But in fact only some children, and some adults, have any special taste for them; and when they have it, it is not exclusive, nor even necessarily dominant. It is a taste, too, that would not appear, I think, very early in childhood without artificial stimulus; it is certainly one that does not decrease but increases with age, if it is innate." See also C. S. Lewis, "Sometimes Fairy Stories May Say Best What's To Be Said" in *On Stories: And Other Essays on Literature*, 72, where Lewis admits, "The Fantastic or Mythical is a Mode available at all ages for some readers; for others, at none."

impression."[611] He explains his reason for taking this position a bit later. He argues:

> Do fairy tales teach children to retreat into a world of wish-fulfillment—'fantasy' in the technical psychological sense of the word—instead of facing the problems of the real world? ... Let us again lay the fairy tale side by side with the school story or any other story which is labeled a "Boy's Book" or a "Girl's Book", as distinct from a "Children's Book." There is no doubt that both arouse, and imaginatively satisfy, wishes. We long to go through the looking glass, to reach fairy land. We also long to be the immensely popular and successful schoolboy or schoolgirl, or the lunch boy or girl who discovers the spy's plot or rides the horse that none of the cowboys can manage. But the two longings are very different. The second, especially when directed on something so close to school life, is ravenous and deadly serious. Its fulfillment on the level of imagination is very truth compensatory: we run to it from the disappointments and humiliations of the real world: it sends us back to the real world undivinely discontented ... The other longing, that for fairy land, is very different. In a sense a child does not long for fairy land as a boy longs to be the hero of the first eleven ... It would be truer to say that fairy land arouses a longing for he knows not what. It stirs and troubles him (to his life-long enrichment) with the dim sense of something beyond his reach and, far from dulling or emptying the actual world, gives it a new dimension of depth. He does not despise real woods because he has read of enchanted woods: the reading makes all woods a little enchanted.[612]

In reading Lewis's words in the above-quoted portion, we hear faintly the voice of Tolkien from his important essay, "On Fairy-Stories." Tolkien also dealt with the charge of escapism. He argues:

> Though fairy-stories are of course by no means the only medium of Escape, they are today one of the most obvious and (to some) outrageous forms of "escapist" literature; and it is thus reasonable to attach to a consideration of them some consideration of this term "escape" in criticism generally.[613]

---

[611] C. S. Lewis, "On Three Ways of Writing for Children," 55.
[612] C. S. Lewis, "On Three Ways of Writing for Children," 56–57.
[613] J. R. R. Tolkien, "On Fairy Stories," 60.

C. S. LEWIS PRE-EVANGELISM FOR A POST-CHRISTIAN WORLD

Tolkien proceeds to agree that fairy-stories are a means of escape, but he casts the term "escape" in a positive rather than a negative light. He employs the analogy of a prisoner, asking:

> Why should a man be scorned, if, finding himself in prison, he tries to get out and go home? Or if, when he cannot do so, he thinks about other topics than jailers and prison walls? The world outside has not become less real because the prisoner cannot see it. In using Escape in this way the critics have chosen the wrong word, and, what is more, they are confusing, not always by sincere error, the Escape of the Prisoner with the Flight of the Deserter.[614]

We see that not all form of escape are equal. The sense in which the term is used disapprovingly of myth does not apply to what Lewis and Tolkien had in mind, if we understood their meaning properly.

Tolkien and Lewis both saw the spirit of the age manifested within their culture as a kind of prison, akin to how Plato viewed the prisoners in his cave analogy. Through the influence of naturalism, the world's real nature had been hidden from those inside the prison walls. In thinking about reality through myth and fairy-tale, in the manner discussed in this chapter, man was escaping in the best sense of the term. He was escaping a lie and proceeding ever closer to the truth. Thus, if we think of escape in the negative sense of a deserter, the kind of imaginative fiction that Lewis and Tolkien had in mind was guilty of providing no such thing. If, on the other hand, we have in mind escape in the positive sense, both men would take such a charge as a compliment.

The importance of Lewis's and Tolkien's aims to help readers gain a clearer grasp of reality through the medium of imaginative fiction, rather than trying to help them to escape from it, accords with what was argued in the previous two chapters. First, in chapter two, I argued that reality is sacramental in nature because it is in some sense a copy of a more real reality. The universals can be conceived as being more real in the sense that they have always existed in the mind of God, *and* they are unchanging. Neither of these notions is true of the particulars. Further, because in the imaginative world we find these universals, though reshuffled into new sorts of arrangements, we have access to this more real reality even while we are in "fairy land." Second, in chapter three, I argued that the imaginative realm depends upon the real world for its content. If the content of the real world from which the imaginary one draws bears a

---

[614] J. R. R. Tolkien, "On Fairy Stories," 60–61.

sacramental quality, the imaginative one will as well. The difference is merely that the universals have been attached to something not created in the physical world but to something in the mind of an author, and then put down on the page for us to enjoy. Importantly, we must maintain that the universals are present in each "realm," the real and the imaginary.

It is true that lies can be told about the real world, and in this way people can be led astray from the truth. The same can happen in the imaginative world when beauty is denigrated and ugliness exalted, when true things are presented as false, and when that which is evil is presented as both desirable and satisfying. In this way, an imaginative story would be escapism, in the negative sense of the term, because the real world does not agree with such perversions. We find none of this is Lewis and Tolkien. On the contrary, they aimed to present virtue as truly virtuous, and beautiful and good things as truly and rightfully desirable. Thus, they champion not the attempt to escape reality, but the aim to go "further up and further in."

LEWIS'S SUPPOSAL AS A PRE-EVANGELISTIC STRATEGY

While some people refer to Lewis's imaginative works such as the Chronicles of Narnia and the space trilogy as allegories, Lewis rejected this categorization and insisted that his stories were more accurately labeled "supposals." In a letter written to Mrs. Hook in December of 1958, Lewis clearly stated the distinction between allegory and supposal, affirming that his Narnia stories fall into the latter category. He writes:

> If Aslan represented the immaterial Deity, he would be an allegorical figure. In reality however he is an invention giving an imaginary answer to the question, "What might Christ become like if there really were a world like Narnia and He chose to be incarnate and die and rise again in *that* world as He actually has done in ours?" This is not allegory at all. So in *Perelandra*. This also works out a *supposition.* ("Suppose, even now, in some other planet there were a first couple undergoing the same that Adam and Eve underwent there, but successfully.") Allegory and such supposal differ because they mix the real and the unreal in different ways. Bunyan's picture of Giant Despair does not start from supposal at all. It is not a supposition but a *fact* that despair can capture and imprison a human soul. What is unreal (fictional) is the giant, the castle and the dungeon. The Incarnation of Christ in another world is mere supposal: but *granted* the supposition,

C. S. LEWIS PRE-EVANGELISM FOR A POST-CHRISTIAN WORLD

He would really have been a physical object in that world as He was in Palestine, and His death on the Stone Table would have been a physical event no less than His death on Calvary.[615]

Lewis was not attempting to allegorize in his stories, making his characters stand for something factual in all instances. Rather, he was simply inviting his readers to suppose, along with him, that the truths of reality had been dressed in different clothes. What might those realities look like in another world of a different kind? In understanding Lewis in this way, we should not try to draw a conceptual line from every character or element in his stories to an instantiation in the real world.

STEALING PAST THE WATCHFUL DRAGONS

Lewis cleverly employed the metaphor of "watchful dragons" to represent the cultural paralysis towards Christianity in his day, made up of both false sentiments and tainted reason, caused by the poison of naturalism.[616] Like a dragon lying on guard atop a mountain of treasure, these false sentiments and tainted reason lie atop the average person's will, preventing an opening for Christianity to enter in and to gain an honest hearing. Regarding reason, if Christianity, which claims to be not simply about spiritual matters but about every facet of reality, is in fact true, it follows that it becomes not only truth to think about but truth with which to think about all things. Lewis found it to be such, which is the point he conveyed when comparing Christianity to the sun by whose light he could see all other things. Right reason, therefore, will align with Christianity.

---

[615] C. S. Lewis, *The Collected Letters of C. S. Lewis*, letter dated December 29, 1958.

[616] See C. S. Lewis, "Christian Apologetics," in *God in the Dock*, 93–94, where Lewis describes some of these watchful dragons. He writes, "I find that the uneducated Englishman is an almost total skeptic about History. I had expected he would disbelieve the Gospels because they contain miracles: but he really disbelieves them because they deal with things that happened 2000 years ago ... He has a distrust (very rational in the state of his knowledge) of ancient texts. Thus a man has sometimes said to me, 'These records were written in the days before printing weren't they? and you haven't got the original bit of paper, have you? So what it comes to is that someone wrote something and someone else copied it and someone copied that and so on. Well, by the time it comes to us, it won't be in the least like the original.' This is a difficult objection to deal with because one cannot, there and then, start teaching the whole science of textual criticism ... A sense of sin is almost totally lacking. Our situation is thus very different from that of the Apostles. The Pagans ... to whom they preached were haunted by a sense of guilt and to them the Gospel was, therefore, 'good news'. We address people who have been trained to believe that whatever goes wrong in the world is someone else's fault—the Capitalist', the Government's, the Nazis', the Generals' etc. They approach God Himself as His judges. They want to know, not whether they can be acquitted for sin, but whether He can be acquitted for creating such a world."

Lewis found that the opposite situation had come to pass for most people in his day—tainted reason had largely prevailed.

Regarding the sentiments, given the enormous claims that Christianity makes about all of life and reality, if it is true, apathetic or antagonistic feelings towards it will be the very kinds of feelings one ought *not* to have. Yet again, these are the feelings that Lewis most often encountered in people's hearts towards Christianity in his day. It may in fact be the case that the dragon who guards feelings is a more formidable foe than the one who guards reason. One of the most significant entailments of his argument in *The Abolition of Man* is that if reality is both objective and knowable, then one's feelings towards the various aspects of it can be either fitting or unfitting. Feelings become, much to the chagrin of the present culture, far from neutral. Along these lines, he makes the very reasonable point, "One must keep pointing out that Christianity is a statement, which, if false, is of no importance, and if true, of infinite importance. The one thing it cannot be is moderately important."[617]

Lewis believed that a percentage of the populace would only give Christian truths some level of a hearing if these truths could somehow circumvent their defenses. What he hoped to accomplish by stealing past these watchful dragons was to contribute to forming favorable conditions within which the message of Christianity might gain such a hearing. The formation of such conditions would be part of the result of successful pre-evangelism. He argues:

> I do not in the least agree with those who therefore conclude that the spread of an intellectual (and imaginative) climate favourable to Christianity is useless. You do not prove munition workers useless by showing that they cannot themselves win battles, however proper this reminder would be if they attempted to claim the honor due to fighting men. If the intellectual climate is such that, when a man comes to the crisis at which he must either accept or reject Christ, his reason and imagination are not on the wrong side, then his conflict will be feud out under favourable conditions. Those who help to produce and spread such climate are therefore doing useful work.[618]

Lewis wrote further of this strategy in his essay entitled "Sometimes Fairy Stories May Say Best What's To Be Said." He explains:

---

[617] C. S. Lewis, "Christian Apologetics," in *God in the Dock*, 102.
[618] C. S. Lewis, "The Decline of Religion," in *God in the Dock*, 241.

C. S. LEWIS PRE-EVANGELISM FOR A POST-CHRISTIAN WORLD

> I wrote fairy tales because the fairy tale seemed the ideal Form for the stuff I had to say ... I thought I saw how stories of this kind could steal past a certain inhibition which had paralysed much of my own religion in childhood. Why did one find it so hard to feel as one was told one ought to feel about God or about the sufferings of Christ? I thought the chief reason was that one was told on ought to. An obligation to feel can freeze feelings. And reverence itself did harm. The whole subject was associated with lowered voices; almost as if it were something medical. But supposing that by casting all these things into an imaginary world, stripping them of their stained-glass and Sunday school associations, one could make them for the first time appear in their real potency? Could one not thus steal past those watchful dragons? I thought one could.[619]

J. T. Sellars writes further along these lines:

> Lewis recognized that how one viewed the world depended upon the philosophy one brought to bear upon it. Lewis argued that the habituation of children in the right type of stories might do much to bring about the acceptance of the divine and miraculous. In Lewis' Narnia tales and his Space Trilogy he attempted to bring a sense of the *possibility* and the reality of the supernatural into the lives of his readers. There is a chance to "steal past the watchful dragons" of our *a priori* assumptions in story. For one, our suspension of disbelief may be in effect when we are reading. We might be more willing to accept something as true in a story if it is coherent, consistent, and flows naturally from the narrative. If we are educated in and experience the possibility of such acts and events (e.g., by the reading and rereading of fairy stories in our youth to our adulthood), the divine and miraculous may appear possible.[620]

Thus, one of the facets of favorable conditions for the Christian message is to help people, especially children from a young age, to see the supernatural view as possible. This can be achieved to some degree through imaginative fiction, when Christian truths are conveyed while being kept at the same time in disguise.

---

[619] C. S. Lewis, "Sometimes Fairy Stories May Say Best What's To Be Said," in *On Stories*, 70.

[620] J. T. Sellars, *Reasoning Beyond Reason: Imagination as a Theological Source in the Work of C. S. Lewis*, 61–62.

One must not misunderstand Lewis's stealing past the watchful dragons as an attempt at deceptive manipulation any more than the prophet Nathan attempted the same in his confronting of David regarding his sin with Bathsheba against her husband Uriah. Like the prophet, Lewis simply understood that some truths are better received when one does not realize at first that one's own worldview or actions are being challenged. In removing Christian truths from their "Sunday school associations," Lewis was able to pre-evangelize effectively by presenting ideas to his hearers in the most palatable of ways. Once the veil is removed and the hearer realizes that he must face truly his own assumptions and worldview commitments, he will have to reckon that he has already found persuasive and perhaps even desirable truths that confront him in the end.

EXAMPLES OF PRE-EVANGELISM IN LEWIS'S IMAGINATIVE WORKS

It will be helpful for us now to examine examples of how Lewis pre-evangelized his readership through his works of imaginative fiction. His pre-evangelistic strategy through this medium can be summed up as follows: Helping people to taste in order that they might know. Or, we might put it this way: Helping people to experience reality (dressed in imaginative fiction) so that they might come to know truth in the real world of daily experience. Lewis adopted this strategy largely in light of his cultural context characterized by an anti-Christian posture that he discerned. He recognized that a full-frontal presentation of explicit Christian truths would receive minimal, if any, serious consideration among some people. Thus, he sought for a "back door" to gain entry into peoples' minds. Phillip Harrold explains:

> Given the pervasive spiritual alienation of his day and, indeed, of his own early life, Lewis advised an indirect or 'latent' approach to evangelism that nurtured, through the poetic and mythic imaginations, a disposition to *hear* (preevangelism) then *believe* (preapologetics) the Gospel ... Lewis hoped his fantasy writing would, at the least, awaken deep longings for transcendence.[621]

This section will examine Lewis's attempts to "awaken deep longings for transcendence" throughout his space trilogy and Narnia stories. Malcolm Guite highlights these same sources from Lewis, adding *Till We Have Faces*, in his essay entitled "Telling the Truth Through Imaginative

---

[621] Philip Harrold, "C. S. Lewis's Incarnational Aesthetics and Today's Emerging Imagination," in *C. S. Lewis: Life, Works, and Legacy*, 185.

C. S. LEWIS PRE-EVANGELISM FOR A POST-CHRISTIAN WORLD

Fiction." He inks Lewis's aims with Coleridge's and Wordsworth's. Guite writes:

[P]erhaps the most helpful mapping of the terrain Lewis was to body forth and explore in books like the Ransom Trilogy and the Chronicles of Narnia and *Till We Have Faces* is to be found in the programme Wordsworth and Coleridge set themselves at the beginning of the Romantic movement.[622]

Following on the heels of these two Romantic poets, Lewis attempted to "excite a feeling analogous to the supernatural" by "awakening the mind's attention" and "directing it to the loveliness and the wonders of the world before us" ... This power of re-enchantment, of removing the "film of familiarity" and "awakening the mind's attention" was something Lewis was striving for in his writing.[623]

---

[622] Malcolm Guite, "Telling the Truth Through Imaginative Fiction: C. S. Lewis on the Reconciliation of Athene and Demeter," in *C. S. Lewis at Poets' Corner* (Eugene: Wifp and Stock Publishers, 2016), 20.

[623] Malcolm Guite, "Telling the Truth Through Imaginative Fiction," 21. Guite is quoting from Coleridge's *Biographe Literaria*, which he provides on p. 20: "In this idea originated the plan of the lyrical ballads in which it was agreed that my endeavors should be directed to persons and characters supernatural, or at least romantic; yet so as to transfer from our inward nature a human interest and a semblance of truth sufficient to procure for the shadows of imagination that willing suspension of disbelief for the moment, which constitutes poetic faith. Mr. Wordwsorth, on the other hand, was to propose to himself as his object, to give the charm of novelty to things of every day, and to excite a feeling analogous to the supernatural by awakening the mind's attention from the lethargy of custom, and directing it to the loveliness and the wonders of the world before us; an inexhaustible treasure, but for which, in consequence of the film of familiarity and selfish solicitude, we have eyes, yet see not, ears that hear not, and hearts that neither feel nor understand." It is important to note, in light of the fact that Guite does not offer a point of needed nuance, that Lewis sides more with Tolkien than with Coleridge as it pertains to the notion of one's "willing suspension of disbelief." Lewis was not asking him readers to suspend disbelief via an act of the will. If one should have to do that, the imaginative tale or the poem is not achieving its intended aim of enchantment. See J. R. R. Tolkien, "On Fairy-Stories," in *Tree and Leaf* (London: HarperCollins, 2001), 37, where Tolkien argues, "Children are capable, of course, of *literary belief*, when the story-maker's art is good enough to produce it. The state of mind has been called 'willing suspension of disbelief'. But this does not seem to me a good description of what happens. What really happens is that the story-maker proves a successful 'sub-creator.' He makes a Secondary World which you mind can enter. Inside it, what he relates is 'true': it accords with the laws of that world. You therefore believe it, while you are, as it were, inside. The moment disbelief arises, the spell is broken; the magic, or rather art, has failed. You are then out in the Primary World again, looking at the little abortive Secondary World from outside. If you are obliged, by kindliness or circumstance, to stay, then disbelief must be suspended (or stifled), otherwise listening and looking would become intolerable. But this suspension of disbelief is a substitute for the genuine thing, a subterfuge we use when condescending to games or make-believe, or

Brian M. Williams

In this section, I will give more treatment to the space trilogy than to the Chronicles of Narnia simply because the former tends to be less familiar to readers. Therefore, conveying the sense of Lewis's pre-evangelistic strategy in these books calls for a more careful and slow walkthrough than his Chronicles of Narnia, as we are likely starting from scratch in terms of many readers' acquaintance with the space trilogy.

As we will see, Lewis's stories are filled with truths that combat familiar falsehoods with which Lewis was facing in his day. Also, because morality, as he makes clear in *Mere Christianity*, *The Abolition of Man*, and *The Problem of Pain*, had come under attack, he presents moral goodness as an objective reality throughout his books. Further, Lewis sought to present beauty in its true light, often allowing the atmosphere or the ethos of his stories to work upon his readers. Finally, the sense of the numinous, which intrigued him throughout his life, haunts his imaginative fiction as a pervasive presence sometimes merely hinted at, and other times showing up in potent manifestations.

Rather than presenting these examples grouped together in categorical sections, we will walk through the stories in their narrative flow. The above qualities are highlighted as we make our way along. The reason for organizing this treatment this way is so that we do not see merely the ideas themselves, but hopefully we gain some sense of the ethos and flow of the stories that, in Lewis's mind, were equally if not more important than the mere ideas. With this explanation set forth, let us turn now to Lewis's space trilogy.

The Space Trilogy

Lewis publishes the first book in his space trilogy in 1938 and the final one in 1945. His attempt to pre-evangelize his readership through these stories is carried out through the use of the literary tools that were examined in detail in the previous chapter - symbol, metaphor, and even mythology. Along these lines, Chad Walsh writes:

> *Out of the Silent Planet*, *Peralandra*, and *That Hideous Strength* were issued as "novels," but in reality they are three installments of one myth ... The critics have treated the three novels all too casually. They cannot be judged as novels: they are a vast myth. Lewis has baptized the solar system and filled it with the radiant presence of Maleldil. I shall not be so bold as to apply to Lewis the words he used to characterize Macdonald ... but I venture

---

when trying (more or less willingly) to find what virtue we can in the work of an art that has for us failed."

C. S. LEWIS PRE-EVANGELISM FOR A POST-CHRISTIAN WORLD

the prophecy that the interplanetary trilogy will be one of the few myths of the century that will firmly grip the imagination of future writers and provide them with a treasure trove of symbols.[624]

Again, if Bevan and Barfield, and Lewis who stands in agreement with them, are correct in holding that these literary tools are in some way connected ontologically with the things in the real world from which they borrow or to which they point, it follows that the same "sacramental" pull that arrests a person who stands in the presence of truth, beauty, and goodness in the real world might do the same in Lewis's imaginative tales. Further, theological truths that would otherwise be rejected right out of the gate might slip past the defenses of the reader if sufficiently cloaked in myth and presented through conversations between the characters. The degree to which these effects are possible, depends in part of course, on how successfully Lewis has accomplished his task as an author.

Out of the Silent Planet

In a letter written on December 28, 1938 from Lewis to his friend Roger Lancelyn Green, he expressed his motivation for writing his space trilogy. He writes, "I like the whole interplanetary idea as a *mythology* and simply wished to conquer by my own (Christian) point of view what has always hitherto been used by the opposite side."[625] By the "opposite side," Lewis was likely referring to Jules Verne, H. G. Wells, J. B. S. Haldane, Olaf Stapledon, and the like.[626] He lamented the fact that science fiction stories had been employed largely in the service of an anti-Christian worldview. He sought to adopt the genre to tell stories consistent with a Christian view of reality.[627]

---

[624] Chad Walsh, *C. S. Lewis: Apostle to the Skeptics* (Eugene: Wipf & Stock, 1949), 39, 47.

[625] C. S. Lewis, *The Collected Letters of C. S. Lewis*, Vol. II, 236–237.

[626] Jules Verne is perhaps best known for his fifty-four novels which make up the *Voyages Extraordinaires*. Most recognizable within this set to most readers are the stories *Twenty Thousand Leagues Under the Sea* and *Journey to the Center of the Earth*. Notable novels from H. G. Wells are *The Invisible Man, The War of the Worlds, The Island of Doctor Moreau*, and *The First Men in the Moon*. J. B. S. Haldane wrote *Possible Worlds and Other Essays*. Lewis takes the views expressed in this book and applies them to the villain Weston in his space trilogy. Olaf Stapledon wrote the book *Last and First Men*, within which the heroes are a barbaric people who destroy those creatures living on Mars and Venus.

[627] By "Christian view of reality," it will be apparent that the author does not mean that all aspects are to be believed as pertaining to the real world. Lewis was not suggesting, for instance, that alien life existed on other planets, and that those creatures remained innocent and therefore lacking the need of a redeemer. Much that comes through his trilogy is fantasy,

Brian M. Williams

The first book in the trilogy is *Out of the Silent Planet*. It is the story of Dr. Elwin Ransom, a Cambridge University philologist who has set out on a walking tour. After being drugged, he awakens to discover that he has been abducted by two men, Dick Devine and Dr. Weston. These men have built a spaceship to travel to the planet Malacandra in order to gain riches and in the process, present Ransom as a human sacrifice. One of the first hints of Lewis's medieval view through which he aims to present creation to his readers, not as a sterile "nature" of resources to be mined and crafted for the perpetuation of the species, but as an enchanted reality full of wonder, beauty, and mystery, comes while Ransom peers out of one of the portholes while on the way to Malacandra. The narrator comments on Ransom's behalf:

> There was an endless night on one side of the ship and an endless day on the other: Each was marvelous and moved from the one to the other at his will, delighted ... There were planets of unbelievable majesty, and constellations undreamed of: there were celestial sapphires, rubies, emeralds and pinpricks of burning gold ... he found it night by night more difficult to disbelieve in the old astrology: he almost felt, wholly he imagined, "sweet influence" pouring or even stabbing into his surrendered body ... "Space" seemed a blasphemous libel for this empyrean ocean of radiance in which they swam. He could not call it 'dead'; he felt life pouring into him from it every moment. How indeed should it be otherwise, since out of this ocean the worlds and all their life had come? He had thought it barren: he saw now that it was the womb of worlds, whose blazing and innumerable offspring looked down nightly even upon the earth with so many eyes—and here, with how many more! No: space was the wrong name. Older thinkers had been wiser when they named it simply the heavens—the heavens which declared the glory ...[628]

We recall that Lewis believed that atmosphere profoundly influences the overall ethos of a story and the corresponding reaction the reader will likely have to it.[629] To draw on a point made in the previous chapter

---

but the basic structure is consistent with Christianity. For instance, Lewis's world is a created one that is populated with angelic beings both good and evil. Humans are not innocent victims; rather, they are fallen and therefore part of the problem. An all-knowing, all-powerful and loving God reigns sovereignly. One finds even a redemption story of God's son come to die for fallen humans. Further, philosophical views that Lewis holds to be inconsistent with humanity's higher purpose of knowing and loving God are shown in their diabolical light.

[628] C. S. Lewis, *Out of the Silent Planet*, 33–34.

[629] See Sarah Clarkson, "The Best Tale Lewis Ever Told," in *C. S. Lewis at Poets' Corner*, edited by Michael Ward and Peter S. Williams (Eugene: Wipf and Stock Publishers, 2016), 104,

C. S. LEWIS PRE-EVANGELISM FOR A POST-CHRISTIAN WORLD

regarding the sacramental nature of *both* reality *and* the imaginative realm, although Lewis was first enchanted by the real Castlereagh Hills of Ireland long before he was by the imaginary ones of Nordic mythology, he found both to be legitimate mediums for the "real joy." Whatever criticisms one might raise against Lewis's space trilogy, one cannot legitimately charge his stories with the absence of atmosphere. Both the heavens and the planet Malacandra are beautiful, mysterious, and delightful.[630]

The narrator comments, referring to Ransom, "But something he learned. Before anything else, he learned that Malacandra was beautiful; and he even reflected how odd it was that this possibility had never entered into his speculations about it."[631] The water on Malacandra "was not merely blue in certain lights like terrestrial water but 'really' blue."[632] Ransom notices "the pinkish-white vegetation [that] went down to the very brink—there was a bubbling and sparkling which suggested effervescence."[633] He sees "rose-colored cloud-like" shapes floating along in the sky, a "purple mass ... like a clump of organ pipes," and "bright, still, sparkling unintelligible landscape—with needling shapes of pale green, thousands of feet high, with sheets of dazzling blue soda-water, and acres of rose-red soapsuds."[634] He later sees mountains that, "in spite of their improbable shape, were mountains; and with that discovery, the mere oddity of the prospect was swallowed up in the fantastic sublime."[635]

---

where she writes, "In his essay 'On Stories,' Lewis wrote of the 'atmosphere' imbuing his favorite 'romances.' Some tales were steeped in a certain air beyond the cycle of mere events, an air that struck the reader with a sense of otherness, a sense of something beyond a plotted sequence. Whether the long, awful dark of 'Outer Space,' or the chill, pure sky of Northern myths, the greatest stories let us enter, for a moment, a 'sheer state of being' that stirs our souls to life with hunger, awe, or wonder."

[630] Lewis was under no illusion that all readers would find similar enchantment in his story, let alone enjoy it. See C. S. Lewis, *The Collected Letters of C. S. Lewis*, Vol. II, 242, wherein admits in a letter written on January 11, 1939 to A. K. Hamilton Jenkin, "If you'd care for a copy of my story (a journey to Mars) let me know and I'll send you one. But I rather think it is not a genre you care for; and I know that if people don't like stories of that kind they usually dislike them very much indeed. These sharp *frontiers* of taste are a very interesting literary fact which I've never seen discussed by any critic, and which are far more important in dividing readers than any of the *formal* divisions, even that of verse and prose. 'Do you like stories about other planet - or hunting stories - or stories of the supernatural - or historical novels?' - surely these are questions which elicit an unalterable Yes or No from the very depth of a reader's heart."

[631] C. S. Lewis, *Out of the Silent Planet*, 43–44.
[632] C. S. Lewis, *Out of the Silent Planet*, 44.
[633] C. S. Lewis, *Out of the Silent Planet*, 45.
[634] C. S. Lewis, *Out of the Silent Planet*, 45–46.
[635] C. S. Lewis, *Out of the Silent Planet*, 54.

Brian M. Williams

One might think of Lewis's argument for objective values in *The Abolition of Man* when reading these descriptions. It would be a monumental stretch indeed to take these descriptions to not pertain to the heavens or to Malacandra but merely to the characters' inner feelings. Lewis would have nothing of this sort in his stories. When Malacandra is called beautiful and the mountains sublime, he means that the reader receives real information about these imaginary locales and very little to perhaps nothing of the characters' inner opinions. These are real universals peeking through the imaginative stage set.

In addition to atmosphere, Lewis presents truth about the fallen condition of humanity, the nature of God with respect to the divine persons, and the reality of angelic beings both good and evil. Of course, all of this remains disguised because Lewis chooses words that would not be associated with the common Christian lingo, and he puts these statements into the mouths of fictional characters wrapped up in an invented plot. Through such disguises, he is able to infiltrate the imaginations of his readers with inklings of facts about the real world.

Regarding humanity's fallen condition, Lewis found himself in a culture that had rejected this notion outright. The suggestion that humanity stands before a divine being with real moral guilt rang hollow in the ears of most in Lewis's day. Consequently, the felt reality of guilt and the attending sense of shame was almost entirely absent from the modern consciousness into which he was hoping to exert some measure of influence. Lewis took up this argument persuasively and in a largely rational way in the first part of his wartime broadcasts which would become the book *Mere Christianity*. He believed deeply that unless the belief in real moral guilt could be recaptured, Christianity would have nothing to say, in the same way that a doctor has nothing to say to a man who is perfectly well, or who at least thinks himself perfectly well.

In his recently rediscovered article "A Christmas Sermon for Pagans," Lewis described this unfortunate situation. He contrasted the Pagan, who was a "pre-Christian" from the modern individual who is a "post-Christian." Of the Pagan, Lewis writes:

> [H]e believed in what we now call "Objective" Right or Wrong. That is, he thought the distinction between pious and impious acts was something which existed independently of human opinions: something like the multiplication table which Man had not invented but had found to be true and which (like the multiplication table) he had better take notice of. And this leads us to the third great difference between a Pagan and a post-Christian man. Believing in a real Right and Wrong means finding

out that you are not very good ... Hence a Pagan, though in many ways merrier than a modern, had a deep sadness. When he asked himself what was wrong with the world he did not immediately reply, 'the social system," or "our allies," or "education." It occurred to him that he himself might be one of the things that was wrong with the world ... Now the post-Christian view ... is quite different ... There is no objective Right or Wrong: each race or class can invent its own code of "ideology" just as it pleases ... Now if the post-Christian view is the correct one, then we have indeed waked from a nightmare. The old fear, the old reverence, the old restraints—how delightful to have waked up into freedom, to be responsible to no one, to be utterly and absolutely our own masters![636]

Lewis ends this section on a note of sarcastic optimism. The important distinction he makes is that older civilizations believed in moral objectivity, and in measuring their own behavior against this objective standard, they concluded that they were guilty before the gods. This belief was accompanied by fitting feelings of shame and fear. Because these beliefs and attendant feelings are nearly totally absent in the consciousness of modern man, and because Christianity is the antidote to the problem of real moral guilt before God, Lewis knew that if modern man was to give Christianity any level of hearing, he would have to be reintroduced to this notion and persuaded of its truth.

In *Out of the Silent Planet*, he reintroduces the story of the fall of humanity in a conversation between Ransom and the seal-like creature named Hyoi, one of the creatures called the hrossa. Hyoi befriends Ransom him early in the story. In one tragic scene, Weston and Divine, Ransom's former captors, shoot and kill Hyoi from a hidden position in the woods. While Hyoi lies wounded in Ransom's arms, with blood sputtering from his mouth and eyes becoming dull, Ransom, grief-stricken and gripped by guilt, confesses to his dying friend:

Hyoi, it is through me that this has happened. It is the other *humans* who have hit you, the bent two that brought me to Malacandra. They can throw death at a distance with a thing they have made. I should have told you. We are all a bent race. We have come here to bring evil on Malacandra ... Hyoi ...[637]

---

[636] C. S. Lewis, "A Christmas Sermon for Pagans," 47–48.
[637] C. S. Lewis, *Out of the Silent Planet*, 82.

Through these final words spoken from Ransom to Hyoi, the reader learns that the human race in Lewis's imaginative tale are all "bent." This was Lewis's way of acquainting his readers with the notion of sin and humanity's fall without using these terms.

Lewis also smuggled into his story theology proper, or theology about God. Hnohra, another one of the hrossa, begins teaching Ransom the language. Through their conversation, Ransom learns of a person named "Maleldil" whom he discovers is both creator and ruler of the world, and lives with "the Old One."[638] When Ransom asks who the Old One is and where he lives, Hnohra responds, "He is not that sort ... that he has to live anywhere."[639] Lewis writes further, "It became plain that Maleldil was a spirit without body, parts or passions."[640]

For one who knows his theology, these divine persons' identity of whom Hnohra speaks becomes clear. Rather than using the title "God the Father," Lewis chooses "the Old One," and in the place of "Christ," or "the second Person of the Trinity," or even "Jesus," Lewis employs the name "Maleldil." Moreover, he affirms Maleldil's non-corporeality, simplicity, and impassibility, classic doctrines that have been long-held by Christians.[641] As impressed as the reader might be when he encounters the "eldils," the mysterious translucent intelligences who populate the heavens and the planets, and especially the "Oyarsa," the ruling intelligences who reign over the planets, he learns that Maleldil's greatness far surpasses theirs.

Ransom inquires of Hyoi in one scene about the nature of the eldila. He recounts, "As we came out today I passed a child who said she was talking to an *eldil*, but I could see nothing."[642] Hyoi then explains:

> One can see by looking at your eyes ... that they are different from ours. But *eldila* are hard to see. They are not like us. Light goes through them. You must be looking at the right place and the right time; and that is not likely to come about unless the *eldil* wishes to be seen. Sometimes you can mistake them for a sunbeam or even a moving of the leaves; but when you look

---

[638] C. S. Lewis, *Out of the Silent Planet*, 69.
[639] C. S. Lewis, *Out of the Silent Planet*, 69.
[640] C. S. Lewis, *Out of the Silent Planet*, 69.
[641] Whether one agrees with the doctrines of divine simplicity and impassibility, Lewis is simply adopting classic views long-held by Christians and writing them into his story. It is beyond the scope of this essay to evaluate these doctrines; rather, the point is to show how Lewis is sneaking in theology under cover of his mythology.
[642] C. S. Lewis, *Out of the Silent Planet*, 77.

C. S. LEWIS PRE-EVANGELISM FOR A POST-CHRISTIAN WORLD

again you see that it was an *eldil* and that it is gone. But whether your eyes can ever see them now I do not know.[643]

Soon after this conversation, Ransom has his first encounter with an eldil. In this scene, Lewis attempts to create a sense of the numinous, which is one of the most significant pre-evangelistic qualities that one finds throughout his stories.[644] Ransom is out to sea with the hunting party of the hrossa, in search of the revered creature called a *hnakra*. While they are waiting for the *hnakra* to emerge, all moving quietly in eager anticipation, Hyoi says softly to Ransom, "There is an *eldil* coming to us over the water." Lewis describes the experience of Ransom thus:

Ransom could see nothing—or nothing that he could distinguish from imagination and the dance of sunlight on the lake. A moment later Hyoi spoke again, but not to him. "What is it, sky-born?" What happened next was the most uncanny experience Ransom had yet had on Malacandra. He heard the voice. It seemed to come out of the air, about a yard above his head, and it was almost an octave higher than the *hross's*— higher even that his own ... "It is the Man with you, Hyoi," said the voice. "He ought not to be there. He ought to be going to Oyarsa."[645]

Later in the story, as Ransom is taken to meet the Oyarsa of Malacandra, he comes to the area known as Meldilorn. Lewis's description of this enchanted place upon Ransom's arrival is striking. He writes:

He did not know what he had expected ... he had not looked for anything quite so classic, so virginal, as this bright grove—

---

[643] C. S. Lewis, *Out of the Silent Planet*, 77.

[644] See C. S. Lewis, *The Problem of Pain*, 5–6, where Lewis explains the term "numinous," writing, "Those who have not met with this term may be introduced to it by the following device. Suppose you were told there was a tiger in the next room: you would know that you were in danger and would probably feel fear. But if you were told 'There is a ghost in the next room', and believed it, you would feel, indeed, what is often called fear, but of a different kind. It would not be based on the knowledge of danger, for no one is primarily afraid of what a ghost may do to him, but of the mere fact that it is a ghost. It is 'uncanny' rather than dangerous, and the special kind of fear it excites may be called Dread. With the Uncanny one has reached the fringes of the Numinous. Now suppose that you were told simply 'There is a mighty spirit in the room', and believed it. Your feelings would then be even less like the mere fear of danger: but the disturbance would be profound. You would feel wonder and a certain shrinking—a sense of inadequacy to cope with such a visitant and of prostration before it—an emotion which might be expressed in Shakespeare's words 'Under it my genius is rebuked'. This feeling may be described as awe, and the object which excites it as the *Numinous*." He later refers to the feeling as "numinous awe," p. 9.

[645] C. S. Lewis, *Out of the Silent Planet*, 80.

lying so still, so secret, in its colored valley, soaring with inimitable grace so many hundred feet into the wintry sunlight. At every step of his descent the comparative warmth of the valley came up to him more deliciously. He looked above—the sky was turning to a paler blue. He looked below—and sweet and faint the thin fragrance of the giant blooms came up to him ... All was solitude; but as he gazed upon it he seemed to hear, against the background of morning silence, a faint, continual agitation of silvery sound—hardly a sound at all, if you attended to it, and yet impossible to ignore. "The island is full of *eldila*," said the *hross* in a hushed voice ... The sense of awe which was increasing upon him deterred him from approaching the crown of the hill, the grove and the avenue of standing stones ... He said to himself that he was having a look at the island, but his feeling was rather that the island was having a look at him. This was greatly increased by a discovery he had made after he had been walking for about an hour, and which he ever afterwards found great difficulty in describing. In the most abstract terms it might be summed up by saying that the surface of the island was subject to tiny variations of light and shade which no change in the sky accounted for. If the air had not been calm and the ground-weed too short and firm to move in the wind, he would have said that a faint breeze was playing with it, and working such slight alterations in the shading as it does in a corn-field on the Earth. Like the silvery noises in the air, these footsteps of light were shy of observation ... He had no doubt that he was "seeing"—as much as he ever would see—the *eldila*.[646]

When the Oyarsa meets ransom at last, the sense of numinous awe is heightened. Lewis describes the meeting thus:

Without being told, he knew that it was his business to go up to the crown of the island and the grove. As he approached them, he saw with a certain sinking of heart that the monolithic avenue was full of Malacandrian creatures, and all silent. They were in two lines, one on each side, and all squatting or sitting in the various fashions suitable to their anatomies. He walked on slowly ... and ran the gauntlet of all this inhuman and unblinking eyes. When he had come to the very summit, he stopped ... All the creatures were looking at him and there was no noise anywhere. He perceived, gradually, that the place was full of *eldila*. The lights or suggestions of light, which yesterday had been scattered

---

[646] C. S. Lewis, *Out of the Silent Planet*, 105, 108–109.

C. S. LEWIS PRE-EVANGELISM FOR A POST-CHRISTIAN WORLD

over the island, were now all congregated in this one spot, and were all stationary or very faintly moving ... afterwards ... there was a noise of movement. Every visible creature in the grove had risen to its feet and was standing, more hushed than ever, with its head bowed; and Ransom saw (if it could be called seeing) that Oyarsa was coming up between the long lines of sculptured stones. Partly he knew from the faces of the Malacandrians as their lord passed them ... Oyarsa passed between his subjects and drew near and came to rest, not ten yards away from Ransom in the centre of Meldilorn. Ransom felt a tingling of his blood and a pricking on his fingers as if lightning were near him; and his heart and body seemed to him to be made of water. Oyarsa spoke.[647]

A conversation between Ransom and Oyarsa ensues, in which Oyarsa tells him of how his planet Thulcandra, which is earth, became "silent" and of how its Oyarsa became "bent." Through his explanation, the reader is offered a mythological retelling of the fall of Satan, cleverly disguised to the degree that only two out of sixty reviewers of Lewis's book discerned that the "Bent One" referred to anything beyond Lewis's own invention. Oyarsa explains to Ransom:

"Thulcandra is the world we do not know. It alone is outside of heaven, and no message comes from it." Ransom was silent, but Oyarsa answered his unspoken questions. "It was not always so. Once we knew the Oyarsa of your world—he was brighter and greater than I—and then we did not call it Thulcandra. It is the longest of all stories and the bitterest. He became bent. That was before any life came on your world. Those were the Bent Years of which we still speak in the heavens, when he was not yet bound to Thulcandra but free like us ... There was great war, and we drove him back out of the heavens and bound him in the air of his own world as Maleldil taught us. There doubtless he lies to this hour, and we know no more of that planet: it is silent. We think that Maleldil would not give it up utterly to the Bent One, and there are stories among us that He has taken strange counsel and dared terrible things, wrestling with the Bent One in

---

[647] C. S. Lewis, *Out of the Silent Planet*, 117–118.

Thulcandra. But of this we know less than you; it is a thing we desire to look into."[648]

Along with the story of the Bent One, Oyarsa hints of Maleldil's incarnation on the planet Thulcandra. Maleldil's taking on human flesh and his death on behalf of bent humanity is the terrible thing he dared in his wrestling with the Bent One to which Oyarsa alludes. A little later in the story, Ransom's captors and the murderers of the hross named Hyoi are brought to Oyarsa. When he speaks to them, though they hear his voice, they do not believe it is a real non-corporeal person speaking to them; rather, they suppose it is a loudspeaker or some trick of ventriloquism.[649]

Nevertheless, Oyarsa tells them of the Bent One's true plans for humanity in contrast to Maleldil's. Through this explanation, Lewis is drawing on the true nature of Satan's aims versus Christ's. Oyarsa says, "The weakest of my people do not fear death. It is the Bent One, the lord of your world, who wastes your lives and befouls them with flying from what you know will overtake you in the end. If you were subjects of Maleldil you would have peace."[650]

The story ends with Oyarsa mercifully allowing the three men to return to Thulcandra, warning Ransom of their plans for evil before allowing them to depart and also promising their protection in his impending war with them and the forces behind them. After this, Lewis writes himself into his story, giving a fictional account of his correspondence with Dr. Ransom. It is in the final two chapters that Lewis expresses explicitly his pre-evangelistic strategy through this story. He writes:

---

[648] C. S. Lewis, *Out of the Silent Planet*, 119–120. This notion of the Oyarsa desiring to look into things regarding Maleldil's dealings with Thulcandra is repeated again later in the conversation. See C. S. Lewis, *Out of the Silent Planet*, 121, where Oyarsa says, "Tow things I wanted to ask of your race. First I must know why you come here—so much is my duty to my world. And secondly I wish to hear of Thulcandra and of Maleldil's strange wars there with the Bent One; for that, as I have said, is a thing we desire to look into." This reminds one of what Peter writes in 1 Peter 1:10-12: "Concerning this salvation, the prophets who prophesied about eh grace that was to be yours searched and inquired carefully, inquiring what person or time the Spirit of Christ in them was indicating when he predicted the sufferings of Christ and the subsequent glories. It was revealed to them that they were serving not themselves but you, in the things that have not been announced to you through those who preached the good news to you by the Holy Spirit sent from heaven, things into which angels long to look."

[649] See C. S. Lewis, *Out of the Silent Planet*, 125. "'God!' exclaimed Devine in English. 'Don't tell me they've got a loud-speaker.' 'Ventriloquism,' replied Weston in a husky whisper. 'Quite common among savages.'"

[650] C. S. Lewis, *Out of the Silent Planet*, 138–139.

C. S. LEWIS PRE-EVANGELISM FOR A POST-CHRISTIAN WORLD

It was Dr. Ransom who first saw that our only chance was to publish in the form of *fiction* what would certainly not be listened to as fact. He even thought—greatly overrating my literary powers—that this might have the incidental advantage of reaching a wider public, and that, certainly, it would reach a great many people sooner than "Weston." To my objection that if accepted as fiction it would for that very reason be regarded as false, he replied that there would be indications enough in the narrative for the few readers—the very few—who at *present* were prepared to go further into the matter. "And they," he said, "will easily found out you, or me, and will easily identify Weston. Anyway," he continued, "what we need for the moment is not so much a body of belief as a body of people familiarized with certain ideas. If we could even effect in one per cent of our readers a change-over from the conception of Space to the conception of Heaven, we should have made a beginning."[651]

Perelandra

The second book in Lewis's space trilogy is *Perelandra*. Walter Hooper once commented to Lewis that of all his books, he thought that *Perelandra* was his best, with which Lewis agreed.[652] Several factors contribute to the excellence of Lewis's second volume. The poetic and beautiful quality of the writing itself and the sublimity of much of the descriptive imagery stand unmistakably above his other works of fiction. This may be explained, in part, by the fact that Lewis began penning the first words to this story in poetic form, perhaps intending to write the whole of it at one time as a poem.[653] This story excels the previous one's aesthetic value because Lewis

---

[651] C. S. Lewis, *Out of the Silent Planet*, 152.

[652] See *Socrates in the City* interview with Eric Metaxas and Walter Hooper on December 4, 2015. Accessed on June 13, 2019 at https://www.youtube.com/watch?v=slMLk4dhh0M. See also Walter Hooper, *C. S. Lewis: Companion & Guide*, 221, where Hooper writes of "*Perelandra*, which is arguably Lewis's most perfect book."

[653] See Walter Hooper, *C. S. Lewis: Companion & Guide*, 220, where Hooper cites Lewis's poem. He writes, "We don't know how long this 'mental picture' had been in Lewis's mind before he wrote this undated fragment of verse, but it was almost certainly the first thing he put on paper about *Perelandra*:
'The floating islands, the flat golden sky
At noon, the peacock sunset: tepid waves
With the land slider over them like a skin:
The alien Eve, green-bodied, stepping forth
To meet my hero from her forest home,
Proud, courteous, unafraid; no thought infirm

aims to describe an unspoiled paradisal planet where the "gods" manifest themselves in visible form to a degree far beyond their prior luminous yet shapeless manifestations in *Out of the Silent Planet*. It would be difficult to improve upon the beauty that an Edenic setting inspires.

Still more, a sense of the numinous is felt more potently in this second story, especially at the climactic scene when Ransom meets Mars and Venus amid numerous eldila during the celebration of Perelandra's salvation through Ransom's help. Finally, Lewis's medievalism is far more explicit here as well, as he identifies the Oyarsas of Malacandra and Perelandra respectively as Mars and Venus.[654] Given that beauty and a sense of the numinous stand as two of Lewis's most relied-upon sacramental tools to pre-evangelize his readership's sentiments via the ethos of his stories, these qualities bear significance for the present argument.

Perelandra begins with Lewis himself making his way to Ransom's home in response to a wire he had received to "Come down on Thursday if possible."[655] The reader is instantly treated to a view of reality that collides sharply with the mechanistic naturalism and scientism in which Lewis's day was steeped. He introduces the reader to a sense of what a world is like that is populated with mysterious and powerful spiritual creatures. In doing so, he invites one to "breath the air" of this imaginary world in the hopes that one might long for such a world, and in so doing, come to see in time that the "air" in the real world is not so different after all.[656]

After discussing the almost sacred privilege of Lewis's getting to meet Ransom, who had met and talked with the mysterious eldila, he writes:

> The distinction between natural and supernatural, in fact, broke down; and when it had done so, one realized how great a comfort it had been—how it had eased the burden of intolerable strangeness which this universe imposes on us by dividing it into two halves and encouraging the mind never to think of both in the same context. What price we may have paid for this comfort

---

Alters her cheek.'"

[654] To clarify, the identification of the planets as powerful beings stretches back to the classical Greek period, being found in Plato's writings, for example. It does, however, carry over into the medieval period, as Lewis points out in *The Discarded Image*, and is thus associated with a medieval cosmological imagination.

[655] C. S. Lewis, *Perelandra*, 10.

[656] His ultimate desire is for his readers to see that Christianity best accounts for a world with such things in it in the hopes that through "tasting" they might come to believe.

C. S. LEWIS PRE-EVANGELISM FOR A POST-CHRISTIAN WORLD

in the way of false security and accepted confusion of thought is another matter.[657]

Lewis goes on to describe the inner struggle he has with both his thoughts and emotions as he presses on making his way to Ransom's home.

Later, he learns from Ransom that it was not merely an overactive imagination that caused him trouble, but the bent eldila doing all in their power to prevent his arrival at Ransom's home. After he arrives, Lewis hears, for the first time, the sound of an elida's "voice" saying Ransom's name. The sense of the uncanny is nearly overwhelming, and he helps the reader to experience this through the use of symbolism, a significant point that was explored in the previous chapter. He writes:

> The two syllables sounded more as if they were played on an instrument than as if they were spoken ... And it went through me from chest to groin like the thrill that goes through you when you think you have lost your hold while climbing a cliff.[658]

The metaphor of an instrument seems a fitting one to Lewis of the eldila's voice to provide the reader with a sense of what he both hears and feels in the story.

The previous chapter's discussion of both Bevan's and Barfield's ideas regarding metaphors and symbols is helpful to recall. Lewis happily employs rich symbolism throughout to convey to his readers things that they have not seen but that he takes to be very real.[659] One would be hard-pressed to convey the sense of holy fear better than Lewis's explanation when he writes of the Oyarsa of Malacandra whom he encounters: "I felt sure that the creature was what we call 'good,' but I wasn't sure whether I liked 'goodness' so much as I had supposed."[660] This description is congruent with the apostles' reaction in their various encounters with angelic beings recorded in the Scriptures, and thus what is imaginary here in Lewis's tale is also simultaneously a window into the real.

This second book's plot centers around the diabolical plans that Ransom reveals to Lewis early in the story. He tells him, "The black

---

[657] C. S. Lewis, *Perelandra*, 11.

[658] C. S. Lewis, *Perelandra*, 16.

[659] This is not to suggest that eldila, spirit-beings who occupy outer space and rule over the planets, are real in Lewis's mind. The suggestion is that spiritual beings who might be very similar in many ways to the eldila are real in Lewis's mind. Every detail need not fit in order for the sacramental pull of the imaginary to the real to "work" to some degree.

[660] C. S. Lewis, *Perelandra*, 17.

archon—our own bent Oyarsa—is meditating some sort of attack on Perelandra."[661] This bent Oyarsa, who is leader of the "Dark Eldila,"[662] is none other than Satan, though Lewis is careful not to use this title for fear that the "stained-glass and Sunday school associations" might creep in and destroy the enchantment.[663] Thus, the stage is set for Ransom's next adventure, which involves his being transported to the planet *Perelandra*, later revealed to be Venus, in order to do battle with the bent Oyarsa whose aim is to corrupt the two innocent humans who thereon make their home. In this plot, Lewis gives to his readers another Eden temptation story, but one in which the outcome is different from the one which took place in history on the real Thulcandra.[664] In this way, the reader is introduced to a crucial moment in human history, albeit dressed in fantastical garb and altered in places; yet, the parallels remain close enough to give one a whiff of reality.

Ransom soon meets the Green Lady, whom he describes initially as a "goddess carved apparently out of green stone, yet alive."[665] They begin conversing, and Ransom learns in time that the Green Lady has not been corrupted as he and the entire race of humanity have been on Thulcandra. She even enjoys a mysterious line of communication between her and Maleldil, in that He speaks to her and helps her to learn by some kind of direct communication. The first time Ransom is present for this communication, it proves to be a sacred and weighty moment. Ransom asks the Green Lady how she knows that Malacrandra is older than Thulcandra, to which she answers, "Maleldlil is telling me."[666] Upon her telling him this, Lewis recounts the scene thus:

And as she spoke the landscape had become different, though with a difference none of the senses would identify. The light was dim, the air gentle, and all Ransom's body was bathed in bliss, but the garden world where he stood seemed to be packed quite full, and as if an unendurable

---

[661] C. S. Lewis, *Perelandra*, 21.

[662] C. S. Lewis, *Perelandra*, 22.

[663] C. S. Lewis, "Why Fairy Stories May Sometimes Say Best What's to be Said," 70.

[664] See Walter Hooper, *C. S. Lewis: Companion & Guide*, 221, where Hooper notes one important influence that likely spurred Lewis on to write this story. Hooper writes, "He had been lecturing in the University on Milton's *Paradise Lost* since 1937 and this, doubtless, furnished him with the basic plot of *Perelandra*. The story itself is taken, as was *Paradise Lost*, from Genesis 1–3. What Lewis does is to re-imagine the story of the Fall of Man and give us the story of Paradise Retained."

[665] C. S. Lewis, *Perelandra*, 47–48.

[666] C. S. Lewis, *Perelandra*, 53.

pressure had been laid upon his shoulders, his legs failed him and he half sank, half fell, into a sitting position.[667]

The unseen presence of Maleldil brings Ransom to his knees, which is a very fitting reaction given the true identity of Maleldil in Lewis's story.[668] When the apostle John sees the Christ in a vision while exiled on the island of Patmos, he falls at his feet, "as though dead" (Rev. 1:17, ESV). The result of this scene for the reader is that, whether he realizes it or not, he has been shown something true of the nature of the divine. One before whom one falls to one's knees as a non-volitional reaction must be someone indescribably powerful, majestic, and perhaps even dangerous.

Eventually, they notice a dark spherical object that has come to Perelandra. To Ransom's surprise and horror, he learns in time that it is Weston who has hazarded the journey to try to do on Perelandra what he had failed previously to do on Malacandra. He tries in vain to prevent Weston from meeting the Green Lady and from talking to her, and is shocked to hear Weston speaking to the Lady fluently in the Old Solar language, given that he had only learned a tiny bit of it and spoke it very poorly, while previously on Malacandra.[669] The reader begins suspecting that forces beyond Weston's own capacity have helped him to acquire such a masterful grasp of the old language in such a short time.

A large portion of the story centers around the ensuing conversation between Weston and the Green Lady, as he tries avenue after avenue of suggestion and argumentation to persuade the Lady to do the one thing that Maleldil has forbidden her to do on Perelandra—spend the night on the fixed island. Serving as the voice of reason, Ransom repeatedly interjects in the hopes of preventing the Green Lady from taking Weston's diabolical advice. Lewis uses this back-and-forth three-way conversation in a two-fold effort to expose various falsehoods and fashionable but flawed philosophies while also presenting a positive apologetic for truths consistent with a Christian worldview. Lewis thus pre-evangelizes his readership with truth, largely through the mouth of Ransom.

Throughout their conversations, Weston undergoes frightening transformations that create suspicion in the reader's mind as to what is happening to him and who has taken control of his body. Lewis describes one such troubling episode as follows:

---

[667] C. S. Lewis, *Perelandra*, 53.
[668] Maleldil is the Christ of the Bible.
[669] In Lewis's story, this is the language spoken before the Tower of Babel.

A spasm like that preceding a deadly vomit twisted Weston's face out of recognition. As it passed, for one second something like the old Weston appeared—the old Weston, staring with eyes of horror and howling, 'Ransom, Ransom! For Christ's sake don't let them—" and instantly his whole body spun round as if he had been hit by a revolver-bullet and he fell to the earth, and was there rolling at Ransom's feet, slavering and chattering and tearing up the moss by handfuls ... The face suggested that either he was in no pain or in pain beyond all human comprehension.[670]

On another occasion, the reader is allowed to peer into Ransom's suspicions regarding Weston's malady. Lewis writes:

On the one hand he was certain, both from the voice and forming of the things it said, that the male speaker was Weston. On the other hand, the voice, divided from the man's appearance, sounded curiously unlike itself. Still more, the patient persistent manner in which it was used was very unlike the Professor's usual alternation between pompous lecturing and abrupt bullying. And how could a man fresh from such a physical crisis as he had seen Weston undergo have recovered such mastery of himself in a few hours? And how could he have reached the floating island? Ransom had found himself throughout their dialogue confronted with an intolerable contradiction. Something which was and was not Weston was talking: and the sense of this monstrosity, only a few feet away in the darkness, had sent thrills of exquisite horror tingling along his spine, and raised questions in his mind which he tried to dismiss as fantastic.[671]

Later, Ransom finds Weston torturing a frog, and his countenance during this encounter disturbs Ransom intensely. Lewis describes the scene the in following way:

What could you say—what appeal or threat could have any meaning—to *that*? And now, forcing its way up into consciousness, thrusting aside every mental habit and every longing to believe, came the conviction that this, in fact, was not a man: that Weston's body was kept, walking and undecaying, in Perelandra by some wholly different kind of life, and that Weston himself was gone. It looked at Ransom in silence and at last began to smile. We have all often spoke—Ransom himself

---

[670] C. S. Lewis, *Perelandra*, 82–83.
[671] C. S. Lewis, *Perelandra*, 91–92.

had often spoken—of a devilish smile. Now he realized that he had never taken the words seriously ... Ransom perceived that he had never before seen anything but half-hearted and uneasy attempts at evil. This creature was whole-hearted. The extremity of its evil had passed beyond all struggle into some state which bore a horrible similarity to innocence. It was beyond vice as the Lady was beyond virtue.[672]

As Ransom perceives with increasing clarity the inhuman qualities of Weston, he begins referring to him as the "Un-man."[673] In time, all doubt as to the identity of the person who has taken over Weston's body is removed from the reader's mind. Ransom confronts the Un-man and proceeds to engage him in physical combat. Before this battle ensues, he and Weston engage in the following exchange:

"So you mean to try strength," it said in English, speaking thick. "Put down that bird," said Ransom. "But this is very foolish," said the Un-man. "Do you not know who I am?" "I know *what* you are," said Ransom. "Which of them doesn't matter." "And you think, little one," it answered, "that you can fight with me? You think He will help you, perhaps? Many thought that. I've known Him longer than you, little one. They all think He's going to help them—till they come to their senses screaming recantations too late in the middle of the fire, mouldering in concentration camps, writhing under saws, jibbering in mad-houses, or nailed on to crosses. Could He help Himself?"—and the creature suddenly threw back its head and cried in a voice so loud that it seemed the golden sky-roof must break, *"Eloi, Eloi, lama sabachthani."* And the moment it had done so, Ransom felt certain that the sounds it had made were prefect Aramaic of the First Century. The Un-man was not quoting; it was remembering. These were the very words spoken from the Cross, treasured through all those years in the burning memory of the outcast creature which had heard them, and now brought forward in hideous parody; the horror made him momentarily sick.[674]

The Un-man serves, for Lewis, as the incarnation of evil and malice, of that angelic being who at one time was good but who had chosen the path of self-destructive pride, revolting against his creator.

---

[672] C. S. Lewis, *Perelandra*, 95.
[673] C. S. Lewis, *Perelandra*, 105.
[674] C. S. Lewis, *Perelandra*, 130.

While one strategy of Lewis's pre-evangelism is to set truth, goodness, and beauty before us by giving various instances of each throughout his stories, another is to set falsehood, evil, and ugliness before us as well, casting all of the above in their true light. He sets the two in sharp contrast in the following description of Ransom's reaction to the devilish face of Weston:

> The children, the poets, and the philosophers were right. As there is one Face above all worlds merely to see which is irrevocable joy, so at the bottom of all worlds that face is waiting whose sight alone is the misery from which none who beholds it can recover. And though there seemed to be, and indeed were, a thousand roads by which a man could walk through the world, there was not a single one which did not lead sooner or later either to the Beatific or the Miserific Vision.[675]

Consistent with Lewis's view on objective values, argued most thoroughly in *The Abolition of Man*, the proper sentiments towards such a ghastly creature are precisely those that Ransom expresses towards the Un-man—horror and repulsion. The shaping of one's sentiments can be helped, Lewis thought, both by stirring attraction for the good and by arousing disgust for the wicked.

In the end, Ransom bests the Un-man in a fight and tosses his body into a pool of subterranean lava, destroying his former captor. The Green Lady also emerges triumphant. Despite all of the Un-man's attempts, she refuses to rebel against Maleldil's command not to sleep on the fixed island. Thus, the "garden temptation" episode on Perelandra ends in victory rather than defeat.

The conclusion of the story stands out as some of Lewis's most beautiful prose. Ransom begins ascending to the tops of the mountains. His journey is accompanied by mysterious singing from a shy creature of Perelandra, flower petals falling on his head, pollen gilding his skin as he walks, and "odours that darted into his brain and there begot wild and enormous pleasures."[676] When at last he comes to take the pass through the red mountains at the summit of the planet where he will come face to face with the Oyarsa of Perelandra and Malacandra, he is struck with competing feelings. Lewis writes:

> He dared not go up that pass: he dared not do otherwise: He looked to see an angel with a flaming sword: he knew that

---

[675] C. S. Lewis, *Perelandra*, 96.
[676] C. S. Lewis, *Perelandra*, 163.

C. S. LEWIS PRE-EVANGELISM FOR A POST-CHRISTIAN WORLD

Maleldil bade him go on. "This is the holiest and the most unholy thing I have ever done," he thought; but he went on.[677]

Ransom comes at last to a valley between the red mountains in the center of which lies a crystal golden pool of water cinctured with lilies. He notices a white coffin lying near the water's edge, its lid set beside it. The coffin is like unto the one in which he first came to Perelandra. As he looks around, he notices a difference in the light falling upon the flowers. Lewis describes the scene thus:

Next, he perceived that the oddity was an oddity in the light; thirdly that it was in the air as well as on the ground. Then, as the blood pricked his veins and a familiar, yet strange, sense of diminished being possessed him, he knew that he was in the presence of two eldila.[678]

These two eldila are not ordinary eldila. They are the Oyarsa of Malacandra and Perelandra. The one says, "In my own sphere I am Oyarsa. Here I am only Malacandra."[679] The other interjects next, "I am Perelandra."[680] A bit later Ransom learns that these Oyarsas' other names are, respectively, Mars and Venus.[681] At this point one can see just how deeply and richly Lewis has infused his story with medievalism, given that the mythological cosmology of the medievals contained the personification of the planets, identifying them with the Greco-Roman gods.[682]

In the presence of these two gods and the great host of the planet Perelandra, Ransom enjoys a magnificent ceremony that ushers in the true "birth" of Perelandra. Mars says to Ransom:

"The world is born to-day," said Malacandra. "To-day for the first time two creatures of the low worlds, two images of Maleldil that breathe and breed like the beasts, step up that step at which your parents fell, and sit in the throne of what they were meant

---

[677] C. S. Lewis, *Perelandra*, 165.
[678] C. S. Lewis, *Perelandra*, 166.
[679] C. S. Lewis, *Perelandra*, 167.
[680] C. S. Lewis, *Perelandra*, 168.
[681] See C. S. Lewis, *Perelandra*, 172, where Lewis writes, "For now he thought of them no more as Malacandra and Perelandra. He called them by their Tellurian names. With deep wonder he thought to himself, 'My eyes have seen Mars and Venus. I have seen Ares and Aphrodite.'"
[682] This mythology was not invented by the medievals. Rather, it comes in the Greek classical period and survives the transition into the medieval period becoming characteristic of that later age.

to be. It was never seen before. Because it did not happen in your world a greater thing happened, but not this. Because the greater thing happened in Thulcandra, this and not the greater thing happens here."[683]

At this point, what Lewis has been hinting at throughout his story becomes nearly explicit. By the fall of Ransom's parents, he is referring to Adam's and Eve's succumbing to the serpent's temptation in the garden of Eden. By the "greater thing" that happened on planet earth, he is referring to the incarnation of the second person of the trinity and his atoning work on the cross on behalf of the human race. Here in Lewis's story, the human race upon Perelandra pass their test. They emerge victorious and thus receive their reward.

Lewis then paints a picture of triumphant humanity that resonates with something he writes in another book he writes. That book is *The Weight of Glory*, and in it Lewis suggests:

> It is a serious thing to live in a society of possible gods and goddesses, to remember that the dullest and most uninteresting person you can talk to may one day be a creature which, if you saw it now, you would be strongly tempted to worship, or else a horror and a corruption such as you now meet, if at all, only in a nightmare ... There are no ordinary people. You have never talked to a mere mortal. Nations, cultures, arts, civilisations—these are mortal and their life is to ours as the life of a gnat. But it is immortals whom we joke with, work with, marry, snub, and exploit—immortal horrors or everlasting splendors.[684]

Ransom observes the wicked Weston becoming the former and the virtuous King and Queen of Perelandra becoming the latter. As he is brought before the triumphant couple, his reaction is the very one that Lewis suggests one might be tempted with when in the presence of humanity made splendid by God. He writes:

> There was great silence on the mountain top and Ransom had fallen down before the human pair. When at last he raised his eyes from the four blessed feet, he found himself involuntarily speaking though his voice was broken and his eyes dimmed. "Do not move away, do not raise me up," he said. "I have never seen a man or a woman. I have lived all my life among shadows and broken images. Oh, my Father and my Mother, my Lord and my

---

[683] C. S. Lewis, *Perelandra*, 169.
[684] C. S. Lewis, *The Weight of Glory*, 45–46.

C. S. LEWIS PRE-EVANGELISM FOR A POST-CHRISTIAN WORLD

Lady, do not move, do not answer me yet. My own father and mother I have never seen. Take me for your son. We have been alone in my world for a great time."[685]

Ransom is not succumbing here to idolatry; rather, he recognizes that the human King of Perelandra is a "copy" of Maleldil, "like and not the same, an echo, a rhyme, an exquisite reverberation of the uncreated music prolonged in a created medium."[686] Soon after the coronation of the King and Queen, a mysterious voice begins speaking poetic phrases of blessing, each stanza concluding with the refrain, referring to Maleldil, "Blessed be He!" and reaching its final crescendo with the triple blessing, "Blessed, blessed, blessed be He!"[687]

Lewis's sacramental theology unmistakably fills the final pages of this second chapter in his space trilogy.[688] For example, the unidentified voice proclaims:

"Where Maleldil is, there is the centre. He is in every place. Not some of Him in one place and some in another, but in each place the whole Maleldil, even in the smallness beyond thought ... Each thing was made for Him. He is the centre. Because we are with Him, each of us is at the centre ... In His city all things are made

---

[685] C. S. Lewis, *Perelandra*, 176.

[686] C. S. Lewis, *Perelandra*, 177.

[687] C. S. Lewis, *Perelandra*, 183–187.

[688] Scott Key agrees with this assessment. See Scott B. Key, "The Moral Aesthetic of Perelandra," in *C. S. Lewis and the Arts*, 18, 26, where Key lists the principles of a sacramental view of reality that he sees undergirding Lewis's story. By the "Great Tradition," Key means the "Great Sacramental Tradition," mentioned on p. 18. He writes, "This understanding of the sacramental informs all of Lewis's work including *Perelandra* and it reflects the great tradition of Christian thinking ... The principles rooted in the Great Tradition that undergird the narrative *Perelandra* can be summarized in the following way: God is the source of value and being; A higher reality in value and being raises the lower reality and gives to the lower its dignity and meaning; Truth, goodness, and beauty are real (not in a purely Platonic sense) and are ultimately rooted in God, and this makes them ontologically related; The longing for beauty can draw us to the source of beauty and beatific vision is a transformative reality that points to God's ultimate mission and purpose; Goodness and beauty are so related that development in virtue can make beauty more discoverable and knowable; The ugly is not outside of the Christian vision nor is the realistic and gritty understanding of human brokenness and sin. But the Christian vision also understands that hope is real, redemption is possible by grace, and that ultimately, the presence of radical evil does not count against the covenantal justice of the Triune God whose love and power is revealed in the resurrection of the crucified One; The mission of the contemporary Church must include the intentional development of all of the Arts understood within the broad contours of a sacramental understanding of the cosmos and an acceptance of the revelatory reality of God's gracious Spirit at work in his people who do all things, in all areas of life, for the glory of God."

for each. When He died in the Wounded World He died not for men, but for each man. If each man had been the only man made, He would have done no less. Each thing, from the single grain of Dust of the strongest eldil, is the end and the final cause of all creation and the mirror in which the beam of His brightness comes to rest and so returns to Him. Blessed be He!"[689]

At last, Ransom is ushered by the King to his coffin that will transport him from Perelandra back to Thulcandra. As the King bids him farewell and closes the lid, he leaves him with these parting words, "Speak of us always to Maleldil as we speak always of you. The splendor, the love, and the strength be upon you."[690] If Lewis ever captures successfully in his imaginative fiction the sense of both the sublime and the numinous, along with intimations of rich theology pertaining specifically to the cross of Christ all in one scene, he does so in this climactic moment that brings the second book to a close.

His theological themes are far more apparent in *Perelandra* than they are in *Out of the Silent Planet*. Reviewers took notice of this, though it did not seem to diminish their enjoyment of the book.[691] Hooper notes an essay written by Victor M. Hamm in which he gives high praise to Lewis's book, particularly the final scene, even comparing him to the great romantic writers. Hamm writes:

> The substance of this wonderful scene ... which culminates in a grand chorus of praises to Maleldil [is] an inspired litany of love and homage. Blake should sound like this, in the *Prophetic Books*, but somehow he never does; there is in them too much of the Ossianic vagueness and verbiage. Keats does, in *Hyperion*, but his allegory is unintelligible. Dante is the man: in the sweep through the gyres of Heaven, to the crowning visit of God as the point that moves the sun and the stars, he is loftier, of course, and more sustained, and he writes poetry instead of prose; but read and see whether the prophetic imagination is not in Lewis too, and something of the high style as well.[692]

As Lewis's culture had rejected much of the truth about reality, such things as Judeo-Christian morality, universals, objective truth and beauty,

---

[689] C. S. Lewis, *Perelandra*, 185–186.

[690] C. S. Lewis, *Perelandra*, 190.

[691] See Walter Hooper, *C. S. Lewis: Companion & Guide*, 229, where Hooper writes, "This time the reviewers were in little doubt of what Lewis intended, and many who disagreed with his Christian orthodoxy nevertheless liked the book."

[692] Cited in Walter Hooper, *C. S. Lewis: Companion & Guide*, 230.

C. S. LEWIS PRE-EVANGELISM FOR A POST-CHRISTIAN WORLD

etc., he pre-evangelizes them by helping them to get reacquainted with them in an imaginative context. There, while their defenses remain down, they may be more receptive to having their affections and even intellects stirred by examples of truth, goodness, and beauty cloaked in imaginative garb. When the explicit gospel comes after this, it may be that they will recognize that much of what they came to love in the imaginative realm can only be realized ultimately by Christianity. Thus, Lewis prepares his readership for an eventual hearing and hopefully and receiving of the truth of the gospel.

That Hideous Strength

That Hideous Strength concludes Lewis's space trilogy. Lewis borrows two lines of poetry from Sir David Lyndsay in his choosing the title of his book. He notes these lines on the title page thus: "The shadow of that hyddeous strength sax mile and more it is of length."[693] The lines, translated, are, "The shadow of that hideous strength, six miles and more it is of length."[694] Lyndsay's poem is referring to the Tower of Babel. From the very title page, Lewis hints to his readers that he is comparing, or even equating, the evil present in the hearts of those who constructed the Tower of Babel with those whose diabolical ambitions in his story are similar. This third book unveils a great cosmic battle between good and evil that appears strikingly close in many aspects to the real battle. Responding to some of the negative reviews Lewis received and demonstrating his belief in the similarity between his fantasy and reality, he writes, "Apparently reviewers will not tolerate a mixture of the realistic and the supernatural. Which is a pity, because (a) It's just the mixture I like, and (b) We have to put up with it in real life."[695]

Lewis stated explicitly that though his story was fantastical, he was communicating truth through it and combatting a certain form of falsehood that he found both prevalent and destructive in his day. In other words, he was doing the work of pre-evangelism, attempting to help his readers to see reality in a way consistent with a Christian worldview so that in time the gospel message might come to them in a more welcome intellectual atmosphere than was presently in the "heads" and "chests" of many. Lewis admits, "This is a 'tall story' about devilry, though it has behind it a serious 'point' which I have tried to make in my *Abolition of Man*."[696]

---

[693] C. S. Lewis, *That Hideous Strength*, title page.
[694] See Walter Hooper, *C. S. Lewis: Companion & Guide*, 232.
[695] Cited in Walter Hooper, *C. S. Lewis: Companion & Guide*, 231.
[696] C. S. Lewis, *That Hideous Strength*, 7.

Brian M. Williams

The story begins in a rather "hum-drum" way, centering on the uneventful lives of the husband and wife pair, Mark and Jane Studdock. Lewis begins this way purposefully, following the classic fairy-tale formula.[697] After the first two chapters, however, the story begins to tie in the plot from the previous two volumes. Though Weston was destroyed in the previous book, the Bent Oyarsa who possessed his body remains and is actively strategizing plans centering on the human race. One eventually realizes that these plans have been building through the previous two books and they coalesce in the final story, revealing a far more disturbing aim than one might have anticipated to this point. In fact, *That Hideous Strength* stands without question as Lewis's darkest book.

Soon after the story begins, we are introduced to a nightmare that Jane recently has had. She dreamt of a prisoner in a room who became intensely frightened upon receiving news from a man with a pointed gray beard. Jane somehow perceived that what the man intended for the prisoner was somehow worse than death. Suddenly, the man took hold of the prisoner's head, gave it a sharp turn, and unscrewed it from his body. Confusion then clouded the scene as it switched to another head. This time, the head belonged to a druidical man with a long white beard, all covered in dirt. Some men out of a churchyard were digging him up. To Jane's horror, the man woke up and began to speak. At that moment, Jane herself awakened.

Jane continues having dream after dream, or rather, receiving vision after vision. She soon learns that her dreams are flashes of events that in time come to pass. Through the counsel of her friends, Mrs. and Dr. Dimble, she learns that she has the power of clairvoyance. She also learns that the Dimbles have joined with Dr. Ransom, who is the head of coalition of individuals committed to waging war against the dark eldila who are led by the Bent Oyarsa himself. They discover that these dark eldila have figured out how to take control of certain humans while remaining largely incognito as they carry out their plans.

---

[697] See C. S. Lewis, *That Hideous Strength*, 7, where he explains, "I have called this a fairy-tale in the hope that no one who dislikes fantasy may be misled by the first two chapters into reading further, and then complain of his disappointment. If you ask why—intending to write about magicians, devils, pantomime animals, and planetary angels—I nevertheless begin with such hum-drum scenes and persons, I reply that I am following the traditional fairy-tale. We do not always notice its method, because the cottages, castles, woodcutters, and petty kings with which a fairy-tale opens have become for us as remote as the witches and ogres to which it proceeds. But they were not remote at all to the men who made and first enjoyed the stories. They were, indeed, more realistic and commonplace than Bracton College is to me; for many German peasants have actually met cruel stepmothers, whereas I never have, in any university, come across a college like Bracton."

C. S. LEWIS PRE-EVANGELISM FOR A POST-CHRISTIAN WORLD

They center their strategy on the "N.I.C.E.," the "National Institute of Co-ordinated Experiments."[698] The N.I.C.E. epitomizes the aim for scientific progress in an effort to perpetuate the human race's existence at all costs. Dick Devine, who now goes by Lord Feverstone and who was Weston's partner in *Out of the Silent Planet* accompanying him to Malacandra, has joined the N.I.C.E. He helps to persuade Mark Studdock to join as well, arguing:

It does really look as if we now had the power to dig ourselves in as a species for a pretty staggering period, to take control of our own destiny. If Science is really given a free hand it can now take over the human race and re-condition it: make man a really efficient animal. If it doesn't—well, we're done.[699]

In order to achieve this, Lord Feverstone explains to Mark that the N.I.C.E. is working towards the "sterilization of the unfit, liquidation of backward races ... selective breeding ... real education, including pre-natal education ... biochemical conditioning in the end and direct manipulation of the brain."[700]

Mark is told that his job will be to market the N.I.C.E. to the general public, massaging the language so as to make their aims sound popular and enticing. Mark takes the job, and one of his first articles to the public reads as follows:

The Institute which has settled at Edgestow is a *National* Institute. That means it is yours and mine. We are not scientists and we do not pretend to know what the master-brains of the Institute are thinking. We do know what each man or woman expects of it. We expect a solution of the unemployment problem, the cancer problem, the housing problem, the problem of currency, of war, of education. We expect from it a brighter, cleaner and fuller life for your children, in which we and they can march ever onward and onward and develop to the full urge of life which God has given each one of us. The N.I.C.E. is the people's instrument for bringing about all the things we fought for.[701]

---

[698] C. S. Lewis, *That Hideous Strength*, 21. One wonders whether or not Lewis gave this sinister organization that acrostic "N.I.C.E." with reference to the "niceness" that he observed had become the supreme ethic, but which was proving devastating to truth and morality, as niceness often does not allow for contradiction of viewpoints.
[699] C. S. Lewis, *That Hideous Strength*, 39.
[700] C. S. Lewis, *That Hideous Strength*, 40.
[701] C. S. Lewis, *That Hideous Strength*, 130.

One cannot fail to notice the parallel that Lewis is drawing from Mark's journalism to the popular media. Lewis believed that the media in his day was working largely for the enemy's side, and in so doing was presenting a great threat to the Christian message, given its pervasive influence. He believed that if Christianity was to make any widespread headway, Christian ideas would have to be circulated incognito to offset the latent naturalism that permeated culture in nearly every form of communication to the masses. Here then, one can see that part of his pre-evangelistic strategy was to show his readership an imaginary account of what a corrupt media output might look like, which would be in a sense like holding a mirror up to society.

Little by little, Mark is drawn deeper into the N.I.C.E., learning only too slowly of their ultimate aim for humanity and the means by which they hope to accomplish it. When he tries to cut ties with them at last, he realizes that unless he conforms and complies, he will be fingered with a murder he did not commit or else be murdered himself. In what is probably the most horrific scene in the book, and perhaps in all of Lewis's literature, Mark is introduced at last "the Head" of the N.I.C.E.[702] To this point, he has been referred to throughout the story simply as "the Head," thus giving the reader faint clues of what is to come.

Mark is led into an area akin to an operating room and is forced to wear sterile white clothes with gloves and a mask. His colleagues bring him to a door covered with dials. As he is taken inside, the narrative shifts suddenly to Jane's recounting the worst of her dreams to this point in the story. It happens to be a dream about what Mark experiences behind the door. She describes her nightmarish vision thus:

> I dreamed I was in a dark room ... with queer smells in it and a sort of low humming noise. Then the lights came on ... I thought I saw a face floating in front of me ... there was a beard and nose and eyes—at least, you couldn't see the eyes because it had colored glasses on, but there didn't seem to be anything above the eyes. Not at first. But as I got used to the light, I got a horrible shock. I thought the face was a mask tied on to a kind of balloon thing ... What it really was, was a head (the rest of a head) which had had the top part of the skull taken off and then ... then ... as if something inside had boiled over. A great big mass which bulged out from inside what was left of the skull. Wrapped in some kind of composition stuff, but very thin stuff. You could see it twitch. Even in my fright I remember thinking, "Oh kill it, kill

---

[702] C. S. Lewis, *That Hideous Strength*, 171.

it. Put it out of its pain." But only for a second because I thought the thing was real, really. It was green looking and the mouth was wide open and quite dry ... And soon I saw that it wasn't exactly floating. It was fixed upon some kind of bracket, or shelf, or pedestal—I don't know quite what, and there were things hanging from it. From the neck, I mean. Yes, it had a neck and a sort of collar thing round it, but nothing below the collar; no shoulders or body. Only these hanging things ... I saw that they were artificial. Little rubber tubes and bulbs and little metal things too. I couldn't understand them. All the tubes went into the wall. Then at last something happened ... Well, quite suddenly, like when an engine is started, there came a puff of air out of its mouth, with a hard dry rasping sound ... Then came a most horrible thing: the mouth began to dribble ... Then it spoke.[703]

This head belonged to the man in Jane's first dream, the prisoner who seemed strangely frightened of something worse than death.

At last, the reader understands that what horrified the prisoner so intensely were the plans for his fate that came from the lips of the man who had come into his room. His future lay in a disembodied existence that was to be perpetuated indefinitely via science and the aid of the "Macrobes,"[704] which are none other than the dark eldils, servants of the Bent Oyarsa. Lewis paints an imaginative picture of the outworking of naturalism and scientism, aligned together towards preserving the human species on earth might look like, set within a story where both the spiritual and the physical stand as real aspects of reality. This "stage set" is consistent with a Christian view of reality, where spirits both benevolent and malevolent participate actively in humanity's affairs. It is conceivable that the strategy of devils in the modern Western world might involve less overt displays of human torment and physical manipulation, and might operate more from the shadows, as it were, through anti-Christian philosophies that incite humans to take the destruction of themselves into their own hands, all the while thinking they are working towards their own liberation. If such a thing should happen, few will likely realize that, far from liberating themselves, they will be increasingly surrendering their freedom into the hands of those who lust for power and control. Like the N.I.C.E., the forces that bring this about will make many of the same promises—public health, a better future,

---

[703] C. S. Lewis, *That Hideous Strength*, 178–180.
[704] C. S. Lewis, *That Hideous Strength*, 330.

more freedom, etc., and they will be successful largely to the degree that they can control the lines of mass communication.

Those behind the N.I.C.E. are deceived into believing precisely this, that they really are helping to bring about man's ultimate liberation. For instance, Straik, one of the leaders of the N.I.C.E., just before leading Mark to meet the "Head," pleads with him:

> Don't you see ... that we are offering you the unspeakable glory of being present at the creation of God Almighty? Here, in this house, you shall meet the first sketch of the real God. It is a man—or a being made by man—who will finally ascend the throne of the universe. And rule forever.[705]

This, in principle, is precisely the end at which Lewis thinks naturalism in the post-Enlightenment age is actually aimed, which he exposes in his book *The Abolition of Man*. In the third and final chapter of this important book, Lewis writes of "Man's conquest of nature."[706] He argues that "what we call Man's power over Nature turns out to be a power exercised by some men over other men with Nature as its instrument."[707] As this power is carried forth from generation to generation, it leads in the end, Lewis argues, to "the last men [who], far from being the heirs of power, will be of all men most subject to the dead hand of the great planners and conditioners and will themselves exercise the least power upon the future."[708]

It would be difficult to conceive of a less powerful "man," than Alcasan, whose existence as a severed head is maintained by the advancements of science and whose animations are brought out by the power of demons. He is a pretty pathetic "God," given that drooling and mumbling out a few discernible words here and there, all against his will, are among the most impressive of his actions. Though the application of these false philosophies in Lewis's story is fantastic and may not be the precise path humanity will choose in time to take, it offers a fitting image of one of the most horrific outcomes of the union of naturalism and scientism, aligned together for the cause of "progress." Lewis chooses the title *The Abolition of Man* for his argument against these philosophies because it is the logical extension of them if carried to their true end. He writes thus:

---

[705] C. S. Lewis, *That Hideous Strength*, 176.
[706] C. S. Lewis, *The Abolition of Man*, 68.
[707] C. S. Lewis, *The Abolition of Man*, 55.
[708] C. S. Lewis, *The Abolition of Man*, 57–58.

C. S. LEWIS PRE-EVANGELISM FOR A POST-CHRISTIAN WORLD

> But as soon as we take the final step of reducing our own species to the level of mere Nature, the whole process is stultified, for this time the being who stood to gain and the being who has been sacrificed are one and the same ... It is the magician's bargain: give up our soul, get power in return. But once our souls, that is, ourselves have been given up, the power thus conferred will not belong to us. We shall in fact be the slaves and puppets of that to which we have given our souls.[709]

The reader of *That Hideous Strength* will find no formal argument along these lines, no prescriptions persuading the reader explicitly to abandon naturalism, scientism, and post-Enlightenment notions of progress and embrace instead traditional values along with a pre-modern understanding of reality within a Christian framework. What he will find is an imaginative tale that presents both sides in their true light, with falsehood exposed as the devilish and repulsive thing that it is and truth as the beautiful and desirable thing that it is. Lewis goes after the reason via the imagination, inviting his readers to taste both evil and good and to see if the former is not bitter and the latter not sweet. We might say that he engages the sentiments, or "the chest" so that in time the reason or the head might be won.

The nature of the true forces behind the N.I.C.E. and of those helping Ransom and his side become increasingly apparent as the novel progresses. One scene in particular paints an eerie picture of what common theological terminology would identify as demon possession. Lewis simply refers to it as the influence of the Macrobes or the dark eldils, avoiding the theological language. Wither and Frost, two of the highest men in the N.I.C.E. are having a conversation about how best to use Mark Studdock for their purposes. Their behavior becomes increasingly strange until at last, Lewis writes:

> They were now sitting so close together that their faces almost touched, as if they had been lovers about to kiss. Frost's *pince-nez* caught the light so that they made his eyes invisible: only his mouth, smiling but not relaxed in the smile, revealed his expression. Wither's mouth was open, the lower lip hanging down, his eyes wet, his whole body hunched and collapsed in his chair as if the strength had gone out of it. A stranger would have thought he had been drinking. Then his shoulders twitched and gradually he began to laugh. And Frost did not laugh, but his

---

[709] C. S. Lewis, *The Abolition of Man*, 71–72.

smile grew moment by moment brighter and also colder, and he stretched out his hand and patted his colleague on the shoulder. Suddenly in that silent room there was a crash. *Who's Who* had fallen off the table, swept on the floor as, with sudden swift convulsive movement, the two old men lurched forward towards each other and sat swaying to and fro, locked in an embrace from which each seemed to be struggling to escape. And as they swayed and scrabbled with hand and nail, there arose, shrill and faint at first, but then louder and louder, a cackling noise that seemed in the end rather an animal than a senile parody of laughter.[710]

Wither and Frost's twisted behavior harken back to some of the ways Weston behaved in the previous story. He too was not entirely himself; rather, his body was hijacked by the Bent Oyarsa and made to do horrific things. Such hijacking is not merely the stuff of fairy tales. On the contrary, Christianity maintains the historical factuality of instances in which demonic beings have taken up residence inside of real people, causing them to do similar things to what Lewis has these N.I.C.E. men do in his story. This is yet another example of Lewis's holding up reality before the eyes of his readership, dressed in fictional garb.

As the plot nears its conclusion, we are introduced to a fictional character from the medieval times—the wizard Merlin. Both sides have been trying to locate his corpse in the hopes of resurrecting him to join their side in the great battle. The N.I.C.E. wants to use Merlin's magic for their sinister purposes, while Ransom and his people want his powers for the cause of good, though they do not understand entirely how this will work. After Merlin rises from his tomb, having been kept for centuries preserved in sleep, he joins Ransom's side. Merlin clearly represents a pre-modern Christian view of reality, and one wonders if Lewis might be making the suggestion that what will save humanity from plummeting to its demise is not only Christianity lived out consistently, but specifically a pre-modern Christianity void of the ills of modernism—in other words, a conception of reality that we have been discussing at length to this point.

One of the final chapters is titled "The Descent of the Gods." In this chapter, Lewis's medievalism comes bursting forth, unrivaled in this sense by any other scene of which he writes in his entire literary corpus. While Merlin and Ransom sit together in the upper "Blue Room" of the house at St. Anne's, awaiting the coming of the great Oyarsa, incredible happenings

---

[710] C. S. Lewis, *That Hideous Strength*, 240.

C. S. LEWIS PRE-EVANGELISM FOR A POST-CHRISTIAN WORLD

begin to take place.[711] While the rest of Ransom's party sit downstairs having their evening tea, the transformation comes.

If one is familiar with the gods and goddesses' characters, one can likely predict who is coming as Lewis describes each scene in elaborate detail. For instance, as Mercury arrives, who is the great messenger and "the lord of Meaning himself," various uses of language break forth among the entire party. Lewis writes:

> Now all of a sudden they all began talking loudly at once, each, not contentiously but delightedly, interrupting the others ... What they said, none of the party could ever afterwards remember. Dimble maintained that they had been chiefly engaged in making puns ... If not plays upon words, yet certainly plays upon thoughts, paradoxes, fancies, anecdotes, theories laughingly advanced ... had flowed from them and over them with dazzling prodigality.[712]

The laughter and gaiety of the downstairs party gives way to a calm silence. Meanwhile, upstairs where Ransom and Merlin wait, Lewis tells us that:

> [A]gitation seized them: a kind of boiling and bubbling in mind and heart which shook their bodies also ... It was well that both men had some knowledge of poetry. The doubling, splitting, and recombining of thoughts which now went on in them would have been unendurable for one whom that art had not already instructed in the counterpoint of mind, the mastery of doubled and trebled vision. For Ransom, whose study had been for many years in the realm of words, it was heavenly pleasure. He found himself sitting within the very heart of language, in the white-hot furnace of essential speech ... For the lord of Meaning himself, the herald, the messenger, the slayer of Argus, was with them: the angel that spins nearest the sun. Viritrilbia, whom men call Mercury and Thoth.[713]

Such was the atmosphere, a very fitting one we can see, for the god who had just arrived.

Next comes Venus, the goddess who is charity personified. Upon her coming, the temperature in the room rises. "Both the humans trembled,"

---
[711] C. S. Lewis, *That Hideous Strength*, 317.
[712] C. S. Lewis, *That Hideous Strength*, 318.
[713] C. S. Lewis, *That Hideous Strength*, 319.

Lewis writes, "Merlin because he did not know what was coming, Ransom because he knew. This was none other than Perelandra herself, whom Ransom has previously met in the planetary journeys. Lewis writes further:

> It was fiery, sharp, bright and ruthless, ready to kill, ready to die, outspending light: it was Charity, not as mortals imagine it, not even as it has been humanized for them since the Incarnation of the Word, but the translunar virtue, fallen upon them from the Third Heaven, unmitigated. They were blinded scorched, deafened. They thought it would burn their bones. They could not bear that it should continue. They could not bear that it should cease. So Perelandra, triumphant among planets, whom men call Venus, came and was with them.[714]

The third to come is the god of war, Mars. As Mars approaches, the party grows in courage and in their willingness to go to physical battle with the opposition if they must. Dimble says, for example, "I'm not like you, MacPhee. I'm not brave. But I was just thinking as you spoke that I don't feel afraid of being killed and hurt as I used to. Not tonight."[715] Meanwhile, upstairs Merlin begins to hear "the snap of the bows, the *click-click* of steel points in wooden shields, the cheers, the howling, and the ring of struck mail."[716] Lewis continues:

> There was no fear anywhere: the blood inside them flowed as if to a marching-song. They felt themselves taking their places in the ordered rhythm of the universe ... Ransom knew, as a man knows when he touches iron, the clear, taut splendor of that celestial spirit which now flashed between them: vigilant Malacandra, captain of the cold orb, whom men call Mars and Mavors.[717]

Saturn comes next, and with him a "cold pressure such as might flatten the very orb of Tellus to a wafer."[718] The atmosphere becomes "like a mountain whose summit never comes into sight."[719] All of the previous gods seem to Merlin and Ransom "young and ephemeral" compared to great Saturn.[720] Yet, for all of his greatness, he is outmatched by the final god to come.

---

[714] C. S. Lewis, *That Hideous Strength*, 320–321.
[715] C. S. Lewis, *That Hideous Strength*, 321.
[716] C. S. Lewis, *That Hideous Strength*, 321.
[717] C. S. Lewis, *That Hideous Strength*, 322.
[718] C. S. Lewis, *That Hideous Strength*, 323.
[719] C. S. Lewis, *That Hideous Strength*, 323.
[720] C. S. Lewis, *That Hideous Strength*, 323.

C. S. LEWIS PRE-EVANGELISM FOR A POST-CHRISTIAN WORLD

The last celestial visitor to Ransom and his party is the father and ruler of the Oyarsa, "known to men in old times as Jove."[721] He is associated with joviality, celebratory cheer, good humor, and kingship. Rightly then does Lewis describe the scene that unfolds upon his coming as follows:

> No one knew afterwards how it happened but somehow the kettle was put on, the hot toddy was brewed. Arthur—the only musician among them—was bidden to get out his fiddle. The chairs were pushed back, the floor cleared. They danced. What they danced no one could remember ... it involved beating the floor, clapping of hands, leaping high ... It seemed to each that the room was filled with kings and queens, that the wildness of their dance expressed heroic energy and its quieter movements had seized the very spirit behind all noble ceremonies ... Before the other angels a man might sink; before this he might die, but if he lived at all, he would laugh. If you had caught one breath of the air that came from him, you would have felt yourself taller than before. Though you were a cripple, your walk would have become stately: though a beggar, you would have worn your rags magnanimously. Kingship and power and festal pomp and courtesy shot from him as sparks fly from an anvil. The pealing of bells, the flowing of trumpets, the spreading out of banners, are means used on earth to make a faint symbol of his quality ... It was like the first beginning of music in the halls of some King so high and at some festival so solemn that a tremor akin to fear runs through young hearts when they hear it. For this was great Glund-Oyarsa, King of Kings, through whom the joy of creation principally blows across these fields of Arbol, known to men in old times as Jove.[722]

The effect of this scene is, in a word, enchantment. The world that Lewis creates in his story is not a closed system whose explanation can be exhausted by the findings of science. Far from it, it is a world that is filled with the supernatural, with beings come from the heavens to help humanity in their struggle against the spiritual forces of wickedness in high places. Admittedly, Lewis takes great liberty with the details at these parts. Nevertheless, the sentiments that he aims to create are most fitting if Christianity is a true account of reality. Through the lenses of naturalism and scientism, those who look upon the world look upon a mechanistic world, a totally closed system that, given enough time, will be fully

---

[721] His Greek name is Zeus and the Roman equivalent is Jupiter.
[722] C. S. Lewis, *That Hideous Strength*, 323–324.

explainable via empirical observation. Once the last bit of explanation is given, the last bit of wonder will disappear with it.

At the close of *That Hideous Strength*, the Christian side, led by Maleldil, emerges victorious over the naturalistic scientism side, led by the Bent Oyarsa. The finale resembles the scene at the Tower of Babel, recorded by Moses. Lewis even refers to what ensues as "the curse of Babel."[723] The entire N.I.C.E. are gathered for a banquet. As Jules, the Director of the Institute, stands up to address those in attendance, his speech becomes meaningless gibberish. The crowd responds with confusion at first but soon thereafter with horror, as person after person is struck with the same malady. Chaos fills the air, and the reader learns that this is brought about by Merlin, who is channeling the power of the gods to bring about the downfall of their enemies. The animals on which the N.I.C.E. have been experimenting are set loose: a tiger, a wolf, a gorilla, an elephant, and a bear, and they begin mauling those attending the banquet.

Many die at the hands of the animals, while others die at each other's hands, their bodies manipulated by the influence of the dark eldils, while through their minds they helplessly watch like imprisoned spectators as they murder and are murdered. Their naturalistic worldview, which leaves them no room for free will or even any sense of something called a "self," seems at last to infiltrate their experience. To their horror, their bodies are taken over completely, and they are destroyed.

In the end, the gods level the N.I.C.E., and goodness prevails. The Bent One does not succeed in destroying humanity after all. Ransom and those on his side enjoy a great celebration as the coming of Venus ushers in a sweeping ethos of love and sexual bliss between husbands and wives. Fittingly, Lewis keeps the enjoyment of the sexual union within the confines of marriage.

In reading the space trilogy, one can see plainly that Lewis looks upon the world with a different set of lenses, namely, those of Christianity and pre-modern thought. The world is full of mystery and wonder. It is an open system in which the natural and the supernatural coexist, relate, and interact. A point is reached at which explanations for the world must look outside the system to a source that has come from without but has broken in and made such explanations known. A word from a privileged position has been sent to humanity in diverse forms: nature itself, miracles of history, inspired Scripture, and finally God made flesh. This is a world that says far more than what mere empirical observation can discern. Meaning, or "patches of Godlight," to use Lewis's terms, peer through the veil at nearly

---

[723] C. S. Lewis, *That Hideous Strength*, 348.

C. S. LEWIS PRE-EVANGELISM FOR A POST-CHRISTIAN WORLD

every turn. Part of the great genius behind much of Lewis's pre-evangelistic strategy through his fictional works is that he invites his readers to look deeper, and even to desire to take this deeper look in the first place.

While employed through his fictional literature, Lewis's mastery of using fitting symbolism and metaphors comes into particularly sharp relief at the close of this series with the coming of the gods. We are met with meaning far richer than lies at the level of the plot, the character development, or even the scenery. Nearly everything invites us to look longer and closer. This phenomenon is similar in form to the nature of the real world itself with all of its sacramental clues. The real world, like Lewis's books, asks us to look, to ponder, and to see if a depth of meaning not yet considered might lie behind, and might be coming through, what we see. By enticing his readers to "look" this way at his imaginary stories, he hopes to help them to gaze similarly at the real world, and in doing so, to know it more truly.

In the same way that a person who has not read Greek and Roman mythology would not be able to succeed at connecting all of the dots between the various qualities and the gods to which Lewis associates them, a person who has not read the Scriptures would not be able to discern rightly the real meaning behind the world. He would miss the Person by whom it is all held together. One needs a map if one is going to find one's way in a mysterious land. Classical mythology and the Scriptures serve as the maps for navigating the meaning behind this scene and the meaning behind the world respectively.

The evangelist's job is to open the "map" explicitly before his hearers. The pre-evangelist does the prior work of giving hints that suggest that one might want to look deeper in the first place. He aims to arouse desire in the heart of the onlooker by allowing him to taste a morsel of truth here, a bit of reality there, little by little leading him to the ultimate truth of the gospel that will make sense of all of the other truths encountered along the way. In Lewis's case as a pre-evangelist, we might say that he aims to enchant "the chest" so that he might in time come to enlighten "the head." Desire provoked is meant to lead to reason embraced, which Lewis maintains will lead one ultimately to Christ, the only source who could reconcile both hemispheres of his mind.

The Chronicles of Narnia

Of all of the stories that Lewis wrote, he is perhaps best known for his Narnia series. Because of this familiarity, these stories will be treated with far more brevity than the space trilogy. This section will provide pre-evangelistic glimpses drawn from each of the seven books. The Narnia stories center around the four Pevensie children, the enchanted land of Narnia, and most importantly, the great lion Aslan. In 1950, Lewis began publishing one book per year, releasing them in the following order: *The Lion, the Witch, and the Wardrobe*, *Prince Caspian*, *The Voyage of the Dawn Treader*, *The Silver Chair*, *The Horse and His Boy*, *The Magician's Nephew*, and finally *The Last Battle*. These books have had on so many people the same effect that MacDonald's *Phantastes* had on Lewis when he first read it—the awakening of a deep sense of longing or enchantment, very near to the experience of worship. Clyde Kilby tells of a letter written from a third-grade teacher in New Jersey who had been reading *The Lion, the Witch, and the Wardrobe* to her students. Her experience further illustrates this point. Kilby recounts:

> She had come to the point where the lion Aslan allowed himself to be killed by his enemies to save a bad boy's life. "The attitude of the room," said this teacher, "was worship, holiness. The rare impression of that moment will never leave me. When I finished the chapter about Aslan's death the room was stunned in disbelief. Aslan dead! And then a child who had read further said, 'Don't give up--something wonderful is going to happen.' It crept through the room and sighs issued. The little people had caught glimpses of the very real, the miracle of spiritual understanding."[724]

These children, though they likely lacked both the concept and the vocabulary to understand what was happening to them at the time, were experiencing the wonder stirred up by effective pre-evangelism.

By the time Lewis began writing these books, he was already well aware of the opportunity to "smuggle" theology into people's minds, to bring them into contact with reality, as it were, through an imaginative tale. In this section, we will explore how he does this through his Narnia books. A far lengthier treatment than this chapter can provide would be necessary to recount all of the "patches of Godlight" that breakthrough in *The Chronicles of Narnia*. That said, the following sampling should suffice to illustrate Lewis's pre-evangelistic strategy throughout these stories.

The Lion, the Witch, and the Wardrobe

In this first book that Lewis writes in the Narnia series, we are introduced to the four Pevensie children who are sent to the large home of

---

[724] Clyde Kilby, *A Well of Wonder: Essays on C. S. Lewis, J. R. R. Tolkien, and the Inklings*. eds. Loren Wilkinson and Keith Call (Brewster: Paraclete Press, 2016), 14–15.

C. S. LEWIS PRE-EVANGELISM FOR A POST-CHRISTIAN WORLD

Professor Kirk in the country to avoid the bombings going on in London by the Germans. While in the professor's home, the children play hide-and-seek. Lucy, who hides in a wardrobe, accidentally enters the enchanted land of Narnia. After having tea with a fawn named Tumnus, she returns and rejoins her siblings, telling them of her adventures. Because of her relentless insistence that she is not inventing a tale, Peter and Susan begin to wonder if something might be wrong with her. They consult the professor for his advice.

During this conversation, Lewis introduces his readers to an argument that has become somewhat well-known—his Lord, liar, or lunatic argument. He makes this same argument elsewhere, suggesting that Jesus has left the world with only three options regarding his true identity. Given the grandiose claims that Jesus made in identifying himself as the Messiah, saying that he had come from heaven to earth and such, Lewis argues that he is either a liar who aimed to deceive people or a lunatic on the level of a man who thinks himself a poached egg, or else the Lord himself. In other words, he is either lying, mad, or telling the truth.

After Peter and Susan explain their predicament about Lucy to the professor, the conversation ensues as follows:

"How do you know ... that your sister's story is not true?" ... Then Susan pulled herself together and said, "But Edmund said they had only been pretending." "That is a point," said the Professor, "which certainly deserves consideration ... does your experience lead you to regard your brother or your sister as the more reliable? I mean, which is the more truthful?" "That's just the funny thing about it, Sir," said Peter. "Up till now, I'd have said Lucy every time." "And what do you think, my dear?" said the Professor, turning to Susan. "Well," said Susan, "in general, I'd say the same as Peter, but this couldn't be true—all this about the wood and the faun." "That is more than I know," said the Professor, "and a charge of lying against someone whom you have always found truthful is a very serious thing, a very serious thing indeed." "We were afraid it mightn't even be lying," said Susan. "We thought there might be something wrong with Lucy." "Madness, you mean?" said the Professor. "Oh, you can make your minds easy about that. One has only to look at her and talk to her to see that she is not mad." "But then," said Susan and stopped ... "Logic!" said the Professor half to himself. Why don't they teach logic at these schools? There are only three possibilities. Either your sister is telling lies, or she is mad, or she is telling the truth. You know she doesn't tell lies and it is obvious that she is not mad. For the moment then and unless any further evidence turns up, we must assume that she is telling the truth."[725]

Though the characters and details are different, this argument is exactly the same in form as Lewis's argument for the identification of Jesus. In this way, he has given his readers the logical form of his argument disguised in imaginative fiction. In the real world, Lewis stands much like Professor Kirk in his story, saying half to himself, "Logic! Why don't they teach logic?" For Lewis, Christianity is not merely irrational wish fulfillment, nor is it a willful embracing of the absurd. Rather, it is reasonable, logical, and mindful of evidence. This is all subtly suggested to his readership in this memorable scene.

The most important character in Lewis's Narnia stories is clearly Aslan, the lion. He ties all of the books together and is the constant focus of each story, even when he remains absent from the foreground. When we come to the end of the final book, we learn that Aslan is not a mere type of Christ, but is Christ himself, who has taken on another form in Narnia to bring to that world the needed rescue. Thus, it is fitting that Lewis pours into Aslan's character, as well as he is able, the character and qualities of Christ.

In the scene where the children are visiting Mr. and Mrs. Beaver's home, the Beavers are telling them for the first time about Aslan. The children ask many questions, one of which, from Lucy's lips is, "Then he isn't safe?"[726] Mr. Beaver responds, "Safe? ... Don't you hear what Mrs. Beaver tells you? Who said anything about safe? 'Course he isn't safe. But he's good. He's the King, I tell you."[727] Anyone who is familiar with the Bible's description of Christ, especially one who has "looked along" rather than "looked at" Christianity merely, will notice how fitting a description of Christ Mr. Beaver provides in his short response to Lucy. The point is this—when we learn about the fictitious Aslan, we are also learning some things about the real Christ.

The final example worth mentioning from this first book is perhaps the most explicit pre-evangelistic glimpse found in all of the series. Edmund has betrayed his brother and sisters to the White Witch, and in doing so, has become the property of the Witch. She lawfully lays claim to his life and may do with him what she chooses, even to the point of killing him. In order to set him free, Aslan exchanges his life for Edmund's. He gives his

---

[725] C. S. Lewis, *The Lion, the Witch and the Wardrobe*, 43–45.
[726] C. S. Lewis, *The Lion, the Witch and the Wardrobe*, 75.
[727] C. S. Lewis, *The Lion, the Witch and the Wardrobe*, 75–76.

C. S. LEWIS PRE-EVANGELISM FOR A POST-CHRISTIAN WORLD

life into the hands of Witch, allows himself to be bound to the sacred stone table, and submits to death by the Witch's knife. While Lucy and Susan watch from a hidden location, just before she plunges the knife into his body, the Witch says to Aslan:

> "And now, who has won? Fool, did you think that by all this you would save the human traitor? Now I will kill you instead of him as our pact was and so the Deep Magic will be appeased ... Understand that you have given me Narnia forever, you have lost your own life and you have not saved his. In that knowledge, despair and die."[728]

Upon finishing her mocking speech, the Witch slays Aslan. As his body lay dead atop the stone table, all hope seems to have faded. Susan and Lucy come after the Witch and her minions have left, and begin to weep over him. While doing so, they notice that mice have come and have begun gnawing away at the straps that hold him down. After walking to the edge of a hill to look out at the castle Cair Paravel, stunned by grief and disappointment, they hear a loud crack behind them. Surprised, they turn around and find the stone table cracked, with no sign of Aslan. Susan, through her tears, asks:

> "Who's done it? ... What does it mean? Is it more magic?" "Yes!" said a great voice behind their backs. "It is more magic." They looked round. There, shining in the sunrise, larger than they had seen him before, shaking his mane (for it had apparently grown again) stood Aslan himself ... "Oh, you're real, you're real! Oh, Aslan!" cried Lucy and both girls flung themselves upon him and covered him with kisses.[729]

Aslan proceeds to explain to the girls the nature of the "Deep Magic,"[730] which causes death to work backward when an innocent person sacrifices his life upon the stone table for a guilty person. The Witch thought that by killing Aslan, she was laying claim for all time to Narnia. Little did she know that Aslan's death would in time prove to be her own undoing. He soon makes his way to the Witch's castle, sets those whom she has turned to stone free, and meets her at last in battle, simultaneously ending her life and her reign over Narnia.

---

[728] C. S. Lewis, *The Lion, the Witch and the Wardrobe*, 152.
[729] C. S. Lewis, *The Lion, the Witch and the Wardrobe*, 158–159.
[730] C. S. Lewis, *The Lion, the Witch and the Wardrobe*, 159.

Brian M. Williams

In Aslan's death and resurrection that sets guilty Edmund free, Lewis gives to us a glimpse of the cross and resurrection of Christ—the innocent dying in place of the guilty which causes death to "work backwards." This is the great eucatastrophe (the "good catastrophe") in Lewis's story—the sudden turn that begins to set wrong things right. It is a shadow of the central event in human history when Christ really did something very much like what Aslan did.

Prince Caspian

In the second book in the series, many years have passed in Narnia since the events of *The Lion, the Witch and the Wardrobe*. Prince Caspian lives with his wicked uncle, Miraz, who, through cunning, has become king of Narnia. Caspian has heard from his nurse of the old days in Narnia when "all the animals could talk, and there were nice people who lived in the streams and the trees. Naiads and dryads they were called. And there were dwarfs. And there were lovely little Fauns in all the woods."[731] King Miraz has eradicated every semblance of the old days from the land and has convinced most people that all of the tales of talking animals and Old Narnia are nonsense.

In King Miraz, Lewis is introducing his readers to something akin to the anti-supernatural viewpoint that had become very prevalent in his own day. After sending away his nurse for filling Caspian's head with "fairy tales"[732] of "Old Narnia,"[733] King Miraz hires another teacher for Caspian, a suspiciously short man named Dr. Cornelius. Unbeknownst to Miraz, the new teacher is half man-half-dwarf, and he promises to tell Caspian the truth about Old Narnia, as soon as the opportunity presents itself.

In what proves to be the most enchanting scene in the second book, Dr. Cornelius tells Caspian to go to bed early so that he can wake him when a certain conjunction of two planets draws near, at which time he will give him a lesson in Astronomy. Lewis describes Dr. Cornelius's coming to wake Caspian thus:

> [H]e soon dropped off and it seemed only a few minutes before he felt someone gently shaking him. He sat up in bed and saw that the room was full of moonlight. Dr. Cornelius, muffled in a hooded robe and holding a small lamp in his hand, stood by the bedside … Caspian followed the doctor through many passages and up several staircases, and at last, though a little door in a

---

[731] C. S. Lewis, *Prince Caspian*, 38–39.
[732] C. S. Lewis, *Prince Caspian*, 39.
[733] C. S. Lewis, *Prince Caspian*, 43.

C. S. LEWIS PRE-EVANGELISM FOR A POST-CHRISTIAN WORLD

turret, they came out upon the leads. On one side were the battlements, on the other a steep roof; below them, all shadowy and shimmery, the castle gardens; above them, stars and moon. Presently they came into another door which led into the great central tower of the whole castle: Doctor Cornelius unlocked it and they began to climb the dark winding stair of the castle. Caspian was becoming excited ... Away on his right he could see, rather indistinctly, the western mountains. On his left was the gleam of the Great River, and everything was so quiet that he could hear the sound of the waterfall at Beaversdam, a mile away.[734]

We remember that Lewis placed great importance upon atmosphere literature. In this scene, he creates an air mystery, intrigue, and enchantment that is fitting for the revelation that Dr. Cornelius is about to make known to Caspian. At last his teacher admits: "I brought you here for another reason ... The virtue of this tower ... is that we have six empty rooms beneath us, and a long stair, and the door at the bottom of the stair is locked. We cannot be overheard."[735] Dr. Cornelius continues, "Listen ... All you have heard about Old Narnia is true. It is not the land of men. It is the country of Aslan, the country of the Walking Trees and the Visible Naiads, of Fauns and Satyrs, of Dwarfs and Giants, of the gods and the Centaurs, of Talking Beasts."[736]

After revealing the truth about Old Narnia to Caspian, Dr. Cornelius tells him that they must be on their way. Delighted by what he has been told, Caspian responds, "Must we? ... I'd like to go on taking about these things for hours and hours and hours."[737] He learned that the nature of reality was not the cold story that his wicked uncle had told him but the enchanted one that had he wished to be true but that had fallen out of fashion. Caspian longed for the conversation to continue. We see that the same spirit of the age that King Miraz brought to pass in Narnia was similar to the one that had taken hold in Lewis's. It was a disenchanted view of reality that had turned its back on the spiritual and the wonderful. Part of Lewis's aim, much like Dr. Cornelius's, was to remedy this disenchantment. The reader can experience something of a sense of re-enchantment vicariously through Caspian as he learns of Old Narnia atop the central castle tower on a moonlit night through the lips of a half-man half-dwarf

---

[734] C. S. Lewis, *Prince Caspian*, 44–45.
[735] C. S. Lewis, *Prince Caspian*, 46.
[736] C. S. Lewis, *Prince Caspian*, 47.
[737] C. S. Lewis, *Prince Caspian*, 51.

teacher. I can remember, very vividly, reading this story to my son before he drifted off to sleep. The wonder that filled his eyes and the longing for me to keep reading more, which he begged for passionately, convinced me that something of the same enchantment that Caspian felt had made its way into my son's young heart.

The Voyage of the Dawn Treader

In *The Voyage of the Dawn Treader*, the reader is introduced to Eustace Clarence Scrubb, cousin of the Pevensies. He is a selfish and bratty young boy strongly dislikes his cousins. The story begins with three children (Edmund, Lucy, and Eustace) entering the land of Narnia through a painting on the wall. Once in Narnia, their adventures commence. At one point in their journey, Eustace slips away from the others and finds himself looking across a little valley with a pool of a water in the center and a cave next to it. As he watches, a dragon slithers out, takes a drink from the pool, rolls over, and then dies. After checking to make sure that the dragon is really dead, heavy rains begin to fall.

Seeking shelter in the cave, Eustace notices that it is full of treasure. He takes a bracelet that is cinctured with diamonds and slips it onto his wrist before nodding off to sleep. He is awakened at last by a sharp pain in his arm. As he looks down in front of him, to his horror, he notices two dragon arms. Mistaken at first, he thinks that a dragon perhaps seized him while he lay sleeping. In time, he discovers that the dragon arms are his own and that he has become the victim of some terrible curse. He realizes that the pain in his arm was caused by the bracelet cutting into his scaly flesh, as his transformation had enlarged his size considerably.

Eustace tries to no avail to tear the bracelet from his forearm and the scaly skin from his body. It is not until he encounters Aslan that his deliverance from the dragon curse comes. Aslan says to him, "You will have to let me undress you."[738] Recounting later to Edmund how Aslan helped him, Eustace explains:

> The very first tear he made was so deep that I thought it had gone right into my heart. And when he began pulling the skin off, it hurt worse than anything I've ever felt. The only thing that made me able to bear it was just the pleasure of feeling the stuff peel off ... Well, he peeled the beastly stuff right off ... And there was I as smooth and soft as a peeled switch and smaller than I had

---

[738] C. S. Lewis, *The Voyage of the Dawn Treader*, 90.

C. S. LEWIS PRE-EVANGELISM FOR A POST-CHRISTIAN WORLD

been ... I'd turned into a boy again ... After a bit the lion took me out and dressed me ... in new clothes.[739]

In this encounter between Eustace the dragon and Aslan the lion, Lewis communicates several concepts inherent within Christianity's teachings. Eustace's transformation into the dragon stands as an outward expression of his inner character. He is dragon-like in his character long before he becomes a dragon externally. What lay on the inside had simply worked its way to the outside, brought about by the cursed treasure. When he tries to cure himself, he lacks the power to do so. It will take claws that can penetrate far deeper than his own dragon claws to turn him back into a human boy. Aslan's claws will have to dig down into his heart in order to tear the scales off of his outer flesh. It was a painful operation, the most painful Eustace had ever felt. Rather than leaving him naked, Aslan dresses him in new clothes. Once Eustace is redressed, he is smaller than he was before, his smallness symbolizing his newly found humility. In fact, when the reader meets Eustace in the next book, *The Silver Chair*, Eustace recalls the boy he once was before he met Aslan. He remembers, "I was a different chap then. I was—gosh! what a little tick I was."[740]

In a way, Lewis was describing the operation of salvation that Christ brings about in a person's life. Like the dragon scales on Eustace's body, removing the curse of sin from one's life proves far beyond all human capacities and resources. Only the work of Christ on the sinner's behalf can provide the needed deliverance. His work must penetrate much deeper than one's outward behavior. It must reach all the way down into the recesses of the human heart. Lewis knew the process of coming to Christ in his own life to be a painful one, and he described his conversion as one who was "dejected and reluctant."[741] The painful tearing away of the flesh from its forbidden loves is an experience known widely among Christians, and Lewis captures this truth vividly in Eustace's experience with Aslan.

The Silver Chair

The fourth book in the series finds Eustace and his friend Jill Pole called by Aslan into his country. Once there, Jill meets Aslan and becomes extremely thirsty. Through this scene, Lewis conveys the truth that only Christ can quench the deepest thirst of the human heart, and that by coming

---

[739] C. S. Lewis, *The Voyage of the Dawn Treader*, 90–91.
[740] C. S. Lewis, *The Silver Chair*, 3.
[741] C. S. Lewis, *Surprised by Joy*, 229.

to Christ, one cannot remain unchanged. Also, Aslan is portrayed again as entirely unsafe, but good. Lewis writes:

> "Are you not thirsty?" said the Lion. "I'm *dying* of thirst," said Jill. "Then drink," said the Lion ... "Will you promise not to—do anything to me, if I do come?" said Jill. "I make no promise," said the Lion. Jill was so thirsty now that, without noticing it, she had come a step nearer. "Do you eat girls?" she said. "I have swallowed up girls and boys, women and men, kings and emperors, cities and realms," said the Lion. It didn't say this as if it were boasting, nor as if it were sorry, nor as if it were angry. It just said it. "I daren't come and drink," said Jill. "Then you will die of thirst," said the Lion. "Oh dear!" said Jill, coming another step nearer. "I suppose I must go and look for another stream then." "There is no other stream," said the Lion. It never occurred to Jill to disbelieve the Lion—no one who had seen his stern face could do that—and her mind suddenly made itself up. It was the worst thing she had ever had to do, but she went forward to the stream, knelt down, and began scooping up water in her hand. It was the coldest, most refreshing water she had ever tasted.[742]

We see through Jill's encounter with Aslan before the pool the same truths that apply to Jesus.

Second perhaps only to *The Screwtape Letters*, in a later scene Lewis captures vividly the nature of temptation, particularly the intellectual kind that aims to make Christianity seem like make-believe wishful thinking.[743] Lewis had faced such a temptation earlier in his life through his encounter with Freud's philosophy. Because people wished for religion to be true, Freud maintained, they had concocted myths that gave them that for which they wished. One can hear not only Freud's voice in the Queen of Underland, who is also called the Witch, but also a complete denial of the point Plato that made in his cave analogy.

Along with the unforgettable Marsh-wiggle Puddleglum, the children have come to rescue Prince Rilian, who has been captured by the Witch.

---

[742] C. S. Lewis, *The Silver Chair*, 16–18.

[743] See Stratford Caldecott, "Speaking the Truths Only the Imagination May Grasp: Myth and 'Real Life'" in *The Pilgrim's Guide*, edited by David Mills, 87, where Caldecott writes differentiates the longing for God from mere wishful thinking. He writes, "This longing ... is a longing for union with something infinitely remote and infinitely beautiful; a longing for self-transformation, for the One who entirely transcends our present state ... This is the longing that myths evoke ... it would be a mistake to dismiss our myths as 'wishful thinking' and nothing more. As J. R. R. Tolkien wrote, 'legends and myths are largely made of "truth," and indeed present aspects of it that can only be received in this mode.'"

C. S. LEWIS PRE-EVANGELISM FOR A POST-CHRISTIAN WORLD

After throwing some magical green powder into the fire and then playing an enchanted instrument that causes drowsiness and forgetfulness, the Witch commences her assault on the rescue party's beliefs. Puddleglum insists that the upper world of Narnia is real, and his conversation with the Witch proceeds thus:

> "There is no land of Narnia." "Yes there is though, Ma'am," said Puddleglum. "You see, I happen to have lived there all my life." "Indeed," said the Witch. "Tell me, I pray you, where that country is?" … "It's in Overworld" … "And what, or where, pray is this … how do you call it *Overworld?*" "Oh don't be so silly," said Scrub … "As if you didn't know! It's up above, where you can see the sky and the sun and the stars."[744]

The Witch's enchantment begins to take hold, and she slowly succeeds in convincing the children that their supposed memory of Narnia is nothing but a dream. Not to be taken in so easily, Puddleglum continues to argue with the Witch, tenaciously resisting the power of her spell. He replies:

> "But you can play that fiddle till your fingers drop off, and still you won't make me forget Narnia … I've seen the sun coming up out of the sea on a morning and sinking behind the mountains at night" … "What is this sun you all speak of? Do you mean anything by the word? … "Please it your grace," said the Prince … "You see that lamp. It is round and yellow and gives light to the whole room … Now that thing which we call the sun is like the lamp, only far greater and brighter" … "You see? When you try to think out clearly what this *sun* must be, you cannot tell me. You can only tell me it is like the lamp. Your *sun* is a dream; and there is nothing in that dream that was not copied from the lamp. The lamp is the real thing; the sun is but a tale, a children's story."[745]

Next, the rescue party tries to convince the Witch that Aslan is real, comparing him to a cat that scurries past them on the ground while conversing. Employing the same strategy as with the lamp, she dismantles their belief in Aslan as well:

> "I see," she said, "that we should do no better with your *lion*, as you call it, than we did with your *sun*. You have seen lamps, and so you imagined a bigger and better lamp and called it the *sun*.

---

[744] C. S. Lewis, *The Silver Chair*, 152.
[745] C. S. Lewis, *The Silver Chair*, 154–156.

You've seen cats, and now you want a bigger and better cat, and it's so called a *lion*. Well, 'tis a pretty make-believe, though, to say the truth, it would suit you all better if you were younger. And look how you can put nothing into your make-believe without copying it from the real world, this world of mine, which is the only world ... There is no Narnia, no Overworld, no sky, no sun, no Aslan."[746]

Finally, Puddleglum stamps out the fire, dispelling the power of the Witch's spell, and he argues back with her:

"Suppose this black pit of a kingdom of yours *is* the only world. Well, it strikes me as a pretty poor one. And that's a funny thing, when you come to think of it. We're just babies making up a game, if you're right. But four babies playing a game can make a play-world which licks your real world hollow. That's why I'm going to stand by the play world. I'm on Aslan's side even if there isn't any Aslan to lead it. I'm going to live as like a Narnian as I can even if there isn't any Narnia."[747]

One must not read into Puddleglum's argument the denial of reason. On the contrary, he makes a very reasonable case that has some affinity to Anselmian thought. The likelihood that four simple young people could fashion out of their imaginations a better world than the real one, a greater ruler in Aslan than the present ruler of the Underworld, and that they would desire this world in first place seemed like an unlikely prospect unless such a world were actually true. Who told them of this better world? If it were not real, why were they longing for it? Contrary to what Freud had argued, might not their longing for a better world not serve as evidence *for* such a world rather than against it? Why must the fact that one desires something lessen the probability of that thing's existence? Is it not just as reasonable, perhaps more reasonable even, that some of the human heart's deepest desires align with, rather than stand at odds with reality? Lewis makes such an argument with respect to one's desire for heaven in *Mere*

---

[746] C. S. Lewis, *The Silver Chair*, 157. One can also see in the Witch's argument a denial of the views affirmed in the previous chapter regarding symbols and metaphors, views drawn from Bevan's and Barfield's books. Again, both writers affirm the view that good metaphors bear an essential affinity to the things themselves. Further, one of the purposes of metaphors and symbols is to shed light on things not seen or experienced. As was mentioned in the previous chapter, the universality of some of these symbols for the divine throughout various ages and cultures seems telling. The reader will recall that Bevan discusses such symbols as height, light, time, and spirit with respect to God.

[747] C. S. Lewis, *The Silver Chair*, 159.

C. S. LEWIS PRE-EVANGELISM FOR A POST-CHRISTIAN WORLD

Christianity, and back of Puddleglum's response to the Witch, one can detect the same sentiments.

The Horse and His Boy

In Lewis's fifth book, the boy Shasta and his friend Aravis are traveling across the desert on horseback. Shasta's horse is named Bree and Aravis's is Hwin. At one point during their journey, they encounter a lion that attacks them. Lewis describes the scene thus:

> Shasta saw all this in a glance and looked back again. The lion had almost got Hwin now. It was making snaps at her hind legs, and there was no hope now in her foam-flecked, wide-eyed face … One of the most terrible noises in the world, a horse's scream, broke from Hwin's lips … the lion rose on its hind legs, larger than you would have believed a lion could be, and jabbed at Aravis with its right paw. Shasta could see all the terrible claws extended. Aravis screamed and reeled in the saddle. The lion was tearing her shoulders.[748]

The two travelers are forced to flee inside a gate in a green wall where they are welcomed and where Aravis's wounds are nursed by a hermit. After helping them, the Hermit says:

> "Now, daughter, you may sleep when you wish … For your wounds are washed and dressed and though they smart they are no more serious than if they had been the cuts of a whip. It must have been a very strange lion, for instead of catching you out of the saddle and getting his teeth into you, he has only drawn his claws across your back. Ten scratches: sore, but not deep or dangerous."[749]

At some time later, the same lion catches up with Shasta while he is traveling along atop his horse Bree on a dark night. He does not know it is a lion at first, because of the darkness, but he feels warm breath beside him. Suddenly, a "large voice"[750] begins speaking to him. The conversation ensues:

> "I can't see you at all," said Shasta … "Oh, I am the unluckiest person in the whole world" … "I do not call you unlucky," said the Large Voice. "Don't you think it was bad luck to meet so

---

[748] C. S. Lewis, *The Horse and His Boy*, 138–139.
[749] C. S. Lewis, *The Horse and His Boy*, 143.
[750] C. S. Lewis, *The Horse and His Boy*, 157.

many lions?" said Shasta. "There was only one lion," said the Voice ... "How do you know?" "I was the lion." And as Shasta gaped with open mouth and said nothing, the Voice continued, "I was the lion who forced you to join with Aravis. I was the cat who comforted you among the houses of the dead. I was the lion who drove the jackals from you while you slept. I was the lion who gave the horses the new strength of fear for the last mile so that you should reach King Lune in time" ... "Then it was you who wounded Aravis?" "It was I." "But what for?" "Child," said the Voice, "I am telling you your story, not hers. I tell no-one any story but his own." "Who are you?" said Shasta. "Myself," said the Voice, very deep and low so that the earth shook ... Shasta was no longer afraid that the Voice belonged to something that would eat him, nor that it was the voice of a ghost. But a new and different sort of trembling came over him. Yet he felt glad too. The mist was turning from black to grey and from grey to white ... Now the whiteness around him became a shining whiteness; his eyes began to blink. Somewhere ahead he could hear birds singing. He knew the night was over at last ... A golden light fell on them from the left. He thought it was the sun. He turned and saw, pacing beside him, taller than the horse, a Lion ... It was from the lion that the light came. No-one ever saw anything more terrible or beautiful.[751]

Through this scene, Lewis conveys once again the goodness and beauty, mingled with the terror and the danger of Christ, through the character of Aslan. He also communicates the providential help of God that attends the Christian throughout life's many twists and turns. Similar to God's workings in the real world on behalf of the Christian, Aslan's help manifests itself at times as danger, obstacles, set-backs, detours, and such. Like the disciples in the Scriptures who question the fairness of God's plan for them compared to what Christ tells John he must face, neither they nor Shasta are given an up-front explanation for the hidden providential purposes in their lives. They only learn these things by looking backwards. Lewis uses this scene as a metaphor, a kind of literary sacramental hint, at some of the ways that God operates in the lives his children.

The Magician's Nephew

When the reader comes to the sixth book in Lewis's Narnia series, he is treated to many explanations of how many things originally came to be in Lewis's imaginary world. The origin of the White Witch, the lamppost,

---

[751] C. S. Lewis, *The Horse and His Boy*, 157–160.

C. S. LEWIS PRE-EVANGELISM FOR A POST-CHRISTIAN WORLD

the wardrobe, and even Narnia itself are explained. Through the founding of Narnia, Lewis offers a story that bears some affinity to the factual story told in the opening chapter of Genesis. The parallels are not difficult to discern. Lewis writes:

> In the darkness something was happening at last. A voice had begun to sing. It was very far away and Digory found it hard to decide from what direction it was coming. Sometimes it seemed to come from all directions at once ... There were no words. There was hardly even a tune. But it was, beyond comparison, the most beautiful noise he had ever heard. It was so beautiful he could hardly bear it ... Then two wonders happened at the same moment. One was that the voice was suddenly joined by other voices; more voices than you could possibly count. They were in harmony with it, but far higher up the scale: cold, tingling, silvery voices. The second wonder was the blackness overhead, all at once, was blazing with stars. They didn't come out gently one by one, as they do on a summer evening. One moment there had been nothing but darkness; next moment a thousand, thousand points of light leaped out—single stars, constellations, and planets, brighter and bigger than any in our world ... But the Witch looked as if, in a way, she understood the music better than any of them. Her mouth was shut, her lips were pressed together, and her fists were clenched. Ever since the song began she had felt that this whole world was filled with a Magic different from hers and stronger. She hated it ... the Voice rose and rose, till all the air was shaking with it. And just as it swelled to the mightiest and most glorious sound it had yet produced, the sun arose ... The earth was full of many colours: they were fresh, hot, and vivid. They made you feel excited, until you saw the Singer himself, and then you forgot everything else. It was a Lion. Huge, shaggy, and bright it stood facing the risen sun ... Thus, with an unspeakable thrill, she [Polly] felt quite certain that all the things were coming (as she said) "out of the Lion's head." When you listened to his song you heard the things he was making up: when you looked round you, you saw them.[752]

Aslan walks to and fro throughout the darkness, singing ever more of the land of Narnia into existence. Like the account in Genesis, the world comes into being through the divine creator's mind and mouth. Narnia is an orderly and beautiful world, not yet stained by evil, as sadly it will come

---

[752] C. S. Lewis, *The Magician's Nephew*, 98–107.

to be in time. Though it gets corrupted, we see that it remains essentially good and worth saving in the final book.

For those who have not joined the Witch's side, the music proves the most delightful thing they have ever heard. However, for the Witch and those aligned with her, Aslan's song strikes them as grating and jarring. They find themselves repulsed by it. Lewis is communicating something that is shown throughout the Scriptures implicitly and is told explicitly in a few places. Those who love the true, the good, and the beautiful naturally are delighted whenever they encounter its varied visitations. On the other hand, for those whose desires have been warped such that they love falsehood, evil, and ugliness, even beautiful things disgust them. John, in his gospel, writes of individuals who love darkness and hate light, for example. Elsewhere one finds that to the perverse, God Himself seems crooked. Lewis expresses this principle in another book, arguing that "the instrument through which you see God is your whole self. And if a man's self is not kept clean and bright, his glimpse of God will be blurred—like the Moon seen through a dirty telescope."[753]

The Last Battle

The story that concludes the Chronicles of Narnia is *The Last Battle*. Significantly, it is also in this final story that Lewis's sacramental view of reality emerges most explicitly. The shadows are revealed to be precisely that, shadows which, while they were wonderful in their own way, were only ever the foretaste of the more solid, more real realities that Aslan had been preparing all along. In addition, *The Last Battle* might be the story in which the human longing for heaven is aroused more potently than in any of his other books.

For those who read the final book for the first time, the experience is one first of intense sadness at what is lost that in time gives way to joyful celebration at what has been restored. The loss is felt as Aslan begins, little by little, unmaking the Narnia that many have come to love. The great forests disappear, the stars fall from the heavens, the mountains are removed, and all in time becomes utter blackness. After Aslan causes final night to fall upon Narnia, bringing it to its intended end, Peter says to Lucy:

> "What, Lucy! You're not *crying*? With Aslan ahead, and all of us here?" "Don't try to stop me, Peter," said Lucy, "I am sure Aslan would not. I am sure it is not wrong to mourn for Narnia. Think of all that lies dead and frozen behind that door." "Yes, and I *did*

---

[753] C. S. Lewis, *Mere Christianity*, 164–165.

hope," said Jill, "that it might go on forever. I knew *our* world couldn't. I did think Narnia might."[754]

Lucy is right to mourn, as what she says goodbye to is good. Yet, as the children and their company continue to go "further up and further in" to the new country to which Aslan has brought them, glimmers of past experiences and a strange sense of familiarity begins slowly to arrest them. Lewis writes:

> It still seemed to be early and the morning freshness was in the air. They kept on stopping to look round and to look behind them, partly because it was so beautiful but partly also because there was something about it which they could not understand. "Peter," said Lucy, "where is this, do you suppose?" "I don't know," said the High King. "It reminds me of somewhere but I can't give it a name. Could it be somewhere we once stayed for a holiday when we were very, very small?" "It would have to have been a jolly good holiday," said Eustace. "I bet there isn't a country like this anywhere in *our* world. Look at the colours? You couldn't get a blue like the blue on those mountains in our world" ... "If you ask me," said Edmund, "it's like somewhere in the Narnian world. Look at those mountains ahead—and the big ice-mountains beyond them. Surely they're rather like the mountains we used to see from Narnia, the ones up Westward beyond the Waterfall?" "Yes, so they are," said Peter. "Only these are bigger." "I don't think *those* ones are so very like anything in Narnia," said Lucy. "But look there ... Those hills ... the nice woody ones and the blue ones behind—aren't they very like the southern border of Narnia?" "Like!" cried Edmund after a moment's silence. "Why they're exactly like" ... "And yet they're not like," said Lucy. "They're different. They have more colours on them and they look further away than I remembered and they're more ... more ... oh, I don't know ..." "More like the real thing," said the Lord Digory softly.[755]

It is Farsighted the Eagle who at last makes the wonderful discovery.

"Kings and Queens," he cried, "we have all been blind. We are only beginning to see where we are. From up there I have seen it all—Ettinsmuir, Beaversdam, the Great River, and Cair Paravel still shining on the edge of the Eastern Sea. Narnia is not dead. This is Narnia" ... "The Eagle is right,"

---

[754] C. S. Lewis, *The Last Battle*, 158.
[755] C. S. Lewis, *The Last Battle*, 167–169.

said Lord Digory. "Listen, Peter. When Aslan said you could never go back to Narnia, he meant the Narnia you were thinking of. But that was not the real Narnia. That had a beginning and an end. It was only a shadow or copy of the real Narnia, which has always been here and always will be here: just as our own world, England and all, is only a shadow or copy of something in Aslan's real world. You need not mourn over Narnia, Lucy. All of the old Narnia that mattered, all the dear creatures, have been drawn into the real Narnia through the Door. And of course it is different; as different as a real thing is from a shadow or as waking life is from a dream." His voice stirred everyone like a trumpet as he spoke these words: but when he added under his breath "It's all in Plato, all in Plato: bless me, what *do* they teach them at these schools!" the older ones laughed.[756]

What was "all in Plato" was the idea which we have already explored—that of a lower world being merely a copy of an upper, more real world. That is to say, in a word, that the lower world bears a sacramental quality that draws our eyes and hearts upward and awakens longing for this more real-world and ultimately for its creator whom we were always meant to enjoy.

As they continue journeying deeper into the real Narnia, they find, to their immense delight, that they can run without growing tired, swim effortlessly up waterfalls, see far off in the distance without need of binoculars. Try as they might, they can feel no fear, only adventurous excitement. Everything wonderful, beautiful, and good, with no mixture of ugliness or wickedness, fills the new world. They find that the Narnia that Lucy had been mourning just moments prior is the very land to which they have come, fully restored. To their increasing pleasure, they discover that Narnia is not the only land in the new world. They see England as well. The worlds have been merged into one everlasting world upon which the darkness of death and cessation will never fall.

In the final pages, they come at last to Aslan, who says to them:

"You do not yet look so happy as I mean you to be." Lucy said, "We're so afraid of being sent away, Aslan. And you have sent us back into our own world so often." "No fear of that," said Aslan. "Have you not guessed?" Their hearts leaped and a wild hope rose within them. "There *was* a real railway accident," said Aslan softly. "Your father and mother and all of you are—as you used to call it in the Shadow-Lands—dead. The term is over: the holidays have begun. The dream has ended: this is the morning."And as He spoke He no longer looked to them like a

---

[756] C. S. Lewis, *The Last Battle*, 169–170.

lion; but the things that began to happen after that were so great and beautiful that I cannot write them. And for us this is the end of all the stories, and we can most truly say that they all lived happily ever after. All their life in this world and all their adventures in Narnia had only been the cover and the title page: now at last they were beginning Chapter One of the Great Story, which no one on earth has read: which goes on forever: in which every chapter is better than the one before.[757]

With these words, Lewis brings his Chronicles of Narnia to a close. Through them, he has offered to his readers not an allegorical tale, but a supposal. He has asked them to suppose that Christ had come as a lion into a world full of talking beasts and mythological creatures that, like the real world, also needed saving. In doing so, he has provided, or at least aimed to provide, an imaginative literary sacramentalism. He wants his readers not only to look *at*, but to look *through*, much as the children in the story pass through the Shadow-Lands of the old world into the real world to which they always pointed. Still more, he wants his readers, as a result of their looking *through*, to come to long—to long deeply for the more real-world and ultimately for the one who is the real Aslan, whose earthly name is Jesus. He wants his stories to do for others what George MacDonald's and many others' had done for him.

As he aims for this, he knows that his role is akin to John the Baptist's, whereas the explicit gospel proclaimer's is more akin to Christ's. Lewis's role, through his fiction, is that of pre-evangelist, the one who does the preparatory work prior to the evangelist's coming. He is hoping to prepare the soil of the imagination and in time the intellect, so that when the gospel message is brought to the individual, it might come to him in "favorable conditions."[758]

CONCLUSION

To return now to the previous chapter's discussion of Bevan's and Barfield's views of symbolism and metaphor, along with Lewis's own argument that in a sense reality and the imaginative world are inseparable, the importance of surveying these pre-evangelistic truths throughout the

---

[757] C. S. Lewis, *The Last Battle*, 183–184.
[758] See C. S. Lewis, "The Decline of Religion," in *God in the Dock*, 241. Though cited earlier in this chapter, it will be helpful to cite here as well. Lewis writes, "The propagandist, the apologist, only represents John the Baptist: the Preacher represents the Lord Himself. He will be sent—or else he will not. But unless he comes we mere Christian intellectuals will not effect very much. That does not mean we should down tools."

space trilogy and the Chronicles of Narnia can be expressed as follows. The separation between the symbolic and the literal is a separation that Lewis lamented, in part due to the influence of Bevan and Barfield. Further, the denial that the imaginative world depends on the real one for its material presents a false separation between what remains essentially linked.

Duriez writes, "Lewis suggested that comparatively recently we (Western people) lost an ancient sense of the unity of the poetic and the prosaic, the symbolic and the literal. It was this unity that Lewis and his friends tried to regain through their fantasy."[759] If this linkage is, as Lewis and his influencers believed, an ontological connection, the separation is an *epistemological*, and not an *ontological* one—that is, it is a separation of what is *known*, not of what *is*. It is a matter of learning to see things as they truly are again. This means that one way that we can help people to see reality as it truly is would be to present them with imaginative stories that employ good metaphors and symbols, enchanted tales that present the structure of reality as it really is, however one may choose to disguise it.

This is the sense in which Lewis's "myths" can help in a pre-evangelistic sense. They bring the reader face-to-face with reality, via the symbol, or the sacrament, to use Lewis's preferred term. In doing so, they begin to acquaint the reader with reality while the defenses remain less alert than they would be if Lewis were to use explicitly Christian language. When, in time, the Christian message is presented plainly, Lewis hoped that the person would recognize that these were the very truths he had been delighting in all along, disrobed of their fantastical costumes, and he would therefore in turn make the rational and finally the volitional move to follow Christ.

This can be illustrated through a letter that Lewis wrote to a concerned mother who feared that her son, Lawrence, might have come to love Aslan more than Jesus. Lewis responds to the mother:

> Lawrence can't really love Aslan more than Jesus, even if he feels that's what he's doing. For the things he loves Aslan for doing or saying are simply the things Jesus really did and said. So that when Lawrence thinks he is loving Aslan, he is really loving Jesus: and perhaps loving Him more than he ever did before ... If I were Lawrence I'd just say in my prayers something like this: "Dear God, if the things I've been thinking and feeling about those books are things You don't like and are bad for me, please take

---

[759] Colin Duriez, "The Romantic Writer: Lewis's Theology of Fantasy," in *The Pilgrim's Guide*, 99.

C. S. LEWIS PRE-EVANGELISM FOR A POST-CHRISTIAN WORLD

away those feelings and thoughts. But if they are not bad, then please stop me from worrying about them."[760]

To recap a bit—in chapters two and three, I have attempted to explain the reasons why this phenomenon not only seems effective in many cases but also why it is a legitimate approach in the overall aim of helping people come to know Christ. As we have seen, it is precisely because of the nature of reality and the human imagination, along with the relationship between the two, that the Christian who possesses the knowledge and the ability to produce such imaginative works should feel both the allowance and the encouragement, as well as the confidence to do so. His confidence can rest on the fact that God has made the world and his image-bearers such that a Lewisian pre-evangelistic approach is both fitting and good.

In the present chapter, I have tried to illustrate Lewis's understanding of his own pre-evangelistic strategy and the impetus behind it. We have looked together at glimpses of his strategy employed through his space trilogy and his Chronicles of Narnia. The "patches of Godlight" that we have seen are expressions of reality dressed in fictional clothing—acts of moral goodness, instances of beauty, encounters with the numinous, and such. In the chapter that follows, we will revisit the argument to this point and consider some concluding suggestions for those who would seek to apply a similar Lewisian pre-evangelistic strategy in the present day.

---

[760] C. S. Lewis, *C. S. Lewis: Letters to Children*, 52–53.

Brian M. Williams

CHAPTER 5

Towards a Lewisian Pre-Evangelistic Approach Today Through the Medium of Imaginative Fiction

Introduction

Before offering points of consideration for our present context drawn from Lewis's pre-evangelistic strategy, it will be helpful for us to review the previous four chapters in order to see clearly how the parts fit together into the whole of the argument. I have sought to develop the argument in such a way that each chapter builds on the former one. My main thesis has been that C. S. Lewis's understanding of both the nature of reality and of the human imagination informs and motivates his pre-evangelistic strategy.

LEWIS IN REVIEW

In the first chapter, we examined Lewis's story, focusing on how imaginative fiction and nature pre-evangelized him, preparing him in a sense for his eventual conversion to Christianity. His life is best understood by exploring the concept of what he calls "Joy," the various experiences of inconsolable longing that stab his heart, awakening within a desire for the transcendent. It might be difficult to make a case for which medium played the more pivotal role, imaginative fiction or nature. Without question from Lewis's own pen, we can know that story, rather than nature, "baptized" his imagination. This profoundly and lastingly altered the way that he viewed the world.[761] Further, Lewis made the point very clearly that one of the last hurdles he crossed before coming to Christ resulted from a conversation he had with Tolkien on the relationship between myth and reality. The great myths and various imaginative stories awakened desire in Lewis, and Tolkien helped him to see that some measure of reality was

---

[761] As recounted in the first chapter, the book that achieved this was George MacDonald's *Phantastes: A Faerie Romance* (Mineola: Dover Publications, 2016).

C. S. LEWIS PRE-EVANGELISM FOR A POST-CHRISTIAN WORLD

being mediated through these stories. Thus, Lewis's thinking about a particular genre of story—namely, mythology—lay at the center of his transformation. For this reason, the concluding section of the present chapter will focus solely on the medium of story as we consider what insights we might gain from thinking about Lewis's pre-evangelistic strategy.

It will be helpful to recall that in telling Lewis's story, the first chapter kept central what Lewis kept central in his autobiography, *Surprised by Joy*. Most important was his search to discover what stood behind, if anything, his experiences of joy. Prior to his embracing a Christian view of reality, all of his attempts to reconcile his reason with his imagination proved fruitless. When he looked to the particulars for satisfaction, they let him down, proving to be "false Florimels." When he turned to the experience of joy itself, he hoped that he might be able to capture it and make it last, hoping that in doing so he might come to secure the very thing for which yearned. This attempt also left him empty. He later concluded, with much help from Samuel Alexander's *Space, Time, and Deity*, that joy was not that for which he longed, as desirable as it may have been, but was rather a pointer to something else.[762] In the end, Lewis came to see that all of his experiences of joy were "sign-posts" leading him in the end to the ultimate object of his desire, which was Christ. Having come to Christ, he finally was able to reconcile his reason and his imagination.

In chapter two, we explored Lewis's view of reality at which he arrived in conjunction with his embracing of Christianity. This chapter connects with the previous one and begins the argument of the dissertation by seeking to answer the question: What conception of reality best explains why Lewis's various encounters with joy, mediated mainly through story and nature, impacted him as they did? Lewis came to understand that nature must be sacramental in the sense that the particulars point beyond themselves to that which is unchanging and eternal. In looking at the matter

---

[762] Chapter one explained that what Alexander's book offers to Lewis is the distinction between enjoyment and contemplation. One can only enjoy something when one is attending to it. The moment one turns one's attention away from the object of enjoyment and contemplated the act of enjoyment itself, one ceases to enjoy the object. Thus, when Lewis turns to contemplate joy in the instant that it is stirred up by some story, the result in the moment is the death of joy. He concludes therefore that joy itself does not satisfy. On the contrary, it points to something else. See C. S. Lewis, *Surprised by Joy*, 219–220, where Lewis envisions joy replying, "'It is not I. I am only a reminder. Look! Look! What do I remind you of?'" ... But a desire is turned not to itself but to its object. Not only that, but it owes all its character to its object ... Joy itself, considered, simply as an event in my own mind, turned out to be of no value at all. All the value lay in that of which Joy was the desiring ... Joy proclaimed, "You want—I myself am your want of–something other, outside, not you nor any state of you."

in this way, we can understand why the universals are more real than the particulars. In addition to truth, goodness, and beauty—universals that presented themselves throughout the world—Lewis encountered scattered fragments of theological truths through mythological tales, fairy stories, and such. For instance, he read about a dying god, and he found in time that this story had a glimmer of real truth to it. He encountered in Plato the concept of the Forms, universals after which the particulars are patterned. In time, this view seemed to answer for him with some satisfaction the problem of being and becoming, with which the pre-Socratics largely wrestled. Through George MacDonald's writings, he saw beauty set before him, and found himself wanting "something else which can hardly be put into words—to be united with the beauty ... to pass into it, to receive it ... to bathe in it, to become part of it."[763]

If humanity truly has been made for God, a view that Lewis eventually embraced, we can understand how Lewis's conception of reality fits the larger story of Christianity. It makes sense why the world would evoke in Lewis inconsolable longings. God has designed His creation such that it conveys something of his nature. According to the psalmist, it conveys information about God. The psalmist writes, "The heavens *declare* the glory of God, and the sky above *proclaims* his handiwork. Day to day *pours out speech*, and night to night *reveals knowledge* ... Their voice goes out through all the earth, and their words to the end of the world" (Psalm 19:1–2, 4, ESV). It is no stretch to restate the psalmist's concept of the world as being sacramental, in a roughly Platonic sense. Many of the early church fathers certainly understood nature in this way.[764] Furthermore, it was noted in the second chapter that Lewis's preferred term to describe the nature of reality was in fact the term "sacramental."[765]

This realization helps to make greater sense of Lewis's biography that was recounted in chapter one in that it sheds further light on his various experiences of joy. Put plainly, the reason that these encounters *seemed* to beckon him towards something beyond the particulars is that they *were* doing precisely that. Reality does include more than merely meets the eye. As chapter two argued, Plato saw this with remarkable insight as well in his own largely pagan context. Lewis had this semi-Platonic kind of a sacramental ontology in mind when he put the line into the mouth of Lord Diggory in *The Last Battle* after the party arrives in the "real" Narnia. Lord Diggory remarks, "It's all in Plato, all in Plato: bless me, what *do* they teach

---

[763] C. S. Lewis, *The Weight of Glory*, 42–43.

[764] Some notable church fathers who held to this view are Justin Martyr, Athenagoras, Clement of Alexandria, and Eusebius of Caesarea.

[765] C. S. Lewis, "Transposition" in *The Weight of Glory and Other Addresses*, 102.

them at these schools!"[766] What was "all in Plato"[767] was the "ectype"[768] mirroring the "archetype"[769] phenomenon that the second chapter discussed at length.

In light of these matters, the best explanation for why nature and mythology could evoked inconsolable longings in Lewis's heart is really two-fold. First, they bear an essential sacramental quality, meaning that the universals in which the particulars participate are in some sense present and can be known to some degree.[770] Second, these universals reside, as Augustine argued, in the mind of God, and given that humanity is made for God, it makes good sense why longing can be stirred when a person encounters these "patches of Godlight."[771] They can be stirred by the particulars but only ever ultimately satisfied in the fountain from which they flow, which is God.

While chapter two explained Lewis's understanding of the nature of reality, which in turn shed further philosophical and theological light on why nature and myth affected him as they did, a crucial piece of the argument still remained. We needed not only to seek to understand reality but also the human person who interacts with this reality. Thus, whereas in chapter we sought to discover what the nature of reality must be that it can serve as a medium for such longings as Lewis experienced. In chapter three, we considered the next question: What must humanity be like that we can be affected in such ways by such mediums as nature and myth? Both questions must be answered if Lewis's experiences, recounted in the first chapter, are to be understood.

---

[766] C. S. Lewis, *The Last Battle*, 170.
[767] C. S. Lewis, *The Last Battle*, 170.
[768] C. S. Lewis, *The Pilgrim's Regress*, 161.
[769] C. S. Lewis, *The Pilgrim's Regress*, 161.
[770] It is worth repeating from chapter two Boersma's helpful distinction between symbol and sacramental, given that Lewis prefers the latter term to the former. See Hans Boersma, *Heavenly Participation*, 22–23, where he writes, "What, then, is so distinct about the sacramental ontology that characterized so much of the history of the church? Perhaps the best way to explain this is to distinguish between symbols and sacraments. A road sign with the silhouette of a deer symbolizes the presence of a deer in the area, and its purpose is to induce drives to slow down ... The former is a sign referring to the latter, but in no way do the two co-inhere. It is not as though the road sign carries a mysterious quality, participating somehow in the stags that roam the forests ... Things are different with sacraments. Unlike mere symbols, sacraments actually *participate* in the mysterious reality to which they point ... For Lewis, a sacramental relationship implies real presence. This understanding of sacramentality is part of a long lineage."
[771] C. S. Lewis, *Letters to Malcolm*, 91.

In particular, we focused on Lewis's thoughts on the human imagination. After all, it was his imagination that was primarily engaged through his various experiences of joy. Whether remembering the day that Warnie brought into the nursery his toy garden, or delighting in the "idea of Autumn"[772] in *Squirrel Nutkin*, or envisioning "pure northernness"[773] through the Nordic myths, Lewis was employing the use, not chiefly of his reason, but of his imagination. He recognized this and wrote at some length about the nature of this vital faculty. It was because of this realization that Lewis set out to make an argument for a "romantic doctrine of imagination."[774] It will be remembered that by the term "romantic," Lewis meant that which produces an "experience ... of intense longing."[775] Again, one sees from Lewis's own pen that a thorough exploration of "romantic" experiences will have to give an account not only of reality but also of the imagination.

In attempting such an account, I emphasized in chapter three the point that the main power of the imagination lies not in the making of images, as is often the point of definitional emphasis, but rather in the making or recognizing of meaning. Lewis even referred to the imagination as the "organ of meaning."[776] It was demonstrated that in imaginative experiences, the image itself is not of *ultimate* importance, as a person may have a different visual image in reading the same scene in a book on different occasions, yet have the same affective experience. Lewis argued that what truly matters is what the reader takes the image to be. Moreover, and very importantly, what one takes it to be will be dependent on one's knowledge of all sort of other aspects of reality. In agreement with this point, Lewis writes:

> You cannot have even a fairy tale unless the reader and writer understand what a castle, or a stepmother, or a giant *is*. Now I have used the word 'is' advisedly. To read the fairy-tale we must know what a castle is; and that would seem to be a bit of knowledge about the real world.[777]

This is one of the most important points of linkage with Lewis's sacramental ontology presented in chapter two, given that the entailment is that the same sacramental quality present in the real world is present in

---

[772] C. S. Lewis, *Surprised by Joy*, 17.
[773] C. S. Lewis, *Surprised by Joy*, 76.
[774] C. S. Lewis, "Image and Imagination" in *Image and Imagination*, 34.
[775] C. S. Lewis, *The Pilgrim's Regress*, 209–210.
[776] C. S. Lewis, "Buspels and Flalansferes: A Semantic Nightmare," 265.
[777] C. S. Lewis, *Image and Imagination*, 38.

the imaginary one. This is the case, we have seen, because the latter borrows its content from the former.

When the fiction writer, for example, sets out to write a fantasy story or a fairy tale, he draws on the knowledge he has received from the real world. He may place "unreal" things into his story such as unicorns, minotaurs, or make-believe lands, and such, but in doing so, he is not imagining *ex nihilo*. Rather, he is drawing, in the case of the unicorn, upon his knowledge both of horses and of horns that he has seen on other animals. His creativity lies not in making a creature out of nothing but in recombining elements of known things into new arrangements. He is offering what Lewis calls "summarized knowledge of the real."[778] The same is true of the minotaur. He is combining man and bull, taking the head and tail from the bull and the body from the man.

Another quality of equal, if not greater importance, is the imaginative story's power to convey universals such as truth, goodness, and beauty through non-factual particulars. When these universals are mediated through the imaginary world, joy can be stirred. The facts need not be true to reality in the sense that the people are real historical figures, or real places, or the actual events that once happened. What must come through, however, in order for a real mediation of reality to occur, is that the universals must be conveyed as they truly are and the characters must respond to them fittingly. For example, a virtuous character must be honored and revered by those who also prize virtue and must be, by way of contrast, hated or scorned by the villainous. A beautiful place such as Rivendell in Tolkien's *Lord of the Rings*, must likewise move its visitors to delightful admiration through its enchanting sublimity. A sound argument must be affirmed as true in the story in order for truthfulness to shine forth in its proper light.

Very often, symbol and metaphor are the tools the imaginative writer employs in his craft. Importantly, the notion of the "true metaphor" posited by Barfield, helped to shed light on a real ontological connection between the symbol and the thing symbolized. This insight is important given that the real power of the imagination is the making or the discerning of meaning. For Barfield, wisdom is the ability to perceive real meaning in the world. The wise person sees three things: the symbol, the symbolized thing itself, and the essential connection between the two. Thus, if one is to understand the world, not only must one's reason be developed, but also one's imagination, in the sense that Lewis and Barfield have in mind.

---

[778] C. S. Lewis, *Image and Imagination*, 49.

Brian M. Williams

Realizing that a great deal of language has a metaphorical quality to it, Lewis argues:

> I confess, it does follow that if our thinking is ever true, then the metaphors by which we think must have been good metaphors. It does follow that if those original equations, between good and light, or evil and dark, between breath and soul and all the others, were from the beginning arbitrary and fanciful—if there is not, in fact, a kind of psycho-physical parallelism (or more) in the universe—then all our thinking is nonsensical. And so, admittedly, the view I have taken has metaphysical implications.[779]

The purpose of restating the above quote from Lewis is to highlight once again for us the connection between the human imagination and the nature of reality. Recognizing this connection is absolutely vital for the argument of this book. It helps to link not only the third chapter with the second, but also with the fourth. If the imagination is tethered to the nature of reality in this way, what follows is that when Lewis attempts to pre-evangelize his readership through imaginative fiction, to the degree that he employs good metaphors, he is helping to convey not only a sense of enchantment through his wonderful tales, but also a sense of reality itself.

The fourth chapter set forth examples of how Lewis carried out his pre-evangelistic work. The argument presented was that Lewis knowingly took this approach because of his understanding of both reality and the human imagination, as well as his insight into the spirit of the age in his day. Those to whom Lewis attempted to communicate the gospel came with their defenses ready, most often refusing to give the explicit gospel message a fair hearing. A Christian view of reality was already quickly fading from the public consciousness due to a willful rejection of what many saw as a dated and scientifically unsophisticated system of beliefs that needed to be jettisoned. Further, the longer that this rejection pervaded, the greater peoples' ignorance of Christian theology became. Lewis believed, in light of these facts, that his conversational starting point needed to be considered carefully and employed strategically.

A great insight into this starting point that would support his pre-evangelistic strategy came, as was shown in the previous chapter, as the reviews began coming in for his book *Out of the Silent Planet*. Lewis commented in a letter to his friend, Sister Penelope, that most of the reviewers completed missed his point about a fall of humanity and his inclusion of the "Bent One" as connecting respectively to the biblical fall of

---

[779] C. S. Lewis, "Bluspels and Flalansferes," 265.

C. S. LEWIS PRE-EVANGELISM FOR A POST-CHRISTIAN WORLD

humanity and to Satan. He told Sister Penelope that "this great ignorance might be a help to the evangelization of England: any amount of theology can now be smuggled into people's minds under cover of romance without their knowing it."[780] Lewis set out to do precisely this for the remainder of his space trilogy, which was surveyed at length in the previous chapter.

Through his pre-evangelistic fiction, Lewis was trusting, in part, in the inseparable linkage between the imaginary world and the real, as well as the ontological connection between good metaphors and symbols and the things they symbolize. We can see quite clearly that Lewis understood this, when we remember in his response to a mother who was afraid that her young son might have grown to love Aslan more than Christ. We recall that Lewis responded to her:

> Lawrence can't really love Aslan more than Jesus, even if he feels that's what he's doing. For the things he loves Aslan for doing or saying are simply the things Jesus really did and said. So that when Lawrence thinks he is loving Aslan, he is really loving Jesus.[781]

Not only did Lewis write into the character of Aslan many of the things Jesus said and did, but also various qualities that are true of the historical Jesus. Along with the space trilogy, we examined Lewis's Narnia books in the fourth chapter, showing how he carried out his pre-evangelistic aims through them.

We know that through Lewis's fiction, he was aiming to evoke the same quality of joy in his readers as was evoked in him on many occasions through various mediums, most notably perhaps through George MacDonald's *Phantastes*. In addition to smuggling in plenty of theology, Lewis devoted the same careful attention as MacDonald to creating atmospheres that might contribute to the reader's sense of enchantment. The result is that all aspects of Lewis's stories work together to produce longing. Most significantly, Lewis knew that this longing pointed to something, or rather someone, very real who alone could satiate it.

To summarize the argument of the book to this point in an attempt to make the connections clearer, let us work backward and end at the beginning. These steps proceed as follows, each notion depending upon the next: from Lewis's pre-evangelism strategy to the reality of longings, from such longings to the nature of the human imagination and of the imaginative world, from these to the nature of reality as sacramental, and

---

[780] C. S. Lewis, *The Collected Letters of C. S. Lewis*, Vol. II, 262.
[781] C. S. Lewis, *C. S. Lewis: Letters to Children*, 52–53.

all of this undergirded by metaphysical realism (the view that universals or essences, or Plato's notion of the Forms, are really real).

We can also note the above points as separate propositional statements. Lewis's pre-evangelism depends upon the possibility of inconsolable longings being stirred through imaginative fiction. Such longings are explained in part by considering the nature of the human imagination, namely its capacity to discern meaning and to apprehend the sacramental reality present in certain fictional stories that convey such to the reader. Finally, the human imagination, as well as the imaginative world, in turn depend upon the nature of reality from which they borrow their content. This reality is sacramental in nature.

Thus, if one wants to know the justification for Lewis's pre-evangelistic strategy, at least three notions require examination: longing, the human imagination, and the nature of reality. I have attempted, to this point, to explain each of these concepts accurately to the way that Lewis understood them. I have also sought to demonstrate the dependence relationship between them that helps to tie the whole argument together. In concluding section of this final chapter, I will offer suggested points of application for the present-day context in light of Lewis's pre-evangelistic work. I would hope to encourage those Christians who have been properly gifted, to take up the task of carrying out similar work today.

LEWIS'S PRE-EVANGELISM APPLIED TO THE PRESENT-DAY CONTEXT

We can draw several points of application for the present day from Lewis's strategy to pre-evangelize his readership through his imaginative fiction. While a much wider treatment could be offered that might touch on various areas of the arts such as music, painting, architecture, sculpture, theater, film, etc., which might prove valuable, this chapter will focus solely on the written word, and mainly the genre of story. The reason for such focus is that this was Lewis's chosen medium for carrying out his pre-evangelistic task, and most of what he has to say on pre-evangelism deals specifically with this medium.

Qualities of Stories with the Potential to Pre-Evangelize

When one evaluates both Lewis's stories as well as those that stirred longing in him, several common qualities begin to emerge, five of which we will consider in this section. These qualities are: the numinous, the sacred, virtue and legal guilt, Christian theology in disguise, and subcreation. Though the specifics vary greatly in terms of characters, setting,

C. S. LEWIS PRE-EVANGELISM FOR A POST-CHRISTIAN WORLD

plot, etc., the common thread between all of these stories is their inclusion of these important qualities.[782] If the Christian writing fiction stories today is to have any success in evoking joy in her readers, and in so doing pre-evangelize them to some degree, she will need to include these same qualities in her own stories. Importantly, our present culture largely rejects several of these qualities in principle. In weaving them into one's story, one will be combatting the current spirit of the age.

Imaginative fiction provides a vehicle to introduce these qualities to people whose defenses are up, without the likelihood of immediate rejection. It must be stated strongly that not just any imaginative story can accomplish, in terms of pre-evangelism, what Lewis's, MacDonald's, and Tolkien's did. Some stories, just like some things in the real world, can lead one away from, rather than closer to the truth. The following discussion highlights qualities that, when included in an imaginative story, can stir the affections towards that which is true to reality.

The Numinous

Lewis writes quite a bit about the quality of the numinous throughout his books. Chapters three and four dealt at some length with this concept, so it does not need a great deal of explanation here, except to offer a description by way of reminder of what one feels in the presence of the numinous. Lewis writes that one "would feel wonder and a certain shrinking—a sense of inadequacy to cope with such a visitant and of prostration before it ... This feeling may be described as awe, and the object which excites it as the *Numinous*."[783] This reaction is not the same as one would have in the presence of a known physical danger such as a bear or a tornado, or in the presence of a great person such as a nation's president. A deep sense of mystery shrouds the object, as though it seems almost not quite to belong to the world of humanity. If one feels fear, it is not the mere fear that physical harm may come; rather, it is the fear that often fails to comprehend with much clarity the nature of the entity that evokes the feeling. The sense is a kind of unpredictability regarding what the entity in question might do, or wish to do, if in fact it is a person with wishes and

---

[782] It is not necessary that every story include every one of the qualities mentioned in order to serve as a useful pre-evangelistic tool; however, if none of the qualities noted are present, it is doubtful whether the story will prove successful at evoking joy. For instance, a sense of the numinous does not seem to play much, if at all, into Lewis's *The Lion, the Witch, and the Wardrobe*, outside of the children's hearing about Aslan before meeting him. That said, one certainly finds a sense of the sacred, virtue, an objective view of morality, beautiful atmosphere, and certainly plenty of smuggled-in Christian theology.

[783] C. S. Lewis, *The Problem of Pain*, 6.

desires. Perhaps a better word than fearful might be unsettled. While the numinous can be either malevolent or benevolent, the common quality is that its very presence sharply conflicts with any naturalistic sentiments about the world. In the face of the numinous, one begins to feel that the world may not, in fact, be a closed system.

Given the pervasiveness of naturalism in the present day, the inclusion of the numinous in imaginative stories offers the reader the opportunity to feel in the imaginary world what he otherwise might not have the opportunity to feel in the real one. Importantly, the Christian view of reality maintains that the real world is populated with mysterious beings whose presence and power have unsettled people on various occasions throughout history. Men have given way to weakened knees and intense trembling as they were greeted by angelic visitors. Prophets have received visions of real things that everyday sight does not perceive. Whether Moses atop Mount Sinai who saw the resplendent tabernacle pattern, or Isaiah who, peering into the temple viewed God sitting on his throne surrounded by the seraphim (literally, "burning ones") who cried out repeatedly "Holy, holy, holy is the LORD Almighty" (Isaiah 6:3), or Jacob who saw the staircase ascending into heaven with angelic beings going up and down upon it, all felt something like what Lewis describes as a "certain shrinking."[784] None of these felt very comfortable. If the old adage "familiarity breeds contempt" is true, contempt was the least likely possible result from these encounters.

The present-day march towards increasing scientific and technological progress can create the false sense that, given enough time, the world can be explained fully and brought into total submission to humanity. This was the precise sentiment that Lewis had in his crosshairs in his space trilogy and that he sought to expose as false. It could be for this reason, in part, that these books present more strongly and consistently than any of this others a sense of the numinous.[785] Moreover, people do not tend to reason about that towards which they lack an affective interest. The sentiment that humanity is not along in a strictly materialistic world but may at any moment be "entertaining angels unaware," as the author of Hebrews writes,[786] is the very sentiment that the numinous seeks to awaken. When such a sense is stirred, it helps one to feel as though materialism is not only

---

[784] C. S. Lewis, *The Problem of Pain*, 6.

[785] It is perhaps debatable whether the space trilogy or *Till We Have Faces* conveys the numinous more potently. Nevertheless, one can see very clearly that Lewis includes this quality in his space trilogy to combat the view that scientific and technological progress will save humanity.

[786] See Hebrews 13:2.

possibly untrue, but also painfully dull. This realization can be a great help to the cause of pre-evangelism.

The Christian who sets out to write imaginative stories today would be wise to set the numinous before her readers. This can be achieved by introducing scenes, characters, and objects that work together to convey a sense of an unsettling, uncanny, mysterious presence. Subtlety is necessary for success. Hints, rather than full disclosure, at least as the author is beginning to introduce her readers to the numinous, are key. The saying, "less is more" is never more true than in crafting this aspect of the story.

When Ransom first meets an eldil, in *Out of the Silent Planet*, Lewis achieves this masterfully. This scene was described in chapter four, but it bears repeating here. While Ransom is in the boat with Hyoi, he thinks that he sees something on the water. A hush comes over the party, and Hyoi says softly, "There is an *eldil* coming to us over the water."[787] Even the soft tone of Hyoi adds to the sense of mystery. Lewis then writes, "Ransom could see nothing—or nothing that he could distinguish from imagination and the dance of sunlight on the lake."[788] He then has a conversation with an eldil whom he cannot see but only hear. Very slowly throughout the story, and continued throughout the entire trilogy, Lewis acquaints his readers with the eldils with increasing clarity—but even in the end, much of their nature lies beyond description. If he had presented the clarity at the beginning, the mystery would have been destroyed, and the sense of the numinous absent.

Let us remember that the numinous can confront the reader either through either good or evil presences. George MacDonald, in the story *Phantastes* which was responsible for baptizing Lewis's imagination, introduces an evil one known as "the Ash." Regarding the Ash's nature, whether tree or person, one cannot be sure. All that MacDonald offers are vague and unsettling glimpses that offer just enough description to distinguish the Ash from other presences in the book but so little as to keep the reader guessing regarding the nature and intentions of the mysterious presence. MacDonald writes:

> What I feared I cannot tell. Indeed, I was left in a state of the vaguest uncertainty as regarded the nature of my enemy, and knew not the mode or objects of his attacks; for, somehow or other, none of my questions had succeeded in drawing a definite answer from the dame in the cottage. How then to defend myself

---

[787] C. S. Lewis, *Out of the Silent Planet*, 80.
[788] C. S. Lewis, *Out of the Silent Planet*, 80.

I knew not; nor even by what sign I might with certainty recognize the presence of my foe; for as yet this vague though powerful fear was all the indication of danger I had. To add to my distress, the clouds in the west had risen nearly to the top of the skies, and they and the moon were traveling slowly towards each other ... At length she was for a moment almost entirely obscured. When she shone out again ... I saw plainly on the path before me—from around which at this spot the trees receded, leaving a small space of green sward—the shadow of a large hand, with knotty joints and protuberances here and there ... I reflected in a moment, that if this were indeed a shadow, it was useless to look for the object that cast it in any other direction than between the shadow and the moon. I looked, and peered, and intensified my vision, all to no purpose. I could see nothing of that kind, not even an ash-tree in the neighborhood. Still the shadow remained; not steady, but moving to and fro, and once I saw the fingers close, and grind themselves close, like the claws of a wild animal, as if in uncontrollable longing for some anticipated prey ... I went forward boldly ... to the spot where the shadow lay, threw myself on the ground, laid my head within the form of the hand, and turned my eyes towards the moon. Good heavens! what did I see? ... I saw the strangest figure; vague, shadowy, almost transparent, in the central parts, and gradually deepening in substance towards the outside ... The hand was uplifted in the attitude of a paw about to strike its prey. But the face ... was horrible. I do not know how to describe it. It caused a new sensation. Just as one cannot translate a horrible odour, or a ghastly pain, or a fearful sound, into words, so I cannot describe this new form of awful hideousness.[789]

In examining the above passage, we notice the following phrases: "I cannot tell"; "of the vaguest uncertainty"; "I knew not"; "I saw the strangest figure; vague, shadowy"; "I do not know how to describe it"; "I cannot describe." The mystery of the description does not stir simply fear of harm in the reader, though such a feeling might be awakened by this passage. Far more potent than fear of physical harm is the sense of the uncanny, of being stalked by a presence that defies clear description, that is vague and shadowy, yet unmistakably present.

The Christian writer who is able to convey similar qualities in her imaginative stories will offer something to the present-day reader that he will not find widely available to him the modern world. On the contrary,

---

[789] George MacDonald, *Phantastes*, 25–27.

most of what he will encounter, whether through the media, the arts, or in many of his day-to-day interactions will strengthen the false sentiment that the physical world is all that exists. He is confronted by a culture that holds scientists, mathematicians and economists, rather than poets, philosophers, or theologians to be the real bearers and tellers of truth. This kind of a world has very little room for wonder, as wonder fits better in a world where the numinous is real. Roger Scruton describes the connection between the view of scientism and a drab and mechanistic view of the world writing, "Scientific explanations of the moral life often exhibit what I call the 'charm of disenchantment.'"[790] All talk of the supernatural will seem to a person who embraces such a view to be detached from his daily experience. He will feel that it does not fit with the world he knows. One antidote to this false sentiment is the presence of the numinous set forth in imaginative fiction that might help to awaken feelings, and perhaps even desire, for reality beyond the senses. This, of course, would be a help to the one who would come nearer to a Christian view of reality.

The Sacred

Not only can the Christian author of fiction today offer pre-evangelistic help through including the numinous in her writings, she can also introduce, or perhaps reintroduce, her readers to the notion of the sacred, which largely has been rejected by the current spirit of the age. In Lewis's article, "A Christmas Sermon for Pagans," he refers to this loss of the sacred, which he sees as a part of the rejected religious sentiments.[791] Very importantly, he contrasts the Pagan from the post-Christian, arguing:

> Now the real Pagan differed from the post-Christian in the following ways. Firstly, he was religious. From the Christian point of view he was indeed too religious by half. He was full of reverence. To him the earth was holy, the woods and waters were alive ... Now the post-Christian view which is gradually coming into existence—it is complete already in some people and still incomplete in others—is quite different. According to it Nature is not a live thing to be reverenced: it is a kind of machine for us to exploit.[792]

The Christian would not agree with the Pagan's account of the divine nor with the reason why nature should be treated with a measure of reverence; nevertheless, both would be well-acquainted with the notion of

---

[790] Roger Scruton, *The Face of God*, 28.
[791] C. S. Lewis, "A Christmas Sermon for Pagans," 47.
[792] C. S. Lewis, "A Christmas Sermon for Pagans," 47.

the sacred, that is, both in concept and in sentiment, which is the point at present.[793] The pre-evangelistic task is, after all, not immediately concerned with correcting bad theology, but with stirring interest so that in time, the reader might think the task of considering theological truth claims a worthy undertaking. Perhaps one of the most powerful sentiments that will need to be reawakened if modern people are to feel such an interest is a sense of the sacred.

The sacred is that which properly is to be revered, cherished, and approached with a measure of solemnity, if such an approach is permitted at all. Scruton helpfully describes various cultures' views of the sacred. He writes:

> The idea of the sacred place seems to be a human universal. Different accounts are given to explain it. For some cultures gods, spirits and other supernatural agents live among us, and must be worshiped or acknowledged at the spot where they reside. For others a place becomes sacred because it is the haunt of a ghost, maybe the ghost of someone who has died with some deep need unsatisfied or some deep love denied, and whose moment of crisis occurred at this very spot: this idea you find in the Shinto religion, and dramatized in the Noh theatre of Japan … Other cultures connect sacred places with the legends of heroes or with great battles of the past, to which we come to pay respects for some patriotic sacrifice. In all societies in which dead people are ceremonially buried, the place of burial becomes "hallowed ground", and ritualized acts and words are deemed appropriate when we walk there … A comparable sentiment attaches to ruins, and it is from the attempt to represent ruins and their meaning that our tradition of landscape painting began.[794]

Scruton goes on to describe a view of nature that is contrary to the sacred, namely the consumerist view that seeks to use the world largely for material enjoyment and gain. This view has captured the imaginations of so many, and in doing so, nearly has wiped out all sense of the sacred. In a way that sounds reminiscent of Bevan's, Barfield's, and Lewis's thoughts on the imagination and meaning, Scruton argues:

---

[793] By "Christian" in this sentence, the notion is of the pre-modern Christian, or the Christian whose sentiments are consistent with how the Scriptures describe nature as a creation of God. The suggestion is not being made that most Christians today revere nature. The contrary is probably true in many cases.

[794] Roger Scruton, *The Face of God*, 115–116.

C. S. LEWIS PRE-EVANGELISM FOR A POST-CHRISTIAN WORLD

It is not just a world of objects to be used and discarded. It is a world of *revealed meanings*, in which the most ordinary thing might suddenly blurt out its secrets, or in which a landscape can burst into tears. Such a sentiment tied the Israelites to the Promised Land, and to the Holy City that was built in it.[795]

One of the most helpful examples of the sacred comes from the Old Testament description of the temple, and in particular from the room called the most holy place which housed the ark of the covenant. One was not permitted simply to stroll casually into this structure, or to do whatever one pleased while inside. God gave to Moses clear instructions as well as sober warnings for how one was to conduct oneself, who was permitted to enter, as well as the overall purpose of the space. One of the marks of Israel's wickedness manifested itself in how they began in time to profane that sacred temple by doing inside of it that which suited their desires, which had been shaped not by the true and good words of God but by the wrongful practices of the wicked nations.

The present situation is similar in that most peoples' imagination have been captured by the spirit of the age in which the sacred is absent from much of modern life. The Christian writer can reintroduce this lost sense of the sacred by writing about imagined sacred places and rituals and also by showing how the characters properly respond to such places and rituals. The strongest sense of the sacred in all of Lewis's books where he accomplishes this comes at the end of *Perelandra* when Ransom arrives at the mountain summit and comes before the gods Mars and Venus who are preparing for the ceremony to usher in the birth of Perelandra. We have already looked at this, but a reminder will serve us well to make the point.

As he approaches the sacred summit, Ransom thinks to himself, "This is the holiest and the most unholy thing I have ever done."[796] It is holy in the sense that he is coming before great, powerful, and good beings, as well as a numerous host of other eldils. He is also approaching the man and the lady whose innocence had been preserved in the face of great temptations from the Unman. Ransom describes it as unholy in the sense that he feels he is unworthy to be present before such beings, in such a place, and at such a ceremony.

Everything in the scene magnifies the sacred, from the beauty of the scenery that Lewis describes, to the nature of the beings present, to the response of all present for the whole ordeal. One could convey similar

---
[795] Roger Scruton, *The Face of God*, 118.
[796] C. S. Lewis, *Perelandra*, 165.

truths in any number of imagination stage-sets. The scene would need to be full of reverence and deep solemnity on the part of the characters present. A great variety of reasons would be available as to why the space might be properly sacred. Perhaps it is the location of where a significant war was fought. It might be the sight of a religious temple. A legendary hero might have died in the place and might be buried in a tomb on the site. A monument that recounts a pivotal event in a peoples' history could serve the purpose well. Certain characters might come into the presence of Godlike beings and fall to their faces. The possibilities are many. The important point is that the quality of the sacred could help to reintroduce people today to something of inestimable value that largely has been forsaken and which fits with a Christian view of reality.

Virtue & Guilt

Virtue, like the sacred and the numinous, has fallen on hard times in our day.[797] Consequently, so has the notion of real legal guilt before God. Most people are more comfortable writing and speaking of values rather than virtue. The implicit shift that occurs in this subtle change of words is of monumental importance. It is the shift from objective to subjective right and wrong. Values tend to highlight the subject who holds them whereas virtue emphasizes the actual moral goodness itself. What one person values another might view with contempt. Virtue, on the other hand, is no respecter of persons.

Out of all of the psychological shifts that have taken place from the pre-modern world to the present one, Lewis seemed to think that the move towards subjective morality that in time sponged away the notion of real guilt before God or the gods, was the most devastating one for the Christian task of evangelism. One can see why he thought this way, given that the front door into Christianity through which one must first enter, is the one that reveals one's guilt before God. Christ will be no help to the individual who thinks he bears no real guilt. Lewis knew this to be the case, and he recognized that before one could be convinced of the relevance of Christ's death and resurrection, one needed to acknowledge his guilt and need for redemption. He writes of the Pagan who differs from the post-Christian thus:

[H]e believed in what we now call an "Objective" Right or Wrong. That is, he thought the distinction between pious and impious acts was something which existed independently of

---

[797] Virtue, here, refers to the cardinal and the Christian virtues, which are: wisdom, justice, temperance, fortitude, faith, hope, and love. These are the universal moral virtues that must be reintroduced through imaginative fiction and shown to be praiseworthy.

C. S. LEWIS PRE-EVANGELISM FOR A POST-CHRISTIAN WORLD

human opinions: something like the multiplication table which Man had not invented but had found to be true ... But though his code included some fantastic sins and duties, it got in most of the real ones. And this leads us to the third great difference between a Pagan and a post-Christian man. Believing in a real Right and Wrong means finding out that you are not very good ... Hence a Pagan, though in many ways merrier than a modern, had a deep sadness. When he asked himself what was wrong with the world he did not immediately reply, "the social system," or "out allies," or "education." It occurred to him that he himself might be one of the things that was wrong with the world. He knew he had sinned ... Now the post-Christian view ... is quite different. According to it Nature is not a live thing to be reverence: it is a kind of machine for us to exploit. There is no objective Right or Wrong: each race or class can invent its own code or "ideology" just as it pleases. And whatever may be amiss with the world, it is certainly not we, not the ordinary people; it is up to God ... or to Government, or to Education, to give us what we want.[798]

One can see that Lewis connected the notion of objective right and wrong with that of guilt. If the former is lost, the latter will have no real support. Thus, Lewis sought to reintroduce these concepts to his readers through fiction. He accomplished this in part, not by arguing explicitly for the virtues, but by assuming them and then creating his heroes such that they exhibit them to a degree. Likewise, when a character failed morally, Lewis presented this failure as something that went against the real objective moral order in his stories.

In *The Lion, the Witch and the Wardrobe*, Edmund's betrayal of his brothers and sisters was not simply a nasty thing from his siblings' perspectives. Rather, he had broken a real law that resulted in tragic legal consequences. Were it not for Aslan sacrificing his life in his place, Edmund would have died at the hand of the White Witch.

Further, the mouse Reepicheep is portrayed throughout the stories, despite his physical stature, as a giant in terms of courage. He is a noble character who also possesses a deep sense of duty to Aslan and to his country. In fact, one sees in Reepicheep a good measure of patriotism, another good moral quality that has been all but lost today. Whenever Aslan praises or condemns one's character or actions, Lewis is presenting

---

[798] C. S. Lewis, "A Christmas Sermon for Pagans," 47–48.

the absolute moral evaluation. No voice can override Aslan's, though the Witch offers her own twisted perspective repeatedly.

The value of Lewis's treatment of morality throughout his fiction stories is that he allows his readers to enter a world where virtue is objective. One finds the same quality present in Tolkien's stories as well, who shared very similar views with Lewis on the power of imaginative fiction to convey virtue. Because of this similarity, what we find in Tolkien's books serves to illustrate the same point we are making here in analyzing Lewis's stories.

The hobbits in Tolkien's tales exhibit great courage and a love of their home, the Shire. It would be difficult to find a more moving expression of friendship love than what one finds between Frodo and Sam. The various kingdoms face the threat of despotic rule, if not outright destruction, at the hands of the evil Lord Sauron. Elves, dwarfs, hobbits, men and others join together to stand against the evil that confronts them. Contrary to many a modern story, Tolkien does not present heroism as one person's setting out to find himself in the face of a scornful community that only wants to hold him back from fulfilling his personal dreams. This individualistic and selfish hero-tale does not fit in Tolkien's world. Rather, each person sacrifices his own well-being and resources for the good of all others. Tolkien saw such true heroism displayed on the battlefields of the Great War, most potently in the lives of the "batmen" who carried the officers' equipment.[799]

In spite of the great virtue that Tolkien's heroes display, fittingly, none is able to rid the world of evil. Whoever wields the great ring, succumbs eventually to its diabolical power. A more powerful hand than any of the visible characters must work to bring about the happy ending. At the end of *The Lord of the Rings*, Frodo, who for the majority of the story has been resisting the ring's temptation, succumbs to it in the end. When at last he has the chance to toss the ring into the fire, he instead turns away and chooses to keep it for himself, just as Isildur, Aragorn's ancestor, had done before him. Both man and hobbit fall. The point is clear—none can defeat evil in his own power. Yet unexpectedly, catastrophe soon gives way to eucatastrophe as the creature Golem, who by the unseen hand of providence was allowed to live, attacks Frodo, steals the ring, and falls to

---

[799] See Colin Duriez, *J. R. R. Tolkien: The Making of a Legend*, 94, where he describes these batmen, who served as Tolkien's inspiration for the hobbits, the real heroes of *The Lord of the Rings*. Duriez writes, "Like all officers, Tolkien had a batman to look after him and take care of his kit, and he remarked in later life that the character of the Hobbit who accompanied Frodo Baggins on his quest to destroy the Ring owed much to his wartime contact with the ordinary 'Tommy': 'My "Sam Gamgee" is indeed a reflexion of the English soldier, of the privates and batmen I knew in the 1914 war, and recognized as so far superior to myself."

C. S. LEWIS PRE-EVANGELISM FOR A POST-CHRISTIAN WORLD

his death in the lava of Mount Doom, destroying both himself and the ring. Evil is vanquished at last, and goodness restored, but *not* ultimately because of man, dwarf, hobbit, wizard, or elf.

Tolkien is setting before his readers a great hint in how he portrays the destruction of evil. He provides a glimpse of the true gospel, though disguised in mythological clothing. He explains this phenomenon thus:

> The consolation of fairy-stories, the joy of the happy ending: or more correctly of the good catastrophe, the sudden joyous "turn" (for there is no true end to any fairy-tale): this joy, which is one of the things which fairy-stories can produce supremely well, is not essentially "escapist", nor "fugitive." In its fairy-tale—or otherworld—setting, it is a sudden and miraculous grace: never to be counted on to recur. It does not deny the existence of *dyscatastrophe*, of sorrow and failure: the possibility of these is necessary to the joy of deliverance; it denies (in the face of much evidence, if you will) universal and final defeat and in so far is *evangelium*, giving a fleeting glimpse of Joy, Joy beyond the walls of the world, poignant as grief.[800]

Thus, we can see clearly that good and evil are objective in both Lewis's and Tolkien's stories. We should expect nothing less given that both men shared much of the same ideas regarding the power of story to convey glimmers of reality. Virtue is praiseworthy and vice is blameworthy, period. If a Christian view of reality with respect to virtue and guilt is to be offered to readers through imaginative fiction, the eucatastrophic turn can offer a helpful hint to the real event in history in which the death of the Son of the God on a cross dealt a fatal blow to evil and ended up being the means through which humanity was given the possibility of one day of being made completely virtuous, where vice would be vanquished once and for all.

If virtue remains largely absent and held in disdain by our modern world, the Christian writer of imaginative fiction can offer to her readers an uncommon opportunity to taste goodness and see that it is truly good. She can also show that in light of this objective goodness, the best characters fall short and thus incur real guilt. Tolkien achieved this with great success, and one can be sure that he did so intentionally in light of what is now known about a fateful meeting that took place over the weekend of December 12th and 13th of 1914. Tolkien and his college friends, G. B. Smith, Rob Gilson, and Christopher Wiseman met together for what they called "The Council of London." While sitting around a fire in a small room

---

[800] J. R. R. Tolkien, "On Fairy-Stories," in *Tree and Leaf*, 68–69.

with pipes lit, the friends discussed how they might use their gifts for the betterment of society, should they survive the war. Colin Duriez notes that this meeting proved to be for Tolkien "a turning point in his creative life."[801] Through Gilson's architecture, Smith's poetry, and Tolkien's mythological tales, the friends would attempt to reintroduce people to "religious faith, human love, duty to one's country, and a nations's right of self-rule."[802] Christians possessing the literary gift today would do well to find inspiration through Tolkien and his friends, and of course through Lewis, and should seek to emulate their aim of setting virtue before a morally decadent culture.

Christian Theology in Disguise

Examples of how Lewis "smuggles in" Christian theology "under cover of romance" have been given in the previous chapter and therefore do not need repeating at length presently.[803] This same smuggling can be done today in various ways. For example, Lewis chose the disguise of a lion to share with his readers the character of Christ in *The Chronicles of Narnia*. In his space trilogy, he introduced Maleldil as the king of eldils, and he is very clearly synonymous with Christ. The "Bent One" is none other than Satan, who did battle with Maleldil on earth but lost. The fall of humanity on Thulcandra is the same historic fall that occurred to Adam and Eve in the garden of Eden. Several strategies emerge as we consider his imaginative fiction works on which Christian authors today might capitalize.

Lewis's genius lay in his ability to present these and many other theological truths clearly while detaching them from their "stained-glass and Sunday school associations" so that they might be seen "in their real potency."[804] He achieved this by changing the particulars while keeping many of the necessary parts. First, he changed the names of characters, especially those who stood for major characters in the Scriptures. If Aslan had been called "Jesus" or "the Christ," it is unlikely that his stories would have reached as far as they have with the result of stirring up love and admiration towards the lion in the hearts of so many.

In addition, he abandoned the use of explicitly religious terms and replaced them with terms that mean the same thing but that do not raise the reader's suspicion that he is encountering anything religious. For example, rather than referring to characters as "sinful" in his space trilogy,

---

[801] Colin Duriez, *J. R. R. Tolkien: The Making of a Legend*, 83.
[802] Colin Duriez, *J. R. R. Tolkien: The Making of a Legend*, 83.
[803] C. S. Lewis, *The Collected Letters of C. S. Lewis*, Vol. II, 262.
[804] C. S. Lewis, "Sometimes Fairy Stories May Say Best What's To Be Said," in *On Stories*, 70.

C. S. LEWIS PRE-EVANGELISM FOR A POST-CHRISTIAN WORLD

he referred to them as "bent." Next, Lewis altered the locations and some of the details of significant historical events but kept enough of the important parts that the truth peeks through the fictional setting. For instance, in *Perelandra* he offered an imagined account of what Satan's temptation of Eve might have looked like if given a more detailed accounting in the Scriptures. He has this unfold on another planet, namely Venus, and he used the medium of the possessed man, Weston, through whom the Bent One carried out his assault. Through the dialogue that ensued, Lewis combatted a great deal of modern thinking that is contrary to a Christian view of truth, goodness, beauty, and the character of God. In Aslan's death, he does not have him nailed to a cross and placed in a tomb. Rather, he has the substitutionary act take place on a stone table. But the important point remains—a substitutionary death by a righteous character is the means by which the guilty one can be set free.

The Christian imaginative fiction writer today, like Lewis, can capitalize on the present cultural theological ignorance and introduce people to Christian truths dressed in fictional disguise. The particulars will change to some degree, as we have seen, though one must not forget what has been argued in chapter three from Bevan's, Barfield's, and Lewis's perspectives regarding symbol and metaphor. Some symbols serve one's purpose better than others depending upon what one aims to convey. For obvious reasons, a lion serves as a very good choice for conveying the qualities of Christ. An ape, whom Lewis chooses for his foolish villain in *The Last Battle*, would not have accomplished the same potent sacramental mediation as the lion. It will take wisdom and creative discernment to decide upon how much disguising is necessary and which symbols and metaphors will give the reader the best sense of the truths one wants to convey without blowing one's cover.

Sub-Creation

The final quality worth mentioning, which is likely the most difficult to achieve with success, is what Tolkien calls "sub-creation."[805] He describes the "successful sub-creator" as one who:

> [M]akes a Secondary World which your mind can enter. Inside it, what he relates is "true": it accords with the laws of that world. You therefore believe it, while you are, as it were, inside. The moment disbelief arises, the spell is broken; the magic, or rather

---

[805] J. R. R. Tolkien, "On Fairy-Stories," in *Tree and Leaf*, 47.

art, has failed. You are then out in the Primary World again, looking at the little abortive Secondary World from outside.[806]

Sub-creation allows the reader to believe that the imaginary world is coherent. Such a quality provides the proper atmosphere within which the previously mentioned qualities can prove most effective. It allows for enchantment to take place. According to Lewis, Tolkien succeeded in his sub-creative aims in *The Hobbit* and in *The Lord of Rings*. In a short review, Lewis writes:

> The publisher's claim that *The Hobbit*, though very unlike *Alice*, resembles it in bring the work of a professor at play. A more important truth is that both belong to a very small class of books which have nothing in common save that each admits us to a world of its own—a world that seems to have been going on before we stumbled into it but which, once found by the right reader, becomes indispensable to him ... To define the world of the Hobbit is, of course, impossible, because it is new. You cannot anticipate it before you go there, as you cannot forget it once you have gone ... Though all is marvelous, nothing is arbitrary: all the inhabitants of Wilderland seem to have the same unquestionable right to their existence as those of our own world, though the fortunate child who meets them will have no notion—and his unlearned elders not much more—of the deep sources in our blood and tradition from which they spring.[807]

Lewis was impressed by Tolkien's ability to craft and to communicate a world whose existence seems surprisingly believable. The power of this achievement, whenever it is found to be true of any story, is that the reader forgets she is reading a made-up tale while immersed in it. Consequently, she need exert no amount of effort at willing suspension of disbelief, efforts which would break the enchantment. One is allowed to enter in and to breath the air, as it were, of fairy land. Whatever one finds while exploring, because the author has proved a successful sub-creator, will seem to exist there fittingly.

In his short review of Tolkien's *The Lord the Rings*, Lewis heaped further praise upon his friend's work, drawing particular attention to the sense of reality and the corresponding believability that it conveyed. Lewis writes:

---

[806] J. R. R. Tolkien, "On Fairy-Stories," in *Tree and Leaf*, 37.
[807] C. S. Lewis, "The Hobbit," in *On Stories*, 123–124.

C. S. LEWIS PRE-EVANGELISM FOR A POST-CHRISTIAN WORLD

This book is like lightning from a clear sky ... Nothing quite like it was ever done before. "One takes it," says Naomi Mitchison, "as seriously as Malory." But then the ineluctable sense of reality which we feel in the *Morte d'Arthur* comes largely from the great weight of other men's work built up century by century, which has gone into it. This utterly new achievement of Professor Tolkien is that he carries a comparable sense of reality unaided. Probably no book yet written in the world is quite such a radical instance of what its author has elsewhere called "sub-creation" ... Not content to create his own story, he creates, with an almost insolent prodigality, the whole world in which it is to move, with its own theology, myths, geography, history, paleography, languages, and orders of beings—a world "full of strange creatures beyond count" ... Despite many a snug fireside and many an hour of good cheer to gratify the Hobbit in each of us, anguish is, for me, almost the prevailing note. But not, as in the literature most typical of our age, the anguish of abnormal or contorted souls: rather the anguish of those who were happy before a certain darkness came up and will be happy if they live to see it gone ... Even now I have left out almost everything— the silvan leafiness, the passions, the high virtues, the remote horizons. Even if I had space I could hardly convey them. And after all the most obvious appeal of the book is perhaps also its deepest: "there was sorrow then too, and gathering dark, but great valor, and great deeds that were not wholly vain" ... This book is too original and too opulent for any final judgment on a first reading. But we know at once that it has done things to us. We are not quite the same men.[808]

Tolkien's stories left such lasting impact upon Lewis in part because they had the ring to truth in them. The sub-creative quality was so potent that, when coupled with the other four qualities mentioned in this final section, the spell proved powerful.[809] While not as dense as Tolkien's sub-creation of Middle Earth, Lewis offered a world to his reader in the Chronicles of Narnia that is coherent, consistent, and enchanted. It stands as a world that one easily forgets is not real whenever one visits that

---

[808] C. S. Lewis, "Tolkien's *The Lord of the Rings*, in *On Stories*, 127–128, 131, 133, 139.

[809] Regarding the quality of smuggled in Christian theology, Tolkien was not attempting to introduce people to the truths of Christianity through these stories. Whether Christian truths come through unintentionally as part of Tolkien's worldview is another matter. The point is that Tolkien does not do this intentionally.

imaginary land. Such is the quality produced in the reader when encountering successful works of sub-creation.

In order to pre-evangelize the modern audience through imaginative fiction, the present-day Christian fiction writer need not feel the burden to create a secondary world with the level of depth and intricacy equal to Tolkien's, though the attempt would be admirable. Yet, the same aim for internal coherence and a sense of reality and believability must be pursued. The sub-creative quality of a work of fiction is what helps to capture the reader's attention and imagination and allows him to engage the imaginative world on its own terms. Perhaps no quality will prove so important in helping to lower the readers's defenses so that sweet desire for the good, the true, and the beautiful can be awakened. That is, after all, our great aim—to awaken such a desire, the fulfillment of which will only ever be satisfied in the Person of Christ.

A CALL FOR CHRISTIANS TODAY TO PRE-EVANGELIZE THROUGH IMAGNINATIVE FICTION

In this book, I have sought to make a case that Lewis understood nature to be sacramental. In viewing nature this way, he began to understand the role that the imagination plays in the awakening of desire for the transcendent that was mediated for him mainly through nature and imaginative fiction. He used this understanding to justify, not just pragmatically but also in terms of ontology (not just because it "works" but because it reveals what truly "is"), his pre-evangelistic strategy through writing his own fiction stories. I am deeply convinced that the same approach is still worthwhile today. We can glean from Lewis, not only through considering his views of nature and the human imagination which philosophically undergird the pre-evangelist task, but also through examining the products of his pre-evangelistic aims, namely his own stories. In doing so, we discover certain important qualities that, if included in new stories yet to be written, can likely help to awaken inconsolable longings in the hearts of disenchanted people today.

A few words of disclaimer are needed before offering, by way of conclusion, a call to Christians to take up the pre-evangelistic task through the medium of imaginative fiction. I am not suggesting here that *all* Christians, or even a majority, need to attempt to write fiction. One need not feel the burden to set out to do that for which one lacks the needed ability and aptitude. I am calling here only those Christians who find within themselves the ability, the desire, and the means, to write new stories that

C. S. LEWIS PRE-EVANGELISM FOR A POST-CHRISTIAN WORLD

can help to evoke a similar desire in people today that Lewis felt and in turn sought to awaken in his own readers.

Just as not all possess the gifting to be able to write imaginative fiction, so also not all enjoy reading such stories. Therefore, the call for some Christians to pre-evangelize through imaginative fiction is not here presented as *the* approach that aims to stir interest in all people. Such a strategy might prove in the end to make only a small contribution towards the present need. Lewis understood this. Even so, he maintained that the work was worth the effort. He writes:

> If the intellectual climate is such that, when a man comes to the crisis at which he must either accept or reject Christ, his reason and imagination are not on the wrong side, then his conflict will be fought out under favorable conditions. Those who help to produce and spread such a climate are therefore doing useful work: and yet no such great matter after all. Their share is a modest one.[810]

We must understand and admit that pre-evangelism is incomplete without the explicit communication of the gospel. A little later in the same article just cited above, Lewis states that the evangelist's work is far more important than the pre-evangelist's. Such being the case, he still affirms once again the preliminary work must be done. He admits:

> Far higher than they stands that character whom, to the best of my knowledge, the present Christian movement has not yet produced—the *Preacher* in the full sense, the Evangelist, the man on fire, the man who infects. The propagandist, the apologist, only represents John the Baptist: the Preacher represents the Lord Himself. He will be sent—or else he will not. But unless he comes we mere Christian intellectuals will not effect very much. That does not mean that we should down tools.[811]

One can see that Lewis was willing to do what he thought a small task for the cause of Christianity. He humbly took up the tools that the Lord had given to him and put them to use.

The concluding call I am sounding for Christians today is to do the same. Imaginative fiction offers a doorway into peoples' desires, which, thanks in part to the pervasive influence of naturalism, are akin to deserts in need of need deep irrigation, to use Lewis's metaphor. If such stories are

---

[810] C. S. Lewis, "The Decline of Religion," in *God in the Dock*, 241.
[811] C. S. Lewis, "The Decline of Religion," in *God in the Dock*, 241.

done well, they can help to awaken dormant desire, "satisfying it while often whetting it unbearably."[812] Not all stories are equal, however, and one might just as easily throw his reader off of the trail that leads to the truth as he might lead them down it. If, however, he succeeds at writing an immersive story that includes the above-noted qualities found in other great pre-evangelistic stories, he will provide some needed help. Those who read such stories may just find themselves stabbed with sickening desire as Lewis was, which may lead them to ask the questions that, if answered truly, will lead them in the end to Christ.

If my case has been made successfully, I have shown that Lewis's views of reality and the human imagination both illuminate and justify the pre-evangelistic strategy he employs through his stories. I have argued that Lewis's sacramental ontology offers the best explanation for why desire can be stirred for the transcendent through the imagination, which Lewis referred to as "the organ of meaning." Thus, when Lewis attempts to sneak past the watchful dragons, he is not relying on mere pragmatics, but on the nature of reality and the human person as an imaginative creatures who has been made for God. The purpose of my argument, in the end, is to persuade talented Christians to rise up and offer needed help towards pre-evangelistic efforts in the present day.

The pre-evangelist, in the Lewisian sense, need not only be a talented individual equipped with great sub-creative capacity. He will also need to be humble enough to be willing to contribute a modest share towards a great cause. The commonly heard exhortation to go out and "change the world" threatens this necessary modesty and places undo pressure upon Christians today. Those who would consider taking up the pre-evangelistic call might be encouraged to hear once again the words of Dr. Ransom from the conclusion of *Out of the Silent Planet*. Let us agree with him, in conclusion, when he says, "If we could even effect in one per cent of our readers a change-over from the conception of Space to the conception of Heaven, we should have made a beginning."[813]

---

[812] J. R. R. Tolkien, "On Fairy-Stories," in *Tree and Leaf*, 41.
[813] C. S. Lewis, *Out of the Silent Planet*, 152.

INDEX

Allen, Diogenes. *Philosophy for Understanding Theology.* Louisville: Westminster John Knox, 1985.

Anscombe, Elisabeth. *Collected Philosophical Papers, Vol 2: Metaphysics and the Philosophy of Mind.* Minneapolis: University of Minnesota Press, 1981.

Aristotle. *The Complete Works of Aristotle.* Vol. 1. The Revised Oxford Translation. Princeton: Princeton University Press, 1984.

———. *The Complete Works of Aristotle.* Vol. 2. The Revised Oxford Translation. Princeton: Princeton University Press, 1984.

Armstrong, Chris R. *Medieval Wisdom for Modern Christians: Finding Authentic Faith in a Forgotten Age with C. S. Lewis.* Grand Rapids: Brazos Press, 2016.

Augustine. *Confessions,* 2nd ed. Translated by F. J. Sheed. Indianapolis: Hackett Publishing Company, 2006.

Bacon, Francis. *The New Organon.* Edited by Lisa Jardine and Michael Silverthorne. Cambridge: Cambridge University Press, 2000.

Baggett, David, Gary R. Habermas, and Jerry L. Walls, eds. *C. S. Lewis as Philosopher: Truth, Goodness, and Beauty,* 2nd ed. Lynchburg: Liberty University Press, 2017.

Barfield, Owen. *Poetic Diction: A Study in Meaning.* Oxford: Barfield Press, 2010.

Barnard, Justin D. "Brains But No Blood: C. S. Lewis' Obsession with Naturalism."*Renewing Minds: A Journal of Christian Thought* 4 (Fall 2013): 27–35.

Barrs, Jerram. *Echoes of Eden: Reflections on Christianity, Literature, and the Arts.* Wheaton: Crossway, 2013.

Beck, Lewis White, ed. *18th-Century Philosophy.* New York: The Free Press, 1966.

Begbie, Jeremy, ed. *Beholding the Glory: Incarnation Through the Arts.* Grand Rapids: Baker Academic, 2001.

———. *Resounding Truth: Christian Wisdom in the World of Music.* Grand Rapids: Baker Academic, 2007.

Brian M. Williams

Bellah, Robert, Richard Madsen, William M. Sullivan, Ann Swidler, and Steven M. Tipton. *Habits of the Heart: Individualism and Commitment in American Life.* Berkeley: University of California Press, 2008.

Bernthal, Craig. *Tolkien's Sacramental Vision: Discerning the Holy in Middle Earth.* Kettering: Second Spring, 2014.

Boersma, Hans. *Heavenly Participation: The Weaving of a Sacramental Tapestry.* Grand Rapids: Eerdmans, 2011.

Bray, Suzanne. "La Dialectique Du Desir Chex C. S. Lewis." *La Conversion Religieuse* (2000): 237–46.

Bunyan, John. *The Pilgrim's Progress.* Oxford: Oxford University Press, 2008.

Carr, Nicholas. *The Shallows: What the Internet is Doing to Our Brains.* New York: W. W. Norton & Company, 2011.

Castleman, Robbie F. *Story Shaped Worship: Following Patterns from the Bible and History.* Downers Grove: IVP Academic, 2013.

Chesterton, G. K. *Orthodoxy.* New York: Snowball Classics Publishing, 2015.

———. *Saint Thomas Aquinas.* Nashville: Sam Torode Book Arts, 2016.

———. *The Everlasting Man.* Middletown: Rough Draft Printing, 2013.

Cobble, William J. "C. S. Lewis' Understanding of God's Work in Paganism." *Journal of Theta Alpha Kappa* 25, no. 2 (Fall 2001): 16–28.

Copleston, Frederick, S. J. *A History of Philosophy.* 9 Vols. New York: Doubleday, 1993.

Coutras, Lisa. *Tolkien's Theology of Beauty: Majesty, Splendor, and Transcendence in Middle-earth.* New York: Palgrave Macmillan, 2016.

Crouch, Andy. *Culture Making: Recovering Our Creative Calling.* Downers Grove: IVP Books, 2008.

Davison, Andrew, ed. *Imaginative Apologetics: Theology, Philosophy, and the Catholic Tradition.* Grand Rapids: Baker Academic, 2011.

Descartes, Rene. *Discourse on Method and Meditations on First Philosophy,* 4th ed. Translated by Donald A. Cress. Indianapolis: Hackett Publishing Company, 1998.

Detweiler, Craig. *I Gods.* Grand Rapids: Brazos Press, 2013.

Downing, Crystal. "Angelic Work: The Medieval Sensibilities of Dorothy Sayers." *Journal of Inklings Studies* 3, no. 2 (October 2013): 111–32.

Dreher, Rod. *The Benedict Option: A Strategy for Christians in a Post-Christian Nation.* New York: Sentinel, 2017.

Dumsday, Travis. "C. S. Lewis on the Problem of Divine Hiddenness." *Anglican Theological Review* 97, no. 1 (Winter 2015): 33–51.

Duriez. Colin. *C. S. Lewis: A Biography of Friendship.* Oxford: Lion Hudson, 2013.

———. *J. R. R. Tolkien: The Making of a Legend.* Oxford: Lion Hudson, 2012.

———. *The Oxford Inklings: Lewis, Tolkien, and their Circle.* Oxford: Lion Books, 2015.

Edwards, L. Clifton. *Creation's Beauty as Revelation: Toward a Creational Theology of Natural Beauty.* Eugene: Pickwick Publications, 2014.

Edwards, Mark. "*Till We Have Faces* as Myth and Allegory." *Journal of Inklings Studies* 6, no. 2 (October 2016): 113–38.

Ellul, Jacques. *The Presence of the Kingdom.* Second Ed. Expanded. Translated by Olive Wyon. Colorado Springs: Helmers & Howard Publishers, 1989.

Feinendegen, Norbert, and Arend Smilde, eds. *The "Great War" of Owen Barfield and C. S. Lewis: Philosophical Writings 1927–1930.* Inklings Studies Supplements No. 1. St. Andrews: Journal of Inklings Studies, 2015.

Fennell, Jon. "A Polanyian Perspective on C. S. Lewis's *The Abolition of Man.*" *Journal of Inklings Studies* 4, no. 1 (April 2014): 93–122.

Ferry, Luc. *A Brief History of Thought: A Philosophical Guide to Living.* New York: Harper Perennial, 2011.

Feser, Edward. *Scholastic Metaphysics: A Contemporary Introduction.* Piscataway: Transaction Books, 2014.

Freud, Sigmund. "A Difficulty in the Path of Psycho-Analysis." *Complete Psychological Works.* Vol. 17. London: Hogarth Press, 1955.

Gay, Craig M. *The Way of the (Modern) World Or Why It's Tempting to Live As If God Doesn't Exist.* Grand Rapids: Eerdmans, 1998.

Gibbs, Lee W. "C. S. Lewis and the Anglican *Via Media*." *Restoration Quarterly* 32, no. 2 (1990): 105–19.

Gilbert, Douglas, and Clyde S. Kilby. *C. S. Lewis: Images of His World*. Grand Rapids: Eerdmans, 2005.

Gilchrist, K. J. *A Morning After War: C. S. Lewis & WWI*. New York: Peter Lang, 2005.

Glaspey, Terry. *C. S. Lewis: His Life & Thought*. Edison: Inspirational Press, 1996.

Glyer, Diana Pavlac. *Bandersnatch: C. S. Lewis, J. R. R. Tolkien, and the Creative Collaboration of the Inklings*. Kent: Black Squirrel Books, 2016.

Goetz, Steward, and Charles Taliaferro. *A Brief History of the Soul*. West Sussex: Wiley- Blackwell, 2011.

Green, Roger Lancelyn, and Walter Hooper. *C. S. Lewis: A Biography*. Revised edition. London: Harcourt Brace, 1994.

Gresham, Douglas H. *Lenten Lands*. New York: Macmillan, 1988.

Grewell, Cory Lowell. "'It's All One': Medievalist Synthesis and Christian Apology in Owen Garfield's Studies of Meaning." *Journal of Inklings Studies* 3, no. 2 (October 2013): 11–40.

———. "Medievalist Fantasies of Christendom." *Journal of Inklings Studies* 3, no. 2 (October 2013): 3–10.

Griffiths, Bede. *The Golden String*. London: Fount, 1979.

Gruenler, Curtis. "C. S. Lewis and Rene Girard on Desire, Conversion, and Myth: The Case of *Till We Have Faces*." *Christianity and Literature* 60, no. 2 (Winter 2011): 247–65.

Guinness, Os. *Fool's Talk: Recovering the Art of Christian Persuasion*. Downers Grove: InterVarsity Press, 2015.

Hart, David Bentley. *The Beauty of the Infinite: The Aesthetics of Christian Truth*. Grand Rapids: Eerdmans, 2003.

Hart, Trevor. *Between the Image and the Word*. Burlington: Ashgate, 2013.

Hasker, William. *Metaphysics: Constructing a World View*. Downers Grove: InterVarsity Press, 1983.

Heck, Joel. "The Liberal Arts: Antidote for Atheism: A Partial Theological Justification for the Liberal Arts." *Lingaculture* 2 (2014): 67–78.

Hein, Rolland. *Christian Mythmakers*, 2nd ed. Eugene: Wipf & Stock, 2014.

Henderson, J. W. *Methodist College, Belfast, 1868–1938: A Survey and Retrospect.* Vol. 1. Belfast: Governors of Methodist College, 1939.

Higgins, Sorina. "Double Affirmation: Medievalism as Christian Apologetic in the Arthurian Poetry of Charles Williams." *Journal of Inklings Studies* 3, no. 2 (October 2013): 59–96.

Hooper, Walter. *C. S. Lewis: Companion & Guide.* New York: HarperCollins, 1996.

Hunter, James Davison. *To Change The World: The Irony, Tragedy, & Possibility of Christianity in the Late Modern World.* Oxford: Oxford University Press, 2010.

Hutchinson, Jamie. "Imagine That: A Barfieldian Reading of C. S. Lewis's *Till We Have Faces.*" *Journal of Inklings Studies* 6, no. 2 (October 2016): 79–111.

Keller, Timothy. *Making Sense of God: An Invitation to the Skeptical.* New York: Viking, 2016.

Kilby, Clyde S. *A Well of Wonder: Essays on C. S. Lewis, J. R. R. Tolkien, and the Inklings*, ed. Loren Wilkinson and Keith Call. Brewster: Paraclete Press, 2016.

Kilby, Clyde S., and Marjorie Lamp Mead. *Brothers and Friends: The Diaries of Major Warren Hamilton Lewis.* San Francisco: Harper & Row, 1982.

King, Don W., ed. *The Collected Poems of C. S. Lewis: A Critical Edition.* Kent: The Kent State University Press, 2015.

———. *C. S. Lewis, Poet: The Legacy of His Poetic Impulse.* Kent: The Kent State University Press, 2001.

Khoddam, Salwa, Mark R. Hall, and Jason Fisher, eds. *C. S. Lewis and the Inklings: Reflections on Faith, Imagination, and Modern Technology.* Cambridge: Cambridge Scholars Publishing, 2015.

Kreeft, Peter. *Christianity for Modern Pagans.* San Francisco: Ignatius Press, 1993.

Lanier, Jaron. *Who Owns the Future?* New York: Simon & Schuster Paperbacks, 2013.

Lee, Seung Chun. "C. S. Lewis' Mythopoeia of Heaven and Earth: Implications for the Ethical and Spiritual Formation of Multicultural

Brian M. Williams

Young Learners." *International Journal of Children's Spirituality* 20, no. 1 (2015): 15–28.

Lewis, C. S. *A Grief Observed.* New York, HarperOne, 1994.

———. *A Preface to Paradise Lost.* Oxford: Oxford University Press, 1961.

———. *All My Road Before Me: The Diary of C. S. Lewis 1922–1927.* Edited by Walter Hooper. San Diego: Harcourt Brace Jovanovich, 1991.

———. *An Experiment in Criticism.* Cambridge: Cambridge University Press, 2015.

———. *C. S. Lewis, Poet: The Legacy of His Poetic Impulse.* Kent: The Kent State University Press, 2001.

———. *Christian Reflections.* Grand Rapids: Eerdmans, 1967.

———. "De Descriptione Temporum: Inaugural Lecture from the Chair of Medieval and Renaissance Literature." Cambridge University, 1954. Accessed on 3/2/19. https://www.romanroadsmedia.com/old-western-culture- extras/DeDescriptioneTemporum-CS-Lewis.pdf.

———. *Dymer.* Originally published under the pseudonym: Clive Hamilton. UK: Crossreach Publications, 2016.

———. *English Literature in the Sixteenth Century: Excluding Drama.* Oxford: Clarendon Press, 1954.

———. *George MacDonald: An Anthology.* San Francisco: HarperCollins, 2015.

———. *God in the Dock.* Grand Rapids: Eerdmans, 2014.

———. *Image and Imagination: Essays and Review.* Edited by Walter Hooper. Cambridge: Cambridge University Press, 2013.

———. *Letters to Malcolm: Chiefly on Prayer: Reflections on the Intimate Dialogue Between Man and God.* Boston: Mariner Books, 2012.

———. *Mere Christianity.* New York: HarperOne, 2001.

———. *Miracles: A Preliminary Study.* New York: HarperOne, 2001.

———. *Of Other Worlds: Essays and Stories.* Edited by Walter Hooper. New York: Harcourt Brace Jovanovich, 1966.

———. *On Stories and Other Essays on Literature.* Boston: Mariner Books, 2002.

———. *Out of the Silent Planet.* New York: Scribner, 2003.

C. S. LEWIS PRE-EVANGELISM FOR A POST-CHRISTIAN WORLD

———. *Perelandra.* New York: Scribner, 2003.

———. *Prince Caspian.* New York: Macmillan, 2003.

———. *Reflections on the Psalms.* New York: HarperOne, 2017.

———. *Selected Literary Essays.* Cambridge: Cambridge University Press, 2013.

———. *Studies in Medieval and Renaissance Literature.* Cambridge: Cambridge University Press, 2013.

———. *Surprised by Joy: The Shape of My Early Life.* Orlando: Harcourt Books, 1955.

———. *That Hideous Strength.* New York: Scribner, 2003.

———. *The Abolition of Man.* New York: HarperOne, 2001.

———. *The Allegory of Love.* Cambridge: Cambridge University Press, 2016.

———. *The Collected Letters of C. S. Lewis: Books, Broadcasts, and the War (1931–1949).* Vol. II. Edited by Walter Hooper. San Francisco: HarperCollins, 2004.

———. *The Collected Letters of C. S. Lewis: Family Letters (1905–1931).* Vol. I. Edited by Walter Hooper. San Francisco: HarperCollins, 2004.

———. *The Collected Letters of C. S. Lewis: Narnia, Cambridge, and Joy, 1950–1963.* Vol. III. Edited by Walter Hooper. San Francisco: HarperCollins, 2004.

———. *The Discarded Image: An Introduction to Medieval and Renaissance Literature.* Cambridge: Cambridge University Press, 2013.

———. *The Four Loves: An Exploration of the Nature of Love.* Boston: Mariner Books, 2012.

———. *The Great Divorce.* New York: HarperOne, 2001.

———. *The Horse and His Boy.* New York: Macmillan, 1970.

———. *The Last Battle.* New York: Macmillan, 1970.

———. *The Lion, the Witch and the Wardrobe.* New York: Macmillan, 1970.

———. *The Magician's Nephew.* New York: Macmillan, 1970.

———. *The Pilgrim's Regress.* Wade Annotated Edition. Grand Rapids: Eerdmans, 2014.

———. *The Problem of Pain.* San Francisco: HarperCollins, 1996.

———. *The Screwtape Letters.* Annotated Edition. New York: HarperOne, 2013.

———. *The Silver Chair.* New York: Macmillan, 1970.

———. *The Voyage of the Dawn Treader.* New York: Macmillan, 1970.

———. *The Weight of Glory: And Other Addresses.* New York: HarperOne, 2001.

———. *The World's Last Night: And Other Essays.* Boston: Mariner Books, 2012.

———. *Till We Have Faces: A Novel of Cupid and Psyche.* Boston: Mariner Books, 2012.

Lewis, C. S., and Charles Williams. *Arthurian Torso: Containing the Posthumous Fragment of The Figure of Arthur by Charles Williams and A Commentary of The Arthurian Poems of Charles Williams by C. S. Lewis.* Oxford: Oxford University Press, 1969.

Lewis, C. S., and E. M. W. Tillyard. *The Personal Heresy: A Controversy.* New York: HarperOne, 2017.

Lewis, W. H. *Brothers & Friends: The Diaries of Major Warren Hamilton Lewis.* San Francisco: Harper & Row, 1982.

Lewis, W. H., ed., *The Letters of C. S. Lewis.* London: Bles, 1966.

Loconte, Joseph. *A Hobbit, a Wardrobe, and a Great War: How J. R. R. Tolkien and C.*

S. Lewis Rediscovered Faith, Friendship, and Heroism in the Cataclysm of 1914–1918. Nashville: Nelson Books, 2015.

MacDonald, George. *Phantastes: A Faerie Romance.* Mineola: Dover Publications, 2016.

MacSwain, Robert, ed. *Scripture, Metaphysics, and Poetry.* London: Routledge, 2016.

Markos, Louis. *From Achilles to Christ: Why Christians Should Read the Pagan Classics.* Downers Grove: IVP Academic, 2007.

———. *Heaven and Hell: Visions of the Afterlife in the Western Poetic Tradition.* Eugene: Cascade Books, 2013.

———. *Literature: A Student's Guide.* Wheaton: Crossway, 2012.

———. *On the Shoulders of Hobbits: The Road to Virtue with Tolkien and Lewis.* Chicago: Moody, 2012.

———. *Restoring Beauty: The Good, the True, and the Beautiful in the Writings of C. S. Lewis.* Downers Grove: InterVarsity Press, 2010.

Martindale, Wayne, and Jerry Root, eds. *The Quotable Lewis.* Wheaton: Tyndale House, 1989.

Mathis, David, and John Piper, eds. *The Romantic Rationalist: God, Life, and Imagination in the Work of C. S. Lewis.* Wheaton: Crossway, 2014.

McGrath, Alister. "An Enhanced Vision of Rationality: C. S. Lewis on the Reasonableness of Christian Faith." *Theology* 6, no. 116 (Nov. 2013): 410–17.

———. *C. S. Lewis: A Life: Eccentric Genius, Reluctant Prophet.* Carol Stream: Tyndale House, 2013.

———. *Mere Apologetics: How to Help Seekers & Skeptics Find Faith.* Grand Rapids: Baker, 2012.

———. *The Intellectual World of C. S. Lewis.* Oxford: Wiley-Blackwell, 2014.

———. *The Open Secret: A New Vision for Natural Theology.* Oxford: Blackwell Publishing, 2008.

Milbank, John, Catherine Pickstock, and Graham Ward, eds. *Radical Orthodoxy: A New Theology.* London: Routledge, 1999.

Mills, David, ed. *The Pilgrim's Guide: C. S. Lewis and the Art of Witness.* Grand Rapids: Eerdmans, 1998.

Moore, T. M. *Culture Matters: A Call for Consensus on Christian Cultural Engagement.* Grand Rapids: Brazos Press, 2007.

Myers, Kenneth A. *All God's Children & Blue Suede Shoes.* Wheaton: Crossway, 2012.

Newbigin, Lesslie. *The Gospel in a Pluralist Society.* Grand Rapids: Eerdmans, 1989.

Ordway, Holly. *Apologetics and the Christian Imagination: An Integrated Approach to Defending the Faith.* Steubenville: Emmaus Road Publishing, 2017.

───. "'Further Up and Further In': Representations of Heaven in Tolkien and Lewis." *Journal of Inklings Studies* 3, no. 1 (April 2013): 5–23.

Packer, J. I. "Living Truth for a Dying World: The Message of C. S. Lewis." *Crux* 34, no. 4 (Dec. 1998): 3–12.

Payne, Leanne. *Real Presence: The Christian View of C. S. Lewis as Incarnational Reality.* Grand Rapids: Baker, 1995.

Pearce, Joseph. *Beauteous Truth: Faith, Reason, Literature, and Culture.* South Bend: Saint Augustine's Press, 2014.

───. *Merrie England: A Journey Through the Shire.* Charlotte: Tan Books, 2016.

Pearcey, Nancy. *Saving Leonardo: A Call to Resist the Secular Assault on Mind, Morals, & Meaning.* Nashville: B&H, 2010.

Pelser, Adam C. "Irrigating Deserts: Thinking with C. S. Lewis About Education for Emotional Formation." *Christian Scholar's Review* 44 (Fall 2014): 27–43.

Phillips, J. B. *Letters to Young Churches.* New York: Macmillan, 1957.

Pieper, Josef. *Abuse of Language, Abuse of Power.* Translated by Lothar Krauth. San Francisco: Ignatius Press, 1988.

───. *Faith, Hope, Love.* San Francisco: Ignatius Press, 1981.

───. *Happiness & Contemplation.* South Bend: Saint Augustine's Press, 1979.

───. *Leisure: The Basis of Culture.* San Francisco: Ignatius Press, 1963.

Plato. *Plato: Complete Works.* Edited by John M. Cooper. Indianapolis: Hackett Publishing Company, 1997.

Poe, Harry Lee. "The Book C. S. Lewis Never Wrote: On Imagination and the Knowledge of God." *Sewanee Theological Review* 57, no. 4 (Michaelmas): 465– 79.

───. "C. S. Lewis and the Inklings on the Importance of Narrative." *Renewing Minds: A Journal of Christian Thought* 4 (Fall 2013): 37–45.

Polanyi, Michael. *The Tacit Dimension.* Chicago: University of Chicago Press, 2009.

Postman, Neil. *Amusing Ourselves to Death: Public Discourse in the Age of Show Business.* New York: Penguin Books, 2006.

———. *Technopoly: The Surrender of Culture to Technology.* New York: Vintage Books, 1992.

Rookmaaker, H. R. *Modern Art and the Death of a Culture.* Wheaton: Crossway, 1994.

Root, Jerry. "C. S. Lewis, Objectivity, and Beauty." 63–78 in *C. S. Lewis and the Arts: Creativity in the Shadowlands.* Edited by Rod Miller. Baltimore: Square Halo Books, 2013.

Root, Jerry, and Mark Neal. *The Surprising Imagination of C. S. Lewis: An Introduction.* Nashville: Abingdon, 2015.

Sayer, George. *Jack: C. S. Lewis and His Times.* San Francisco: Harper & Row, 1988.

Schakel, Peter J. *Reason and Imagination in C. S. Lewis: A Study of Till We Have Faces.* Grand Rapids: Eerdmans, 1984.

Scruton, Roger. *An Intelligent Person's Guide to Modern Culture.* South Bend: St. Augustine's Press, 2000.

———. *Beauty: A Very Short Introduction.* Oxford: Oxford University Press, 2011.

———. *The Face of God.* London: Continuum International Publishing Group, 2012.

Selby, Gary S. *Not with Words of Wisdom: Nonrational Persuasion in the New Testament.* Grand Rapids: Eerdmans, 2016.

Sellars, J. T. *Reasoning Beyond Reason: Imagination as a Theological Source in the Work of C. S. Lewis.* Eugene: Pickwick Publications, 2011.

Sertillanges, A. G. *The Intellectual Life: Its Spirit, Conditions, Methods.* Translated by Mary Ryan. Washington, D.C.: The Catholic University of America Press, 1998.

Sire, James W. *Apologetics Beyond Reason: Why Seeing Really is Believing.* Downers Grove: IVP Academic, 2014.

———. *The Universe Next Door*, 5th ed. Downers Grove: InterVarsity Press, 2009.

Smith, James K. A. *How (Not) to Be Secular: Reading Charles Taylor.* Grand Rapids: Eerdmans, 2014.

———. *Imagining the Kingdom: How Worship Works.* Grand Rapids: Baker Academic, 2013.

Taliaferro, Charles, and Jill Evans. *The Image in Mind: Theism, Naturalism, and the Imagination.* New York: Bloomsbury Academic, 2013.

Taylor, Charles. *A Secular Age.* Cambridge: Belknap Press, 2007.

Taylor, W. David O., ed. *For the Beauty of the Church: Casting a Vision for the Arts.* Grand Rapids: Baker, 2010.

Thorson, Stephen. *Joy and Poetic Imagination: Understanding C. S. Lewis's "Great War" with Owen Barfield and its Significance for Lewis's Conversion and Writings.* Hamden: Winged Lion Press, 2015.

Tiffany, Grace. "C. S. Lewis: The Anti-Platonic Platonist." *Christianity and Literature* 63, no. 3 (Spring 2014): 357–71.

Tolkien, J. R. R. *The Letters of J. R. R. Tolkien.* New York: Mariner Books, 2000.

———. *Tree and Leaf.* New York City: Harper Collins, 2001.

Travers, Michael, ed. *C. S. Lewis: Views from Wake Forest.* Wayne: Zossima Press, 2008.

Tyson, Paul. *Returning to Reality: Christian Platonism for Our Times.* Portland: Cascade Books, 2014.

Walsh, Chad. *C. S. Lewis: Apostle to the Skeptics.* Eugene: Wipf & Stock, 2008.

Ward, Michael, and Peter S. Williams, eds. *C. S. Lewis at Poet's Corner.* Eugene: Cascade Books, 2016.

Ward, Michael. *Planet Narnia: The Seven Heavens in the Imagination of C. S. Lewis.* Oxford: Oxford University Press, 2008.

Weaver, Richard M. *Ideas Have Consequences.* Chicago: The University of Chicago Press, 1984.

———. *The Ethics of Rhetoric.* Chicago: Henry Regnery Company, 1953.

———. *Visions of Order: The Cultural Crisis of our Time.* Wilmington: Intercollegiate Studies Institute, 1995.

Wells, David F. *Above All Earthly Pow'rs: Christ in a Postmodern World.* Grand Rapids: Eerdmans, 2005.

———. *God in the Wasteland: The Reality of Truth in a World of Fading Dreams.* Grand Rapids: Eerdmans, 1994.

———. *Losing Our Virtue: Why the Church Must Recover its Moral Vision.* Grand Rapids: Eerdmans, 1998.

---. *No Place for Truth Or Whatever Happened to Evangelical Theology?* Grand Rapids: Eerdmans, 1993.

---. *The Courage to be Protestant: Truth-lovers, Marketers, and Emergents in the Postmodern World.* Grand Rapids: Eerdmans, 2008.

Wells, H. G. *The New World Order.* London: Secker and Warburg, 1940.

White, Roger, Brendan N. Wolfe, and Judith Wolfe, eds. *C. S. Lewis & His Circle: Essays and Memoirs from the Oxford C. S. Lewis Society.* Oxford: Oxford University Press, 2015.

Wilde, Oscar. *The Letters of Oscar Wilde.* Edited by Rupert Hart-Davis. London: Butler & Tanner, 1967.

Williams, Charles, and C. S. Lewis. *Arthurian Torso: Containing the Posthumous Fragment of The Figure of Arthur by Charles Williams and A Commentary on The Arthurian Poems of Charles William by C. S. Lewis.* Oxford: Oxford University Press, 1969.

Williams, Clifford. *Existential Reasons for Belief in God: A Defense of Desires & Emotions for Faith.* Downers Grove: IVP Academic, 2011.

Williams, Donald T. *Deeper Magic: The Theology Behind the Writings of C. S. Lewis.* Baltimore: Square Halo Books, 2016.

Wolfe, Gregory. *Beauty Will Save the World: Recovering the Human in an Ideological Age.* Wilmington: ISI Books, 2014.

Wolterstorff, Nicholas. *Art in Action: Toward a Christian Aesthetic.* Grand Rapids: Eerdmans, 1996.

Wooddell, Joseph D. *The Beauty of the Faith: Using Aesthetics for Christian Apologetics.* Eugene: Wipf & Stock, 2011.

Yandell, Stephen. "*The Allegory of Love* and *The Discarded Image*: C. S. Lewis as Medievalist." 117–141 in *C. S. Lewis: Life, Works, and Legacy.* Edited by Bruce Edwards. Vol. 4. Santa Barbara: Praeger, 2007.

Zaleski, Philip, and Carol Zaleski. *The Fellowship: The Literary Lives of the Inklings.* New York: Farrar, Straus, and Giroux, 2015.

Printed in Great Britain
by Amazon